Gavin Souter is the author of several narrative histories, including *Heralds and Angels*, *Acts of Parliament* and *A Peculiar People*.

Lion and Kangaroo received the Foundation for Australian Literary Studies award.

To Anne and Gretel

LION AND KANGAROO

The Initiation of Australia

GAVIN SOUTER

SUN
AUSTRALIA

First published in Australia 1976 by
William Collins Publishers Pty Ltd.

This edition published 1992 by
Pan Macmillan Publishers Australia
a division of Pan Macmillan Australia Pty Ltd
63-71 Balfour Street, Chippendale, Sydney
A.C.N.: 001 184 014

National Library of Australia
cataloguing-in-publication data:

Souter, Gavin, 1929-
Lion and kangaroo: the initiation of Australia.
Bibliography.
Includes index.
ISBN 0 7251 0696 4.

1. Australia - History - 1901-1922. I. Title.

994.041

Printed in Australia
by The Book Printer

CONTENTS

ACKNOWLEDGMENTS

I wish to thank the Literature Board of the Australia Council for its one-year fellowship and special purposes grant, without which this book could not have been written; Conzinc Riotinto of Australia Ltd, for its valued assistance; Qantas Airways Ltd, for enabling me to visit Britain and France; and John Fairfax and Sons Ltd, for allowing me to take leave from *The Sydney Morning Herald*.

I also thank the libraries from which I received so much help: the State Library of New South Wales, and particularly its Mitchell Library; in Canberra the manuscript branch of the National Library of Australia, the Australian Archives and the Australian War Memorial; in Melbourne the La Trobe Library and the Archives of the University of Melbourne; the Oxley Memorial Library, Brisbane; the J. S. Battye Library, Perth; the State Library of South Australia; in London the Public Record Office, the House of Lords Record Office, the National Army Museum, and the British Library's State Paper Room and Newspaper Library; and in Oxford the Bodleian Library, for permission to see the Asquith and Bryce papers.

My indebtedness to many workers in this period of Australian history will be apparent from the bibliography. I am grateful to those who read and commented on parts of the manuscript, or helped in other ways. In particular, and without attempting to be exhaustive, I wish to thank Professor P. H. Lane, Professor Geoffrey Sawer, Professor R. M. Crawford, Dr C. Cunneen and Professor D. J. Mulvaney.

I am also grateful for help received from the Commonwealth War Graves Commission at Çanakkale, the Central Army Records Office in Melbourne, the Royal Military College of Australia, the Department of the Special Minister of State and the Department of the Capital Territory in Canberra, the Reserve Bank of Australia, the Australian Electoral Office, the Lutheran Church of Australia, the High Court of Australia, Prince Alfred College in Adelaide, the Australian Institute of Aboriginal Studies, the NSW Department of Education, Mr J. D. Burke, Mrs Helga Tukk, and several people with longer memories than mine, who dispelled some of the period's mystery for me: Pastor F. W. Albrecht, Mr R. Avison, Professor A. P. Elkin, Mr Jack Flower, Mr Jack ('Snowy') Howe, Mrs H. Jones, the late Mr Jack Lang, the late Mr Jack Sheridan, Mr Jack Tarrant, Mr Tom Thick and Lady White (née Deakin).

So far as copyright is concerned, I offer the following thanks for permission to quote from various sources. Melbourne University Press, for permission to quote from *Alfred Deakin: A Biography* by J. A. La Nauze and *The Emergent Commonwealth* by Ronald Norris; Oxford University Press, to quote from letters in *Isaac Isaacs* by Zelman Cowen; Angus and Robertson Ltd, to quote the poem 'Who Are These?' from *Prosper The Commonwealth* by R. R. Garran; Patrick Young, to quote from an unpublished journal of Sir Baldwin Spencer held by the Mitchell Library; Mrs Jessie Clarke and Mr A. D. Brookes, to quote from Alfred Deakin's letters at the National Library of Australia; Miss Margaret Fisher, to quote from her reminiscences of her father, Andrew Fisher (NLA); Miss Helen Palmer, to quote from the letters of Nettie Palmer (NLA); Mrs Joy Higgins, to quote from the letters of Esmonde Higgins (NLA); Lord Tennyson, to quote from the papers of Audrey, Lady Tennyson (NLA); and Mr R. J. McKimm, to quote from the manuscript autobiography of John Shaw Neilson (NLA). The coats of arms on the endpapers are reproduced by permission from the Australian Archives.

The illustrations are reproduced as follows by courtesy of the National Library of Australia (NLA), the Australian War Memorial (AWM), the National Gallery of Australia (NGA), the Historic Memorials Committee in Canberra (HMC), the Government Printer of NSW (GP), the Mitchell Library (ML), the National Museum of Victoria (NMV), the Archives of the Reserve Bank of Australia originally Commonwealth Bank of Australia (RBA), and the *Bulletin* (B).

For groups, as well as for individuals, life itself means to separate and to be re-united, to change form and condition, to die and to be reborn ... And there are always new thresholds to cross: the thresholds of summer and winter, of a season or a year, of a month or a night; the thresholds of birth, adolescence, maturity and old age.

THE RITES OF PASSAGE
Arnold Van Gennep 1909

FOREWORD

There is something familiar, and quite appropriate for this reprinting, about the final escalation of the 1990s towards another century and a new millennium. This time last century Britain's six Australian colonies, beset by depression and drought, were beginning a process destined to bring them into federal union on the first day of the 20th century, 1 January 1901. Having no wish to break their ties with the mother country, they planned to federate under the British Crown as a constitutional monarchy. One hundred years later, as an economically distraught and drought-stricken Commonwealth of Australia approaches another temporal threshhold, debate is under way on the need to repudiate the monarchy and declare Australia a republic on the centenary of Federation, 1 January 2001.

Although I count myself a republican, convinced about the desirability and feasibility of such a change, *Lion and Kangaroo* is not about republicanism. On the contrary, it is about British-Australian sentiment – a sentiment which, although it has weakened in the course of this century, may still be a stumbling block on the road to a republic. It need not be. Surely, one would think, the crimson thread of kinship is now sufficiently faded, and the well of Anglo-Celtic identity sufficiently diluted by exogamous blood, for Australia to make do without an hereditary British monarch.

But only a referendum will tell. For the last thirty years, opinion polls have been showing a gradual decline in support for the monarchy, and a somewhat steeper republican rise. In the latest poll (June 1991) 34 per cent favoured a republic, and 52 per cent of adult respondents were still opposed to the idea.

How different such a poll would have been during the first two decades of this century! In spite of new nationhood, the result would have been a walkover for Crown and Empire. *Lion and Kangaroo* is about those decades of Federation and the Great War, a period when most of Australia's national institutions came into being. The period is still close enough to be reached in memory by some Australians, but to anyone born well and truly in the 20th century it seems infinitely remote. Nothing demonstrates this more plainly than an Australian prime minister of that time, Alfred Deakin, referring to himself as an 'independent Australian Briton'. Deakin scarcely knew whether he was one thing or the other, or both.

While the Commonwealth of Australia was passing through various formalities of birth, infancy and adolescence, the imperial and national sentiments of its people were indeed close to equilibrium. Since then, the British component has been dwindling with each successive generation. I started thinking about this book in the late 1960s, when Australian theatres were at last mercifully abstaining from *God Save The Queen*; and I was writing the last chapter when the Queen's representative in Australia dismissed a prime minister who held a majority in the House of Representatives.

Sir John Kerr's unfortunate action, combined with prudent avoidance of intervention by the Queen of the United Kingdom in her capacity as Queen of Australia, had certain beneficial side effects. It generated republican discussion, and showed furthermore how much Australia already resembled a republic. The Governor-General handled the 1975 constitutional crisis without the slightest reference or accountability to Britain, and to that extent he might just as well have been the president of a republic.

In the fifteen years since *Lion and Kangaroo*'s first publication, Australia's few remaining formal links with the United Kingdom have further diminished, and the republican debate has gained new vigour. Such matters are summarised in a postscript at the end of this edition.

I

INITIATION

BY THE LUCK of geography and chronology, it happened that the last continent to be explored and colonized by the British people, or indeed by any Europeans, was the first to enter the 20th century. Australia's precedence in this regard consisted only of a few hours, but the fact remains that while the clocks of Sydney, Melbourne, Brisbane and Hobart ticked away the first hour of 1 January 1901 those of London, Berlin, Washington and even Tokyo still had various distances to go before they reached the last midnight of an old era. Another hour brought South Australia into the new day ahead of all its fellow British colonies in Asia, and one more hour, by encompassing the colony of Western Australia, completed the southern continent's change of century. This minor distinction could hardly have been more appropriate, for it meant to anyone with an eye for symmetry, and perhaps prognostication too, that the first substantial land mass to be revealed by the first light of the 20th century was also that century's first new nation. Before the day was out, the six British colonies into which geographical Australia had been subdivided would be proclaimed the Commonwealth of Australia. In the words of Edmund Barton, who was to be sworn in that afternoon as Australia's first Prime Minister, there was something new under the sun: 'a nation for a continent, and a continent for a nation.'

As the light of day moved westward it unveiled the triumphal arches of Sydney, garlanded in readiness for a military procession and proclamation ceremony; it played over the eucalypt gorges and wind-scoured sandstone caves of the Blue Mountains, a barrier which the colonists of New South Wales had forced only eighty-eight years before; over the western slopes and plains, tawny as a lion's flanks in the heat of midsummer; and, west again, over the desolate superstructure of Broken Hill's silver and lead mines. Here the Caledonian band would soon be tuning its pipes for a parade down Argent Street, and at 12.30 p.m. the unofficial Federal flag would be saluted with an artillery piece made by some of the men at North Broken Hill mine.[1]

[1] This quite attractive flag was widely flown during the 1890s as the ensign of the Australian

North of Broken Hill the light was moving out over the veined Channel Country of Queensland, where a million empty watercourses waited for the wet season to begin; out across the Simpson Desert of the Northern Territory of South Australia, where ridges of red sand ran like corrugated iron from one horizon to the next; across gibber plains strewn with brown and purple stones; and so to the very centre of the continent, a region of astringent splendour whose inhabitants by and large were little affected by the coming of either the 20th century or Federation. These two manifestations meant something to the eighty inhabitants of Alice Springs and the few miners at Arltunga goldfield, 100 kilometres away; but they meant nothing at all to some 2000 Aborigines of the Aranda group who wandered the dry steppes and quartzite ranges south and west of Alice. The Aranda, like the Luritja people to the west of them and the Kaitish to the north, were not counted when it came to nationhood. The censuses taken in 1901 by New South Wales, Victoria, Queensland, South Australia, Tasmania and Western Australia – which together recorded a combined Australian population of 3,756,894 – probably counted no more than a quarter of the Aborigines whose ancestors had preceded the British Australians by many thousands of years. When the Commonwealth of Australia conducted its first national census ten years later, it omitted full-blooded Aborigines from national population figures for Constitutional reasons which will be explained later in this chapter. These people, who were thought to number about 67,000, were also excluded by the Constitution from those races for which Federal Parliament could make special laws, and to all intent they were denied the vote. If for no other reason than to make amends for such exclusion, it seems a good idea to start this narrative with the Aborigines of Central Australia as they were seen in 1901 by two of the very few white Australians who then took them seriously – Walter Baldwin Spencer, Professor of Biology at the University of Melbourne, and Francis James Gillen, a former post telegraph master at Alice Springs.

For most of that year Spencer and Gillen travelled northward from one Aboriginal group to the next, observing and recording ceremonial life. Neither man was immune from the prevailing racial attitudes of the time (Gillen referred to Aborigines as 'niggers' and 'darkies', and Spencer seemed to regard them as a somewhat more interesting species of Australian fauna than the platypus or the kangaroo); but both were

Federation League. It was based upon the British white ensign, with a large cross of pale blue instead of red. The cross was charged with five white stars, one in each arm of the cross and one in the centre, and the Union Jack appeared in the hoist. The official Australian flag, which will be referred to in Chapter 9, was chosen by competition in September 1901 and gazetted officially in 1903.

fascinated by the intricate web of ritual with which the Aborigines reconciled their present and their past and the land to which they and their ancestors had adapted so harmoniously. After twenty years in the Centre, Gillen had come to be held in high regard both by the Aborigines, who allowed him to attend some of their most sacred ceremonies, and by Australia's nascent circle of anthropologists. In 1900 he was elected president of the Anthropological Section at the Melbourne meeting of the Australasian Association for the Advancement of Science. It had been Gillen, the experienced amateur, who suggested seven years earlier to Professor Spencer, the professional scientist, that they should work together on the Aborigines.

As the result of a petition sent by British scientific societies to the Governments of Victoria and South Australia, both men were given twelve months' leave of absence from official duties so that they might continue their research on an overland expedition to the Gulf of Carpentaria. The cost of this was met by £1000 from David Syme – proprietor of the Melbourne *Age*, which boasted the largest newspaper circulation in the British Empire outside London (more than 100,000) – and £500 from Spencer's father in England; the South Australian Government also provided an express wagon, a team of horses, and the services of a mounted trooper. The expedition's equipment included a kinematograph camera and a large Edison phonograph, and the motion pictures and cylindrical recordings produced by them in 1901 survive to this day as evidence of Spencer's thoroughness. 'You may rest assured,' he wrote to Sir James Frazer, who had sent him a second edition of *The Golden Bough*, 'that at least Gillen and myself will do our best, and will not disregard the smallest trifles.'

The way north from Adelaide was by train to Oodnadatta, then by horse and wagon along a track following the route of the Overland Telegraph. Over this telegraph's two wires, strung between ceramic conductors on poles of metal pipe which marched 3200 kilometres to Palmerston (later renamed Darwin), went all the morse traffic between Australia and Britain, at 4s 10d per word. In Gillen's time at the Alice Springs repeating station, Aborigines sometimes impeded the flow of traffic by breaking off conductors and making them into scraping tools. He responded sensibly to this by providing a free supply of broken bottles. From Palmerston telegraph messages went by submarine cable to Java, Singapore, Penang, Madras, Bombay, Aden, Suez, Alexandria, Malta and Gibraltar to the office of the Eastern Extension Telegraph Co. in London. On this 24,000-kilometre route only Java lay outside the sway of the Empire to whose heart and soul Australia was linked so tangibly.

Spencer and Gillen left Oodnadatta on 19 March. They met their first wild 'niggers' two days later, and by April were well into Aranda country, a vast area of wiry and tussocky scrub, dry river-beds emblazoned here and there with the brilliant white trunks of ghost gums, and eventually the red gorges and bluffs of the MacDonnell Ranges. The Aranda people were dark brown, and heavily marked with ceremonial scars. They had broad noses and sloping foreheads, and although bodily graceful were 'somewhat under the average height of an Englishman', according to Spencer. Even in winter, when the night temperature fell below freezing point, they wore nothing that could have been described as clothing. The men, well endowed with wavy hair and frizzy beards, usually wore a forehead band of fur string, perhaps also a shock of emu feathers, and sometimes a long nose-bone supporting a bunch of parrot feathers. Their only other trappings were a waist belt of human hair provided by the wearer's mother-in-law, and a small pubic tassel whitened with pipeclay. The women wore necklets of bright red beans and perhaps a small apron of fur string.

In the early hours of 25 April, a date which later in Australian history would seem to have been strangely appropriate, Spencer and Gillen sat shivering in pre-dawn darkness waiting to see their first initiation ceremony on this expedition. While camped at Ellery River, a dry tributary of the Finke, due west of Alice Springs, they had been invited to attend a *quabara undattha* for the benefit of two young men who were then to undergo, as every Aranda male was required to do, the extraordinary rite of subincision. *Quabara undattha* was a general name for certain ceremonies performed away from the women by dancers wearing patterns of bird's down stuck to their bodies with blood. It is still possible to watch some of these innumerable ceremonies on film developed from Spencer's nitrate negatives. Because his camera was stationary, he set it up in front of the ground upon which most of each ceremony would take place. As the dancers move out of nowhere on to the screen, weirdly marked with pipeclay as well as bird's down, and then pass abruptly out of camera range again, they seem all the more to represent, as they were meant to do, the totemic ancestors who first had their being in the mythic past.

Every individual in Aranda society was born into some totem, and each of the tribe's many local groups was composed largely of individuals who associated themselves totemically with the same animal, plant, in-animate object or natural phenomenon: they were people of the kangaroo, emu, honey ant, white bat, eaglehawk, frog, hakea flower, dingo, echidna, crow, green cicada – even wind or sun, and fire or water. The most extensive totemic group among the Aranda in 1901, the forty-odd witchetty grub people, occupied an area of about 260 square kilometres near Alice Springs. Another totem, the plum tree, was represented by only one reincarnation. He lived alone and was the sole proprietor of several square miles of bush, including all its marsupials and reptiles, acacia seeds, wild honey, grubs and certain edible flies.

The *quabara undattha* near Ellery River was devoted to one of the most important totems – the white-spotted native cat. In its mythic wanderings, the first native cat was believed to have crossed Australia from south to north, populating the land not only with its own progeny but with kangaroos and emus as well, shaping many mountains and rivers, and instituting the rite of subincision. In a *quabara* the native cat wore a vest-like covering of bird's down and a tall tasselled hat of similar material.

Late on the night of 24 April, Spencer and Gillen were led in solemn procession to a site which had been prepared for the initiation. Spencer, wearing a heavy English overcoat, lay down in the bed of a sandy creek and tried to get some rest before the ceremony began at daybreak. 'I didn't get to sleep much,' he wrote in his journal. 'Every now and then someone would suddenly spring up and dance around the fire yelling "Wah! Wah!" with his hand moving quickly backwards and forwards in front of his mouth. You have no idea what a wild weird kind of shout this makes especially when it is made by a blackfellow amongst the rocky hills in the darkness of the night.' Gillen, huddled under a rug and suffering the onset of a bilious attack, had even less chance of sleep. 'The scene is a wild one,' he wrote, 'the blacks are squatting in clusters of three or four around small fires, the background of the camp is formed of lean long spectral-looking young gum trees. Would that I had the gift to transfer the scene to this page but I haven't. The din is fearful.'

Soon after dawn the native cat ceremony took place near a long spear in the ground ensheathed with hair string and rings of white and red bird's down, surmounted by a tuft of eaglehawk feathers, and hung with a number of sacred stones. The two young men for whom the *quabara* had been performed were then advised to embrace the feathered spear for several minutes in order to prevent pain during the surgical operation which now awaited them. Shortly before sunrise two men lay down, one on top of the other, and on this improvised altar the first of the young men lay supine. An operator took the young man's penis and with a quartzite knife slashed its underside, laying open the full length of the urethra from glans to scrotum. The initiate, his faith in the analgesic property of feathered spears somewhat diminished, was led away to squat over a shield until his bleeding had stopped. His relatives tied on his pubic tassel, telling him that he had now achieved the status of *atua-kurka* in the long procedure of initiation, and that, although more rites of passage were still ahead of him, he had no more operations to fear. During the three or four weeks which it took the *atua-kurka* to recover from subincision, he was forbidden to eat the flesh of opossum, snake, echidna or lizard, for to do so would be certain to inflame his wounds.

This surely was one of the most remarkable rites ever devised by the human mind. Neither the Aranda nor any of the other Central Australian tribes by whom it was universally practised, could or would explain to Professor Spencer why the native cat had seen fit to institute it. Yet the cat's mysterious decree had been observed faithfully for untold centuries. No male could take a wife before becoming *atua-kurka*, and infringement of that rule was punished by death. The Aranda did not associate subincision with the idea of preventing procreation, which was just as well, for it was no guarantee against that. It interfered with urination (*atua-kurka* usually squatted like women) but did not prevent insemination. In any case, the Aranda saw no direct connection between sexual intercourse (which merely, as they saw it, prepared the mother for the later implantation of a child by spiritual agency), and pregnancy (which was regarded as the direct consequence of a totemic ancestor entering her body). Some *atua-kurka* told later inquirers than Spencer that subincision increased coital pleasure by widening the penis, and that the easily opened urethral wound provided a ready source of the right kind of blood for bird's down. Arm blood was not sufficiently potent for this sacred purpose.

These sound more like rationalisations than origins, and it would seem that the underlying purpose of subincision must be sought elsewhere. The practice was only one, though an important one, of many initiation rites through which all Aranda males had to pass between the ages of ten or twelve and somewhere in the twenties. In the first of these rites, while women danced and sang, the boy was tossed into the air several times by the men, who caught him as he fell and then painted him with red or yellow ochre. He was told that henceforth he would no longer play with the women and girls, but would instead hunt with the men. His nasal septum was bored through by his father or paternal grandfather, and he began wearing a nose-bone.

At any age after puberty at which his elder male relatives decided that he was ready, the boy was shown certain totemic ceremonies for the first time and then, at a secret bush camp, amid the booming of unseen bull-roarers, he was circumcised. While the initiate was recovering from this operation, he also underwent a painful rite called 'head-biting'. As he lay face downwards several men bit deeply into his scalp, each man biting two or three times until blood poured and the initiate was screaming with pain.

The object was to make his hair grow abundantly.

Next came the rite of subincision, and finally the *engwura* – a series of initiation ceremonies which imparted totemic lore principally to do with the native cat, white bat and frog. One *engwura* attended by Spencer lasted four months and ended with what he called an ordeal by fire. Fire played an important part at various stages of the *engwura* (in one ceremony at night the initiates hurled hundreds of firesticks over the camp, sending them flying through the darkness like rockets to the accompanying screams of women and children and the howling of dogs), and an astonishing amount of blood was also used. One man bled more than two pints into a wooden shield while Spencer watched him. On the last day of the *engwura* a fire of logs and branches was burnt to a diameter of about three metres and covered with green boughs. Each initiate was then made to lie on the smoking leaves and endure the heat of the embers underneath for about five minutes. Every so often one of the older men would lift the boughs with a long pole to fan the fire.

The initiate – parboiled, subincised, scarred of scalp, circumcised and septum-pierced – was now a fully mature member of his society. Some of Spencer's informants told him that the *engwura* had the effect of strengthening all who passed through it, and imparted both wisdom and courage. Even after maturity the Aranda continued to mark their bodies with parallel ridges of keloid tissue which they raised by cutting the skin and rubbing ashes or bird's down into the wounds. Their bodies were in fact their scripture: a living record, inscribed for all to see, of rites performed and status honourably acquired. According to one of Spencer's contemporaries, the Dutch ethnologist Arnold Van Gennep, the initiation rites of all races and societies were concerned basically with separation and incorporation. The initiate, he said, was removed from the common mass of humanity by a rite of separation which automatically incorporated him into a defined group. The boy thrown up into the air and painted with ochre was thus separated from the world of women and children, and incorporated into the world of men; with each new rite he changed condition again, but was always vouchsafed the complementary guarantee of incorporation. The rite was both a permit to cross a new border and a defence against the anxiety of separation.

While Spencer and Gillen were testing the truth of these assertions among the Aranda, other rites were being performed in a wider Australian setting. On 30 March 514,400 Australians (56 per cent of the total enrolment) voted in the first election for a Federal Parliament. Spencer and Gillen were able to observe a microscopic part of this performance at the Charlotte Waters telegraph station. At 8 a.m. the telegraph master, in his capacity as assistant returning officer, placed a tin box on his office table and declared the poll open. 'There is no inrush of eager electors,' wrote Gillen, who had taken the precaution of casting his absentee vote before embarking on the expedition, 'indeed there are only three electors on the roll on this station: the cook and the assistant operator have never troubled to place their names on the roll. At breakfast I say a word in favour of the men I am supporting . . . [The telegraph master] stigmatizes my nominees, with one or two exceptions, as fools or worse. After breakfast I promptly interviewed the two free and independents outside and I am glad to be able to record that they went for my men.'

On 9 May, as if to reassure the young Commonwealth of its incorporation in the British Empire at another level, the Duke of Cornwall and York, who was later to become King George V, opened the first Australian Parliament. 'Neither of us would care to be present at the great function of which not even the faintest rumble reaches us here,' wrote Gillen at the Ellery River camp. That afternoon, the camp was startled by the sudden appearance in full regalia of twenty-five men from the eastern MacDonnell Ranges. 'They arrived in full dress,' wrote Gillen, 'each with a bunch of Eaglehawk or Emu feathers in his waist girdle and armed with spears boomerangs and shields. As soon as the local men heard that the party was approaching they hurried to their camps and decorated themselves with yellow ochre and charcoal and mustering together all fully armed they marched to meet the visitors . . . An hour or two was spent in raking up old grievances and discussing them in furious tones all speaking at once. Boomerangs were on several occasions thrown and with one exception cleverly parried. Some men foaming and quivering with rage tried to use their spears but the women rushed in and with the assistance of the more peaceful of the men stopped them . . . Things calmed down by degrees and after the more belligerent characters had grown too hoarse to make themselves heard I served out a stick of tobacco to each man which put them all in good humour.'

Had Spencer and Gillen been present in Melbourne's Exhibition Building, they would have found themselves in an assembly less turbulent but hardly less bizarre than the one at Ellery River. They would have seen the Duke of Cornwall, wearing the cocked hat and epaulettes of a British admiral and flanked by various vice-regal dignitaries splendid in gold braid and scarlet tunics, addressing the assembled members of the House of Representatives and the Senate in the name of his father, King Edward VII. 'The Duke of Cornwall read his message well,' noted the Governor of South Australia, Lord Tennyson, in his diary. 'Not very well stage-managed as there were long pauses. The Hallelujah chorus feeble. Told that our dais with its various uniforms looked splendid. "Rule Britannia" and "God Save The King" sung with fervour.'

This kind of imperial fervour – its ebb and flow with the passage of time, and its changing accommodations with Australian nationalism – will be the principle theme of the narrative soon to begin. The decade from which Australia had just emerged had not been an exclusive domain of nationalism. Admittedly the *Bulletin*, with its sustained antagonism towards the British Vampire and Union Jackals, had been fostering the nationalism of such writers as Henry Lawson, Joseph Furphy and Banjo Paterson. Looking back through the pages of the *Bulletin* during the 1890s, one could easily gain the impression that Australia, seething with radical and optimistic impulses, was about to strike out on its own. It should be remembered, however, that the twine of Australian identity had another strand to it: 'the crimson thread of kinship' which Sir Henry Parkes, the patriarch of Federation, found running through us all.

This thread was a genetic reality, for in 1901 more than 98 per cent of the Australian population was of English, Irish, Scottish or Welsh descent, and eighteen per cent had actually been born in the British Isles. Sixty-two per cent of Australia's imports came from Britain (eight out of ten grocery lines were British; even a certain amount of English butter was shipped out in salt casks), and in return the mother country took the lion's share of Australia's exports. Seventy-three per cent of the capital invested in Australian joint stock companies and public bonds was British rather than Australian; the coins in circulation were British coins bearing the likenesses of Queen Victoria and Britannia; and for defence the six Australian colonies relied not on their own miniature navies and armies ('painted soldiers', Parkes had called them) but on the might and mobility of the Royal Navy.

Such dependence on Britain could well have been resented by Australians if they had not been so British themselves, and if the British Government has responded less promptly to their pressure for Federal union. Britain's concessions were still a far cry from independence, but they were enough to satisfy most Australians. As the day of Federation approached, one of the founding fathers, B. R. Wise, wrote: 'I certainly did not anticipate [in 1888] that in so short a period of twelve years the then prevalent indifference on the part of Great Britain and suspicion on ours would have given place to the mutual confidence which is now so significant of the relations between the two countries.'

During the 1880s many nationalists were uncertain whether Australia ought to remain part of the British Empire much longer; but, as one historian has put it, 'schizoid love-hate' for Britain was an important part of Australian reality, and the loyalties of imperialism and nationalism were by no means mutually exclusive. By the end of the 19th century – in spite of the rising tide of Federation, which to a large extent was the product of nationalism – there was no longer much question about Australia's place in the British Empire. The republican leagues had withered away; the nationalist *Boomerang* had failed to return in 1892; and the Australian Natives' Association, numbering 20,000 members in 1900, had altered course from possible separation to positive imperial loyalty. Any doubts about that loyalty were stifled, for the time being at least, by the enthusiasm with which Australia sprang to Britain's aid when the Boer War began in 1899.

Australia's schizoid condition at the turn of the century consisted not simply of love and hate for a far distant progenitor, but also of dual loyalty. Alfred Deakin, one of the founding fathers who was now about to be sworn in as the Commonwealth's first Attorney-General, and would later serve three times as Prime Minister, considered himself to be an 'independent Australian Briton'. A Prime Minister of even longer tenure, William Morris Hughes, was to express much the same sentiment: 'A man may be a very loyal and devoted adherent to, and worshipper of, the Empire, and still he may be a very loyal and patriotic Australian all the time.'

Well, not quite all the time. As no one knew better than Deakin and Hughes, there were times when loyalties inevitably came into conflict and were inclined to chafe. One such occasion was a climactic series of meetings in London during March, April and May of 1900 between five Australian delegates and representatives of the British Government to negotiate the terms of a *Commonwealth of Australia Constitution Bill* which would bring Federation into being. These meetings at the Colonial Office were marked less by the mutual confidence which had impressed Bernhard Wise than by what Alfred Deakin now called 'polite antagonism'. The Australian delegates were Barton, a former Acting Prime Minister of New South Wales (Parkes, his predecessor at the head of both the New South Wales Government and the Federation movement, had died five years earlier); Deakin, representing Victoria; Sir James Dickson, a former Premier of Queensland; Charles Kingston, a former Premier of South Australia; and Sir Philip Fysh, a former Premier of Tasmania. Western Australia, which still had marked reservations about Federation, was represented by an observer, S. H. Parker. The principal negotiator for Britain's Conservative Government was the proud and combative Secretary of State for the Colonies, Joseph Chamberlain. The Queensland and Tasmanian delegates were inclined to be deferential towards

Chamberlain, but the same could not be said of their colleagues, all of whom were better acquainted with the constitutional points at issue. '[Dickson and Fysh] were visibly apologetic,' wrote Deakin, always an uninhibited chronicler of his contemporaries' foibles. 'Chamberlain was almost tart in manner.'

So far as the Australians were concerned, they already had a Constitution Bill of their own drafting; their task, according to instructions from a conference of the colonial premiers, was to secure the enactment of that bill by the British parliament without amendment. Chamberlain, for his part, proceeded to seek amendments which he said the British Government regarded as essential. Before describing this encounter more fully it is necessary to trace the steps by which the Australian colonies – each with its own customs tariff (travellers between Sydney and Melbourne, for example, had to go through customs at Albury), its own railway service, post office and postage stamps, defence force, parliament and governor – had come to the threshold of Federation.

As early as the middle of the 19th century, while the six colonies were pressing for more legislative autonomy, it was being suggested both in Australia and Britain that for reasons of geography, common ancestry, defence, economics and administrative convenience some form of colonial union was desirable. The most persistent advocate of this was the leonine giant Sir Henry Parkes, who, in a memorable speech at Tenterfield in 1889, had called for a conference of Australasian governments (which meant New Zealand's as well as Australia's, though it seemed doubtful that New Zealand had any intention of uniting with the Australian colonies) to explore the possibility of real federation. An earlier convention in 1883 had brought into being a Federal Australasian Council which was severely limited in power, did not include New South Wales or New Zealand (South Australia did not join until 1889, and dropped out again in 1891), and had no independent financial resources. It was little more than a debating society.

The first National Australasian Convention, meeting at Sydney in 1891, drafted a Federal Constitution which among other achievements seemed to find a way around the complex subject of customs tariff, once described by a former Premier of Victoria, James Service, as 'the lion in the path' towards Federation. It reassured the free traders of New South Wales with the promise of a common market between the colonies; and the protectionists of Victoria, anxious to shield their industries against overseas competition, left Sydney feeling confident that an external tariff framed by a Federal Government would be adequately protective. The draft Constitution, inspired partly by American, Canadian and Australian colonial examples, provided for two Houses of Parliament, a Governor-General to represent the British Sovereign in Australia, and a Federal court to hear all Australian appeals. It conferred upon the Federal Government some carefully defined powers, including the power to control all armed forces, and what was not so defined was to reside with the Colonies, or 'States' as they were to be known. The drafting was done mainly by Sir Samuel Griffith, then Premier of Queensland and later to become first Chief Justice of the Federal court; Andrew Inglis Clark, the Attorney-General of Tasmania; Kingston and Barton. But the style (such as it was, for neither this nor the final version of the Constitution had the literary quality of their American model), given its final polish during a cruise on Broken Bay and the Hawkesbury River in the Queensland Government's steam yacht *Lucinda*, belonged almost entirely to Griffith.

Not the least of this Convention's achievements was a decision that the new Federal union should be called the Commonwealth of Australia, a term suggested by Parkes, supported enthusiastically by Deakin, and narrowly adopted by the Constitutional Committee in preference to 'Federal Dominion'. Parkes's choice of 'Commonwealth' was inspired not only by Cromwell's use of the word, which endowed it with disturbing overtones of republicanism, but also by his awareness that it had been used earlier by Shakespeare and Milton. He may also have been guided by American precedent, for James Bryce's *The American Commonwealth*, published only three years before, was obligatory reading for framers of the Australian Constitution.

Another National Australasian Convention, attended by representatives from all colonies except Queensland, met at Adelaide during 1897 and Melbourne early in 1898. Guided by the 1891 draft, the Convention's Constitutional Committee – consisting of Barton (chairman), his close friend Richard O'Connor from New SouthWales, and Sir John Downer, a former Premier of South Australia, all of whom were assisted in their deliberations by Barton's secretary, Robert Garran – produced a Constitution which gave the Commonwealth a few more specific powers but in some respects was more decentralized than its forerunner. One subject which was never at any stage discussed constructively by the founding fathers was the position of Australia's Aborigines. The only references to them in the Constitution were highly negative in character: Section 51 Sub-section (xxvi) made Aboriginal questions a matter for the States rather than the Commonwealth (the Federal Parliament was empowered to make laws with respect to 'the people of any race, other than the Aboriginal race in any State'), and Section 127 directed that 'in reckoning the numbers of the people of the Commonwealth, or of a State or other part of the Commonwealth, aboriginal natives shall not be counted.' The Commonwealth Franchise Act of 1902 specifically excluded Aborigines from the vote unless they already had it for a State lower house, which very few of them did. Section 127 of the Constitution was inspired not by racial prejudice or by the physical difficulty of including Aborigines in a census, but rather by the need to allocate seats in the House of Representatives according to the population of each State, and to share between the States on a population basis certain revenues collected by the Commonwealth. This section was not intended to qualify the taking of censuses or the publishing of population figures, but it had that effect nonetheless. It does not seem to have occurred to any of the Constitution's framers that the two Aboriginal provisions, which were emended from the Constitution after a referendum in 1967, bore the implication that Aborigines were less than human beings.

The Constitution of 1898 was submitted for consideration by the Parliaments of the five participating colonies; the Convention re-convened to consider the suggestions made by these Parliaments and, unofficially, by the Colonial Office; and at a final session the *Constitution Bill* was adopted in a form ready for submission to the voters of all Colonies. In June and July of 1898 referendums were held in Victoria, South Australia, Tasmania and New South Wales. The required affirmative majorities were easily achieved in the first three colonies, but not in New South Wales, where the ante had been raised by the Reid Government's amendment of the NSW Enabling Act requiring a 'Yes' vote to exceed 80,000. The affirmation in New South Wales, although a majority of those voting, failed by 5,000 to reach this figure, and early in 1899 the Premiers of all six colonies met in Melbourne to try to break the deadlock. This conference amended the Bill to meet criticisms that it was too conservative and too heavily weighted in favour of the less populous colonies, mollified New South Wales and its Premier, Sir George Reid, by deciding that the site of the Commonwealth capital should not be more than 160 kilometres from Sydney, and lessened the financial anxieties of the future States by adding a federal power to make conditional grants to them – a power which would later be used as an instrument for Commonwealth 'intrusions' into State fields.

Back to the polling booths. A second referendum held in all colonies except Western Australia between April and September 1899 produced 'Yes' verdicts in all cases, though the majority was narrow in Queensland. In total, about 40 per cent of those entitled to vote supported Federation, and 16 per cent rejected it. Western Australia, the most apprehensive of the 'small States', still demanded concessions before passing its Enabling Act.

The goldfields of Coolgardie and Kalgoorlie, heavily populated with 'T'othersiders' from the eastern colonies, wanted to federate, and were even talking of doing so if necessary without the rest of the colony; but the conservative Western Australian Government, dominated by the massive figure and feudal character of its Premier, the former explorer Sir John Forrest, was alarmed by the threatened loss of its right to impose customs duty, which provided about 90 per cent of the Colony's revenue.

Any revenue misgivings held by the other colonies had been assuaged by the so-called 'Braddon Clause' of the *Constitution Bill*, which provided that the Commonwealth Government, although collecting all customs and excise duty, would, for the first ten years of Federation at least, spend no more than one-fourth of that revenue on its own affairs and would distribute the balance to the State Governments. Western Australia, unconvinced, continued to bargain with the other colonies and with Britain for the right to levy customs for five years after the creation of the Commonwealth. Despite this lingering unevenness in the Federal ranks, the British Government indicated its willingness to discuss the *Constitution Bill* with those colonies which had already dressed in line. Western Australia and New Zealand also sent observers to this conference.[1]

At the first meeting in the Colonial Office, Joseph Chamberlain insisted upon four amendments to the Bill. He, or rather his law officers, objected first to a phrase in one of the Bill's introductory clauses, *This Act shall bind the Crown*; and secondly to the Bill's provision that Commonwealth laws should operate *on all British ships, the Queen's ships of war excepted, whose first port of clearance and whose destination* lay within the Commonwealth of Australia. Chamberlain's law officers professed to be concerned about the possibility that some colonial laws might be in conflict with the body of law already applying to British vessels around the world. This raised a third point: would the Colonial Laws Validity Act

---

[1] Although New Zealand suggested some amendments to the Bill, it had little real interest in joining the Federation. A ten-man Royal Commission which spent the first five months of 1901 inquiring into the arguments for and against New Zealand membership concluded its report with this resounding sentence: 'Your Commissioners, after giving the fullest consideration to the evidence before them, and with their knowledge of the soil, climate and productiveness of New Zealand, of the adaptability of the lands of the Colony for close settlement, of her vast natural resources, her immense wealth in forest, in mine, in natural scenery, of the energy of her people, of the abundant rainfall and vast water-power she possesses, of her insularity and geographical position; remembering, too, that New Zealand as a Colony can herself supply all that can be required to support and maintain within her boundaries a population which might at no distant date be worthily styled a nation, have unanimously arrived at the conclusion that merely for the doubtful prospect of further trade with the Commonwealth of Australia, or for any advantage which might reasonably be expected to be derived by this Colony from becoming a State in such Commonwealth, New Zealand should not sacrifice her independence as a separate Colony, but that she should maintain it under the political Constitution she at present enjoys.'

(designed to avoid any such legislative collision by affirming imperial supremacy whenever British and colonial laws contradicted one another) apply to the laws of the Commonwealth? The Colonial Office thought the answer was 'Yes', and that it should be clearly written into the Constitution.

Fourthly, Chamberlain objected to Clause 74 of the proposed Constitution which prevented (except for the Queen's right to grant special leave by Royal prerogative, which in any case the Federal Parliament would be empowered to limit at its legislative discretion) appeals proceeding from the Federal High Court to the British Privy Council on matters involving interpretation of the Constitutions of the Commonwealth and any State, unless those matters involved the public interest of some part of the British Empire other than the Commonwealth or State. Despite its safeguards, this clause was regarded by the Colonial Office as a threat to imperial interests *inside* the new Commonwealth. To Chamberlain, these interests meant not only matters affecting Britain's foreign relations but also 'the private interests of investors . . . a very large class . . . of British subjects interested in Australia.' Their interests might be affected by Constitutional cases, it was felt at Whitehall, and should therefore be protected by leave to appeal.

The Australian delegates gave in quietly over *This Act shall bind the Crown*; and, when it came to the point, Britain did not insist upon either deletion of the maritime clause or obeisance to the Colonial Laws Validity Act. The Colonial Office's enthusiasm for the latter amendment cooled considerably when the Australian delegates seemed about to raise the more basic question of whether the *Validity Act* should apply at all to 'such great self-governing communities as the Dominion [of Canada] and the Commonwealth.' The safer course, Britain decided, was not to press for a formal declaration of imperial supremacy but to rely upon the strong probability that, in the event of any legal ruling on whether the *Validity Act* applied to a Commonwealth law which was in conflict with an imperial Act applying throughout the Empire, the Commonwealth would be found subordinate.

On the final amendment, both sides compromised. Chamberlain proposed that Clause 74 should leave Constitutional cases of distinctively Australian interest to final settlement by the High Court while at the same time permitting appeal to the Privy Council in all matters involving imperial interest. But who was to decide which cases were 'Constitutional'? The answer – suggested by Griffith, Downer and O'Connor among others, but given precise form by a British official, and accepted by the British Government while the Bill was on its way through the House of

Commons – was that only the High Court itself should have authority to grant or withhold leave to appeal from its own decisions in Constitutional cases involving the relative powers of the Commonwealth and States. In other matters the Judicial Committee of the Privy Council would be at liberty to issue special leave to appeal to itself from the High Court, though the Commonwealth would also have power to bring down legislation restricting the kind of matters on which these non-Constitutional appeals could be made by leave from the Privy Council.

This was the 'golden bridge' across which the Australian Colonies finally passed to Federation. When the British delegates left the meeting which finalised Clause 74, there took place a curious little ceremony which Deakin, who had been suffering badly from carbuncles in the last days of the conference, later described with his customary frankness. 'Splendid!' he wrote. 'When the door closed upon [the Australian delegates] and left them alone, they seized each other's hands and danced hand in hand around the centre of the room to express their jubilation.'

The *Commonwealth of Australia Constitution Act*, assented to by Queen Victoria on 9 July 1900, began by noting that the people of New South Wales, Victoria, South Australia, Queensland and Tasmania had agreed 'to unite in one indissoluble Federal Commonwealth under the Crown of the United Kingdom of Great Britain and Ireland.' It went on to empower the Queen to declare by proclamation that on and after a certain day the people of those five colonies – 'and also, if Her Majesty is satisfied that the people of Western Australia have agreed thereto, of Western Australia' – should be united in a Federal Commonwealth. The rest of the Act consisted of the eight chapters and 128 sections of the Constitution.

In the nick of time, and not without some anxious prodding by the Secretary of State for Colonies, Western Australia toed the line. In March, as Barton and his colleagues were coming to grips with the British Government, the 'T'othersider' faction on the Western Australian goldfields presented to the Queen a petition of 27,733 signatures requesting the union of their region with South Australia. Chamberlain at about this time urged the Federal delegates to give special consideration to Western Australia's request that, if it entered the Commonwealth as an original member, it should be allowed to retain its present tariff for five years. The delegates felt, however, that their common market concept had already been compromised as far as was reasonable by the Bill's concession that Western Australia could impose customs duty on goods from other States at a rate which would diminish by one-fifth each year, thus ceasing altogether after the fifth year of Federation.

In April Chamberlain brought his influence bluntly to bear upon the

Forrest Government with a cable urging Western Australia to join as an original State on the existing Constitutional terms, and hinting that unless this happened sympathetic consideration would be given to the goldfields petition. The game was up, and the Parliament at Perth passed its Enabling Act. At Western Australia's referendum on 31 July, 46 per cent of those eligible to vote, and 69 per cent of those actually voting, said 'Yes' – the highest affirmative vote from any of the Colonies. Thus satisfied that Western Australians were at one with the people of the eastern colonies, Queen Victoria proclaimed on 17 September 1900 that 'on and after the first day of January one thousand nine hundred and one' the people of all six colonies would be united in a Federal Commonwealth under the name of the Commonwealth of Australia.

Symmetry would have its way, and the initiation of the 20th century would coincide with what Deakin called 'the birthday of a whole people.' In the flush of optimism, it was possible to overlook the extent to which the new Commonwealth would remain subordinate to the old imperial power; but subordinate it would be without any doubt. The Federal Parliament would have power to make laws for the peace, order and good government of the Commonwealth with respect to naval and military defence, for example, but nevertheless it could not authorize the declaration of war or the making of peace with a foreign power. These were prerogatives of sovereignty, and, as constitutional lawyers agreed, the Commonwealth of Australia would not be a sovereign State. As the position was described some years later by one constitutional authority – Sir Arthur Berriedale Keith, a dignitary at the Colonial Office during the early years of Federation – the Commonwealth could not even declare itself neutral, for such a declaration would be to deny that it was a dependency of the United Kingdom, and such a denial would be *ultra vires* the Federal Parliament. 'It is perfectly clear,' wrote Keith, 'that in international law the whole of the Empire is at war if the United Kingdom is at war, and that it lies in the hands alone of the Imperial Government to declare war or to make peace.'

Although empowered by its Constitution to make laws for its own peace, order and good government with respect to external affairs, the Commonwealth would have no power to make the more formal kinds of treaties with foreign States, and would have no diplomatic status abroad. The executive power of the Commonwealth, extending to the maintenance of its Constitution and laws, would be vested in the Queen, but exercised formally on her behalf by the Governor-General with the advice of his Australian ministers. That advice would of course carry great weight, and in practice the executive government of the Commonwealth would be almost exclusively the province of elected politicians; but the final say, if it ever came to that, would in theory rest with the representative of the Sovereign. In many matters the prime minister and his parliament would be plainly subservient to the Governor-General and the British institutions which he represented. If the Australian Prime Minister wished to communicate officially with his opposite number in a foreign country, or even in Great Britain, he would have to do so first through the Governor-General and thence through the Colonial Office. The Parliament of Westminister could pass legislation applicable to the Commonwealth, and, as we have seen, under the doctrine of colonial repugnancy any Commonwealth law at odds with that legislation would almost certainly be void and inoperative. Furthermore, the Queen would appoint the Governor-General of Australia on the advice of her own imperial ministers, and that gentleman could, at his discretion, withhold assent from any of the Commonwealth Parliament's Bills or reserve any of those Bills for the Queen's pleasure. In other words, he could stop them becoming law. Even where the Governor-General had granted assent in the Queen's name, Her Majesty would still be able to disallow the law at any time up to a year after assent.

For all these reasons it was clear to anyone who thought about the matter that the Commonwealth of Australia would still be what its constituent members had been hitherto, and what the Colonial Office was going to call it for several years to come: a self-governing colony. Yet clearly also, the whole would be more than its parts. The gap between Commonwealth power and full sovereignty was not so wide that it could not one day be bridged, and in the exercise of vice-regal discretionary powers the Governor-General would have his Australian ministers to think of as well as Her Majesty's ministers at home. Eventually the Commonwealth would become whatever Australia could make of it, and in the give and take of that continuing process the Australian-British relationship would be exposed to many subtly changing pressures at levels of both public and private life.

The Australian Britons who were about to become a 'whole people' would have many thresholds to cross during the first two decades of Federation. In that respect they were not so different from the Aboriginal societies which they had displaced, or the still untouched tribes visited by Spencer and Gillen in Central Australia. Despite their continuing Colonial status, the Australian Britons were about to experience a kind of separation and rebirth. In their new form they would be incorporated into the British Empire with appropriate ceremonies of the lion and unicorn, and as subsequent changes of status occurred there would be other rites of passage sacred to the kangaroo and emu. The initiation of Australia may indeed be considered in much the same terms as initiation among the Aranda: a succession of shock-absorbing, status-confirming rites all the way from the first jubilant throwing of the child into the air to the young man's final ordeal by fire. In the chapters to come we shall travel across an historical landscape from 1901 to 1919, observing the rites of passage as we go. The rites will be associated with many totems, but the most important by far will be those of the lion and kangaroo.

2

MOTHER AND DAUGHTER

AT THE TOP of its regular column entitled 'Today's Arrangements' – where readers turned to see what was going on in Royalty, Parliament, sport and society – the London *Times* of Tuesday, 1 January 1901, announced grandly, almost permissively: 'The Twentieth Century begins.' In fact, of course, that century had already begun elsewhere in the world. The Lord Mayor of London had acknowledged as much by ordering the Bow Bells to be rung and the unofficial Australian flag to be hoisted over the Mansion House at two o'clock the previous afternoon, the Greenwich Mean Time equivalent of the moment at which the east coast of Australia had passed into the 20th century and the Commonwealth of Australia had entered history.

The day's arrangements for the Commonwealth involved every corner of the continent. At Geraldton – a sugar-cane community on the far north coast of Queensland, later renamed Innisfail, numbering about 200 white Australians and 1500 Chinese, Japanese, Malays and Kanakas – schoolchildren were presented with Commonwealth medals and addressed by two clergymen. The Reverend J. Massingbred Teale told his young listeners that in future, instead of being Queenslanders, they would be Australians; they must not, however, forget that they were also children of the great British Empire of which the Commonwealth formed a part. The next speaker, Father Clancy, made no mention of the Empire.

Another Geraldton, a wool port over 3000 kilometres away on the shore of the Indian Ocean, had voted against Federation at the Western Australian referendum; but its townspeople now put their heart into a Commonwealth Day procession led by mounted police, and at night there was a fireworks display at sea. The little mining town of Southern Cross, 320 kilometres northeast of Perth, raised the unofficial Australian flag and sang *The Sons Of New Britannia*. Then it raised the Union Jack, whose 100th anniversary also happened to fall on that very day, and sang *Where The Flag Of England Flies*. At the centre of the goldfields, and of the Federal movement in Western Australia, Kalgoorlie staged a procession cheered by 15,000 people. The first vehicle was a drag drawn by eight greys and carrying officials of the Goldfields Reform League which had helped to prod the Western Australian Government into holding a referendum; it was followed, among other less impressive vehicles, by a large float in the form of a Japanese battleship made, and manned in immaculate naval uniforms, by the Japanese residents of Kalgoorlie. The *Kalgoorlie Miner* conceded that 'the little brown men' had produced the best display of all, but at an open-air concert that evening one speaker from the Reform League reminded his listeners that they had to declare firmly for a white man's Australia. The Commonwealth, he said, should not be peopled by 'a mongrel or piebald race.'

At Gould's Country, in the northeast corner of Tasmania, bands of young men walked from house to house playing music. One settler who welcomed the strolling players with cakes said he was glad to see them – firstly, because it was New Year's Day; secondly, because it was the beginning of a new century, which none of them was likely to see again; and thirdly, because it was 'our first birthday as a nation.' There was less enthusiasm at Hobart, where the Chief Justice of Tasmania, Sir John Dodds, after being sworn in as Administrator of the new State, read Queen Victoria's proclamation of the Commonwealth before a crowd which the *Mercury* described as neither large nor demonstrative. Hobart was feeling snubbed by the apparent failure of the Prime Minister-designate, Edmund Barton, to include a Tasmanian in his first Cabinet. 'This seemed to have completely damped the ardour of all who assembled,' said the *Mercury*, 'and prompted such remarks as, "We would have stood out of it if we could; but unfortunately we could not afford to." ' The Constitution provided for only seven paid ministers (combined salaries, £12,000), and Barton had decided that the claim of Western Australia to one of these positions was stronger than Tasmania's. His ministry consisted of Deakin; the Prime Minister of New South Wales, Sir William Lyne; the Premiers of Victoria and Western Australia, Sir George Turner and Sir John Forrest; the former Prime Minister of South Australia, Charles Kingston; and the former Premier of Queensland, Sir James Dickson. At the last moment, in time for the swearing in of the Executive Council on Tuesday afternoon, he included two more ministers without portfolio and without salary – Richard O'Connor from New South Wales, and the Premier of Tasmania, Neil Lewis. But Hobart, which claimed to have been staunchly pro-Federation while Perth wavered, was still sulking.

In Adelaide town hall at 12.30 p.m. Lord Tennyson, the hearty, gouty Governor of the Province of South Australia, was sworn in as Governor of the Federal State of South Australia – a change of title which brought Tennyson, who was the senior Colonial Governor, a dormant commission to administer the Government of the Commonwealth in the Governor-General's absence. Tennyson and the only other State Governor then in residence, Lord Lamington at Brisbane, had absented themselves from the day's most important proceedings at Sydney because, as Tennyson explained in a cable to the Colonial Office, 'the States would resent any appearance of subordination of States to Governor-General.' After Lord Tennyson had concluded his swearing-in address with three blessings – 'God bless the Queen [cheers], God bless the Mother Country [cheers] and God bless our Commonwealth of Australia [loud cheers]' – the Adelaide Choral Society sang a musical setting of *Hands All Round*, a poem by his father, the late poet laureate:

> First pledge our Queen, my friends, and then
> A health to England every guest,
> He best will serve the race of men,
> Who loves his native country best.

The Adelaide procession, unlike those in other capital cities, included a motor car. There were at that time little more than sixty motor vehicles in the whole of Australia, and not only did they frighten horses but most of them, because air and benzine were fed separately into their carburetors by two levers, were hard to drive sufficiently slowly for a procession. They kept overtaking everyone else. The Lewis car in Adelaide completed the distance discreetly, however, and was reported to have been 'excellently got up.'[1]

Melbourne, which had influenced the Federal cause more than any other capital, was not yet the centre of Commonwealth affairs which it would soon become. Many of its leading citizens had gone to Sydney for the principal inauguration ceremony, and the city was not so lavishly decorated as it would be when Federal Parliament opened there later in the year. The Victorian House of Parliament, already designated as the temporary seat of Federal Parliament, was surmounted by a pictorial representation of Rudyard Kipling's poem *The Young Queen*, and on its ample steps, surrounded by banks of fern, were gigantic models of the

---

[1] Although few in number, these precursors of what was sometimes called 'automobilism, were gradually getting around the continent. Only recently a 2¼ horsepower De Dion Voiturette had travelled from Melbourne to Sydney in 38 hours' actual riding time, leaving in its wake clouds of dust and sensations of wonder. So clean was the atmosphere in 1901, and so still the night air of southern New South Wales, that some people who had seen the Voiturette pass during the previous afternoon could still detect the unfamiliar odour of benzine next morning. The first car in Australia – the Knight Eaton, a tricycle car built at Brisbane in 1893 – was not a great success. By 1901 Sydney had twenty-eight cars, and was able to muster six for a trial run to Botany Bay. The first breach of law by a motorist appears to have been in 1903, when Charles Kellow, a well known cyclist, was fined for 'furiously driving a motor car' along the Toorak Road in Melbourne.

Crown of England and the British Coat of Arms. Above the steps, along the Roman Doric colonnade in large gold letters, ran the message: 'Federated Australia – One Flag, One Hope, One Destiny.'

In New South Wales schoolchildren at Deniliquin were being given medals to commemorate the relief of the British garrison at Mafeking, and at Condobolin, on the western plains, a Commonwealth sports carnival was enlivened by an event called 'Cleaving The Boer's Head'. Australians were at war not only in South Africa but to a token extent also in China. In South Africa the Commonwealth was toasted at the messes of some imperial regiments with which Australian troops were serving, and in China, where men of the New South Wales and Victorian Naval Brigades were helping in their small way to put down the Boxer Rebellion, a grand review of all British forces was held on New Year's Day at Peking for the joint purpose of commemorating Queen Victoria's proclamation as Empress of India, twenty-four years before, and honouring the inauguration of the Commonwealth. The Chinese adventure was hardly more gruelling for Australia than the New South Wales Contingent's almost bloodless taste of war in the Soudan had been sixteen years previously; but for the Chinese it was not without some hazards.[1] The 100-strong Victorian Naval Contingent had recently served with a British column which had occupied the walled city of Pao Ting Fu and arranged for the decapitation of thirty prominent Boxers.

Grand though the review at Peking may have been, it was outstripped as a military spectacle by the procession through Sydney which led up to the reading of the Queen's proclamation and ceremonies of oath-taking at Centennial Park. The Sydney procession was made up not only of soldiers and civilians from all over the Commonwealth, but also – as a sort of stiffening and embellishment – an imperial contingent of one thousand men drawn from most of the better regiments of the British and Indian armies. After disembarking from the *Britannic*, these Dragoon Guards, Hussars, Fusiliers, Highlanders, Bengal Lancers, Sikhs and Gurkhas set up camp on Sydney's Agricultural Ground, where they immediately became the centre of admiring attention from local soldiers

[1] A New South Wales contingent of 750 men and 200 horses reached the Soudan in March 1885, but Britain's war against the Mahdi was almost over by that time and the New South Welshmen saw hardly any fighting. Three men were slightly wounded in a single skirmish, and six died of fever. Nobody won the stipend of 20 guineas a year for five years which an Australian jingo had offered to the first New South Welshman to win a Victoria Cross, but nonetheless one member of the Legislative Assembly welcomed the troops back with the words: 'God bless old England; well done Australia!' Australia's only other military experience had been during the Waikato War of 1863–4, the biggest of the Maori Wars in New Zealand. About 2600 volunteers, mainly Victorians and New South Welshmen, took part in this war as military settlers. Many of them saw sporadic action, and they suffered some casualties.

and journalists. New South Wales regimental parades were postponed so that colonial officers could watch the imperials at drill, and the *Sydney Mail* informed its readers that the average chest measurement of the 2nd Battalion Queen's Own Cameron Highlanders was 38 inches.

The Commander-in-Chief of the Commonwealth's military forces, by virtue of his office as the Queen's representative in Australia, was the slim, elegant but rather sickly Governor-General: John Adrian Louis Hope, 7th Earl of Hopetoun, Viscount Aithrie, Baron Hope and Baron Niddry. Lord Hopetoun, then in his 41st year, had been a popular Governor of Victoria during the early 1890s. 'A *grand seigneur* to the tips of his fingers,' as one visitor to the colony described him, Hopetoun nonetheless had an easy manner in all kinds of company. One day in 1892 two bush workers engaged on a fencing contract, John Neilson and his son Shaw Neilson, were camped at a water tank in Karkarook County, northwestern Victoria, when Lord Hopetoun and his entourage stopped there for a midday meal. While the Vice-Regals were dining, one of their horses bolted into the scrub. Young Shaw Neilson, who was later to be acclaimed as one of Australia's best lyrical poets, went after the horse and took it back to its owner. 'He was a big stout chap,' wrote Neilson many years later. 'He did not even say thank you. I was rather surprised that such a fine gentleman should behave so badly. After dinner Lord Hopetoun himself came over. He began to chat with my father just as if they had known each other from boyhood. What a charm the man had. He spoke of everything that would interest us, the future of the Mallee, the possibility of the depression ending, the improvement of the gold mining industry in Bendigo. There was no nonsense about the Earl. He seemed to be every inch a man. He was a fine sport.'

During the depression of 1892–3, Hopetoun gave cases of champagne to the unemployed and, more to the point, used his influence to find employment for some of them. He had spent considerably more than his official salary on the Governorship of Victoria, and was now about to do the same on the Governor-Generalship. He had sent seventeen horses and thirteen stablemen ahead of him to Melbourne, and eventually came to have thirty horses in his stables. The Tennysons in South Australia were astounded at the extravagant demands made upon their kitchen by the Governor-General's valet when, after a brief stay at Government House in Adelaide, the Hopetouns and their accompanying staff of two prepared to face the rigours of an overnight train journey back to Melbourne. The valet's list of requirements, as recounted by Lady Tennyson to her mother in England, read as follows: '2 bottles of whisky, 2 bottles claret, 1 bottle port, 9 bottles spa water which costs I don't know what out here! Then he took a menu to Mrs Bates saying they required "Fish, 2 chickens – a tongue, ham, fillet of beef and other things I forget – dessert, pears, apples, grapes and bananas, bacon and eggs to fry for their breakfast – though they stop at an excellent station for breakfast and are due at Melbourne at 10 – tea, coffee, 2 large bottles of cream, milk, rolls, bread, 1 lb butter etc." All these things and quantities ordered by the valet if you please.'

Apart from this raid on their pantry, the Tennysons found the Governor-General 'full of fun, a wonderful mimick and extremely kind and thoughtful and open.' At their first meeting, Hopetoun asked Tennyson why certain young ladies with bare shoulders were like bad photographs. Answer: because they were too much exposed and ill-developed. On the other hand, recorded Lady Tennyson after one meal with the Governor-General and his lady, 'we had a good deal of one of his favourite topics, his health and his sufferings and awful depression of spirits when he feels he would like to lie down and die.' Hopetoun once expressed the opinion to Edmund Barton that the Governor-Generalship did not require extreme cleverness but did want 'a reasonably sound stomach and lots of energy.' In both these essentials he was wanting. On the voyage out he had suffered so badly from a tropical fever that after landing at Sydney on 15 December he still required three days of rest to recuperate.

He was clever enough, certainly more so than one of his rival candidates for the Governor-Generalship, Lord Brassey, who had succeeded him as Governor of Victoria. There was some feeling in Australia that the job should go to a member of the Royal Family, perhaps the Duke of Cornwall or Duke of Connaught; but once the Queen had made it known that she did not want any of her grandsons taking up residence so far from England, the field narrowed to three former Australian governors – Hopetoun, who had recently been serving as Lord Chamberlain in Queen Victoria's household; another 7th Earl, Lord Jersey, a former Governor of New South Wales; and Brassey. The latter was not highly regarded at the Colonial Office ('The man is an ass,' minuted someone on one of his despatches), and when the appointment was finally announced on 18 July 1900 it went to the Queen's Lord Chamberlain.

Whether because of illness or bad advice, the Governor-General began his term of office by making what came to be known as the Hopetoun Blunder. His first task was to invite some Australian citizens to form a ministry which would act as a caretaking 'government' until the normal parliamentary machinery began to function at a Federal election. This had to be the Governor-General's decision, and to the astonishment of most Australian politicians he chose not Barton – as Barton, Deakin and others confidently expected he would – but Sir William Lyne, the 'crude, sleek, suspicious, blundering, short-sighted' Prime Minister of New South Wales. The description was Deakin's, but even those more tolerant of Lyne were hard put to understand why Hopetoun had chosen him. He was a big, shambling man with features half-hidden by whiskers and a chest-deep beard which might almost have belonged to one of the Boer leaders whose likenesses were then to be seen in Australia's newspapers. In moments of tension it was Lyne's habit to pull his beard, sometimes sharply, and sometimes – as his fellow parliamentarian, W. M. Hughes, observed – 'with the gentle rhythmic movement of a man milking a good-tempered cow.'

Hopetoun quickly realised that he had made a grave error of judgment. 'Great surprise expressed at choice of Lyne instead of Barton,' read a cable to him from the Secretary of State for the Colonies. 'Please give reasons.' What Hopetoun had apparently decided was that the first Prime Minister, who in any case would soon be either confirmed or replaced after the first election, should be the Prime Minister of the senior colony, New South Wales. There was Canadian precedent for such an *ex officio* choice, and it just might have worked in Australia if the wily but popular Sir George Reid had still held that office, for at least Reid had been half-heartedly in favour of Federation. Lyne, although a Protectionist unlike Reid, had consistently opposed the Federal cause.

How could Barton serve under such a man? Both he and O'Connor declined the invitation promptly, and although Lyne continued the attempt to form a ministry his hopes steadily declined. If Deakin had agreed to work with him, he might have brought it off, for he would then have had a fair show of securing the other leading Victorian, Sir George Turner; Sir Frederick Holder, the Premier of South Australia; and perhaps also Sir John Forrest of Western Australia. But Deakin would serve under no one but his leader in the Federal movement, and on Christmas Eve Sir William Lyne advised the Governor-General to send for Barton.

'Toby' Barton, as his friends had called him since childhood, was a well-rounded man in every respect. At the age of fifty-one, with the Speakership and Attorney-Generalship of New South Wales behind him as well as years of devoted work for the Federal cause, he was an imposing figure of 100 kilograms; tall and dignified, with heavy but clearly chiselled features and a head of thick brown hair streaked with one lock of white above the forehead; an excellent cricketer in his day, and now a *bon vivant* and convivial clubman. Barton was a pillar of the Athenaeum Club, where he was regarded as one of the best talkers among a company which included the editor of the *Bulletin*, J. F. Archibald; the artist Julian Ashton;

the editor of *The Sydney Morning Herald*, Andrew Garran, whose son had been Barton's secretary; the Professor of English Literature at Sydney University, Mungo McCallum; and finally the Professor of Latin, Tom Butler, who Barton said was 'all meat'. Barton himself had graduated from Sydney University with first-class honours in Classics before going to the Bar, and while he was Prime Minister he still possessed sufficient Latin to converse briefly in that language with Pope Pius X at the Vatican. He was later to regret this feat when he received a petition of protest from 30,000 angry Australian Protestants.

Because of his clubbable temperament and liking for good food and drink (the *Bulletin* called him 'Toby Tosspot'), it was sometimes said that Barton did not bring to the Prime Ministership quite the amount of energy which that office required. This reputation was undeserved. Barton had worked passionately for Federation (in four years, he addressed no fewer than 300 public meetings), and as Prime Minister he worked long into the night when necessary. He enjoyed a good working relationship with the Governor-General, but in the end, as we shall see later, he unintentionally repaid poor Hopetoun for his blunder.

It was still New Year's Day in Sydney: a day as hot and humid as the tropics. The sky had at first been overcast after a storm the night before, but during the morning it cleared to a soft blue mirrored in a deeper shade by the wide waters of Sydney Harbour. No fewer than eleven warships of the Royal Navy lay at anchor in the harbour, and around Circular Quay one could see the masts of some of the sailing ships which still carried about one-fifth of the port's total cargo. The presence of so many sailing ships was a palpable reminder of how little time had passed since the British Australians first settled on the shores of this cove. 'Old Charlie', an Aboriginal living near Kempsey on the north coast of New South Wales in 1901, was popularly believed to be 117 years old; if this was true, he would have been alive, in fact four years of age, when the first convict fleet dropped anchor in Sydney Cove on 26 January 1788. Transportation was gone but not forgotten, and at Fremantle in 1901 two old men named Duggan, the last surviving convicts sent from Britain to Western Australia before transportation ended there in 1868, were still earning an honest penny by exhibiting the scars on their backs to hotel patrons.

As Lord Hopetoun's valet laid out his clothes for the first ceremony of the day – Court dress richly embroidered with gold lace, a gilt sword and the various gilt and enamelled insignia of the Order of the Thistle, the Knight Grand Cross of St Michael and St George and the Grand Cross of the Royal Victorian Order – the larger part of Sydney's 488,000 people were travelling to the centre of the city or were already stationed there between the elaborate arches which had been erected on behalf of foreign countries and Australian industries. George M'Clure, a bank clerk at Wallsend, had been staying with his brother Charles in the new northern suburb of Turramurra. On New Year's Eve, while wind and rain were thrashing the bush at Turramurra, George M'Clure had written in his diary: 'A real wild night. How much we should pray for the guidance of the Holy Spirit in the affairs of Federated Australia that she may be an example to all sections of the British Empire.'

On New Year's morning the M'Clure brothers caught the 7 a.m. steam train to Milson's Point, crossed the harbour by ferry, attended Holy Communion at St Mary's Cathedral, and then, after some light refreshment, took their places on a balcony near the American Arch. George M'Clure left no record of how he and his brother were dressed on this occasion, but to judge from photographs taken of the crowd that day they may well have been wearing bowler hats, dark serge three-piece suits with narrow trouser-cuffs, and buttoned-up boots. Their shirts would probably have had high winged collars, and hanging from each of their waistcoats would have been a heavy gold watch-chain. Many men, and women too, preferred straw boaters for their headgear. Women also wore picture hats and chiffon toques, bodices with insertions of Chantilly lace, and below the waist metre upon metre of chiffon, voile, Indian muslin or guipure.

At 10.20 am a section of mounted police and a squadron of New South Wales Lancers led the procession out of the Domain and past a statue of Queen Victoria into Macquarie Street. First to appear, but lowest in precedence, for the Governor-General would come last, were the trade unions: thirty mounted shearers in bush attire; ten Broken Hill silver miners in dungarees, carrying hammers and drills; ten coal miners from Newcastle and Bulli, with lamps and picks; ten slaughtermen with knives and pole-axes; ten wharf labourers with wool hooks; ten glass blowers with blowpipes and ring irons; ten plasterers, ten iron moulders, ten tailors and so on through the trades.

The shearers, who stole the show from their pedestrian fellow unionists, had been provided with mounts by Billy Hughes, who was then a member of the NSW Legislative Assembly and general secretary of the Sydney Wharf Labourers' Union. 'My idea was to get together a goodly band of shearers,' wrote Hughes, '– all mounted, each man with a pack-horse carrying his swag; real shearers from the Never-Never, with horses of the kind one meets in the back country – not those well-groomed, well-mannered animals that canter sedately round Centennial Park.' Hughes, a sallow, scrawny and hyper-active little man, had himself been an organiser for the shearers before taking up with the waterside workers. He persuaded the Australian Workers' Union to bring some shearers to Sydney, and then arranged to have forty young horses, fresh from Queensland with not a nail mark in their hooves, sent by goods train to Darling Harbour. Hughes and the shearers rode and drove these unbroken horses through the city to Moore Park where, after many dress rehearsals, they were trained sufficiently – while still far from being well-groomed or well-mannered – to bring an authentic touch of the back country to the procession.

After the trade unions came the lodges, Oddfellows, Loyal Orange, Rechabites, Druids and Royal Foresters; then the churches. There were three Church of England bishops, three Jewish rabbis, and various silk-hatted, frock-coated representatives of the Congregational, Lutheran and Baptist Churches, the Church of Christ and the Salvation Army. The Roman Catholics, Presbyterians and Wesleyans should have been there too, but all had withdrawn because of arguments about precedence. The Presbyterians – whose Moderator-General, the ferocious Dr William Dill Macky, carried a revolver as protection, so he said, against Catholic attack – complained that they had not been accorded equal status with the Anglican and Roman Catholic Churches. So did the Wesleyans.

The Catholics, for their part, complained that they had been deceived at the last minute on matters of precedence and public prayer. In consequence they refused to take part in either the procession, the swearing-in ceremony at Centennial Park, or the official Commonwealth banquet that night. Although the Catholic Church in Australia had welcomed the coming of Federation, its abstention from these national rites was hardly surprising. Its very absence could be seen as a way of representing the sectarianism which had characterized Australian life throughout the 19th century, and would continue to do so during the first two decades of the Commonwealth.

The leader of the Catholic Church in Australia, scholarly Cardinal Moran, was as much European as Irish; although born in Ireland, like most of his fellow-prelates in Australia, he had lived in Rome from the age of 12 to 36. But in the See of Sydney, to which he had been translated in 1884, the Cardinal could no more ignore the mean-spirited politics of Catholic-Protestant, Irish-British rivalry than could the grubbiest of New South Wales politicians. It had been his understanding from the Premier, Sir William Lyne, that as a prince of his church he would take precedence over all other churchmen during the Commonwealth celebrations. Although the Catholic Church enjoyed the allegiance of only 22 per cent of Australians professing religious faith, compared with the Church of England's 41 per cent, St Mary's Cathedral contended that cardinals were accorded precedence over archbishops, even at the Court of St James. This had been conceded in the British Government's communication to Lord Hopetoun on the order of precedence for the procession, and it was on this under-standing, after having had the order of precedence read to him by Lyne, that Cardinal Moran had accepted invitations on behalf of his Church.

On New Year's Eve, however, the Premier's office informed the Cardinal's private secretary, Father Denis O'Haran, that priority had been awarded to the Anglican Primate of Australia and Archbishop of Sydney, Dr William Saumarez Smith, and that furthermore it would not be pos-sible to have a Catholic prayer at the swearing-in ceremony. An editorial in *The Catholic Press* later described these decisions as a gratuitous and painful insult to the Catholic people of the Commonwealth. 'At the be-ginning of Australian life Catholics were persecuted,' it said, 'and it would seem that the State Premier would be pleased to humiliate them on the day of the foundation of the Commonwealth, in the creation of which Catholics have taken such a prominent part, consistently fighting against the nefarious anti-Federal schemes of men like Sir William Lyne. We thought, in our simplicity, that all the ocean of rant and cant about fair play, honour, British liberty, with which we have been deluged for the past hundred years, and the statement of the Irish patriot, Curran, that everyone standing on the soil over which waves the British flag must feel himself "redeemed, regenerated, disenthralled" had at least something of semblance and reality, but we were deceived.'

Yet how could a Protestant government such as Lyne's have allowed a cardinal to outshine the Primate at any time, let alone a time of strong anti-Catholic feeling in New South Wales? This feeling, always flickering beneath the surface of colonial life, had been fanned into sudden flame by newspaper reports of a sermon delivered by Archbishop Redwood of Wellington, New Zealand, at the official opening of St Mary's Cathedral, which had been attended by the Governors of New South Wales and Queensland on 9 September 1900. His Grace said next day that the sermon had been written in New Zealand for a purely Catholic audience, and that the words objected to had not in fact been uttered by him at St Mary's. But neither had they been deleted from printed copies of the sermon supplied to the press, and readers of Sydney's newspapers were fully apprised of the Archbishop's views on Protestantism. 'The leaders and founders of Protestantism – Luther, Calvin, Zwingli etc – were notorious for their vices . . . Among Protestants the most effectual means of sanctification have disappeared – abstinence, fasting, mortification, con-fession, communion etc. Both the Greek Schism and Protestantism have rather obstructed than promoted true civilization. The first had brought despotism upon the east, the second covered Europe with blood and ruins in the sixteenth century, and has ever since been the helper and instrument of the worst foes of Christianity. It desecrated the home, it polluted the nuptial bed, it lowered the dignity of womanhood, it devastated the school, and stopped the progress of science.'

Cardinal Moran's assurance to his 'separated brethren of the Anglican communion' that the Bishop had been referring only to 'the so-called Reformation in Europe' did little to calm those brethren. 'Men must be mad,' said His Eminence, 'or ripening for madness, or, at least, very foolish, if they attempt to deny the truth of the charges made as to the immorality which was the result of the so-called Reformation in Europe.' Dr Saumarez Smith, who was once described as being humble to a fault, did not attend a meeting of enraged Protestants which filled the Town Hall; but a statement from him read to the audience referred to Bishop Redwood's words as 'libellous, unhistorical and needlessly offensive.' The Grand Master of the Loyal Orange Lodge rebuked the Governor of New South Wales, Lord Beauchamp, for having been among those present at the Cathedral when he should have remembered that the Sovereign whom he represented in the colony was the defender of the Protestant faith, and the Reverend J. W. Gillett provided the Town Hall audience with numerous examples of Papal immorality. 'There was Pope John, the 23rd I think it was, but I'm sure it was a John . . . ' 'John Chinaman!' called a voice, to loud laughter. The sermon next Sunday at St Thomas's Church of England, Balmain, was entitled 'Rome's Insult To The Crown, The Country And The Church', and at Waverley Wesleyan Church the title was 'Protestantism And Its Popish Slanderers.'

This uproar was nothing, however, compared to the sensation caused soon afterwards by *Coningham v. Coningham*, a divorce action brought by Arthur Coningham, a bookmaker and Protestant, against his wife Alice. Public interest in the case was almost as great as in Federation, and the reason was not hard to find. Arthur Coningham had cited as co-respondent Cardinal Moran's private secretary: the handsome, Irish-born Reverend Dr Denis O'Haran, who was said to have been recommended to the Cardinal by the Pope himself. Coningham was seeking divorce on the grounds of his wife's alleged adultery with Father O'Haran in St Mary's Cathedral and adjacent buildings. He claimed £5000 from the co-respondent, and custody of two of his three children – but not the third, whom he alleged had been fathered in more ways than one. Mrs Coningham's evidence, delivered with great self-possession to an all-Protestant jury, supported her husband's allegations but was otherwise uncorroborated. Dr O'Haran denied everything. The jury was unable to reach a decision, and was discharged on 14 December. Thus the prospect of a second court hearing would have been regarded by the Lyne Government as yet another reason for denying precedence to the Cardinal.[2]

Although neither Cardinal Moran, the Archbishop of Melbourne nor any of several other Catholic prelates who were in Sydney at the time, took any direct part in the New Year's Day proceedings, the Cardinal with 2000 Catholic children and a large number of clergy watched the procession from a platform erected outside the cathedral. As the Governor-General passed by, their choir sang *Hail To The Commonwealth Mighty And Free*. Before that climax, they had seen the robed and chained mayors of all State capitals, carriage-loads of politicians from all State parliaments, justices of the Supreme Courts, new ministers-designate of the Commonwealth, and, galling as it must have been to them, the red and white robed Anglican Primate of Australia.

Then came the military: sixteen New South Wales Lancers in khaki and felt slouch hats, 305 school cadets, a Royal Australian Artillery band and guard of honour, and veterans from the Soudan Contingent and the New South Wales South African Contingent. There were detachments from the military forces of all other Australian colonies and New Zealand, and finally the gorgeously accoutred imperial contingent led by Lt-Col W. G. Crole Wyndham of the 21st Hussars, a hero of the Zulu War, the Nile Expedition and the Battle of Khartoum. It is still possible to watch this procession on a ten-minute cine film shot by Joseph Perry, a maker of Biblical films for the Salvation Army. As the British and Indian regiments swing through Martin Place past the crowded steps of the GPO, one can imagine the crash and blare of *The British Grenadiers* and the brilliance of the uniforms after so much Colonial khaki: the First Dragoon Guards in scarlet with blue facings, brass helmets with panaches of red horsehair, and white leather gauntlets; the Queen's Own Hussars in blue jackets with white plumed busbies and scarlet busby bags; the Coldstream Guards in scarlet and blue, with a scarlet feather on one side of their bearskins and a white rose embroidered on their shoulder straps; the Northumberland Fusiliers in scarlet with white facings and fusilier caps; the King's Own Rifle Corps in green and scarlet; the Black Watch in scarlet jackets and dark tartan kilts; the 9th Bengal Lancers in blue with white facings; the

[2] In the second case, three months later, a jury of eight Protestants, two Catholics and two Jews decided in favour of Dr O'Haran. Arthur Coningham was so incensed by the verdict that while still in court he fired a revolver which had been lent to him, as protection against the Catholic foe, by the Presbyterian gunman Dr William Dill Macky. No one was hurt. Dr O'Haran made a triumphant return to the Cathedral accompanied by his counsel and friends. From a window in the presbytery, Cardinal Moran waved to them and acknowledged their cheers with a raised biretta.

Hyderabad Cavalry in dark green; the 16th Bombay Infantry in red and yellow; and the 5th Gurkhas in dark green and black. One of the spectators – Henry Bournes Higgins, a former Member of the Victorian Legislative Assembly and soon to stand for Federal Parliament although, in an excess of Federal enthusiasm, he had spoken against the Federation Bill on grounds that it did not go far enough – would have paid particular attention to the Gurkhas, for he had recently received a letter from his schoolboy son, Mervyn: 'Have you seen the English and Indian troops yet? In this week's *Australasian* there is a picture of the Gurkha Major Thaba, Lord Roberts's devoted orderly during the Afghan War'.

At last, escorted by lancers and mounted infantry, came His Excellency the Governor-General seated opposite his private secretary, Captain E. W. Wallington, and personal physician, Major S. C. Philson, in an open landau drawn by four horses with two postilions and two grooms in caps, wigs and embroidered livery. Captain Wallington was an old hand at serving colonial governors. His professional caution at Government Houses in Sydney, Melbourne and Adelaide had earned him the nickname of 'Mr Better Not', but not even this negative counsel would save Lord Hopetoun from the error of judgment which was later to bring him down.

And so the eight-kilometre-long procession wound its way through the city and out along sealed roads to Centennial Park, which had been officially opened in 1888 to commemorate the arrival of the First Fleet. 'Came first a troop of Australian cadet-boys,' wrote the *Bulletin*, confining its comment to the military part of the procession, and getting that somewhat out of order, '– they might have seemed to image our country still in her cradle of infancy, her pride of youth. Came last, after many uniformed soldiers, many gowned dignitaries, after the small fry of officials and politicians – Governor-General Hopetoun, the legacy of persistent British rule. In the official mind, the order of precedence fell from end to beginning, the best was last; in the natural order, in the order of Australia the nation, the British representative came at the tail because he was the least necessary, the most insignificant of all the procession's components . . .' At Centennial Park, the *Bulletin* noted sourly, 'the foreign troops marched into the reserved enclosure; to give point to the British character of the procession the Australian troops remained outside . . . Our own men fell away from cheek-bone to pointed jaw, and their mouths were often curiously slack. The Britishers were squarer in the jaw, and their lips set tightly. They looked less intelligent, more dogged, not more determined . . . the Governor-General at the tail looking so puny, so wan – as if in his own person he figured the wan and puny basis of the idea of monarchy which he represented.'

No such sentiments were discernible at Centennial Park, where 7000 invited guests, two choirs (one of 10,000, the other of 1000) and 60,000 spectators covered a natural grassy arena and the surrounding slopes of tall brown grass broken here and there by outcrops of ancient sandstone. There was loud, prolonged cheering as the Governor-General, leaning on a malacca cane, walked from his coach to a seven-sided white pavilion, pillared and domed like an 18th century folly, and surmounted by the Royal coat of arms. While he acknowledged the greetings of judges and ministers, and waved to the crowd, the choir sang *O God Our Help In Ages Past*. It was now almost one o'clock, and the heat was insufferable. When the choir finished, the Primate offered up a prayer composed by the Governor of South Australia beseeching the Lord God Almighty to grant unto the Commonwealth His Grace and heavenly benediction, and to 'make our Empire always a faithful and fearless leader among the nations.' Some time before, Lord Tennyson had rashly offered his prayer to the Catholic Archbishop of Adelaide for use in Catholic churches on New Year's Day. The Archbishop had replied that, although it was 'everything that a prayer should be', only the Supreme Pontiff could 'change a single syllable in the wording of the liturgy.'

The clerk of the South Australian Parliament – Mr E. G. Blackmore, later to become clerk of the Federal Parliament, and reputed to have the most sonorous voice in Australian public life – now read the Queen's proclamation of the Commonwealth, the letters patent constituting the office of Governor-General and Commander-in-Chief of the Commonwealth, and the Governor-General's commission. His place was then taken by the Lieutenant-Governor of New South Wales, Sir Frederick Darley, who spoke briefly to Lord Hopetoun and handed him documents from which he read, in a clear and high-pitched voice, the judicial oath, the oath of allegiance and the oath of office. All these he signed in turn at a table, in the centre of the pavilion, at which Queen Victoria had given her assent to the *Commonwealth of Australia Constitution Bill*. When Lord Hopetoun signed the last oath at 1.25 pm, the royal standard was unfurled above the pavilion, a royal salute of 21 guns signalled the Governor-General's assumption of office and the inauguration of the Commonwealth. Next Mr Justice Owen of the NSW Supreme Court administered oaths to Edmund Barton and eight other members of the Executive Council, whose Constitutional duty it would be to advise the Governor-General in the government of the Commonwealth. These Councillors were in fact the Prime Minister and his Cabinet, though the Constitution made no mention of a Cabinet; it provided merely that the Governor-General might appoint Executive Councillors to administer departments of State of the

Commonwealth. The band played *God Save The Queen*, the Governor-General read out a telegram from that revered old lady herself, and the massed choir sang *Federated Australia*.

By now the crowds in the city had somewhat dispersed, though Sydney was to remain in festive mood for several days to come. Charles M'Clure went home with a bad toothache, leaving his brother to stroll about the city for a while longer admiring the decorations. A certain John Swales made himself so obnoxious in the Royal Standard Hotel that he was arrested, and then tried to bash the arresting policeman. His excuse was that he had been celebrating the birth of the Commonwealth. A man sailing in Farm Cove capsized his yacht and was drowned, and a police constable fell from the footboard of an electric tram in Oxford Street and fractured his skull. The Governor-General was 'so thoroughly tired out' by his day's work that he was unable to attend a State banquet at the Town Hall that evening. There was so much noise in the Chief hall that the Justice of Queensland, Sir Samuel Griffith, could hardly be heard as he proposed the toast to the Commonwealth. Now and again, through the hubbub, Sir Samuel was heard to say that he came from a State as large as France, Germany and Austria combined, or to hope that the Federal Government would show the Australian people that they were not an unworthy branch of the British race. Sir George Reid, in the course of his speech, managed to incorporate the late Sir Henry Parkes's 'crimson thread of kinship' which, he said, made every official and every subject 'loyal and staunch in the maintenance of the institutions of the Empire.' As the guests made their way home from the Town Hall that night they were greatly impressed by the electrical illuminations which bejewelled the city and the ships on its harbour. Many of those who lived in darker, less privileged parts of Sydney also dined well, or at least were entitled to obtain food on this auspicious occasion. The Sydney RescueWork Society had drawn up a list of 7000 needy families and supplied them with grocery vouchers. 'It is expected,' said the Society, 'that every poor person in the city and suburbs will be furnished with sufficient food for his or her immediate wants on the day that ushers in the new year, the new century and the Australian Commonwealth.'

This triple coincidence demanded and received expressions of optimism and confidence from Australia's conservative daily newspapers and also, in more guarded vein, from its few working class journals. Although the Brisbane *Worker*'s cartoon showed a champagne bottle exploding with a froth of bubbles labelled 'Claptrap', 'Guzzle', 'Booze' and 'Hang The Expense', its editorial conceded that no nation had ever before been launched under such happy auspices. It remarked disapprovingly, however, on the spirit of militarism which had characterised the inaugural celebrations, and warned that the only way to avoid the pitfall of plutocracy was to base the Commonwealth upon 'the hopes and needs and aspirations of the people.'

Australia's oldest newspaper, *The Sydney Morning Herald*, said that seldom in the world's history had 'a people entered into full possession of their heritage under circumstances so auspicious and with an outlook so full of dazzling promise.' 'We inherit to the full those proud traditions which have made the statesmanship and the policy of Britain the admiration of philosophic historians and the models of constitution-makers. We share the national life and thought of an Empire of which the peer has yet to make itself known. We are guarded in our isolation by the iron wall of a navy which is admittedly incomparable, and by a military prestige built up on a record which has never known complete defeat. We have within our borders, in our but partly discovered and exploited natural resources, all the material guarantees for prosperity and greatness. We enter on the new year and the century a united Australian nation.'

Conceding that the isolation in which Australia had grown to nationhood was not likely to remain undisturbed, the *Herald* nonetheless looked forward confidently to 'that alliance of English-speaking peoples which will one day hold with secure and loyal hands the balance of the world's peace in the interests of civilization and progress.' Like other newspapers in Australia and England, the *Herald* regarded Australian federation as a forerunner of the imperial federation under which Canada, Australia, South Africa, and even India and Egypt would eventually have a bigger say at the board meetings of John Bull and Co. 'These daughters of the Imperial mother will share in the greater conclave of the nation,' said the *Herald*, 'and make manifest in counsel the blood-tie and common racial instinct already proved on the South African battlefields.'

The theme of blood, both racial and martial, ran not only through editorials but also through many of the exquisitely bad odes and hymns which hailed, blessed and lauded the new Commonwealth. Some idea of the prevailing standard may be conveyed by the opening lines of a poem with which George Essex Evans of Toowoomba won a fifty-guinea prize offered by the New South Wales Government for the best *Ode On The Inauguration Of The Commonwealth*:

> Awake! Arise! The wings of dawn
> Are beating at the Gates of Day!
> The morning star has been withdrawn,
> The silver vapours melt away.

William Allen's *Australia Fœderata* addressed itself to the new nation with equal directness ('A nation amongst nations thou dost stand,/ Australia Fœderata! What fitlier could grace/the century's beginning?'), and Robert Garran began his *Song Of The Commonwealth* with some comparisons between the Plough and the Dragon of northern skies and our own Magellanic Clouds and the Southern Cross ('Circles and sparkles, ere night darkles, Lo! the starry Cross').[3] Garran, tall and rather stork-like, had been appointed permanent head of the Federal Attorney-General's Department. In that capacity it was his task on New Year's Day to write in longhand the first number of the Commonwealth Gazette, and personally take it to the Government Printer. This Gazette, headed with the British coat of arms, contained the Queen's Proclamation, the Governor-General's Letters Patent and Commission, and lists of Executive Councillors, Federal departments and their respective ministers, and the Governor-General's staff.

Garran's ode, published in the *Herald* of 2 January, spoke of 'the blood of ancient races' and 'the blood that brooks no master'; another poem in the same issue, by A. Nugent Robertson, sang the praises of an Australia 'calm, with the pride of blood she shared.' But the most crimson as well as the best turned celebration of the Commonwealth was Rudyard Kipling's widely published *The Young Queen*. The Old Queen, receiving her daughter mounted high on a 'red-splashed charger,/beautiful, bold and browned,/ Bright-eyed out of the battle', addressed her as follows:

> Blood of our foes on thy bridle and speech of our friends in thy mouth,
> How can I crown thee further, O Queen of the Sovereign South?
> Daughter no more but Sister, and doubly daughter so –
> Mother of many princes – and child of the child I bore . . .

As usual, Kipling's imperial imagery brought into sharp focus the diffuse sentiments of a thousand after-dinner speeches. Sister rather than daughter was precisely what Australia aspired to become; but that change of condition would take some time to bring about, and in the meantime the roles of mother and daughter would have to suffice. The mother was Britannia made flesh in the 81 years-old person of Queen Victoria, who thought of herself, and liked to be thought of, as imperial mother rather

---

[3] This was not Garran's only contribution to the literature of federation. On 1 January Angus and Robertson Ltd published *The Annotated Constitution Of The Australian Commonwealth*, by the Victorian lawyer and federationist, Sir John Quick, and R. R. Garran. Quick and Garran, as it became known, worked its way through the Constitution, phrase by phrase, for 1008 large pages. It took four pages to explain how the preamble of the Constitution came to invoke the deity (*humbly relying on the blessing of Almighty God*), and devoted three pages to the history of the word *Commonwealth*, citing its use to mean a State or community in no fewer than seven of Shakespeare's plays.

than Empress of her 398 million subjects. The Queen had occupied her throne for the last sixty-three years, longer than any other British monarch, and despite her failing health it was difficult to conceive of the Empire without her. Yet empires were no more exempt from change than queens were from natural law, and on New Year's Eve there was a curious omen of impending disaster. A gale of wind and torrential rain swept over southern England, and next morning it was found that two stones in the outer circle of Stonehenge – one of the great uprights, and a lintel mortised into its top – had fallen to the ground. They were the first to have fallen since the winter of 1797.

The British Empire, embracing one quarter of the earth's land surface and one quarter of its population, offered some parallels to the seeming constancy and unsuspected vulnerability of Stonehenge. In the late 19th century, Britain was not only being overtaken industrially by the United States and Germany but was also, for the first time in a century, being challenged militarily by some of her European rivals. Anyone watching the old Queen on New Year's Day as she drove out from Osborne House with Princess Christian of Schleswig-Holstein and the Duchess of Connaught, escorted by the burnished and plumed Household Cavalry, would have found it hard to believe that the Empire had reached its peak some years before and, appearances notwithstanding, was now in decline. Yet this was the truth.

The world was changing, and changing fast. In the last few months there had been several instances of real or attempted violence against established rule, and seen later in retrospect these appeared to portend even greater disturbances yet to come. The King of Italy had been assassinated, the Prince of Wales had escaped two bullets fired through his railway carriage window by a young anarchist in Brussels, the Russian police had uncovered a plot to wreck Czar Nicholas's train, and in Germany a woman had thrown a hatchet at Kaiser Wilhelm but succeeded only in hitting his carriage. On New Year's Day the Kaiser, who was Queen Victoria's grandson, held a levee at the Imperial Castle in Berlin and later, accompanied by a party which included Queen Victoria's 15-year-old great grand-daughter from England, Princess Alice, attended a command performance of Albert Lortzing's opera *Tsar and Carpenter*. It was not surprising that the Kaiser had chosen this work, which had been inspired by Peter the Great, who worked briefly as a carpenter in a Dutch ship-building yard during his grand tour of Europe and later founded the Russian navy. Kaiser Wilhelm was himself obsessed by an urge to strengthen Germany's navy, which was already the third largest in the world. The German people, he said, was preparing to forge itself an arm with which the black, white and red flag would to all eternity, at home and abroad, maintain the dignity of the Empire to all eternity.

In Japan, where a navy of mainly British-built battleships was also being enlarged, the Emperor Mutsuhito and his Empress were both indisposed and unable to attend the opening levee of the year. The ships in port at Yokohama carried bunches of evergreen at their mastheads in salute to the new year and new century. On the far side of the Pacific, the ships of yet another modern navy lay at anchor off Mare Island, California. In Washington, President McKinley spent two and a half hours of New Year's Day standing in the Blue Room of the White House shaking hands with a continuous line of civil, military and naval guests.

On 20 January 1901 telegraph cable stations throughout the British Empire received the news that Queen Victoria was again gravely ill. 'Oh God grant Her precious life may be spared to us,' Lady Tennyson wrote to her mother from Adelaide. 'One cannot for a moment realize England without Her.' Two days later the Queen was dead. 'Dear "Mother Queen",' wrote Lady Tennyson, 'it is just what one feels I think, that one has lost a "Mother" and as Lord Richard [the Governor's secretary, Richard Plantagenet Nevill] said yesterday it is almost as if the sun had gone out.' At Wallsend, George M'Clure wrote in his diary: 'Of all the imporatnt records I have made in my various diaries none can surpass the one I now make – *the death of our Sovereign Queen Victoria, our Mother Queen*. The sad news reached our office at noon today. A blank seemed to come over me and felt almost too upset to continue my duties. I involuntary prayed 'God Save Our Empire!' The cablegrams for days were alarming and we were not unprepared for the sad news. Still it is a great shock. She was our Queen from our infancy, our fathers' and back to our grandfathers' time. We were taught to love her before we could barely lisp her name . . . I wrote [my brother] at length about her death.'

At Moree the town crier walked down the main street calling, 'Oyez! Oyez! Her Majesty Queen Victoria died this morning!' Shop fronts were draped with black and purple crêpe; the young New South Wales cricketer, Victor Trumper, wore a black armband when he made 230 runs against Victoria in the final match of the season; at an afternoon tea given by Mrs Barton, only three out of eighty frocks worn by the guests were anything but black; suburban houses flew the Union Jack at half mast, and the Queen's statue in Sydney was encircled by palm fronds and a sea of wreaths. 'From the Waverly Volunteer Cadet Corps,' said the card on one wreath. 'We young soldiers loved our beloved Queen, and mourn that Her Majesty should be taken from us.' There were wreaths from the ship's company of HMS *Royal Arthur*, flagship of the Australian squadron ('We all loved Her'), from Her Majesty's 'loyal subjects in Boggabri'; and from the Daughters of Ulster, Loyal Orange Lodge 304.

Grief was unfeigned and widespread, but not universal. 'Some fiendish ghoul,' as a newspaper described him, tore the mourning crêpe down from several shops in Brisbane, and in one of Brisbane's hotels a man named McCarthy used abusive language to the publican for wearing black bands of crêpe on his hat and arm. This was dangerously provocative of McCarthy. He was flung out of the bar with such force that his head cracked open on the pavement and he died soon afterwards. The Brisbane *Worker* managed to abstain from grief more respectfully. 'A good woman, a good wife and mother has passed away,' it wrote. 'But, happily, the world still contains many more such. She was of the same flesh as all other women, and subject to the same natural law . . . For the adversity or the prosperity of the British nation during her reign . . . the dead Queen is not to be regarded as responsible. As a ruler she had to do as she was instructed by her Ministers. As a woman it is that Her Majesty is to be judged. And in this respect, when all is said and done, she was no better or no worse than most women.'

As if to emphasise the sense of deprivation and separation felt personally by many Australians at this time, there was a halt in the telegraph traffic across what Kipling called 'the great grey level plains of ooze where the shell-burred cables creep.' The cable connecting Australia to Britain ceased to function on 25 January because of a break between Java and Singapore. Wireless communication had not yet been developed over long distances, and the Pacific telegraph cable would not open until 1902. For three days Australia received no news about the accession of Edward VII, or indeed about anything else that was happening in the Empire and the wider world. At 4.20 pm on 28 January the cable came back into service and the Commonwealth of Australia was once again plugged into the imperial network.

The death of the Mother Queen and the break in the shell-burred cable were symbolic reminders, if such were needed, of how quickly the world could change and how far the bereft daughter was from her ancestral home. The Queen of the Sovereign South, partly illusory though her sovereignty was as yet, had nonetheless assumed some new powers and would in due course assume more. In some ways she was now a little more on her own; but, as solace for whatever loneliness this might entail, she held an honoured place in what Kipling called the 'Hall of Our Thousand Years.' This was a reference to still another chronological milestone with which the inauguration of the Commonwealth had coincided. The year 1901 was not only the 100th anniversary of the addition of the cross of St Patrick to the Union Jack but also the 1,000th anniversary of the death of Alfred, King of the West Saxons, who had been elevated in recent imperial rhetoric to the title of founder of the Empire. The Victorian correspondent of *The Sydney Mail* wrote, 'There is a wild enthusiasm in this State at the present moment about the virtues of Alfred the Great. Archdeacon Tucker of Ballarat writes to a morning journal that October 26 next will be the thousandth anniversary of the death of King Alfred, and suggests that the University professors should celebrate the occasion.' Mr J. C. Williamson staged *The Most Christian King*, an English play about King Alfred, and when Lord Tennyson addressed the boys of Prince Alfred College, Adelaide, at their Speech Day, he took as his subject the school's illustrious namesake. This Methodist boarding school had in fact been named after Queen Victoria's second son – the late Prince Alfred, Duke of Edinburgh – but, as the Governor pointed out in his speech, the Duke himself had been named after Alfred the Great.

Lord Tennyson was a zealot for the Empire. His father, whose secretary and biographer he had been, was not only the most popular poet of the Victorian age but had also in his last years embraced and publicly supported the idea of imperial federation. One of his verses – 'One life, one flag, one fleet, one throne!' – became the anthem of the Imperial Federation League. Hallam Tennyson (he had been named after his father's great friend, the subject of *In Memoriam*) became a member of the League's council, and it was mainly through this connection that he was offered the Governorship of South Australia. In his speech at Prince Alfred College in December 1901 Lord Tennyson enumerated the solid Anglo-Saxon virtues of King Alfred in war as well as in peace; he congratulated those 'Old Reds', as the College's Old Boys called themselves, who had recently been decorated for gallantry in South Africa; and adjured his young listeners to seek even greater distinction for themselves in the future. 'Boys who are leaving Prince Alfred this term,' he said, 'boys who are remaining on at this great school, stand firm like King Alfred in the difficulties and dangers – the irreverence and immorality of our age – "stand firm; quit you like men." Do you recall to mind that story of Wellington at Waterloo? The issue of the battle was uncertain, the 95th Regiment was wavering – Wellington rode up to them and shouted – "Stand firm 95th! We must not be beaten, else what would they say in England?" The men stood firm, Waterloo was won. Stand firm, then, like King Alfred; like the men of the 95th; like your own football team in the Royal match last July, and you will win even greater victories than that which Wellington won at Waterloo.'

The sports report was delivered by the captain of the cricket XI, 18-

year-old Alec Raws, whose own Waterloo loomed fifteen years ahead of him. Raws should be noted here, for we shall meet him again later. Born in England, he was brought at the age of ten to Adelaide where he won a scholarship to Prince Alfred and, although not physically very strong, managed to do extremely well at cricket and tennis. In his Speech Day report, Alec Raws told how the football team had won a brilliant victory at a match before the Duke and Duchess of Cornwall and York; how the cadet corps had formed part of the guard of honour for Their Highnesses when they arrived at Government House; how the gymnastic class had won an inter-collegiate shield; and how the cricket team under his captaincy had lost its final match of the season. He congratulated one of his batsmen and two of the bowlers on their good showing in the lost match, but made no reference to his own even better performance. When Raws had finished reading, Lord Tennyson drew attention to this modesty by calling out: 'Three cheers for Raws and his fine score!'

3

WILMANSRUST

THE BLOOD on the Young Queen's bridle, and on the altar of Federation too, was Boer's blood. In all their encounters with that hardy foe until 1901, the various Australian contingents serving under British command in South Africa had managed to justify, or at least not to tarnish, Kipling's image of an antipodean Boadicea. 'All the Colonials did extremely well,' said Lord Roberts late in 1900 before handing over command to Lord Kitchener and returning in triumph to London under the mistaken impression that – Ladysmith and Mafeking having been relieved, and Johannesburg and Pretoria captured – the war in South Africa was almost over. 'They were very intelligent,' said His Lordship of the colonials, 'and they had what I want our men to have, more individuality. They could find their way about the country far better than the British cavalrymen could do.' The New South Wales Mounted Rifles had also shown the Coldstream Guards how to take Diamond Hill – a victory in June 1900 which moved their British commanding officer, Lieut-General Sir Ian Hamilton, to issue a General Order in praise of 'the gallant way the regiment pushed forward beyond the crest under murderous fire.'

Two months later a mixed force of 300 Australians from every colony except South Australia covered itself with glory in the western Transvaal. Together with 200 Rhodesians, these Australian Bushmen were besieged at Elands River staging camp by a force of 1800 Boers armed with heavy guns and pom-poms. Although more shells were fired into their camp than into Mafeking during its siege, and all drinking water had to be carried nearly a kilometre from the river, the defenders held out for twelve days until a relieving force arrived. By that time seventy-five of the Australians were either dead or wounded. 'When the ballad makers of Australia seek for a subject,' wrote Sir Arthur Conan Doyle in *The Great Boer War*, 'let them turn to Elands River, for there was no finer fighting in the war.'

This was exactly what Australia had hoped for in South Africa: a worthy showing by its own troops alongside seasoned Imperials, and a mother country properly grateful for prompt assistance loyally given. So consistently had expectations been satisfied that the Commonwealth was quite unprepared for some bad news which grew progressively worse during the second half of 1901. Here for a change was everything which Australia had not expected: inefficiency and surrender by its own troops, and in place of maternal gratitude, allegations of cowardice and mutiny. After the accolades, these shocks were rude but illuminating. Some aspects of the British-Australian relationship were lit more clearly by the harshness of Wilmansrust than by the radiance of Diamond Hill.

The Fifth Victorian Contingent, as its number implied, was not the finest unit to have left Australia for South Africa. There had been four earlier contingents, and it stood to reason that, for the Fifth, Victoria must have reached further down in the supply and quality of recruits. The medical officers who examined recruits for this regiment, referred to as both the Fifth Mounted Rifles and the Victorian Rangers, said that physically they were not inferior to their predecessors; the fact remained, however, that within two months of arriving in South Africa their number was reduced by sickness from 1000 to about 700. Proportionately they had far more men in Pretoria Hospital than any other Australian contingent. Another of the Fifth's misfortunes was that previous contingents had all but exhausted Victoria's supply of trained non-commissioned officers; it was said later that if the Fifth had included eight company sergeant-majors and one regimental sergeant-major, as it should have, the trouble at Wilmansrust and afterwards would never have arisen. The regiment included a few regular soldiers, a few veterans who were returning to South Africa, and a somewhat larger number of men who had served in the Victorian military force. But the great majority of its recruits, including many of the NCOs, were without previous military experience.

The term 'contingent' was used to identify a unit or group of units despatched at a particular time, first at colonial expense, but later – when Britain needed reinforcements more urgently, and had become convinced of the colonials' worth – at imperial expense. In the second month of the war, November 1899, an Australian regiment under Australian command was formed at Capetown out of companies from all colonies except Queensland; but this exercise in nationalism lasted only six months, and the regiment was absorbed by the Imperial 1st Mounted Infantry Brigade under Major-General E. T. H. Hutton, a former British commanding officer of the New South Wales military forces.[1] Thereafter the fifty-odd

---

[1] Once the unification of Australian military forces had begun after Federation, contingents for South Africa were formed of representative squadrons from each State and designated as consecutive battalions of the Australian Commonwealth Horse. There were nine such battalions, but only four of them saw any fighting.

Australian contingents – Mounted Rifles, Mounted Infantry, Imperial Bushmen, and such smaller units as Cameron's Scouts and Doyle's Australian Scouts – were used wherever and however the Imperial staff thought best, usually under British command and on British pay. There was little objection from the Australians to being cast in what others might have regarded as the role of mercenaries; on the contrary, some troops had complained at being posted to the short-lived Australian Regiment instead of a British unit. By the time the Fifth Victorian Contingent reached South Africa, the nature of the task before it was fairly predictable. For the mounted columns of khaki-uniformed British troops in sun helmets or slouch hats, the war had entered a phase described by *The Times History Of The War In South Africa* as 'running down with an infinity of toil the broken handfuls of Boers who fled before them or hid in their very midst.' The word 'Boer' was Dutch for 'farmer', and the mounted commandos led by de Wet, Botha and Hertzog knew their native terrain as intimately as a farmer knew his soil. The military importance of that terrain was written all over South Africa's campaign maps in such suffixes as *kopje* (hill), *laagte* (valley), *nek* (pass) and *kloof* (ravine). Trained from childhood to use their Mauser rifles and ride their Cape ponies, the men and boys of the Boer republics were not an enemy to be underestimated, even when reduced to commandos. Wearing khaki or motley civilian clothes, crossed bandoliers and wide-brimmed hats, the Boers were not unlike the armed shearers who had ridden the western plains of Queensland during the shearers' strike of the early 1890s. Even the grass of the veldt seemed to Banjo Paterson, who reported zestfully on the war for *The Sydney Morning Herald* and *The Argus*, 'almost exactly like our kangaroo grass.' 'This is something like sport,' he wrote in one of his early despatches, 'this shooting at human game with cannon over three thousand yards of country. "Hooray! Give 'em another!"' Week after week the columns went out from base camps into the brown countryside, burning disaffected farm houses, consigning their former occupants to concentration camps, commandeering livestock and crops, and wherever possible driving the enemy in towards wire and blockhouse lines.

The Fifth Victorian Contingent was not very proficient at this work. 'There is no disguising the fact they are not a good lot,' said an Australian officer who served near them. 'I saw them do things on active service for which, in our own defence force and in peace time, they would have been instantly cashiered.' Even one of the Contingent's own sergeants, in recounting the achievements of its first trek in the Transvaal (in three weeks it has killed six Boers, taken 124 prisoners and captured 2460 cattle and 5600 sheep) admitted that Imperials did most of the night picket work, and were better at it than the Victorians, who were 'too careless, and inclined to light their pipes.' This was not a frame of mind likely to pass without comment from the Indian Army regulars under whose exacting command the Victorians had been placed. Together with one company of Argyll and Sutherland Highlanders and another of the Duke of Cornwall's Light Infantry, they formed one of several columns with which General Sir Bindon Blood was clearing the country around Carolina and Amsterdam in the eastern Transvaal. Their commanding officer was Acting Major-General Stuart Beatson, whose career until then had been spent mainly with the Bengal Lancers in India and Egypt, and whose brigade major also came from that regiment. Between them, the two Bengal Lancers set an austere standard.

'We have had a lot of humbugging,' wrote one of the Victorians in a letter home. 'First they divided us into two battalions, and then put Imperial officers over us who have tried to bring in barrack room discipline, which does not work with our grain . . . When General Beatson took command he ignored the Australian officers, and went round complaining of want of drill and smartness to the men. General Beatson made no secret of his dislike for volunteers, and wanted them to be as smart and rigid in discipline as a crack cavalry corps.' If there were many sore backs among the horses, everyone was made to march for a day on foot – those who had looked after their mounts along with those who had not. During their first week in the field, one trooper was court-martialled and sentenced to 12 months' imprisonment for refusing to obey a sergeant's instruction to come away from a Boer farmhouse. Two others were sentenced to two years' imprisonment for surrendering to the Boers, and it was said that for some unspecified offence another trooper had been spreadeagled with horse pegs and ropes and left lying on the ground all night.

This was the state of affairs when General Beatson's force halted for several days at Vandyke's Drift, using it as a base from which to send search columns out in every direction. One such column – consisting of the second battalion Fifth Victorian Mounted Rifles (270 men) and two Vickers-Maxim guns in Cape carts, under the command of an Imperial officer, Major Morris – was ordered to look for a Boer commando which had been reported at Boschfontein on the Middleburg road east of Vandyke's Drift. Finding nothing at Boschfontein, the column halted on the afternoon of 12 June at Wilmansrust and pitched camp near a farm with a substantial stone cattle kraal. One picket of twelve men was posted in the kraal, and other pickets, including one of thirty men, at distances of up to 1500 metres from the main camp. The pickets were too large and too far apart, and they had been posted in daylight when any Boers in the neighbourhood could hardly have missed observing them. In the camp itself, about 100 metres square, many Victorians were lying down in the darkness, perhaps drawing on their pipes, at some distance from their stacked Lee Metford rifles. The scene was set for disaster.

At 7.45 pm a whistle was blown and heavy rifle fire began from a range of no more than 40 metres. A commando under Vecht-General C. H. Müller had surrounded Wilmansrust as soon as darkness came, and had managed to approach between the pickets without being seen. 'The horses that were not shot down by the first volley stampeded over the men', said Major W. McKnight, the Australian officer in charge of the 1st Battalion, in his report to the Commandant of Victorian military forces in Melbourne. 'The Boers were advancing smartly almost at a run, firing rapidly from the hip . . . The Boers had evidently located the position of the piles of rifles, as many of the men were hit when grasping their weapons. I got my carbine and bandolier and ran across to H Company, endeavouring to get the men to lie down, as some were excitedly running about not knowing where the enemy were. On getting past H Company I came to a group of men – whom I mistook for Victorians, as they were dressed in khaki and wore hats turned up similar to ours. One asked me in good English what I said, and then I received two hits with carbines and found I was a prisoner. I should say this was seven or eight minutes from the opening of the firing. After ten minutes I was released and then found that Major Morris had surrendered.'

The Boers disarmed and released their prisoners, looted the camp and made off with the two guns and 100 horses which had survived the attack. Fourteen Victorians were dead, and more than sixty wounded; according to Major McKnight, the Boer casualties were ten dead and thirty wounded. A few of the Victorians managed during the night to reach General Beatson's main column, which was only 20 kilometres away, and the General himself arrived at Wilmansrust soon after daylight. He conferred with Major Morris, and could not have been too pleased by what he heard. 'As I was not present,' reported Major McKnight, 'I do not know what transpired.' After a long trek on foot with his battalion to Middleburg, which had become the main base for General Blood's operations, McKnight received a second-hand but accurate account of General Beatson's displeasure. Major Samuel Harris of the Fifth Western Australian Mounted Infantry told him that on the march one day the General, during a conversation within the hearing of himself and another Australian officer, had described the Fifth Victorian Mounted Rifles as 'a fat-arsed, pot-bellied, lazy lot of wasters.'

'I'm sorry to hear you say that,' said Major Harris to the General, 'and I intend to take down your words.'

'Do by all means,' replied the General, 'and you can add if you like that in my opinion they are a lot of white-livered curs.' He also remarked to Major Harris that the Victorians had another colony to keep them company in running away from the Boers. When Harris asked which colony that might be, the General said Western Australia. This was a reference to some events on 15 May at Grobler's Recht, when the Fifth and Sixth Western Australian Mounted Infantry had lost six men. The General made no secret of his feelings. Four days after the debacle at Wilmansrust, he happened to ride past some of the Victorians while they were clumsily using their bayonets to stick pigs for fresh meat. 'Yes, that's just about what you men are good for,' yelled the General. 'When the Dutchmen came along the other night you didn't fix bayonets and charge them, but you go for something that can't hit back.'

General Beatson later apologized to Major Harris for his remarks about the Western Australians, and, after hearing that McKnight had taken offence, asked Harris to go to him with an apology. Taking the view that it was too late for apologies, since the General's remarks had become the talk of the camp, McKnight applied for leave to go to Pretoria, saying that he wished to ask for inquiries into the affair both in South Africa and Victoria. Before he could do this, General Beatson sent Major Harris with an apology to Major T. F. Umphelby, the Australian officer nominally in command of the Fifth Victorian Mounted Rifles. Although Umphelby was off duty and in hospital, he accepted the apology. As Umphelby was his senior officer, McKnight was now compelled to let the matter drop. 'I called the officers together,' he reported, 'and showed them a memo from Major Umphelby. They were indignant about it. I tried my best to keep matters straight, as I knew it was the intention of the men to lay down their arms unless they could get under another command. I also spoke to a number of NCOs, advising them to be careful what they did.'

One night soon after this, six Victorian troopers were discussing the matter around a campfire at Middleburg when one of their number, Private James Steele, was heard by an Imperial officer to say: 'We'll be a lot of fools if we go out with him again.' Whatever else may have been overheard was never officially made public, but it was said later that Steele had urged his companions to pile arms and not to go out with General Beatson until he apologised for his remarks about the Victorians. As a result of that campfire conversation Private Steele, aged 29, Private Arthur Richards, 23, and Private Herbert Parry, 24, were tried by Field General Court-martial for inciting to mutiny. On 11 July, all three were found guilty and sentenced to death. Two weeks later the British Commander-in-Chief, Lord Kitchener, confirmed the verdicts but commuted the sentences to prison terms of ten years in the case of Steele and one year with hard labour for each of the others. The three prisoners had already begun serving their sentences in England before anything was known about the case in Australia.

The first the new Federal Government knew of it was when the Melbourne *Age* on 28 September published a photograph of Private Steel's court-martial schedule, complete with the words 'To suffer death by being shot', 'I commute the sentence to one of ten years penal servitude', and Lord Kitchener's signature. The photograph, taken from the original document at Middleburg, had been placed at the *Age*'s disposal together with a letter from an unidentified soldier in South Africa giving a slightly inaccurate account of the charges and sentences imposed on Steele and two other unnamed privates, and of the remarks alleged to have been made by General Beatson.

The news of Wilmansrust three months earlier had been bad enough, but this was worse. It provoked in Australia a sense of outrage tempered uncomfortably by guilt. How could a British general be so grossly offensive to Australian troops, and how could the British Army sentence Australians to death in such an arbitrary and secret manner? On the other hand, who could wholeheartedly defend what was said to have been incitement to mutiny?

The Wilmansrust affair brought national pride into collision with imperial loyalty ('A fine reward for a man who volunteered to give his life for the service of the Empire!' said one Federal parliamentarian), and it raised again some basic questions about Australia's participation in the war. These questions deserve some attention before we return to the court-martial prisoners. 'Why am I going to the war?' asked a popular poem of the day, going on to answer its own question without the slightest reference to any of the facts about British-Boer rivalry in South Africa:

> Fitzwalter, Drake and Hampden are but elder brethren dead,
> And that's why you are going to the war!

The Governor of New South Wales, the young Earl Beauchamp, was also moved to verse when farewelling the first South African contingent to ail from the colony in 1899:

> Like young lions to help the old one,
> Swift of footfall and firm of poise,

By jove, that foeman will be a bold one,
Who'll face us banded, my boys, my boys.[2]

Trite though they may have been, these two quotations went a long way towards conveying the majority view of why Australia took part in the Boer War. Other issues which were raised by a dissenting minority were regarded as irrelevant by most Australians. The war began ostensibly over Britain's insistence that an independent foreign State – the South African Republic, also known as Transvaal – should extend its own franchise to a large number of British subjects who had gone there to look for gold. 'You see that flag?' said the President of the Transvaal, Paul Kruger, pointing to the quadricolour flying over his Government buildings in Pretoria shortly before the war. 'If I grant the franchise I may as well pull it down!'

Of course there was more to it than this question of votes for Uitlanders, as the Boers called their importunate visitors. The real issue was who should control South Africa: the British, who had two colonies there, the Cape Colony and Natal; or the Boers, who had trekked north to establish their own states, the South African Republic and the Orange Free State. As Britain's Secretary of State for the Colonies, Joseph Chamberlain, told the High Commissioner in Cape Colony, Lord Milner, most people in Britain recognised that 'our supremacy in South Africa and our existence as a great power in the world are involved in the result of our present controversy.' Milner was pushing Kruger hard on the Uitlander issue, and Kruger was not a man to be pushed. Deciding to take the offensive rather than wait for a probable attack, the Transvaal Government issued an ultimatum which it must have known would be unacceptable to Britain. The ultimatum expired on 11 October 1899 and on the following day, hoping for a repetition of their success against Britain in a brief conflict eighteen years before, the Boers invaded Cape Colony and Natal.

When, six days after the invasion, the New South Wales Legislative Assembly debated a motion that the Colony should despatch a military force for service with the Imperial Army in South Africa, the young Labor member for Grenfell, William Holman, drew the attention of the

---

[2] Despite the forced rhymes, this was a more felicitous choice than the patronising snatch of Kipling which Lord Beauchamp sent ahead of him by radio from the ship which brought him to Sydney in 1899:

> Greeting! Your birthstain have you turned to good
> Forcing strong wills perverse to steadfastness,
> The first flush of the tropics in your blood,
> At your feet success.

House to the fact that many thousands of English artisans were employed at bicycle works in Germany. These Britons had to submit to German law, he said; they could not speak their own language in German courts; and they had no vote. Why, he went on to ask, was New South Wales not sending a contingent of Mounted Rifles to coerce the German Government into granting the same rights to these bicycle mechanics as were being demanded for the Uitlanders from the Transvaal Government? 'Because they are not oppressed!' interjected a future Prime Minister of Australia, Joseph Cook.

'That is not oppression in Germany which is oppression in the Transvaal,' replied Holman, one of the Assembly's most adroit debaters. '*That in the captain's but a choleric word/which in the soldier is flat blasphemy.* That is not oppression in Germany, because the Germans are too big, too formidable to be coerced. But with an insignificant little state like the Transvaal every patriot in the House, swelling into importance with the jingo emotions which possess his little twopenny-halfpenny soul, feels called upon in the interests of humanity and freedom to go to the relief of his oppressed and downtrodden countrymen.'

In this debate, the opposition to the war was rationally strong but numerically weak. Such Labor speakers as Holman, Hughes and Arthur Griffith managed to preserve a posture of imperial loyalty while roundly condemning the South African adventure; but this was too subtle an exercise for most of the Honourable Members. In declaring the war to be 'ill-advised, ill-judged and immoral', Billy Hughes aligned himself with such patriots of the past as the Earl of Chatham, who had warned the House of Commons against war with the American colonies; John Bright, who protested against the Crimean War; and Gladstone, who had restored the Boers' independence in 1881. The greatest enemies of the British race, said Hughes, were those who would plunge the Empire into any dispute so long as 'a handful of powerful syndicators' were to be served. The pro-Boers maintained that Britain was fighting to secure control of the gold mines of the Rand, to redden the territorial lacuna between its central and southern African colonies, and to avenge the indignity of 1881.

The anti-Boer view, insofar as it needed any justification, was that the Boers were fighting to establish Afrikaner domination of Southern Africa, and that such domination would mean the imposition of a despotic, retrogressive culture upon Uitlanders and native races alike. More importantly, Britain was meeting a challenge to the British Empire. Was it not a fact that the Boers had invaded the Cape and Natal? How, then, could any British subject hold back. The imperviousness of these questions to rational reply was nicely illustrated by an exchange between Holman and Edmund Barton during the Assembly debate:

> *Mr Holman*: There was a time when English statesmen and English politicians did not fear – I will not say to draw the sword – but, at all events, to measure their forces with the proudest and mightiest empires on the continent . . . But today the English race has fallen on a time when apparently the utmost it can do is to bully weak and struggling powers. England can threaten a country like Venezuela; it can send an expedition into the Soudan. It can fight the Zulu; and it can now, after a long process of negotiation, finally draw the sword against the Boer.
>
> *Mr Barton*: Would the hon. member mind telling us one thing – whether he wants the Boers to win or the British?
>
> *Mr Holman*: I am not to be alarmed at any question of that kind. Whilst my country is fighting in a just cause I hope I shall be as ready to support its claims as any other member. But as I believe from the bottom of my heart that this is the most iniquitous, most immoral war ever waged with any race, I hope that England may be defeated.
>
> *Hon. Members*: Shame! Shame!

To Barton and many other intelligent Australians, including Alfred Deakin in the Victorian Assembly, the question was no more complicated than that. 'When our Empire is at war with any other power whatever,' said Barton later in the debate, 'it becomes our turn to declare the motto, "The Empire, right or wrong." That, at any rate, is the view which I have a right to express . . . and I believe it is the attitude taken by an enormous majority of the inhabitants of the Empire.' When the motion was put, there were seventy-eight Ayes and only ten Noes. All the honourable members then rose in their seats, cheered the Queen and sang the National Anthem.

With few exceptions, the press was unquestioningly pro-war. One dissident was the *Bulletin*, and another was Holman's little newspaper at Grenfell, the *Vedette*. Dissent in the universities was even more isolated; indeed its only prominent expression came from Sydney University's English-born Challis Professor of History, George Arnold Wood, who conducted a lively but polite correspondence in the columns of the *Daily Telegraph* with a self-appointed spokesman for the University's pro-war majority, the Scottish-born Professor of Modern Literature, Mungo MacCallum. Although describing himself as 'a fervid Imperialist', Professor Wood rejected the notion of 'Empire right or wrong'; as he saw it, the duty of an Imperialist was to try to stop the Empire damaging itself. '[Professor MacCallum's] argument,' he wrote, 'means that if we see Englishmen engaged (as it seems to us) in robbing and murdering foreigners, patriotism demands that we should do all we can to assist them to complete the robbery and murder. I, on the other hand, think that patriotism demands that we should do all we can to put an end to the robbery and murder, and I feel sure that in doing so we shall be doing good service not only in the cause of humanity, but also in the cause of England, and in the cause of Empire.'

Professor MacCallum's argument came down to one sentence: 'The war is begun and we must be undivided.' This simple argument was strengthened immeasurably by the unexpected British reverses of 'Black Week' in December 1899, and all but the most recalcitrant sources of dissent fell silent. In any case, there were more subjective influences at work: young Australians were enlisting out of nothing more complicated than a desire for adventure, and many of their elders looked forward to seeing Australia's Britishness tested under fire. The English historian J. A. Froude had remarked in the 1880s that Australians had reacted *ipsis Anglicis Angliciores* to the death of General Gordon at Khartoum, as if 'the life of a nation, like the life of a tree [was] in its extremities.' And so it was also with the Boer War. In the two and a half years of the war, Australia sent 16,175 men to South Africa. This was only a small fraction of the 448,725 who fought on Britain's side, but it was more than twice as large as Canada's contribution (6313), and the Australian casualty rate (588 killed, or died of wounds or sickness: 3.6 per cent of total enlistment) was proportionately not much lower than that of the total British force (4.6 per cent).

Just as 'Black Week' had stiffened support for the war in 1899, so did some of the events of 1901 tend slightly to erode it; there was never any question of a basic change in attitude, but public reaction to such matters as the Wilmansrust Court Martial and Britain's increasing resort to pillage and concentration camps persuaded the Prime Minister in January 1902 to seek from the House of Representatives a re-affirmation of Australia's readiness 'to give all requisite to the mother country in order to bring the present war to an end.' Barton's motion, seconded by the Leader of the Opposition, Sir George Reid, also expressed 'its indignation at the baseless charges made abroad against the honour of the people and the humanity and the valour of the soldiers of the Empire.'

The *Bulletin*'s distaste for the war had kept pace with the growing harshness of policies pursued in the field by Lord Kitchener, whose name it preferred to spell *Ketchener*. 'Truly,' one of its editorials said in December 1901, 'it is time for England to burn the Bible publicly by the hands of the common hangman, and go back to the worship of THOR and ODIN, so that its faith may square with its foreign policy, and its creed and its KETCHENER'S gallows won't look so hopelessly incongruous.' In the same month Professors Wood and MacCallum resumed their correspondence, and once again – to the latter-day reader, though not to most readers of his own time – Professor Wood came off better. MacCallum defended Britain's farm burning and concentration camp policies on grounds that the first would shorten the war, and that the second was well intentioned (where else could women and children go after the roofs had been burnt over their heads?). Wood objected strongly to Australian soldiers being ordered 'to do business which Professor MacCallum describes as "sickening work", and which I, if it were permitted, would describe by a far stronger phrase. "The generals," writes Corporal Thompson of the Queensland Bushmen, "will get a shock if we have to go on burning houses over women and children. We will mutiny some of these days and refuse to do it." For saying less than this Australian soldiers were the other day sentenced to death by Lord Kitchener's Court. I protest against Australian soldiers being compelled, by fear of death, to commit acts which they themselves recognise to be both sickening and atrocious.'

In the Federal Parliamentary debate, H. B. Higgins spoke of the shame which he felt at seeing a French illustrated paper's depiction 'of a number of Australians – fellows with broad hats and feathers – burning Boer houses.' He went on to raise a point which had received scant attention so far and the importance of which was to be borne out some years later by events of greater magnitude. 'The only ground on which the Prime Minister has urged the sending of [another] contingent is that Great Britain is at war, and that, therefore, we should help her . . . I apprehend that the Prime Minister is making a very difficult position for himself and his successors in connexion with future wars – that he is making a very difficult position for Australia. Are we, without going into the causes of the wars of Great Britain, to adopt the principle that we should actively side with Great Britain, no matter what is done? The adoption of such a course will commit Australia to the principle that she must aid the Imperial Government in all wars with her young lives . . . although she has no voice in the negotiations which precede war, and is not to be consulted in regard to its expediency or necessity.' He added that if ever Britain needed help in an honourable cause he would advocate the spending of 'every man and every shilling . . . in defending the Empire.'

As far as most members of the House of Representatives were concerned, Higgins might just as well have been talking Dutch, or double Dutch. 'The Australian bushman,' said a more orthodox speaker, the former Premier of Victoria, Allan McLean, 'is the equal of the Boer in horsemanship, in marksmanship and in bushcraft, and therefore his aid is invaluable to the mother country; and I am perfectly sure that no considerable section of the people of Australia would tolerate anything in the way of refusing aid that the mother country is now asking for.' He was perfectly right. The part of Barton's motion dealing with help to Britain was passed with forty-five Ayes and five Noes, which was rather a low vote for a House of seventy-five members. Many Labor MHRs were absent, but the issue of the Boer War was not one which neatly followed party lines. The future Labor Prime Minister, J. C. Watson, voted with the Ayes, and Hughes, although absent from the House, was paired as an Aye with the Labor member for Coolgardie, Hugh Mahon, whose opposition to the war sprang from much the same source as his support for Home Rule in Ireland. The rest of the motion was resolved in the affirmative without a division, and at Barton's suggestion both sides of the House gave three cheers for King and Empire.

Minuscule though organised opposition to the war may have been, it was increasingly resented in loyalist circles as the war ground brutally to a close. Holman was physically attacked; Arthur Griffith was asked by a committee of electors to resign his seat in the New South Wales Assembly, but cheerfully declined to do so; and Professor Wood, who was president of the Australian Anti-War League, came close to losing his University Chair. In February 1902 the University Senate resolved that Wood's letters and speeches about the war were 'unworthy of a Professor of History whose utterances ought to be marked by strict impartiality and freedom from passion' and tended to 'encourage the enemies of the country . . . and impair the value of his teaching in the university.' This last phrase was indeed ominous, and it was probably only the Prime Minister's intervention which saved Professor Wood from the academic firing squad. Barton, who was himself a member of the University Senate, wrote to the Chancellor, Sir Normand MacLaurin, urging that Wood be accorded the right of free speech.

The intervention came just in time, for Professor Wood had shown no inclination to trim his sails. On the very day that he heard about the Senate's censure resolution, he posted to the *Manchester Guardian* an article which was to rekindle controversy when it was published in April and promptly telegraphed to the Australian press. The chief reason why Australians had taken part in the war, said the article, was that they considered their help a good investment and a good advertisement. 'A few of the volunteers have been inspired by self-sacrifice,' it added, 'but most of them by sheer love of adventure and the desire to escape from the monotony of bush life.'

What of those three volunteers whose service in the Transvaal had been rewarded by the death penalty? On 2 October 1901 a Western

Australian Labor member of Federal Parliament, J. M. Fowler, asked a series of questions on notice to ascertain whether the press reports about the Wilmansrust sentences and commutations were correct, whether General Beatson had used the words ascribed to him, whether such language was subversive of discipline and calculated to produce mutiny, and whether officers guilty of conduct calculated to produce mutiny were punishable under military law. If the answers to all these questions were affirmative, would an inquiry be made into the General's conduct, and would the Victorians' sentences be reconsidered? All the Minister for Defence, Sir John Forrest, could say in reply was that he had asked the Prime Minister to ask the Governor-General to ask the Secretary of State for the Colonies to ask the War Office for full information on 'these very regrettable matters.' So far the Commonwealth Department of Defence knew nothing whatever about them.[3]

'Mr Barton presents his humble duty to Your Excellency,' read the Prime Minister's minute to the Governor-General, Lord Hopetoun, 'and desires to direct your attention to a question asked today in the House of Representatives . . .' Barton's official tone to Government House was more supplicatory than the forms of address used later by his successors. Lord Hopetoun's brief cable to Chamberlain, asking merely for 'any information possible as to matter', was despatched on 3 October; but five weeks were to pass before any reply was received from London. The cabled reply disclosed the names of all three men, confirmed their original and commuted sentences, then stated that the Judge Advocate General had found legal flaws in their convictions. Because of this, the War Office on 26 October had quashed the men's convictions and ordered their immediate release from prison. This was good news for Private Parry's father, who had been trying in vain for several weeks to find out from the Department of Defence and the War Office why his son had stopped writing letters home. 'I am not altogether astonished that he is mixed up in the matter,' he said in a letter to *The Age*, 'as I know him to be a true Briton, and one who would stick to a chum or tent mate to his last drop of blood.'

One reason for the Colonial Office's delay in answering Lord

[3] Sir John Forrest had more reason than most to resent General Beatson's alleged aspersions, for his 16-year-old nephew, Lieutenant Anthony Forrest, had been one of the six Western Australian fatalities at Grobler's Recht where, according to the General, the Western Australian Mounted Infantry had run away from the Boers. The *Sunday Times* in Perth had claimed earlier in the year that Lt Forrest had obtained his commission through family influence, and to judge from his age this would indeed seem to have been the case. His father—Alexander Forrest, a former Mayor of Perth—was suffering from inflammation of the kidneys when Anthony's death was announced. His constitution was said to have been further weakened by grief, and he died on 20 June.

Hopetoun's cable, apart from the tortuous channels of communication, may have been the fact that by this time the War Office had another and more serious judicial problem involving Australians in South Africa. On the day after a reply was sent to Lord Hopetoun, a committee of inquiry began investigating certain activities in the wild Spelonken district of northern Transvaal during July, August and September by a specially enlisted commando corps known as the Bush Veldt Carbineers. As a result of this inquiry, three Australian lieutenants – H. H. Morant, P. J. Handcock and G. R. Witton – were charged with the murder of several Boer prisoners and a German missionary who was said to have inconveniently witnessed some of the shootings. After a series of courts-martial conducted in secrecy, all three were found guilty and sentenced to death. Witton's sentence was commuted to life imprisonment, and he was later pardoned; but Morant (who was well remembered in Australia for some ballads he had contributed to the *Bulletin* under the pen-name of 'The Breaker') and Handcock were executed by a firing squad of Cameron Highlanders at Pretoria gaol on 27 February 1902. Nothing was heard of these charges or sentences in Australia until after the executions.

In the Victorian and Bush Veldt cases alike, Australian misgivings about British military justice were increased by the War Office's reluctance to answer questions and its refusal to disclose details of the courts-martial. Mr Barton presented his humble duty to Lord Hopetoun again on 22 November, after the release of the Victorians had been announced; advised him that the Australian people felt 'that their honour [had] been implicated by the charge which was brought against the men in question'; and courteously asked if the remainder of Mr Fowler's parliamentary questions might now be answered by the War Office. Apparently no answer to that request was ever received from London, and the Commonwealth Government allowed the matter to drop.[4]

When Steele, Richards and Parry began to seek redress for their detention without pay, the Commonwealth washed its hands of them. Parry, a seasonal bush worker with a dark, drooping moustache, wrote to the Commonwealth Department of Defence in January 1902 on behalf of himself and his two companions in misfortune, one of whom was shortly

---

[4] The proceedings of the Bush Veldt Courts-Martial, if they still exist, have never been made public despite at least two formal requests. A request to the British Ministry of Defence in 1974 for access to the Wilmansrust proceedings brought the following reply: – 'The Judge Advocate General's Department select court-martial proceedings which they consider worthy of retention and transfer them to the Public Record Office. The remainder are destroyed after seven years. Enquiries at the JAG's Department and at the Public Record Office have, I am afraid, revealed no trace of these court-martial proceedings.' The Australian Archives file on Wilmansrust contains the Prime Minister's minute of 22 November to the Governor-General, but no trace of any answer.

to land in gaol again for a civilian offence. 'I should like to know,' asked Parry, 'if anything has been done or will be done by the Commonwealth . . . as I have been to the Barracks and have finally been told they know nothing concerning us except that we have been discharged . . . We do not wish to go to any heavy legal expense until we know the attitude the Commonwealth Department and the War Office intend to assume in the matter as to repudiating our claim [for back pay] or not.' Any hope of help from the Commonwealth was dispelled by the secretary of the Department of Defence, Captain R. M. Collins. 'I am directed to state,' he replied to Parry, 'that the things to which you refer occurred during the men's service in the Imperial Army. The Commonwealth Government did not act as agents for the Imperial Government in raising or despatching the Contingent, and neither the State nor the Commonwealth have any responsibility whatever for any military discipline or treatment to which the members of the Contingent had to submit in the service they undertook.'

By the time their old battalion returned from South Africa three months later, the three black sheep had become a fit subject for military reproach. With no satisfaction forthcoming from General Beatson, it seemed as though the good name of the Fifth Victorian Contingent required condemnation of the three men who had added the slur of mutiny to the slur of cowardice. The First Battalion of 200 officers and men landed in Melbourne on 25 April, a date which will acquire further connotations of national honour later in this narrative. The Battalion was cheered through the city and accorded an official lunch at Victoria Barracks with speeches by the State Military Commandant, Colonel Tom Price, and his predecessor in that post, Major-General Francis Downes. In its report next morning *The Age* managed to convey both the wariness of the two speakers and the touchiness of their audience.

> They had had the bad fortune to strike a very sad disaster [said Colonel Price], but through whose fault it was not for him to say. (Cheers; and a voice: 'Good old Tom!') But he would say that he offered them his warmest and deepest sympathy. (Cheers) Unfortunately for them they had had associated with them certain men – one of whom, the principal one, was now in gaol – who had helped to drag their good name through the dirt, and now they had had to work to recover it. (Cheers) Too much had been said of the matter (Cheers) and a great deal of idle and silly talk had been heard of it in Melbourne. One of the principal men he had met himself, who, although he (Colonel Price) did not know him any more than he knew Adam – (laughter) – had told him that he thought he knew what it was up to an Australian to do. 'I said to him,' continued the Commandant, 'that if I had been there you should have dug your own

grave, and then I would have shot you like the cur you are. Australia wants no blackguards like you! (Great cheering) I saw the man afterwards going into Colonel Otter's [a former commanding officer of the Fifth Victorian Mounted Rifles] room, and I asked 'Who is that man?' Colonel Otter told me and I said, 'Well, he has heard my opinion of him and I don't think he'll forget it in a hurry!' (Cheers and laughter).

[Major-General Downes then said] the Wilmansrust disaster had happened through no fault of theirs. (Cheers) He knew that (Cheers) and was sure of it. When they found themselves in that terrible hole they had done all that could be expected of them, and despite everything that was said at the time and the obloquy heaped upon the Contingent, he had never believed it – (Cheers) – and he had taken the first opportunity to state his disbelief. (Cheers) Time had proved him right (Cheers) and he hoped that they would all live for many years to be proud of having served in the Fifth Contingent in South Africa. (Loud Cheers)

A voice: The doughty Fifth! (Uproar, and cries of 'Chuck him out!')

An officer: It's all right; he only said 'the doughty Fifth.'

Colonel Price rose amid the confusion and reminded the men that they were in an enclosed room. They must keep their tongues between their teeth when they went outside, and were not to talk about themselves.

A voice: Our noble selves! (Laughter)

What are we to make of that last discordant voice? There is a sardonic, self-mocking quality about it which is more appealing than either the blandishments of commandants adroitly shifting blame, or the conventional jingoism of Young Lions and Red-Splashed Chargers. Across the distance of three-quarters of a century, it sounds like the voice of experience and self-knowledge: the voice of someone who has learnt the hard way that there is more to war than such abstractions as national honour and imperial loyalty. It is a voice we shall hear again more frequently when next Australia goes to war.

4

PARLIAMENT

IN SEPTEMBER 1901 Tom Roberts started work on a painting which was to keep him busy in Australia and Britain for the best part of two years. This was a different proposition from such works as *The Breakaway* and *A Mountain Muster*, which had brought a touch of Impressionism to the Australian bush and made a name for Roberts as the father of Australian landscape painting. For a fee of 1000 guineas he had undertaken to paint in oils, on a canvas measuring not less than 5.083 metres by 3.325 metres, the social and political muster before which His Royal Highness the Duke of Cornwall and York opened the first Federal Parliament at the Exhibition Building in Melbourne. The painting had to contain 'correct representations of the Duke and Duchess of York, the Governor-General, the various State governors, the members of both Houses of the Federal Parliament, and other distinguished guests to the number of not less than 250.' When *Opening of the First Federal Parliament of the Commonwealth of Australia, May 9, 1901* eventually came off the easel, it was 5.043 metres long, 3.584 metres high, and contained 258 identifiable dignitaries.

'The big picture', 'the C. opus' and 'the gem', as Roberts called it on different occasions, was less a work of art than a feat of organisation. Although Roberts had been an invited guest at the opening ceremony, he did not observe the scene as closely as he would otherwise have done, for no one had yet asked him to paint it. 'It was very solemn and great,' he said later of the view from his seat in the gallery, which he captured with great economy and charm in a small, impressionistic oil sketch. 'The heads on the floor looked like a landscape stretching away.' Once officially embarked upon the project, he had to reconstruct many of the details of that human landscape: rows of vice-royalty resplendent with gold braid, ministers of State in black coats and hirsute dignity (only Barton, book in hand ready to read the response, was clean shaven), MHRs and senators, their wives still dressed in mourning for the dead Queen, bishops and professors, and altogether a host of some 14,000.

Roberts took great trouble to compile statistical information about his cast of identifiable figures, and prevailed upon many of them to sit for him although the space available for their features in the C. opus was no larger than ten centimetres square. Lord Hopetoun did not enjoy sitting, but told Roberts he would rather do it than go to a Liedertafel concert, Gregor McGregor, Labor leader in the Senate and a former iron ship-plate worker in Scotland, was so blind that he stumbled against a table in the studio. For many of his subjects, Roberts kept statistics in tabular form: Barton, 54 years, 5 ft $9\frac{1}{8}$, 14 stone 8 lbs, hat size $7\frac{1}{8}$, born NSW; C. C. Kingston, 51, 6 ft 1 in, 16 stone, $7\frac{3}{8}$, S. Aust.; W. M. Hughes, 38, 5 ft 6 ins, 9 stone 1 lb, 7, England; David Syme, 75, 6 ft $1\frac{1}{2}$ ins, 12 stone, $7\frac{3}{8}$, Scotland; Joseph Cook, 41, 5 ft 9 ins, 12 stone, 7, England; Josiah Symon, 56, 6 ft, 13 stone, $7\frac{1}{4}$, Scotland. Sir John Forrest was 6 feet 1 inch tall, admitted to a weight of 18 stone, but declined to be weighed. Roberts thought he would have tipped the scales at more like 20 stone. 'The C. opus goes on,' he wrote to Alfred Deakin in the second year of his labours, 'it's getting like pumping up a bike, the first filling is very easy but to get it really tight is where the difficulty comes, but it's the same in everything – it's the test of a man to get the last bit in – just that little that raises above the ruck, eh?' From London his friend and fellow artist Arthur Streeton wrote suggesting tactfully that perhaps Roberts was taking his task a little too seriously. 'There's a feeling with others and with me that you're putting *too* much time into your big Gem of the Opening. Still you understand best.'

Looking back at that first Parliament, the writer feels something of the painter's dilemma in the face of so much human material. How does one pump them all in? To start with, of course, there were only the ministers chosen by Edmund Barton (who by convention was called Prime Minister) to administer the Commonwealth until Parliament could be elected. This 'Cabinet of Kings' contained some of the strongest and most truculent politicians in the country, and it was a tribute to Barton's pre-eminence among his colleagues and the easiness of his manner that he was able to keep them working together in reasonable harmony. As there was no Cabinet secretariat, the only record of early Cabinet meetings was that kept in an exercise book by Barton himself. Sometimes Deakin's diary recorded the word 'scene', or 'squabble K & L.' The initials stood for Charles Cameron Kingston, the tall, easily impassioned ex-Premier of South Australia, who was Barton's Minister for Trade and Customs, and Sir William Lyne of New South Wales, big, slow but cunning, who held the portfolio of Home Affairs. Kingston was the son of an Irish father and a mother who was half Scottish and half Portuguese. Ten years earlier he had been arrested while on his way to a duel with a loaded revolver in his pocket. In 1896 he engaged in a furious exchange of letters, through the columns of the *South Australian Register*, with his fellow barrister and political foe, the Scottish-born Josiah Symon. Their letters set a standard of invective which has rarely been surpassed in Australian political life. 'Mr Symon's letter is a choice specimen of epistolary ruffianism,'wrote the Premier, 'requiring for its proper punishment a temporary removal of the literary gloves. So here goes . . .' He called Symon 'a death's head at the wedding feast, a gruesome ghoul with lips reeking with mendacity and foetid with malice, prostituting public opportunity to poison with malignant spite every drop and dreg of the festive cup which he hypocritically pretended to drain to the good health of his friend and guest . . . This forensic compound of squid and skunk has ejected three columns in the hope of escaping in his offensive cloud from the gaff of truth.'[1]

To the explosive mixture of 'Charlie' Kingston and 'Old Bill' Lyne was sometimes added the pride and wrath of another massive ex-Premier, Sir John Forrest, 'The Emperor Of The West' who had been Premier of his colony since its achievement of responsible government in 1890. He was Postmaster-General until the untimely death of Sir James Dickson (Queensland) during the third week of the Commonwealth. Forrest took over Dickson's portfolio (Defence), and the PMG went to a replacement from Queensland, J. G. Drake. The Premier of Tasmania, Neil Lewis, had said when joining Barton's ministry that he would not stand for Federal Parliament. His place was therefore taken in April by another Tasmanian – a member of the 1900 Federal delegation to London, Sir Philip Fysh – and like Lewis he held no portfolio. Richard O'Connor (NSW) was Vice-President of the Executive Council, Sir George Turner (Victoria) was Treasurer, Alfred Deakin (Victoria) was Attorney-General, and Barton (NSW) held the portfolio of External Affairs. Until permanent offices were obtained in Melbourne, which was to be the seat of Federal Parliament for the next twenty-six years, Barton transacted most of his official business on a partially closed-in verandah at one of the NSW Government offices in Sydney. The Governor-General visited him there almost every day, or telephoned him, and the Prime Minister in his daily round was ably assisted by the newly appointed permanent heads of the Prime

---

[1] Symon had asked for this by calling Kingston 'a social pariah . . . cowed by the execration of all decent people.' 'I do not hate Mr Kingston,' he said. 'He is not worthy of that feeling. I despise him.' Lyne could lay about himself too. In the course of an attack on Deakin's 'fusion' ministry in 1909 he told the Minister for External Affairs, Littleton Groom—a Free Trader whose support had helped the Liberal Protectionist Deakin to regain office—that if Groom's father could see the company his son was in his bones would turn in their grave. Groom was much affected by this remark, Deakin responded to it with great heat, and the Speaker, Sir Frederick Holder, who was in the chamber though not in the Speaker's Chair, said 'Dreadful! Dreadful!' and suddenly fell forward with a cerebral haemorrhage. He was carried from the chamber and died soon afterwards.

Minister's and External Affairs Department, Atlee Hunt, and the Attorney-General's Department, Robert Garran.[2] The Commonwealth public service started life on 1 January with a staff of little more than 1400, consisting almost entirely of the colonies' customs officers who, under the terms of the Constitution, transferred immediately to the Commonwealth, which henceforth was to be responsible for the collection and disbursement of all customs and excise duties. Two other departments (Posts and Telegraphs, and Defence) were transferred from the States by proclamation two months later, but other Commonwealth departments – Prime Minister's and External Affairs, Attorney-General's, Home Affairs and Treasury – all had to be created from scratch. How small were these beginnings! When the time came to move to Melbourne, Barton took all his official files in one black bag. By 1905, however, the number of public servants had risen to 22,300.

Among the Prime Minister's files from his pre-election period was a curious minute to the Governor-General which deserves to be recorded as Australia's first juvenile step in the realm of external affairs. 'Mr Barton presents his humble duty to Your Excellency,' he wrote on 15 April, 'and requests that Your Excellency will be so good as to inform the Right Honourable, the Secretary of State for Colonies, that Ministers have had under their consideration the subject of the acquisition by Great Britain of Kerguelen Island in the Southern Indian Ocean. Ministers are deeply impressed with the desireableness of taking measures for the greater security of one of the most important trade routes of the Empire, and respectfully suggest that, if possible, steps be taken by His Majesty's Government which will lead to the acquisition by Great Britain of an island from which the ships passing to and from England to Australia and New Zealand would otherwise be so open to danger in time of war.' The only trouble with this idea was that Kerguelen – a treeless, mountainous island 3700 kilometres southwest of Perth, swept by sub-Antarctic gales,

[2] Communications were better than one might have thought. The Governor-General's official residence in Sydney had three telephone numbers, and Barton naturally had the telephone at both his office and home. Australia's first telephone exchanges opened in Melbourne, Sydney and Brisbane in 1880, and by 1901 the Sydney telephone directory, although small in dimensions, contained 496 pages. The most common handset in use was the oak-panelled Ericsson wall telephone. Beyond reach of the telephone service, which was still largely a city convenience, there was the telegraph system which had been growing steadily since the 1850s. Mr Tom Thick of Sydney recalled more than seventy years later how, as a 14 year-old telegraph messenger in 1903, he rode his bicycle 30 kilometres one day in mid-summer to deliver a telegram to a bush homestead on the road from Horsham to Dimboola in western Victoria. The temperature was 46°C, and on the way he had to skirt a tiger snake lying in the middle of the road. At the homestead he walked about 50 metres through long grass to the front door. He delivered the telegram and was picking his way back to the road, thinking of snakes, when from the house behind him he heard a woman scream. He could still remember that scream in 1975.

split by fjords and strewn with blocks of broken basalt – had been annexed by France eight years before. 'HMG will probably not be disposed to approach the French Government with a view to the acquisition of Kerguelen Island,' minuted one of the Colonial Office mandarins who considered Lord Hopetoun's despatch. Another minute was more per-emptory: 'There would not be the least chance of getting France to give up the island. The Australians must get up a navy and take it on the out-break of war if they want it.'

The first Federal elections, for seventy-five seats in the House of Representatives and thirty-six in the Senate, were held on 29 and 30 March 1901. Voting was not compulsory (the first compulsory election was not until 1925), and most women could not have voted even if they had wished to. The elections were held under the electoral laws of the various States, and only in South Australia and Western Australia did women have the franchise at that time. The Commonwealth Franchise Act of 1902 enfranchised all persons aged 21 years or more, and thus all women were entitled to vote at the next Federal elections in 1903. But many Australians could not be bothered exercising that right. The pro-portion of enrolled voters who voted in 1901, excluding those in un-contested electorates, was 56.68 per cent. In New South Wales 68 per cent voted, and in Western Australia only 36 per cent. In all States except Queensland, where a form of preferential voting had been introduced nine years before, and Tasmania, which used a system of proportional representation, voting was first past the post. Neither Tasmania nor South Australia had completed electoral distribution into Federal divisions, and so for the House of Representatives they each voted as one electorate, just as all States did for the Senate.

And so we come to that landscape of heads mustered for the first time in the Exhibition Building, and then turned out to Parliamentary business in the two ornate chambers of Victoria's Parliament House, from which the Victorian Parliament had moved to the Western Annexe of the Exhibition Building. Few of these Federal politicians were strangers to politics. Of the seventy-five MHRs, fifty-eight had served in colonial parliaments, ten had been Premiers and twelve others had held ministerial rank. Most of them were Australian born, or at least Australian bred; but about twenty of the MHRs had reached Australia in young adulthood, in most cases from the British Isles. Two exceptions to this were the Labor members J. C. Watson (NSW), who had been born at Valparaiso, Chile, while his Scottish father and English mother were en route to New Zealand; and King O'Malley (Tasmania), who said he was born in Canada but was more likely born on the United States side of the

Canadian border. O'Malley, wearing a brown frock coat and ten-gallon hat, had all the spiel and showmanship of a snake-oil salesman or revivalist preacher. He claimed to have founded an institution known as the Waterlily Rock-Bound Church in Texas, and would usually open his political meetings with some such outlandish flourish as: 'Brothers, sisters, fellow Christians. I don't see any profiteers, racketeers, boodleiers or gilt-spurred Brahma-pootra roosters in this meeting . . .' He often used the word 'rooster' with derogatory intent, but was in fact something of a brightly plumaged, gilt-spurred rooster himself.

Needless to say, there were no women in either parliamentary chamber. The first woman to stand for Federal Parliament, and indeed for any parliament in the British Empire, was a Victorian Protectionist named Vida Goldstein, who ran for the Senate in 1903. Miss Goldstein was terrified of mice, and secretly feared that one night her opponents would let some of the creatures loose on her platform while she was speaking. This did not happen, but she was not elected either. Roman Catholics were also under-represented in the first Parliament. Of the 111 members in both Houses, only five are known to have been Catholics – Paddy McMahon Glynn (Free Trader, S.A.), Hugh Mahon (Labor, W.A.), Austin Chapman (Liberal-Protectionist, NSW), Senator D. J. O'Keefe (Labor, Tasmania) and Senator Richard O'Connor (Liberal-Protectionist, NSW). O'Connor – 'one of the type of the Spanish Irish,' as Deakin once described him, 'dark of complexion, deep chested' – was solidly practical and one of the most popular men in Parliament. O'Connor, Deakin and Forrest often gathered in Barton's Parliamentary office and talked late into the night. Before leaving, they sometimes cooked chops and made billy tea at the open fireplace. Forrest in particular was fond of his food. His favourite dishes were devilled oysters, corned beef and marrow bones.

Of all heads in the big picture, none is as hard to portray in miniature as that of Alfred Deakin, the most atypical and multifaceted of all Australian politicians. In 1901, at the age of 45, Deakin was already a seasoned veteran of Victorian politics and the Federal movement. Born in Melbourne of English parents, he qualified at the Bar, but then became a leader writer on the Melbourne *Age*. Under the tutelage of that newspaper's proprietor, David Syme – who, fortunately for Deakin's political future, converted him from Free Trade to Protection – he entered the Victorian Legislative Assembly as a Liberal, which also meant Protectionist. He was 24 years of age. This event, in 1880, had been predicted by one of the spirit mediums Deakin had met during the previous few years, a period when he was fascinated by spiritualism and served as president of the Spiritualist Association in Melbourne. In later years he cited two other predictions which had come true for him: his attendance at an important gathering (which turned out to be, he thought later, the first Colonial Conference in London, 1887), and his marriage to Pattie Browne, the daughter of another keen spiritualist. At the age of 21 he published *A New Pilgrim's Progress*, which he believed at the time had been communicated to him, if not by the spirit of John Bunyan, then at least by some intelligence other than his own.[3]

From spiritualism he moved through theosophy to membership in the Australian Church, a congregation founded by Dr Charles Strong, who had been dismissed as a Presbyterian minister for promulgating unsound and heretical doctrine. His regular attendance at this church fell away sharply after Federation, but not his interest in matters of the spirit. For most of his life Deakin was a prodigious reader, and a prolific recorder of his own reflections. He admired Disraeli, who 'always had another side to his nature, an inner life removed from the crowd', and he jealously guarded and cultivated his own version of that kind of life. At 'Ballara', his holiday home at Point Lonsdale on Port Phillip Bay, Deakin read and thought and wrote as if consciously to hold back the inroads of his public life. He kept books of handwritten prayers, and a series of notebooks entitled *Clues*. Between 1884 and 1914, he recorded 852 consecutively numbered clues. Clue No. 814, written soon after he became Prime Minister for the first time, was: 'Death-it-must-be. O the exquisite relief. The burning pain of millions of nerves throbbing with feverish [*illegible*] and stinging shoots of suffering. The leaden limbs . . . all this sloughed off. O exquisite relief. Elysium. Then freedom. The thrill of life in every nerve and fibre but apart from nerves and fibres – of [*illegible*] and acuteness of delighted activity . . . an ecstasy as of Heaven – health and supremacy – no resistance – no reaction – a floating in a void and slowly a melting as of one organism into cloud – mist . . . insubstantial filmy fading wraith.'

One of his notebooks contained 367 pages of closely written comment on Marlowe, Webster, Ford, Chapman, the ethics of Shakespeare, Beaumont and Fletcher, Kant, Arnold, Mazzini, Massinger, Ben Jonson and Shakespeare's sonnets. He was one of the few people in Australia to have read everything Wordsworth ever published, prose as well as poetry;

[3] Deakin believed in 'ghosts' or 'shells' animated directly or indirectly by souls which had been relatively undeveloped when they 'passed over' from life on earth. In 1909 he wrote: 'These ghosts are undeveloped souls able under certain conditions to discover themselves in their own physiques . . . But in any case the dead who 'return' visibly are not the real personalities of developed souls. They are undeveloped "personalities", largely sportive and sometimes mischievous . . . My own experiences tho they became rarer after I entered public life in 1880 were often striking and suggestive, affording foundations for much theorising. They continuously impressed upon me the actuality of disembodied intelligences . . .'

and on his voyage to England in 1900 he read *The Brothers Karamazov* in French. He read a good deal of French literary criticism, and it was said that his rapport with the British Conservative leader, A. J. Balfour, sprang initially from their shared enthusiasm for the criticism of Sainte-Beuve.

As a public figure, Deakin was characterised as 'Affable Alfred': 180 centimetres tall, trim in figure and face, with a neat Van Dyke beard and animated eyes, he was courteous, even chivalrous. Walter Murdoch, who corresponded with him on literary matters, thought he could have been cast in a pageant as Drake, Raleigh or Spenser. By general consent he was the finest orator of his day – certainly in Australia, and perhaps anywhere in the English language. As J. A. La Nauze remarked in his biography of Deakin, such excellence is surpassingly rare in Australia. In Professor La Nauze's words, Deakin had 'a handsome presence, a manner that could range from passionate earnestness to light humour without loss of dignity, a rich musical voice best described as a light baritone. His speaking was extraordinarily rapid – sometimes in excitement more than 200 words a minute – but his articulation was always perfect; he never hesitated for a word. His complex sentences, with their parentheses and suspended clauses, inevitably swooped to their appointed end on the appropriate principal verb.'

The same fluency and precision were to be found in the extraordinary journalistic career which Deakin managed to combine with all his offices in the Federal Parliament, even those of Attorney-General and Prime Minister. From 1901 to 1914 he was the anonymous – and, to his political colleagues and opponents, quite unsuspected – 'Australian Correspondent' of the *Morning Post* in London. For a fee of £500 a year he wrote a weekly letter, usually on a political subject. Whatever one may think about the propriety of a Prime Minister writing for a wide audience in closely guarded anonymity, his *Morning Post* articles form an intelligent and on the whole responsible account of the period. Deakin enjoyed explaining Australia to a British audience, passing judgment on himself, and drawing attention to the foibles of his opponents.

Sometimes, however, fluency can be the enemy of decision; and so it proved to a large extent with Deakin. 'There was this fatal flaw about Mr Deakin,' wrote Malcolm Shepherd, who was private secretary to him as Prime Minister. 'He was too indefinite when it came to action; he could not do what was wrong, and he could not make up his mind as to what was right.' One of Deakin's daughters, Vera, remembered late in life an incident which may serve now as a parable for the charm and hesitation of her remarkable father. Early one morning, from her window at 'Ballara', Vera Deakin watched her father walk down a narrow bush track that led to the sea. When almost out of sight he turned around, came back towards the house, and then took another, longer track to the water. When her father returned, she asked him why he had changed his mind. There had been a spider's web across the first track, he said, and it looked so beautiful beaded with dew that he had not wanted to disturb it.

The antithesis of Deakin in many respects, although he could be indecisive too, was George Reid. As the Australian Correspondent of the *Morning Post* once wrote, 'Mr Deakin' and 'Mr Reid' were too unlike to be measured against each other, 'for they [belonged to] different species.' Where Deakin was trimly handsome, the 57-year-old former Premier of New South Wales and future Prime Minister of the Commonwealth was obese (five feet eight inches [173 cm] and 18 stone six pounds [117 kg], according to Tom Roberts's statistics for the big picture). Reid was so fat that he had to use a long-handled buttonhook to do up his boots; sometimes, indeed, he needed help. Where Deakin devoted leisure time to his precious 'inner life', Reid unashamedly took his ease. He once told another Minister, Andrew Fisher, that while Premier of New South Wales he 'used to be a regular home vegetable Friday to Monday, and thus [kept himself] fresh.' It was his boast that he never read a book unless it was 'a sensation novel.'

Where Deakin was the polished orator, Reid was a platform speaker of great wit and common touch. His heavy Germanic moustache concealed, as Deakin put it, 'a mouth of considerable size from which there emanated a high, reedy voice rising to a shriek or sinking to a fawning, purring, persuasive orotund with a nasal tinge.' His domelike head and bulging blue eyes, his several chins and immense stomach all combined to produce an air of drowsy lethargy – an air which could be dispelled in an instant, however, by the speed of his repartee. On one occasion hecklers began calling him 'Yes No', the nickname which Reid had acquired during the first New South Wales referendum on the Constitution Bill by stressing the Bill's defects from a New South Wales point of view and then declining to desert the Federal cause himself. When the hecklers called him 'Yes No', he came back at them with: 'That is absolutely false, the exact opposite of the truth – I was "No Yes".'

It was said that no one slept more than Reid, or was more wide awake. He could fall asleep anywhere, publicly and in the most disgraceful attitudes; but unless he was snoring, which of course he often was, it was a mistake to assume that closed lids necessarily indicated unconsciousness. Sometimes he would doze for a few seconds during the dealing of cards for whist on the train journey between Sydney and Melbourne, or even during play; but he never forgot the state of the game, or made a revoke.

Sir George Reid, Prime Minister and High Commissioner in London.

After sleeping in Parliament, he would often keep his eyes closed for a while, picking up the thread of debate and then, by timely interjection, appear not to have been sleeping at all. 'Mr Speaker,' he said once in the New South Wales Assembly, 'I was not asleep. I was merely endeavouring to become mentally oblivious to the honourable and financial nuisance opposite.'

Deakin neither liked nor trusted Reid, and consequently the portrait which he left of his political opponent was less than just. Others spoke of Reid's vitality and generosity, and the public adored him. Reid never spoke over anyone's head, and he was always good for a laugh. He was sometimes referred to as 'Dry Dog' Reid, but this was an allusion to his Free Trade belief that industries should not be pampered. If you had a dog, he once said – employing the familiar kind of imagery that marked all his speeches – you did not teach it to swim or supply it with supports; you just threw it into the water and let it strike out for itself. Protectionists believed in keeping the dog dry.

Should Australia protect its industries by setting a tariff higher than was strictly necessary for the purpose of providing Government revenue, or should it leave them to sink or swim in competition with imports? This was the principal touchstone by which Federal Parliamentarians could be classified politically. There was no fully developed party system during the election campaign, though elected Labor members quickly formed themselves into a disciplined party. During the campaign, candidates were called firstly either protectionists, high tariffists or ministerialists; secondly free traders or oppositionists; and thirdly protectionist Labor, free trade Labor or independent Labor. Those in the first category supported Barton, and in the second Reid. It was not immediately easy to tell which faction had won the elections, but it soon became apparent that Labour would generally support Barton's liberal protectionism rather than Reid's free trade policies. In the House of Representatives there were 31 Protectionists, 28 Free Traders, 14 Labor and two Independents, including one Independent Labor. In the Senate it was the other way round: Protectionists, 11; Free Traders, 17; Labor, 8. Both major factions were confident of having their way with the tariff: the Protectionists felt sure they would be able to guard native industries against the outside world, and the Free Traders, while conceding that some tariff was essential to provide revenue, felt they could stop the Bartonites raising it beyond that minimum.

Labor, the third and smallest force in Parliament, had been only half-hearted about Federation; but although the various trade union-supported organisations in each State had been ill-prepared for the first election campaign, twenty-four of their candidates secured seats in the new Parliament. This was sufficient to exact concessions at different times from both the two major factions in return for support, and to that end the Labor members quickly bound themselves together to observe rigid voting discipline. Two days before the opening of Parliament nine of the Labor members met at Parliament House under the chairmanship of Senator Anderson Dawson for a preliminary discussion about the formation of a party.[4] On 8 May a more representative meeting formed the Federal Parliamentary Labor Party and elected J. C. Watson as its leader. The Labor members also decided to vote as a bloc according to majority decisions taken by themselves in caucus. The titles of Labor organisations varied from State to State until 1918, when all adopted the name 'Australian Labor Party.'

Chris Watson, only 34 years old, was a newspaper compositor by trade. He became president of the NSW Trades and Labour Council at the age of 26; helped Hughes, Holman and others to form the first Labor Leagues which supported electoral candidates bound by a Labor pledge; and was himself elected to the Legislative Assembly for the rural electorate of Young. He used to say that he retained this seat by rendering small services to his constituents; if they wanted a piece of whipcord, for example, he sent it to them. In the Federal Parliament, services were more often rendered to Chris Watson and his party by solicitous ministers of the day. George Reid once said he would not be surprised if some non-Labor ministers were saying 'Yes, Mr Watson' in their sleep. The neatly bearded Mr Watson was personable and quietly astute, but it is not clear why the party preferred his leadership to that of the more aggressive W. M. Hughes or the Scottish-born ex-coalminer, Andrew Fisher, who had been one of Dawson's five-day Ministers in Queensland. Both Hughes and Fisher were five years older than Watson.

These labor members did not differ markedly in their politics from some of the more liberal members of the Protectionist and Free Trade groups. They were not particularly socialist in outlook, and to most of Barton's platform they could quite happily say amen. During the campaign Barton had promised to create a public service and High Court, to extend conciliation and arbitration beyond the limits of any one State in the event of a national industrial crisis, to select a site for the Federal capital as soon as possible, to build a railway to Western Australia, to

---

[4] Two years earlier Dawson had become briefly the first Labor Premier of Queensland, or indeed of anywhere in the world. 'Labor' will be used here to distinguish political 'Labor' from general 'labour', for although the party used the 'our' spelling when it adopted the name 'Australian Labour Party' in 1908, 'Labor' gradually prevailed over 'Labour'.

establish a Federal age pension, to introduce female Federal franchise, and to protect White Australia against the racial and economic threats perceived as being posed by Asian and Pacific Islands labour. No one expected these promises to be fulfilled overnight; indeed it was generally assumed before Federation that the Commonwealth Parliament would proceed at a leisurely pace, meeting less frequently than the State parliaments. Once the Commonwealth Parliament had settled on a uniform tariff, it would soon exhaust its prescribed powers; it would have little to do with other functions, as those belonged to the States, and would therefore have little impact upon most Australian citizens. Even such a centralist as H. B. Higgins expected Parliament to sit for only about two months of the year.

These assumptions were eventually found to be grossly mistaken, and even in its first year of existence the Parliament sat for 191 days. The first session was taken up largely with supply and machinery legislation of the kind necessary to start the Commonwealth moving. Act No. 1 authorized the Treasurer to issue the sum of £16,903 to the Minister of External Affairs, £518 to the Attorney-General, £22,917 to the Minister for Home Affairs, £8496 to himself, £31,523 to the Minister for Trade and Customs, £163,825 to the Minister for Defence, and £237,700 to the Postmaster-General. Act No. 2 was 'An Act for the Interpretation of Acts of Parliament and for Shortening Their Language', and Act No. 5 was 'An Act to Provide for the Recognition Throughout the Commonwealth of the Laws, the Public Acts and Records, and the Judicial Proceedings of the States.' It was not until Acts 16 and 17, assented to in December 1901, that the Parliament came to its first policy legislation: the Pacific Island Labourers Act and the Immigration Restriction Act.

The Barton Government had a clear mandate to bring down this racially discriminatory legislation; indeed it could not have avoided doing so. 'Any Ministry that drops the [White Australia] policy,' said Higgins, 'will be dropped by the country.' The dangers against which the two racial Bills were directed may have been more nightmare than reality, but what political imperative has ever been stronger than nightmare? Reality hardly supported fears that Australia was being infiltrated by an inimical, wage-debasing population of non-whites. The census of 1901 showed that of a total Australian population of 3,788,204, only 29,907 were Chinese. During the previous five years restrictive colonial laws had ensured that the Chinese population (by far the largest Asian group in Australia), increased by only 1307; in New South Wales, Chinese departures had actually exceeded arrivals by 1968. Queensland's sugar planters depended heavily for labour upon Pacific Islanders, generally called Kanakas; yet of the State's 503,266 people in 1901, no more than 9327 were Kanakas. Australians, conscious of themselves as a British enclave dangerously close to unlimited alien millions, were worried not about what *had* happened but about what *might* happen. Although Asians were no present danger, the example of South Africa convinced such men as Deakin and Reid that Australia should at all costs beware of non-white 'uitlanders', particularly Japanese. The Asian was a threat – part real, part bogey – against which Australians flexed their race consciousness, and by so doing asserted their place both in Australia and in the British Empire. Apprehension of the yellow peril was at the root of Australian nationalism, performing much the same function in that context as the threat of foreign conquest had done for European nationalist movements. It also reminded Australians of the Empire to which they belonged. 'Australia and New Zealand are determined to keep their place in the first class,' wrote the Australian Correspondent of the *Morning Post* while he was also Prime Minister of Australia, 'and in order to secure that pride of place agree in putting racial purity before economic gain . . . Those States of the American union which are without a noticeable Negro population are better governed and more efficient members of the Union than those in which there are two separate peoples. The ambition of the Australasian States is to keep within the Empire a place parallel and equal to that of the Mother Country. . .'

The main economic gain which took second place to racial purity was in North Queensland. 'A Kanaka cost $\frac{1}{2}$ crown a day including wages, food, clothing, cost of introduction from the islands and return journey thither,' wrote Lord Hopetoun to Barton from Cairns, where he had sailed for a rest cure in 1901. 'A Jap costs about 3s a day on the same basis. A Chinaman about 4s 4d. An Indian about 5s. [A white Australian labourer's wage was about 7s per day.] While I sympathize with the sentiment of the people which is, rightly I think, in favour of a White Australia, I don't want to see a great industry brought to a standstill and I know your feelings are the same as mine.' But the sugar industry had already become less reliant on Kanakas (between 1885 and 1900, while sugar acreages doubled, the number of Kanakas employed on the canefields fell from 11,745 to 8795), and had been pretty well resigned to the fact that if Queensland joined the Commonwealth the Kanaka trade would come to an end. In any case, protective tariffs and bonuses for 'white' sugar would provide the means and the incentive for conversion to white labour. The end of Kanaka labour was not abrupt, for the Pacific Island Labourers Act provided a winding-down period of five years before deportation would begin. As the *Bulletin* said after the first Commonwealth elections, Barton could write on his fork-handle 'The Kanaka goes as quickly as possible', and on his knife-handle 'The Asiatic goes at once.' The latter inscription was not quite correct, for the Immigration Restriction Act did not affect Asians who were legitimately resident in Australia. It did, however, affect illegal residents and intending immigrants. 'We continue to eject the industrious Jap and the wily Chow,' wrote the permanent head of the Department of External Affairs, Atlee Hunt, to Barton in May 1902. 'The I.R. Act has not yet exhausted its possibilities.'

There were reasons for the racism which existed at all levels of Australian society. Although some of these reasons seem inadequate when considered three-quarters of a century later, it would be rash to conclude from such inadequacies that the legislators of 1901 were over-reacting to what they and their electors perceived as economic, social and eugenic dangers. One can, however, sympathize with the often persecuted Asian inhabitants of Australia. The Japanese and Chinese were industrious, and their living standards were lower than the average Australian's; to that extent they were indeed a potential economic threat. The Chinese smoked opium, and that was offensive to a wholesome, alcohol-drinking society. Sometimes in the polyglot communities of Northern Australia there were outbreaks of inter-racial violence: Japanese against Malays or Manilamen, Kanakas against Indians or Cingalese, White Australians against Chinese. These eruptions may have disturbed the peace, but it was nearly always coloured men who were hurt. Most sizeable towns in Australia had their Chinese market gardeners who performed a useful function quietly and with infinite care. Ah Quey and Ah Duck were two such gardeners in Toowoomba. One afternoon in 1902, for no apparent reason, they were beaten unmercifully with sticks by four drunken young men named William Jones, Thomas Connors, Frank Kimmins and William Parsons. The two Chinese made no attempt to defend themselves, and by the end of the assault they were so badly injured that the police took their dying depositions. They recovered, however, and later gave evidence against their assailants.

Jones had taken off his coat and said to Ah Quey: 'Can you fight?' When Ah Quey replied 'No', Connors said: 'Give it to them; we'll put them out; it's them that's ruining the country.' Connors later said to the police, 'It is not myself I care about, it's my people I am thinking of. If they had been white men we would have treated them like white men; I was not going to let a Chow get the best of me; he hit me and I know I gave the tall Chow a proper one, and I know he went down.' To another witness who met him soon after the assault, Connors boasted, 'We've been having a —— fight with the invaders of our country.' 'Did you get the best of it?' asked the witness. 'We beat them every time, didn't we boys!'

86

Connors and his patriotic companions were tried before a judge and jury. Despite an adverse summing up by the judge, the twelve jurymen of Toowoomba took only 25 minutes to acquit all four of them.

John Chinaman was not always an object of suspicion and persecution. The Sydney tea merchant and tea room proprietor, Quong Tart, was 'as well known as the Governor himself,' according to the *Daily Telegraph*, and 'quite as popular among all classes.' Quong Tart came to Australia at the age of nine, prospered by hard work, embraced the Christian faith, married an English woman and fathered six children, and gained partial admission to Anglo-Saxon society by a combination of good nature and philanthropy. His Elite Hall was a fashionable venue for balls and parties, and he frequently staged free banquets for deserving guests: 250 newsboys, 40 Aborigines, and on other occasions the inmates of the Parramatta and Liverpool asylums. For several years he was official starter for the NSW League of Wheelmen, and wore Highland dress as he flagged the racers on their way. One day in 1902 a man walked into Quong Tart's office, beat him about the head with an iron bar, scooped up £20 from the desk and disappeared. Quong Tart never fully recovered from the attack, and died eleven months later. A 32-year-old engineer named Frederick Duggan was convicted and sentenced to imprisonment for twelve years.

The published evidence at Duggan's trials did not reveal whether the attack was to any extent racially inspired. It is true, nonetheless, that for whatever reason the most distinguished and best assimilated Chinese in Australia met the same fate as many lowlier members of his race.

Respectable and indeed obligatory though racial discrimination may have been in Australia, Parliament still had to dissemble when closing the door on coloured immigrants. During the late 1890s, most of the Australian colonies had passed Bills extending the force of existing Chinese Immigration Acts to all coloured races – even Indians, who were British subjects. On advice from the Secretary of State for the Colonies, however, Royal Assent was withheld on the ground that legislation of this kind would conflict with 'the traditions of the Empire, which makes no distinction in favour of, or against race or colour.' 'To exclude, by reason of their colour, or by reason of their race,' said Chamberlain, 'all Her Majesty's Indian subjects, or even all Asiatics, would be an act so offensive to those peoples that it would be most painful . . . to Her Majesty to have to sanction it.' It was not that Britain disapproved of any people's determination to remain white (the same English statesmen who referred piously to 'the traditions of the Empire' held similar racial views themselves), but rather that the British rulers of India were obliged by the Indian nationalist movement to concern themselves about the treatment of Indian emigrants by the self-governing, which was to say white, members of the Empire. Britain also received strong complaints from Japan about Australian parliaments discussing its citizens as if they were 'on the same level of morality and civilisation as the Chinese and other less advanced populations of Asia.' In fact it had been the sudden need to determine a policy towards Japan which prompted the Australian colonies to extend their racial laws. They had been invited by Britain to adhere to the Anglo-Japanese Treaty of Commerce and Navigation, which offered tariff preferences for Australian primary products on the Japanese market at the probable cost of greater Japanese immigration. Alarmed by Japan's military success against China in 1895, and by the influx of Japanese migrants in Hawaii, all Australian colonies except Queensland rejected the treaty invitation and decided to legislate against coloured immigration. Explaining why Assent had been witheld from the first Bills, Chamberlain urged the Colonial Premiers to adopt an 'education test' like the one used in Natal to bar unwanted immigrants without the appearance of racial discrimination. They did this, and were gratified to find themselves subsequently immune from the kind of diplomatic pressure which Japan exerted upon Queensland, the only colony to have supped with the devil without a long spoon.

The lessons of general restriction by 'education test' were not lost upon Federal Parliament when it came to Bill No. 17. 'Mr Chamberlain long ago laid down the principle that no discriminations could be authorized if they applied by name to particular peoples or complexions,' wrote Alfred Deakin in his *Morning Post* guise. 'It is for this reason that our Immigration Act sanctions in unlimited phrases the exclusion of all comers, although designed and used only to exclude the coloured races . . . In fact and in effect our colourless laws are administered so as to draw a deep colour line of demarcation between Caucasians and all other races. No white men are stopped at our ports for language or any other tests. . . On the other hand all coloured men are stopped unless they come merely as visitors.'

Only two members spoke against the principle of White Australia, and they were Free Traders who believed that Australia should not rock the Imperial boat by giving to Indians and Japanese such offence as might still be taken despite the mollifying effect of an 'education test'. To most members, however, this was a matter in which Australia could legitimately ignore Britain's wishes, for another imperial consideration was involved: Australia's own place in the Empire as an equal (that is, all-white) member with Britain. As Deakin said, the one way in which Australia could most strengthen herself and the Empire was by 'the multiplication of her citizens of British descent.' 'The more Britons, the more British that Empire must become . . .' For once, it seemed, the Young Queen knew better than her Mother.

During the debate the 'education test' was made progressively harder until its real intention became quite obvious. It was to be a dictation test of fifty words in any European language chosen by the examining officer, it would not be applied to 'qualified European immigrants', and the examining officer would select a language with which the unwanted immigrant was unfamiliar. Fearing that such thinly disguised discrimination would offend Japan, whose friendship Britain valued as a counterpoise to Russian influence in the Far East, Lord Hopetoun asked the Colonial Office for instructions. He wrote rather than cabled, however, and by the time the Colonial Office wrote back instructing him to defer Assent until he received further advice, it was too late. The Governor-General had already given Assent on behalf of the King.

Four weeks after the Act became law, a Japanese steamer arrived at Townsville with two intending immigrants on board. They were Pathans from northern India: British subjects who had served in the British Army, and had started their journey in ignorance of the Immigration Restriction Act. The Customs officer at Townsville, finding they did not speak English, gave them an English dictation test. At Brisbane they were again denied landing rights, but made a dash for it down the gangway. Japanese sailors pursued the fugitives, and forced them back on board. One was so distraught that he had to be roped and dragged. When the ship reached Sydney these two British subjects were said by the press to have been sitting despondently on deck watching the crowds on the wharf. Whereever they ultimately found landfall, it was not in Australia.

During 1902, 618 intending immigrants were turned away from Australian ports because they were not sufficiently well educated to write out dictation in an unfamiliar European language. Among them were 459 Chinese, 21 Tonkinese, 6 Egyptians, 3 Kurds, 2 Chileans and one Seychelle Islander. Thirty-three people passed the test, including 8 Japanese, 6 Hindus and 4 Assyrians. It must be assumed that these thirty-three had influential friends in Australia, that they wrote English or some other European language, and that the language chosen for dictation was the language they knew. In 1903, 140 coloured immigrants failed and 13 passed; in 1904, 104 failed and 3 passed; in 1905, 61 failed (including 2 Chaldeans) and none passed; and so it went on year after year, with the standard of English spelling by dark-skinned foreigners remaining predictably low.[5]

[5] And not only dark-skinned ones. In 1913 a Hungarian named Alexander Kellerman, who

Even more important to the Commonwealth than racial legislation was the uniform customs tariff which, under the Constitution, had to be settled by the end of 1902. What good to Federated Australia were restrictive racial laws if the new Government had no adequate and regular income with which to carry out its policies? The Treasurer, Sir George Turner, introduced the Barton Government's tariff proposals as part of his budget in October 1901, but so at odds were the Protectionist and Free Trade factions, each of which found support among Labor members, that the matter had still not been resolved eleven months later. Should moleskins, corduroys and blue frocking carry an import duty of 15 per cent, or less? Should clothes wringers carry 20 per cent, or more? And what about laundry blue, biscuits and toothbrushes? To those who were not particularly interested in such details, or in hearing the traditional Protectionist and Free Trade arguments expounded yet again, the tariff debates were ordeals of paralysing boredom. 'With varying fortune,' wrote Deakin, who had no such interest, 'but with unvarying regularity, a frittering struggle over details and a shameless repetition of stock fiscal arguments has proceeded until to the public the whole debate has become a nightmare – as oppressive, mysterious and unintelligible as the last battle of Arthur in its Tennysonian version.' Bored though he was, Deakin could not ignore the dangerous position of deadlock towards which the tariff debate had drifted late in 1902, for in Barton's absence at the Colonial Conference in London Deakin was Acting Prime Minister.

To Deakin and his fellow Protectionists, the proposed tariff was a very moderate exercise in protection beyond the strict revenue function; but to the Free Traders who controlled the Senate, even a moderate exercise was the thin end of a wedge. Although the Senate had no power to amend taxation Bills, it could, and did, 'request' the House of Representatives to do so. Should the Government modify even further the proposals which it already regarded as moderate, and thereby concede that the Senate could virtually amend money Bills? Or should it stand up for the rights of the Lower House, keep sending the Bills back to the Senate, and run the risk of failing to secure a uniform tariff by the 'end of the year? To Deakin, the first course seemed the lesser of two evils. On 2 September he urged the House of Representatives to receive and consider the Senate's requests, and to refrain for the time being from determining

had been charged with vagrancy in Newcastle, was excluded by dictation test and deported to Hong Kong. In 1914 Ellen Fitzgibbon, a young Irish girl 'of rather attractive appearance', was deported after failing a test in Swedish. The only clue we have to the reason for this churlish reception is that the captain of her ship, as a consequence of something he was told during the voyage to Australia, had caused Miss Fitzgibbon to be examined by a medical officer.

its Constitutional rights *vis-a-vis* the Senate. The Senate was satisfied, and on 16 September 1902 the Customs Tariff Act, with a 38-page schedule of import duties back dated to 8 October 1901, became law. 'The country drew a deep breath of relief,' wrote Deakin in the *Morning Post*, 'simply because, at last, after months of turmoil, a tariff was passed, but the few onlookers who realised all the consequences of failure drew a deeper breath still, and felt a more profound relief as they became assured that the Commonwealth itself was out of the toils at last, and fast escaping beyond the reach of its enemies.'

As the first session of the first Parliament ended in October 1902, Tom Roberts was still only halfway through his Herculean painting of the opening ceremony. On he went, in Melbourne and later in London, pumping more and more heads into that historic moment. In September 1903 he wrote: 'Am still working hard at the "gem" with so accustomed eyes that they leave me in doubts, or with the dread of a sad certainty, when the uninterested many come to see the work of so long a time.' But the end was near, and on 17 November he was able to write to Alfred Deakin, who by that time was Prime Minister, Barton having resigned and taken a seat on the new High Court of Australia. 'At last my task is through,' wrote Roberts, more in exhaustion than triumph. 'Got the "gem" off to Paris for the reproducers yesterday, and I don't know what to say to you for I'm a little tired of thinking of the one thing for so long. . . .'

The big picture had been a commercial venture by the Australian Art Association Pty Ltd, which had commissioned Roberts and persuaded the Federal Government to accept the original painting for presentation to the King – but not before photogravure reproductions had been made for public sale. Artist's proofs went on sale for thirty guineas on parchment and fifteen guineas on Japanese paper, and prints on India paper cost three and a half guineas. The original was presented to King Edward as a memento of his son's role in the opening ceremony, and remained in the Royal collection until Queen Elizabeth made it available on permanent loan to Federal Parliament. Roberts's misgivings about his gem were unfortunately quite justified. Gigantic and lacklustre, the picture hangs now in a cramped corridor of the basement of Parliament House, no more exciting than a tariff debate or the last battle of King Arthur. If the Australian Art Association had only settled for Roberts's first impressionistic sketch, the Commonwealth would have been better served.

5

THE HIGH COURT

WHEN EDMUND BARTON went from the Prime Ministership to the bench of the High Court of Australia, he moved into congenial company. The Chief Justice, Sir Samuel Griffith – vastly learned in the law, and slogging away for years at his spare-time translation of Dante's *Divine Comedy* – was not the warmest of men; but Barton, who was warm, established a good working and personal relationship with the Chief Justice, deferring to him at first, and eventually matching opinions more equally. Griffith did not like being called 'Chief', which he said reminded him of Pharaoh's chief baker, who was hung from a tree; yet he seems to have tolerated letters from Barton beginning, 'My Dear Chief . . .' The third and only other member of the bench when the Court sat for the first time in November 1903 was Barton's friend and former colleague in Parliament, Richard O'Connor. The three of them lunched together every working day until 1906, when they were joined by two other justices: Isaac Isaacs and Henry Bournes Higgins. Abruptly the lunch-time foregathering stopped.

It is not hard to understand why. The five of them knew each other from Parliament, and knew that for all their respective merits they were like oil and water. Not only did the two component groups find it hard to mix socially, but their legal-political attitudes were often at odds. The main source of dissonance was Isaacs, though Barton also had little liking for Higgins. With Isaacs it was not anti-Semitism, though here again Barton did not scruple to call a Jew a jewling. It was a matter of personality and philosophy. Isaacs differed so extremely from the three founding members in personal and judicial style that there was never much chance of harmony.

This did not harm the Court; indeed the conspiring, the backbiting and the dissenting opinions may all be said to have enlivened its proceedings. The High Court's most important function was to interpret the Constitution. Griffith, Barton and O'Connor were all fathers of that document, and their conservative approach to its Federal spirit was not to be wondered at. The Constitution bestowed certain specific or defined powers upon the Commonwealth, leaving the undefined residue to the States. There was still plenty of room for finer definition, of course, and in their early essays at this the first three justices tended to be centrifugal: they preferred not to strengthen the centre if they could help it, but to protect the separate interests of Commonwealth and States. Isaacs and, to a lesser extent, Higgins had also taken part in the framing of the Constitution; but their Federal feeling was not in the least paternal. When it came to the fine-tuning of specific powers, Isaacs and Higgins tended to be centripetal. They were prepared to let power flow to the centre, and never mind the States.

Before the arrival of these centralists the High Court usually found itself in placid, conservative agreement, with Barton and O'Connor tending at first to take their lead from the experienced 56-year-old Chief Justice, who had been Premier of Queensland for seven years and Chief Justice of that Colony for eight. Barton made a slow start, but the combination of health and financial problems which had contributed to his departure from Parliament soon disappeared in his new surroundings, and he began to exert considerable influence on the bench. Whereas counsel in the High Court found Barton and O'Connor the most charming of men, Griffith was coldly courteous. He was 180 centimetres tall, fair-complexioned, with a full beard of fair hair, a big nose and short-sighted eyes. He always wore two pairs of spectacles attached by thin gold chains to the lapel of his coat, and on formal occasions he was always careful to see that his Grand Cross of St Michael and St George appeared at just the right place and angle. His knighthood meant a lot to him. At the age of twenty-one he had recorded in his diary the arms and motto which he wanted to have one day: a shield with wyvern surmounted by a helmet and supported by lions rampant, with the motto *Espérance sans Peur*. And so it came to pass, for Sam Griffith usually got what he wanted.

He was born at Merthyr Tydfil, South Wales, and was brought to Australia at the age of eight. At twenty, after having taken his BA at the University of Sydney, he won a travelling fellowship which enabled him to visit Italy, where he acquired his passion for – or, more correctly, his pedantic devotion to – the works of Dante. In 1903 he published *Draft of a Literal Translation of Dante's Inferno In The Original Metre*, by SWG; in 1908 *The Inferno of Dante Alighieri – Literally Translated into English Verse in the Measure of the Original*, by the Right Honourable Sir Samuel Walker Griffith, GCMG, MA, Chief Justice of the High Court of Australia; and in 1912 *The Divina Commedia of Dante Alighieri – Literally Translated into English Verse in the Hendecasyllabic Measure of the Original Italian*. The final volume, consisting of 525 pages, included the *Purgatorio* and *Paradiso* as well as the *Inferno*. Sir Samuel's preface quoted approvingly a remark by the Bishop of Ripon that 'a translation should present a true photograph of the original', and that was the trouble with Griffith's *Divine Comedy*: it was too literally correct. Each word was a carefully chosen equivalent of the original Italian, but the sum total was both flat and unprofitable. The 1912 publication cost Griffith £126 7s 6d, and his royalties from it were less than £20.

Someone once said that he translated the *Inferno* in Brisbane, the *Purgatorio* in Melbourne and the *Paradiso* in Sydney. This was not beyond possibility, for the Chief Justice enjoyed travelling and made the High Court as mobile as he could, with sittings in Melbourne, Sydney, Brisbane and Hobart. These judicial travels were partly responsible for a remarkable feud between the Commonwealth's fourth Attorney-General, Sir Josiah Symon, and the first three justices of the High Court. The feud – which involved the exchange of more than eighty letters and telegrams over a period of about six months, and what amounted virtually to a strike by the High Court – had none of the verbal extravagance of Symon's correspondence with Charles Kingston in Adelaide; rather it was marked on both sides by suppressed fury and deadly, icy courtesy. Symon was a man who never forgot an injury, and he had been offended by Griffith's criticism of the wording of the Judiciary clauses which were drafted under Symon's chairmanship by the Judiciary Committee at the 1897 Constitutional Convention. Griffith said that their 'catalogue style of drafting' was not 'compatible with the dignity of a great instrument of government.' It also seems probable that Symon regarded himself as having been unfairly passed over for the first bench of the High Court, and perhaps even for the Chief Justiceship. Nor was he without claims, for he was leader of the Bar in South Australia.

The question of the High Court's travelling expenses had already been raised cautiously by the third Attorney-General, H. B. Higgins, in July 1904. The Judiciary Act stated that the principal seat of the High Court should be 'at the seat of Government', and that seat for the time being was Melbourne. For this reason, Higgins felt justified in querying the expenses which had been incurred by the justices and their staffs in sitting at other State capitals as well. In December the Chief Justice wrote to the new Attorney-General, Symon, informing him that he proposed moving his residence from Brisbane to Sydney, and would therefore require about 90 metres of shelving to accommodate his law library in that city by February. Symon's reply on 23 December was nothing less than a declaration of war: 'The travelling expenses of the High Court have attained a magnitude which lately, both inside and outside Parliament, has occa-

The first three justices of the High Court, caricatured by Low: Barton, Griffith (Chief Justice) and O'Connor. In 1906 they were joined by (*below*) Isaacs and Higgins.

sioned remark and evoked sharp criticism – with some of which I confess I sympathize . . . In the meantime perhaps it will be convenient to defer consideration of the request as to shelving.' Symon was on good ground, but he had taken on a tough adversary. Griffith wrote straight back to him saying that the policy of holding sittings of the High Court as a Court of Appeal in all the State capitals had been adopted after full consideration, 'and while it [had] entailed some inconvenience upon the Judges, which they [had] been willing to bear in the interests of Federal unity, it [had] . . . received the approval of public opinion throughout the Commonwealth.' He also appears to have complained to the Prime Minister, George Reid, who would surely, as a 'regular home vegetable', have resented such an intrusion upon his Yuletide leisure. On New Year's Day Reid wrote to Symon: 'I hope there is no truth in a suggestion made to me that you are going to centralize the High Court on Melbourne. The true seat of Government is NSW although Parliament is specially provided for; at least that is my view. But Sydney is the place where the most work is. Don't add to the soreness of NSW and the troubles of,. Yours Sincerely, G. H. Reid.'

Symon replied: 'I am sorry anyone should have been so meddling or ill-natured as, at this restful season, to make you uneasy with apprehensions of "soreness in N.S.W." on my account – Immediately before Xmas I wrote the learned Chief Justice at some length upon various matters to which I invited consideration, chiefly affecting the heavy and as I think unnecessary travelling expenses, and I am certainly surprised to observe how the contents of my letters appear to have reached or filtered to you in concentrated form that I am "going to centralize the High Court in Melbourne".' His answer to Griffith on 13 January made the valid points that policy-making was a matter for the Executive and Parliament, not the High Court; that it was no part of the High Court's duty as the supreme appellate tribunal to concern itself with travelling at great expense 'in the interests of Federal unity'; and finally that any inconvenience to the Justices was irrelevant to the argument.

Griffith in turn was aghast at this Executive intrusion into the Court's exercise of its discretionary powers. 'You will, I am sure, on reflection, be the first to admit,' he wrote to Symon, 'that it is not for the Executive Government to instruct the Judiciary, or to intimate either approval or disapproval of their action . . . With regard to your remark that it is no part of the duty of the High Court to travel from State to State, you cannot fail to notice that the existing Rules of Court, which have the force of law, plainly impose that duty upon the judges.' This was hardly worthy of the Chief Justice; as Symon well knew, the Rules of Court had been framed by the justices themselves, and could just as easily be amended by them. In conclusion, Griffith wrote: 'I think it right to inform you that I shall feel bound to take an early opportunity of offering a public explanation of the absence of my library from Sydney, where it will naturally be expected to be.'

'I note with amazement,' replied Symon, 'the minatory sentence with which you conclude your letter . . . and I regret you should think it wise or worthy of the High Court or of yourself as its President. Happily, it is, I think, without example in British courts for a Judge to reinforce some demand upon the executive which may seem to them unreasonable, by threatening, if refused, to appeal to the public against the economy or decision of the Minister . . .' On 1 March the three justices wrote to the Attorney-General saying they did not think 'that any useful purpose would be served by prolonging a discussion which has assumed, on your part, a tone unusual in official correspondence.' Symon then took direct action. He refused to approve expenses for travel away from Melbourne, and informed Griffith that five telephones in the Court's Sydney premises were four too many; one was enough, and he had ordered the others to be taken out. He also objected to Barton and O'Connor spending £5 and £7 10s respectively on ship fares from Sydney to Hobart when they could have used their free rail passes to Melbourne and taken the Bass Strait steamer from there.

The dispute involved not only the Court's sittings in capital cities other than Melbourne but also the justices' travelling expenses when the Court sat in Melbourne, for all three justices now resided in Sydney. On 29 April Griffith announced from the bench in Sydney that a Melbourne sitting listed for 2 May would be postponed because of continuing uncertainty about the recouping of travel expenses. 'We regret the inconvenience that may be caused to the parties by the postponement of the Court,' he said, 'but we think this a lesser evil than for a judge presiding at the trial of causes to be in a position of a claimant against the Government for his travelling expenses incurred while holding the Court, not knowing whether his claim will be favourably or unfavourably considered, or on what principle his claim, if allowed, will be treated.' This point was neatly emphasized by the fact that in each of the causes postponed in Melbourne the plaintiff was the Commonwealth. On 22 May Griffith sent a telegram to the Prime Minister, who was visiting Moree, asking for assurances on several points including the matter of travelling expenses to Melbourne. Reid replied that the telegram should have been addressed to the Attorney-General, and took exception to the 'peremptory terms in which compliance with your wishes is demanded.' All this was recounted by Sir Samuel Griffith from the bench in Sydney on 23 May, with an implied threat that the Court might also have to postpone hearings listed for Brisbane during the following week. The Government paid an advance to the Court on account of travelling expenses to Brisbane, and the hearings went ahead as planned.

Symon continued to harry the three justices until the Reid-McLean ministry was replaced on 5 July 1905 by the second Deakin ministry, whose Attorney-General was Isaac Isaacs. For reasons which are not hard to divine, Isaacs had the interests of the High Court at heart. Symon may have been right in contending that the Court's travels were against the spirit of the Constitution, but his method of attack led to unnecessary acrimony and probably, by provoking so strong a reaction from the justices, strengthened the Court's position with the new Government, which hastened to settle the matter as quickly as possible. Symon was no longer a factor in the situation, and the justices had made their feelings perfectly clear. Before long, they had everything they wanted, including the Chief Justice's bookshelves. 'On behalf of my learned colleagues and myself,' wrote Griffith to Isaacs on 23 August, 'I have pleasure in saying that we concur in the opinion of the Government that the conclusions set out in your letter constitute a satisfactory, and, as we trust, a permanent solution of the matters in question.'

The solution was permanent, and henceforth the founding justices were able – the Constitution notwithstanding – to hear causes wherever they wished without interference from the Attorney-General's Department. The general tenor of their work during the Court's early years was illustrated by a series of tax cases involving the respective rights of the Commonwealth and the States. The first of these – *D'Emden* v. *Pedder*, April 1904 – was the Court's first major constitutional decision. It dealt with the specific question of whether Commonwealth employees were subject to State stamp duty on receipts for salary paid to them by the Commonwealth paymaster, but it also came to grips with a broader question already debated in Parliament: were the States and the Commonwealth entitled to interfere in each other's activities? The Supreme Court of Tasmania, before which the case began, held that the Tasmanian Government could impose its tax on a Commonwealth officer; in so doing, it rejected a doctrine of 'mutual non-interference' which had been propounded by the United States Supreme Court. When the High Court heard the case on appeal, however, it took the American view and ruled that State tax was not applicable to a Commonwealth activity.

It re-affirmed this doctrine of the 'implied immunity of instrumentalities' in *Deakin* v. *Webb*, a case which reached it in the same year from the Victorian Supreme Court, which had ruled that the State of Victoria could tax Alfred Deakin's salary as a member of the House of Representatives and Minister of State (£1883). The importance of these and subsequent cases of a similar nature was not only that they raised the question of 'the limits *inter se* [between themselves] of the Constitutional powers of the Commonwealth and those of any State', a question upon which the Constitution permitted the High Court to have the last say if it so wished, but that they brought the High Court into conflict with its only rival as a court of appeal: the Judicial Committee of the Privy Council. It will be remembered that at the London conference on the *Constitution Bill* in 1900 the Secretary of State for the Colonies had sought the right of appeal from the High Court to the Judicial Committee of the Privy Council, normally a bench of five appointed by the Lord Chancellor from the Lord Justices of Appeal. The Judicial Committee had been a necessary court of appeal from the Supreme Courts of the various Australian colonies, but in the Federalists' eyes it would no longer be necessary when the High Court came into being. This difference of opinion was apparently resolved by agreement that on *inter se* Constitutional matters only the High Court could issue a certificate permitting appeal from its own decision to the Privy Council, but that the Privy Council could grant special leave to appeal to the Sovereign in Council (which was another way of describing itself) from the High Court in matters other than *inter se*.[1] What had been overlooked, however, was that *inter se* cases might reach the Privy Council directly from a State Supreme court, thus bypassing the High Court. This happened in 1906, when the Victorian Government appealed to the Privy Council against a decision of the Victorian Supreme Court in another *inter se* tax case, *Webb* v. *Outrim*. In this appeal the Privy Council disagreed with the High Court's decision in *Deakin* v. *Webb*, and by inference also with *D'Emden* v. *Pedder*, by ruling that the doctrine of the immunity of instrumentalities did not apply to the Australian Constitution, and that Commonwealth officials were liable to obey the tax

---

[1] The High Court was to issue a certificate for appeal to the Privy Council only once, in *Colonial Sugar Refinery* v. *Attorney General*, 1913. This case, which arose out of a Royal Commission into the sugar industry, concerned the extent of the Commonwealth's power to authorise such inquiries. A High Court bench of four held that the Royal Commissions Act was in general valid, but Griffith and Barton were of opinion that the Commission in question could not lawfully demand information from the Colonial Sugar Refinery concerning matters of internal management. The other two justices (needless to say, Isaacs and Higgins) thought such questions could lawfully be put. The Judiciary Act provided that in such a tied judgment the Chief Justice's opinion should prevail. But because of 'the very great importance' it attached to the case, the Court issued a certificate for the Privy Council. The Judicial Committee upheld the High Court's prevailing decision, but on different grounds.

laws of the State in which they lived. The Privy Council was correct in basing its decision partly on the Australian Constitution's restriction of mutual interference between Commonwealth and State Governments, but, as Professor Geoffrey Sawer has remarked in his *Australian Federal Politics and law*, 'the standard of reasoning throughout the opinion was poor, and provided support for the view of the Australian Founders who had urged that Constitutional questions would be better decided by an Australian tribunal.'

The High Court had to take this Privy Council decision into its reckoning when the question of State taxing rights over Commonwealth officers came before it again in *Baxter* v. *Commissioners of Taxation (NSW)*, 1907. This was an appeal from a decision by a NSW District Court judge in an action by the Commissioners of Taxation to recover State income tax amounting to £23 18s 8d from a Federal Customs officer. Relying on the Privy Council's judgment in *Webb* v. *Outrim*, the District Court judge found for the Commissioners. The High Court, on the other hand, held that since the case involved boundaries of power between the Commonwealth and States, and so could not go on appeal from the High Court to the Privy Council without the High Court's permission, the Court was not bound to follow the Privy Council's decision in *Webb* v. *Outrim*. It reaffirmed (by three to two) the non-interference doctrine of *D'Emden* v. *Pedder*, and refused to grant a certificate of appeal to the Privy Council.

Reading the majority judgment, the Chief Justice re-asserted the High Court's primacy in *inter se* cases. 'For the first time in the history of the British Empire,' he said, 'a Court has been established as to which it has been declared that no appeal shall be permitted from its decisions on certain questions unless the Court itself certifies that the question is one which "ought to be determined" by the Sovereign in Council.' At the High Court's suggestion, the Commonwealth removed the State Governments' grievances about tax immunity by legislation expressly authorizing the States to tax Federal employees, while at the same time protecting the Commonwealth's Constitutional rights. This was a useful excuse for the Privy Council, whose difference of opinion with the High Court had encouraged the NSW Government to petition for special leave to appeal in the Baxter case. In January 1908 the Judicial Committee withdrew from the *inter se* argument by refusing the Commissioners' petition on the rather specious grounds that the amount at stake was inconsiderable and that in any case the controversy had been closed.[2]

[1] Between 1903 and 1919, the Judicial Committee granted leave to appeal from the High Court in non-*inter se* cases on seventeen occasions. In nine of these cases it affirmed the

The doctrine of implied immunity worked both ways, and although the tax cases had dealt only with State interference in Commonwealth activities, the first three justices were equally concerned about Commonwealth encroachment on the States. In 1906, for example, they held back the operation of federal industrial awards on State railways. In *Peterswald* v. *Bartley*, 1904, they established a wider but analogous doctrine, the doctrine of implied prohibitions, by holding that the Commonwealth could not use its specific power over excise duties to collect brewers' licence fees, even though some State Acts referred to these as duties of excise. Griffith, Barton and O'Connor subscribed to the proposition that the Commonwealth should not use its specific powers to encroach upon areas which the Constitution had by implication reserved to the States; Isaacs and Higgins, who joined them in 1906, thought otherwise. In almost every respect the two newcomers differed from their learned colleagues. Who could have differed more bizarrely from them than Isaac Issacs, the brilliant and beloved first child of Jewish parents, Alfred, a tailor born in Russian Poland, and Rebecca, a strange mixture of intellect and sentiment who was born in England? Isaac was born in Melbourne and reared in the Yackandandah-Beechworth district of Victoria. He had a highly retentive memory, and it was said that at his Bar examination he cited so many cases with such accurate volume and page references that his examiners asked the supervisor whether he could have had access to notes. He spoke Russian, French and Italian at the family table, could converse with Italian and Greek shopkeepers, and correspond in Russian, German and French. Although not practising the Jewish religion, he was widely read in both the Old and New Testaments, in religion generally, and in science. He corresponded regularly on these subjects with his mother, even after his marriage and elevation to the High Court.

Hardly a day went by without an exchange of letters, telegrams or telephone calls between Isaac and Rebecca. The letters showed not only that Isaac was a Jewish mother's boy but that Rebecca was the intellectual equal of her son.

'My sweet darling blessed Mammie,' he wrote in 1909, at the age of fifty-four. 'It seems an awful long time since I saw your darling face and yet it is only a few minutes since I heard your dear voice saying "Spiffin" and all sorts of nice things to your big baby boy. I was a bit surprised this afternoon when I phoned, and Bella told me you were out for a drive. Of

High Court's judgment, and in eight it overruled the High Court. Avoidance of the High Court in *inter se* cases by proceeding direct to the Privy Council from a supreme court was stopped by an amendment to the Judiciary Act in 1907.

course there was a lovely change in the weather, and as the Schnorrer says in our friend Zangwill's book "If you don't do it then when you can . . ." You recollect the salmon story don't you?' Another letter the following day ended with: 'Now there's the gong sounding for Breakfast, and you know how I have to take every moment to gormandise and so I shall just say Ta Ta Chummie Girl. God bless and keep you darling, and with kisses and hugs and love galore I am yours ever – Isaac.' Rebecca's letters to Isaac invariably opened with a blend of prayer and baby talk, but thereafter consisted of astute comment on the legal profession, politics and Biblical exegesis. '. . . I am very glad Isaac pet that you like the Trowsers daddy thought they would be your style,' she wrote to him when he was twenty-nine. 'In regard to the Amalgamation of the [legal] profession I remember the late Mr Ramsey fighting against it some years since I know Gaunson and McKeen were very much in favour of it and I know that Quick and Wrixon spoke on the subject but whether they spoke in favour of or against the bill I don't know. My opinion is that Kerford is vexed that he has not been patronised and thinks the lawyers have been neglecting him and out of jealousy he is trying to reduce both branches and Dr Hearn is helping him. Pray God keep Kerford from being a judge.' And pray God make Isaac one!

To those who did not suspect the 'spiffin', 'gormandising' side of Isaacs's nature, he was an intellectual lone wolf, ferociously learned, and never hesitating to set his own opinion at the throat of a majority judgment. He singled out the Chief Justice – seeming to compete with him whenever possible, and sometimes brushing fiercely with him in Court – and it was said by Counsel that if he and Griffith ever agreed on a judgment there was no point in going to the Privy Council. He was a spare, dark-skinned man with protruding lips, incandescent eyes and a high, receding forehead; his hands, like those of Billy Hughes in Parliament, were so knotted and knuckled as to be almost deformed. During the early years of the High Court, the justices used to read their judgments from the bench. Barton was often content to concur in a majority judgment, but Isaacs, even when he was in agreement, insisted upon saying so at great length and with a wealth of rhetorical emphasis. And with Isaacs, agreement was not always what it seemed to be. In 1913 Barton, who was Acting Chief Justice, reported as follows to Griffith in London: 'Isaacs used his opinion which ostensibly agrees with mine to put his own interpretations on questions so as to give some answer, and just the answer Higgins wants: but in the second of the two cases he has been unable to escape a refusal to answer two of Higgins's questions – out of five. The whole affair is just a piece of manipulation however – I don't think there is the least bit of sincerity in the jewling's attitude.' In other letters to Griffith that year, the year in which the number of justices was increased to seven, Barton wrote: 'It is plain to me, and I think to others, that Isaacs is building his hopes on your remaining in England and is trying to make such a big splash that he will make himself manifest as the right C.J. . . . His judgments are swelling to bigger proportions than ever – in fact they are very weighty – in respect of paper; and he has assumed an oracular air in Court that is quite laughable. . . Isaacs of course has his jaws slavering for the devouring of some decision of yours. . . Isaacs seems to be always trying to collogue with our colleagues apart from me. . .'

Much of the colloguing took place with Higgins, his ally against established Constitutional doctrine. Both men were nationalists, and Isaacs was a confirmed imperialist as well. When Beatrice and Sidney Webb dined with him in 1898, he treated them to 'a rhapsody over the Empire.' 'He is the only man we have met in the colonies,' wrote the condescending Mrs Webb, 'who has an international mind determined to make use of international experience.' The Irish-born Higgins could hardly have been called an imperialist, for his sustained opposition to the Boer War had cost him his seat in the Victorian Legislative Assembly. Although never a member of the Labor Party, he had served as Attorney-General in the Labor ministry which briefly succeeded that of Deakin in 1904. He was a radical who did not shirk unpopular causes (he was one of the few to protest against the expulsion of a Labor member, Edward Findley, from the Victorian Assembly in 1901 for publishing a libel on the British Royal Family), and was firmly committed to the extension of Commonwealth power, particularly in the field of industrial arbitration. Although a firm supporter of Federation, Higgins had opposed the Commonwealth Bill in 1900 because in his view it did not provide the Federal Government with sufficient power. He was well placed to try to remedy this in the High Court, for in 1906 he succeeded Mr Justice O'Connor as the High Court judge presiding over the Commonwealth Court of Conciliation and Arbitration.

The best opportunity to extend the central power was provided by the second Deakin Government's policy of New Protection, a policy of using Federal tariffs to protect employees as well as their employers. The 'old' protection of manufacturers against overseas competition would be made conditional upon their charging a reasonable price for their products and providing 'fair and reasonable' wages and working condition for their employees. Despite its lack of specific Constitutional power to interfere with the internal industrial affairs of the States, Federal Parliament passed several Acts which attempted to apply the principle of New Protection on a national scale. In this connection the Commonwealth Court of Conciliation and Arbitration was asked to declare what ought to be 'fair and reasonable' wages for various industries. The most significant of these cases, heard by Mr Justice Higgins in 1907, was *Ex parte H. V. McKay* – an application by Hugh Victor McKay, manufacturer of agricultural machinery at Sunshine, Victoria, for a declaration by the president of the Arbitration Court that conditions of remuneration in his factory were fair and reasonable, thus entitling him to exemption from excise duties of £6 on stripper harvesters, £3 on strippers and 12½ per cent on stump jump ploughs, disc cultivators and winnowers. Higgins chose to hear McKay's application out of many similar ones because the Sunshine Harvester Works was the Commonwealth's largest industrial plant, employing 500 men in a wide range of trades.

Hugh McKay had started in business by building his first successful stripper harvester at the age of nineteen. It combined the stripper and winnower, and gave the wheat farmer his grain free of chaff and bagged, all in the one operation. The stripper harvester was quick as well. In the Wimmera district of Victoria it was not uncommon for one of them, hauled by three horses, to harvest six hectares of wheat in a day. By 1907 McKay had produced 19,670 'Sunshine' harvesters and had sold them not only throughout Australia but in Argentina, Canada and Siberia. His plant at Sunshine was just far enough out of Melbourne, so he thought until New Protection came along, to be outside the ambit of the city's wages board. He was not a bad employer by the standards of his day, but neither was he more generous than the skinflint norm. 'In fixing the wages,' said his brother George, who looked after personnel, 'I have endeavoured to get labour at the cheapest price that I honestly could.' The company helped its employees to build homes on parcels of land around the plant, and discouraged trade-unionism as much as it could.

Self-made man though he was, and resenting interference when it did not suit him, Hugh McKay was only too glad to accept the protection of a Federal £12 import duty on overseas harvesters. But were his wages fair and reasonable enough to fend off the excise duty of £6 which would otherwise halve his protection by import duty? As Mr Justice Higgins pointed out in his judgment, the legislature had been extremely vague about the phrase 'fair and reasonable'. 'It would be almost as reasonable,' he said, 'to tell a Court to do what is "right" with regard to real estate, and yet lay down no laws or principles for its guidance. I cannot think of any other standard appropriate than the normal needs of the average employee, regarded as a human being living in a civilised community.' The dominant factor in this determination, he decided, was the cost of living as a civilised being; wages should be sufficient to buy food, clothing and 'a condition of frugal comfort estimated by current human standard.'

Having thus set his own terms of reference, Higgins proceeded to take evidence on the condition of the average working man in a supposedly civilised community. A blacksmith named William Keating, with a wife and five children, told the Arbitration Court that he earned nine shillings a day, or 54s for a six-day week. The family's weekly housekeeping expenses were as follows: Rent for a four-roomed house without bath (the laundry tub served for ablutions), 7s; groceries, 13s; meat, 8s; milk, 3s; bread, 3s; vegetables, 2s 6d; fruit, 1s; sewing machine hire, 2s 6d; tobacco, 1s 5d; boots, 3s; clothes, 4s; medicines, 1s; insurance against accident, 5d; trade union membership, 6d; clothing club, 1s; firewood, 3s; total, £2 12s 10d. The clothing club had been formed by thirty employees at Keating's blacksmith shop, each of whom contributed one shilling a week. 'Every fortnight we have a draw,' he explained. 'The one whose name comes out first has the right to go to the Union Tailoring Company and get a £3 suit of clothes. He continues paying until he has put in 60s.' Keating had previously belonged to a medical benefit society too, but he had dropped out because he could not keep the payments going, and was now unable to save the 10s entrance fee.

The medical vulnerability of the working man was described in another context by the poet Shaw Neilson, who worked during this period at various low-paying rural occupations in Victoria. People like the Neilsons were victims of their poverty and the quality of medical advice available to them; sickness came, and people died, and often they did not even know what the trouble was. Two of Shaw Neilson's sisters died of tuberculosis, and a niece and a nephew died of meningitis. A doctor had been treating one of the Neilson girls for sores on her neck, but did not at first tell the family how dangerous her condition really was. 'We did not attach much import to these [sores],' wrote Neilson, 'as we all seemed frighteningly ignorant of the different ailments that attack humanity.' Owbridge's Lung Tonic, Vitadatio, and Hudson's eumenthol jujubes were all advertised in the press as being 'good for consumption', but they were of no avail to Maggie Neilson. She ended her days in a little hut outside the family home, ringing a hand bell whenever she needed help. Shaw himself had bad eyesight, and at the age of 38 he went into Bendigo to buy some reading glasses from an optician. 'He told me to wear them all the time,' he wrote, 'and that I would soon get used to them. He made a pretence of testing my eyes and he said that these glasses would do both for distance and reading. I went back and attempted to wear those glasses all the time. I wore them for a fortnight. If I had kept them on any longer I would probably have gone blind.' Eventually he found an oculist in Melbourne who prescribed glasses which slightly improved his reading vision.

If Neilson had been a family man instead of a bachelor, he might well have been unable to spare the price of reading glasses. As was amply demonstrated by evidence in the Harvester case, the margin between weekly income and essential expenditure was fearfully narrow. A Port Melbourne couple supported six children on £2 15s per week. Their weekly expenses were: rent, 12s 6d; lodge, 1s 3d; firewood, 3s 6d; milk, 2s; meat, 5s; groceries, 12s 6d; newspapers, 6d; vegetables, 2s; bread, 5s; boots, 2s; clothes, 2s; school requisites, 6d; total, £2 9s 9d. They had not been able to buy any furniture since they were married.

The wage for an unskilled labourer at the Sunshine factory was 6s per eight-hour day, or 36s per six-day week. On the basis of evidence put before him, Mr Justice Higgins estimated that the weekly expenditure necessary for a labourer's home of about five persons left only a few shillings out of that sum. 'I have confined the figures to rent, groceries, bread, meat, milk, fuel, vegetables and fruit,' he said in his judgment, 'and the average of the list of nine housekeeping women is £1 12s 5d. This expenditure does not cover light, clothes, boots, furniture, utensils (being casual, not weekly expenditure), rates, life insurance, savings, accident or benefit societies, loss of employment, union pay, books and newspapers, tram and train fares, sewing machine, mangle, school requisites, amusements and holidays, intoxicating liquors, tobacco, sickness and death, domestic help, or any expenditure for unusual contingencies, religion or charity. If the wages are 36s per week, the amount left to pay for all those things is only 3s 7d, and the area is rather large for 3s 7d to cover – even in the case of total abstainers and non-smokers – the case of most of the men in question.' After declaring that the Sunshine remuneration was not fair and reasonable, Mr Justice Higgins went on to fix rates of pay which in his opinion would meet that imprecise description over a wide range of employment. The excise tariff standard, as it became known, ranged from 7s per day for unskilled labourers to 8s for ironbenders, 9s for furnacemen and sheet ironworkers, and 10s for fitters and turners, blacksmiths and carpenters. In the case of an unskilled labourer supporting a wife and three children, this rate meant a theoretical increase from 3s 7d to 9s 7d in the weekly residue after essential expenditure. That was little enough to cover the range of expenses listed in the Harvester judgment, but it was a distinct advance nonetheless. Although New Protection was found to be unconstitutional by the High Court, Mr Justice Higgins's needs-based minimal wage was to remain an article of industrial faith for the next sixty years.

Hugh McKay, happy though he was to continue sheltering behind the tariff, stood upon his rights as a sturdy individualist and refused to pay the excise duties to which the Harvester judgment had rendered him liable. The Federal Government took him to the High Court, but the Court ruled three to two in McKay's favour on grounds that the Excise Tariff Act was not a taxing Act because it assumed to regulate conditions of employment at large, and was therefore beyond the Federal Parliament's competence. The McKay case was heard together with *The King* v. *Barger*, in which the Federal Government sought to recover excise from another 'unfair and unreasonable' manufacturer of agricultural machinery, William Barger. Isaacs's dissenting opinion was almost twice as long as the majority judgment, and in the long run it would be seen to have been the more significant. Many of his observations in *The King* v. *Barger*, 1908, foreshadowed a basic change of direction which the High Court was to make twelve years later. He began his opinion with a quotation from the United States Supreme Court: 'The power to tax is the one great power upon which the whole national fabric is based. It is as necessary to the existence and prosperity of a nation as is the air he breathes to the natural man. It is not only the power to destroy, but it is also the power to keep alive.' That power had been granted to Federal Parliament, said Isaacs, and it could be used as Parliament thought fit. 'A Federal power may be exerted to the full,' he wrote, 'for it is either paramount or exclusive, and the grant of the power is incompatible with a restraining or controlling power.'

These words would not have been out of place in the majority judgment which Isaacs wrote and delivered in the climactic Engineers' case of 1920. Griffith, Barton and O'Connor had all gone from the bench by that time, and in *Amalgamated Society of Engineers* v. *Adelaide Steamship Co. Ltd* Mr Justice Isaacs – with appropriate rhetorical emphasis – virtually threw after them the doctrines of implied immunity of instrumentalities and implied prohibitions. The basic question before the High Court was whether a dispute between a trade union and a State-owned sawmilling enterprise in Western Australia came within the ambit of the Federal arbitration power. The Court could have held that because sawmilling was a trading function it did not enjoy the protection against Commonwealth interference which had been established in *D'Emden* v. *Pedder* and other cases. Instead, a majority of four (the new Chief Justice, Sir Adrian Knox, and Justices Isaacs, Rich and Starke) reassessed the doctrines of implied immunity and implied prohibitions and found them both wanting.

Not only was the rule in *D'Emden* v. *Pedder* found to be without constitutional justification, but the decisions in that case, in *Deakin* v. *Webb* and in *Baxter* v. *Commissioners of Taxation* were all formally overruled to the extent that they depended upon the doctrine of implied immunity of instrumentalities. The thrust of the *Engineers* majority judgment went further. Its language was sweeping enough to condemn also the more general doctrine of implied prohibitions.

This was a milestone comparable in some ways to the tariff Bill with which the Commonwealth had avoided economic crisis in the Parliament of 1902. Now the Commonwealth was out of the toils constitutionally, and fast escaping beyond the reach of its legal enemies. It is not hard to imagine the triumph felt by Isaacs as he overturned the orthodoxy from which he had been dissenting for so many years; henceforth Federal powers would be given the fullest amplitude of meaning before anyone considered what powers were left to the States. This time Isaacs's oracular tone was not ludicrous. 'It is apparent,' he said, 'that if, as we have stated, the true basis of *D'Emden* v. *Pedder* is the supremacy of Commonwealth law over State law where they meet on any field, there can be no possible reciprocity. Mutual supremacy is a contradiction of terms. . . We have anxiously endeavoured to remove the inconsistencies fast accumulating and obscuring the comparatively clear terms of the national compact of the Australian people; we have striven to fulfil the duty the Constitution places upon this Court by loyally permitting that great instrument of government to speak with its own voice, clear of any qualifications which the people of the Commonwealth or, at their request, the Imperial Parliament have not thought fit to express. . .' He could also have added that he, Isaac Isaacs, had at last devoured Griffith.

6

THE EMPIRE

Vampire Day

ON 24 MAY 1905, which was the closest approximation Australia had yet found to a national day, the Prime Minister delivered a panegyric upon the British Empire. There was nothing paradoxical about this, for nationalism and imperialism beat side by side in many Australian hearts, and that went for George Reid's fat, indolent heart as well. In any case, this was the first Empire Day. It was the biggest day of its kind since 1 January 1901, with rites of passage performed all over the continent, and such was the duality of Australian self-perception that the nation did not seem to be diminished by this celebration of Empire. On the contrary, it was enhanced: as far as most Australians were concerned, to praise the whole was automatically to praise the part.

And what a whole it was! George Reid, touring New South Wales on an Anti-Socialist campaign which he mistakenly believed would win the next election for him, delivered his Empire Day address in Peel Street (named after a British Prime Minister), Tamworth (named after that Prime Minister's electorate in Staffordshire), a thriving pastoral centre at the foot of the Moonbi Range in northern New South Wales. The venue was as good as any, for Tamworth was an imperial-minded community. Its principal hotels were the Imperial, Royal, Caledonian and Norfolk; and three years earlier its citizens had anticipated Empire Day with a 'loyal demonstration' which, according to the *Sydney Mail*, was 'worthy of any city of the world.' The demonstration consisted mainly of horse-drawn tableaux entitled 'God Save The King', 'Britannia's Sons', 'The Empire On Which The Sun Never Sets', 'Britannia's New Daughters' and 'Britain's Bulwarks.'

The Empire upon which Mr Reid discoursed in Peel Street had sown the world with Tamworths and other communities modelled in varying degrees of verisimilitude upon ancestral originals: there was another Tamworth in Canada; there were five Londons in North America and one on Christmas Island in the Indian Ocean; fourteen Newcastles in North America, two in the West Indies and one each in South Africa and New South Wales; six Sheffields in North America, one in New Zealand and one in Tasmania. When the chief founder of Empire Day – the president of the British Empire League, the Earl of Meath – spoke in London on 24 May, he was able to read aloud a sheaf of cablegrams from Ottawa, Sydney, Natal, Mauritius, Sierra Leone, Jamaica, Capetown and Gibraltar: a representative roll-call from the extraordinary claim which Britain had staked out with flagpoles across the surface of the earth.

'Just let us think of the little spot of earth in the North Sea,' said George Reid in Tamworth, 'from which this enormous power radiates – 120,000 square miles of land in England, Scotland and Ireland. It is only one-eightieth of the size of the Empire which it rules. The British people own or protect half of Africa and one-fifth of the whole globe. If you take the enormous mass of humanity that people the earth, one-fifth of that total – about four hundred millions of human beings – live under the British flag. Only 60 millions of that number are white, and 340 millions are coloured. Now is it not a marvellous thing when you think of that handful of people having not only the power to extend their sway over 340 millions of coloured races but, grander than all, that they have such a genius for governing and administration upon humane lines that all that mass of humanity has practically the same peaceful possession of the rights of property which the people in the streets of London have today.' The speech would hardly have stood up to close analysis, but it is doubtful whether many of George Reid's listeners were that way inclined: Empire Day was an occasion for anthems and collective self-esteem, not objective criticism. 'I am grateful for the marvellous change that has come over us,' said Reid, 'that we are not what we were sixty or eighty years ago, when there could not even be a small appointment made without an emissary from Downing Street sent to direct us on the spot. In those days the Australian people were loyal, but were full of discontent. The tie between Great Britain and Australia was more one of strength of dependence then than of loyalty and affection; but we got the grant of independence, and instead of Australia proving ungrateful and wishing to cast off the tie which unites her to the motherland, there never was a time when Australia clung to her with a feeling of warmer and closer loyalty and affection.'

Before moving on to the 'Anti-Sosh' part of his speech, Reid castigated a recent statement by the Labor member of the NSW Legislative Assembly, Arthur Griffith, to the effect that Labor hoped Australia would eventually cut the painter with Great Britain. 'What marvellous depths of meanness this sentiment represents!' said the Prime Minister. 'He is that sort of Australian – I don't believe he is an Australian – who depicts Australia while she is at her mother's knee clinging for protection against danger, as harbouring in her secret soul a longing for the time when she can tear away from her parent and cease to stand by her side.'

Loud cheers in Peel Street, and indeed in almost every city and town of Australia. Despite his glib assumptions about the Empire's coloured subjects and the realities of Australian independence, Reid was right about the loyalty and affection of most Australians. These feelings were sometimes curbed, of course, by considerations of business. In 1904 the Governor-General, Lord Northcote, wrote to the British Prime Minister, A. J. Balfour: 'The most that can be said of Australian sentiment is that they would rather sell to the Mother Country than to a Foreign, if this can get as much for their article. Sentiment will come in again, if we were landed in another war; but not in matters of business. Of course if we are prepared to give Australia a pull over foreign countries in matters commercial they will respond, and, if we give them a shilling, they will, or may, give us ten pence.' Against this sort of canniness – which surely existed as much in Tamworth, Staffordshire, as in Tamworth, New South Wales – there were factors more conducive to imperial loyalty. Lord Northcote remarked upon 'a strong feeling of devotion to the Throne, rather than to Great Britain, which is odd, since the King is personally unknown.' Within a few months of Edward VII's accession to the throne in 1901, the Victorian Legislative Assembly demonstrated its loyalty by expelling the Labor member for East Melbourne, Edward Findley, for reproducing in his newspaper, *Tocsin*, an article which had recently caused the *Irish People* in Dublin to be suppressed for libelling His Majesty. The vote for expulsion was 64 to 17, and Findley was soundly defeated at the by-election for his seat.

The main thrust of the *Irish People*'s article was against some English Catholics, headed by Cardinal Vaughan and the Duke of Norfolk, who had presented a loyal address to the King despite certain anti-Catholic remarks which His Majesty had made recently. The paper then went on to libel the King with considerable verve: 'Down upon his knees before the old and bald-headed roué – the "lover" of every woman of fair features who has appeared in English "Society" for forty years, including titled dames and (as yet) untitled actresses – the "English gentleman" – perjurer of a historic divorce case – the polluted "hero" of one of the most malodorous scenes in Zola's rotten novel "Nana" – the centre of a score of disgraceful scandals of the most contemptible type – down in front of this English KING, whose latest public performance was to stigmatize on his solemn "oath" the whole Catholic world as "superstitious idolators" – knelt an English-born Cardinal – a Prince of the Church – with a document that might have been presented to a Legree in a Southern "Plantation" fifty years ago.' It was strong stuff: no stronger then could be supported by fact and gossip, but stronger than most of His Majesty's Australian subjects wished to hear.[1]

Even stronger than loyalty to the Throne was their loyalty to the Empire, for this in part meant loyalty to themselves. The Empire was a protective shield and a context within which the new Commonwealth could assert itself on more equal terms than in the larger world. Within the Empire it could aspire to be an equal partner with Great Britain, and in some respects the independent Australian Briton might even be able to teach his northern archetype a thing or two. One of the Australian Britons' most admiring chroniclers was Charles Edwin Woodrow Bean, a young journalist who had been born of English parents at Bathurst, taken to England at the age of ten, and educated at Clifton College and Oxford. In his last year at Clifton, one of Bean's predecessors there, Henry Newbolt, published *Vitaï Lampada*: 'Play up! Play up! and play the game!' Clifton was that kind of school, and Bean that kind of young man. He returned to Australia at the age of twenty-five, in 1904; worked on the land; and then, in 1908, joined the editorial staff of *The Sydney Morning Herald*.

Before joining the *Herald* he had contributed to its pages a series of articles about Australia under the pseudonym of 'C.W.'. The most illuminating of these presented a rather Newbolt-like version of his fellow countrymen. 'At home,' he wrote, meaning England, 'we liked to consider [the Australian] an Englishman, and it cuts against the grain when he draws a distinction. But the truth is that he is only an Englishman in the same way as Englishmen are Angles... The Australian is a tall, spare man, clean and wiry rather than muscular; in face, not your well-filled-out American, full-lipped and round-chinned, but of a certain refined ascetic strength. You would expect him tanned, but he is often fair. In the bush he is generally bearded, though the younger men shave clean. His

[1] Alfred Deakin's private opinion of the King, written while that personage was still the Prince of Wales, was only a little less opprobrious than the *Irish People's*. 'Always in bad company,' he wrote, 'and not too proud to borrow from the shadiest nouveaux riches, he was yet surrounded in England with an atmosphere of reverent admiration almost amounting to worship by a society in which he was *distinctly below the average in morals and ability*; and absolutely deified by many of the middle class who were unaware of and the masses who ignored his protracted devotion to the idlest and most unintellectual pleasures.' The Duke of York was 'a still more commonplace edition of his father', and his wife 'reported to be but little more individual than that palest of pale personalities, the altogether artificial modiste the Princess of Wales.'

character is the simplest imaginable. The key to it is just this – that he takes everything on its merits, and nothing on authority. The Australian from the country is, I suppose, the only Briton outside of Canada who possesses the vigour and the verve which are the hallmarks of a young civilisation; he is the Briton reborn, as it were – a Briton with the stamina and freshness of the 16th century living amongst the material advantages of the 20th century.'

The Briton reborn! Was it any wonder that Australians had welcomed the advent of Empire Day? A day of celebration throughout the Empire was first proposed in 1902 by the Earl of Meath, who had earlier founded such institutions as the Fresh Air League, the Lads' Drill Association, and the Duty and Discipline Movement, and was the author of a five-volume work entitled *Our Empire: Past and Present*. The founding president of the British Empire League in Australia – Canon F. B. Boyce of St Paul's Church of England, Redfern – supported the Earl's proposal in a letter to the *Herald*, and also wrote to the London *Times* suggesting as an appropriate date 24 May, the birthday of the late but not forgotten Queen Victoria. Largely as a result of Canon Boyce's campaigning, but also in the knowledge that other parts of the Empire were moving in the same direction, a conference of State Premiers early in 1905 endorsed 24 May as Empire Day – not a public holiday, but a day on which patriotic functions would be held, small Union Jacks worn in coat lapels, patriotic advertisements placed in the newspapers ('Empire Cocoa, like the Empire itself, lives up to its reputation'), and, above all, appropriate instruction given in the nation's schools. Imperial indoctrination of school children received strong emphasis in Britain as well as Australia, and in this undertaking both countries were inspired partly by the example of Britain's new ally, Japan. In his Empire Day address the Earl of Meath disclaimed all sympathy with 'jingoism or State aggrandisement', and then proceeded to contradict himself. 'The best step towards the world's peace,' he said, 'is to consolidate the Empire so that no power will dare to attack it. The promoters of Empire Day hope to breathe into the souls of Britons a spirit of patriotism more powerful for noble deeds than even the spirit of Bushido for Japan.'

This theme was repeated by the Prince of Wales, who said at an Empire Day service in St Paul's Cathedral that imperial instruction in the schools was 'merely following the example of the practical Japanese who based their successes on the battlefield on lessons of patriotism and devotion inculcated in the schools.' In New South Wales the *Sydney Mail* observed that as the State had long since taken 'one step which the Japanese have found of inestimable value as a basis of their national defence, the training of school children in cadet corps', the addition of direct lessons in patriotism was 'but another step already anticipated by Britain's progressive Eastern ally.' The cadet system was well established in Australian schools, juvenile marksmen competed each year with rifle teams from other parts of the Empire for the Meath Trophy, and from 1904 onwards the estate of the late Empire builder, Cecil Rhodes, enabled one Rhodes Scholar to be sent to Oxford every year from each Australian State. Rhodes had hoped that this ambitious Anglo-Saxon program, drawing its candidates from the United States and Germany as well as from the British colonies, would find 'the best men for the world's fight', and perhaps even 'another Cecil Rhodes'. There was not another Rhodes among them, as it turned out; and just as well too. By that time, the scope for Rhodesian achievement had all but disappeared.

The sort of instruction to be given at public schools on Empire Day was defined by the New South Wales Director of Education, Peter Board, in 1908. 'The history of the British race in many lands furnishes ample material for the instruction required,' he said in a departmental circular, 'in the lives of men and women whose heroism or self-sacrifice, or enterprise or scientific skill, or literary power has helped to build the Empire. While pride in the achievement of the race may thus be stimulated, it is not desirable that it should be stimulated by any disparagement of other countries. The practical outcome of the lessons of the day should be the deepening of a patriotic regard on the part of the pupils for the portion of the Empire that lies nearest to them and of a sense of their duty to their own Australian land . . .' The dualism of Board's approach was endorsed by the architect of the NSW Catholic school system, Cardinal Moran, who at this time was under pressure to comment upon certain statements reported to have been made by Cardinal Logue, the Cardinal Primate of All Ireland, predicting the dissolution of the British Empire and rebellion in Australia. In making an affirmation of Catholic loyalty, Cardinal Moran used the opportunity provided by Mr Board's circular to direct that loyalty as much towards Australia as towards the Empire. 'In [his circular] Mr Board told the teachers that in their patriotism they were to remember that they were Australians,' he said, 'and that the true interests of the Empire lay in developing Australian resources and promoting Australian interests. I endorse that to the fullest extent. Mr Board also said, "Unfurl the banner on the 24th", and I quite agree that every banner should be unfurled on that day. But let it be the Australian banner.'

The growing emphasis on patriotism at Australian schools after 1905 was a change in degree rather than direction. For many years history and geography texts, story books and school magazines had been encouraging loyalty to the Empire and pride in the British race; now the message became more strident, particularly in school magazines.[2] The *Commonwealth School Paper* published by the NSW Department of Public Instruction inundated its young readers with stories and verse about the Victoria Cross, the white man's burden, Queen Elizabeth and Queen Victoria, Shakespeare and Dr Livingstone, Admiral Nelson and General Gordon. 'Gordon may die,' it said, 'other Gordons may die in the future, but the same clean-limbed brood will grow up and avenge them.' For Empire Day the magazine blossomed into colour with vivid images of dual patriotism: Union Jack and Southern Cross, rose and wattle, lion and kangaroo. The 1905 Empire Day issue contained a fable in which the Lion went to visit his cousin the Kangaroo. The Bear, Eagle and Dragon, noticing the Lion's absence from his island, assumed that he was dead. Acting on this assumption, the Dragon took a boat with a yellow sail to Australia with the intention of killing the young and presumably now friendless Kangaroo; but the Lion, with help from the Kangaroo, sent the Dragon packing. 'I think you have learned a lesson, friend Dragon,' said the Lion. 'In future you will know better than to come to my kinsman's country.'

'I didn't know *you* were here,' gasped the Dragon.

'No, I know you didn't. And you thought that because the Kangaroo was young you could easily steal his land. But understand this: while there is a breath of life in me, the animal that attempts to fight the Kangaroo will have to fight me also. He is my nearest and dearest kinsman, and as long as we both live we will fight together against the world. And you may tell that to the Bear and the Eagle and the other animals too. Now go!'

Imperial fervour bore some relationship to social-economic position; it existed to some extent at all levels, but was stronger at the top of society and weaker at the bottom. The fervour of the middle class was well documented, and although the working class left less trace of its attitude towards Empire Day a healthy cynicism could sometimes be discerned. At a 1908 meeting of Braybrook Council, whose area included the Sunshine Harvester Works on the edge of Melbourne, Councillor Hopkins said: 'Empire Day is only for kids.' He moved that the Council's contribution to the celebration be reduced from £10 to £5, and the motion was carried. In the working-class Melbourne municipality of Richmond,

---

[2] The Rev. W. H. Fitchett, president of the Methodist Ladies' College in Melbourne, had achieved such a wide following with his *Deeds That Won The Empire* and *Fights For The Flag* that in 1901 Lord Northcliffe paid him 300 guineas and full travelling expenses between Melbourne and London to write one newspaper article about the Coronation of Edward VII.

Councillor Heagney opposed a motion that the Council should stage an Empire Day celebration. Imperialism was only another name for jingoism, he said. Councillor Heagney deprecated the practice of teaching the young about England's wars and bloodshed, and said that it was wrong to present England as a better state than, say, Germany or France. He favoured a celebration on 26 January, the anniversary of the first British settlement at Sydney Cove, so that Australian and cosmopolitan sentiments might be created. The Empire Day motion was passed, with Councillor Heagney and one other alderman dissenting.

Almost alone among the Australian press, the *Bulletin* criticized Empire Day – or 'Vampire Day', as it sometimes called it – on the ground that glorification of the blood-sucking 'British Vampire' was un-Australian. 'Identify patriotism with "the Empire" in the mind of the Australian child – the Empire of JINGO ideals – and patriotism is at once dissociated from a love for Australia,' said the *Bulletin* in 1905. 'For there is nothing more certain than that the British Imperialism of today – the Imperialism of the Boer War, of the Chinese slave-trade, and of the Japanese Alliance – is utterly antagonistic to White Australian ideals. The fact does not lack recognition from Australian Imperialists. It is, indeed, often the sole reason why they are Imperialists. Australian nationalism stands for democratic equality; for the fostering of home industries; for such extension of State Socialism as will give to the people control of great national services and monopolies; for making the hire worthy of the labourer; for white-race purity. Therefore there are ranged against Australian nationalism all the weak-minded snobs who can see no other hope of standing out a little from the ruck than by securing an Imperial bauble; all the Free Trade importers to whom an Australian industry represents an injury, and who look upon this country as a satrapy of London, to be exploited for the extension of its markets; all the foes to liberal industrial legislation who see in "the Empire" the best hope of the sweater; all the cheap labour advocates, who hope to see this country given over to the coolies and their slave drivers. From these, the Tories, the snobs and the sweaters, are the ranks of the Jingo-Imperialists recruited.'

This was the *Bulletin*'s first and last Vampire Day attack on imperialism. During each of the next few years it remained editorially mute while the Empire had its day, and by the time it weighed national and imperial interests again in 1914 the *Bulletin*'s attitude had changed completely. Empire Day managed to combine national and imperial pride, for, as we have seen, the one fed upon the other. In 1908 the British Empire League of Australia asked the Minister for Defence to direct that the Union Jack should take precedence over the Australian flag at Empire Day celebrations. The Minister replied that the Union Jack might be flown in addition to, though not in place of, the Australian flag; but for many and perhaps even most Australians the question of flag priorities was summed up in 1913 by a *Daily Telegraph* cartoon of a Catholic prelate, waving an Australian flag in each hand, and a sailor-suited boy holding a Union Jack and wearing a hat marked 'Australia'. *His Eminence*: 'Come with me, and you may wave this flag.' *Young Australia*: Why don't you come with me? You must be lonely. You've got a good flag, but this is my flag's day.'

Vampire Day was really not such a bad name for the day of the Union Jack. Australia's nationalism drew strength from the imperial connection, and Australian Britons also liked to think that in return their own youthful blood nourished and revitalised the old Mother Country. An allusion to this circulation of blood was made by Alfred Deakin while he was attending the 1907 Imperial Conference as Prime Minister of Australia. 'We propose a closer partnership,' he told his audience in London, 'not the dissolution of the partnership that we now enjoy. That, thank heaven, we mean to maintain. Today, even with our existing means, the blood which goes from the heart here in the United Kingdom to the furthest extremities of Empire and returns again does so, not debilitated, but invigorated by hope and faith in our national stock and national life. We believe in you, even if you should doubt your own destiny.'

Going Home

If for no other reason, the voyage from Sydney to Southampton was always a voyage home because the ship was either British, French or German; there was an outward voyage and a homeward voyage, and this, for ship and passengers alike, was the homeward one. It was homeward in another sense as well, because even Australian-born passengers making the month-long voyage for the first time were almost certain to have had British parents or grandparents; they were corpuscles travelling from an extremity of Empire to the heart, and the fact that they had never been there before scarcely diminished their sense of homecoming. 'London!' wrote Louise Mack, a young Tasmanian-born journalist who went to England for the first time in 1901. 'I see it every night. I have been there hundreds of times already. I see a great impossible mass, and grey smoke, smoke, smoke. What I see is so large that it would probably cover all England.'

Another journalist, John Adey, who went to Fleet Street from Western Australia, expressed this sense of *déjà vu* in his response to the statue of Boadicea near Westminster Bridge, and its inscription from William Cowper: *Regions Caesar never knew,/Thy posterity shall sway.* 'The loneliness has vanished now,' wrote Adey in 1913. ' " Regions Caesar never knew". Ay, from one of those regions [the visitor] has come; he is one of the great posterity of Boadicea that has Imperial sway beyond the seas. He is not an Englishman perhaps; but he is something greater – he is an Empire man, one of the children of silence and slow time, returned in the eternal cycle to worship at this shrine. It is his.'

His for the price of a ticket to Southampton – £75 first class, or £42 second class, including table wine; and anything from £19 to £25 steerage, without table wine. 'Heavens! The sort of people that travel,' wrote Miss Mack in her memoir *An Australian Girl in London*. 'What a disillusionment! They who travel from Australia are the money-makers, the business people – butchers and bakers and ironmongers. . . The First Class, which always represents Fashion, gives a Ball, and doesn't invite the Second Class. The Second Class, which invariably represents Intellect, gives a Party, and hangs up the notice of it in *Greek*. The First Class doesn't know Greek. It comes, and looks at the notice, and goes away baffled.' There were cricket matches and bottle-driving tournaments on deck, card games in the saloon, an orchestra playing *The Blue Danube* in the breathless furnace of an Indian Ocean night, and one afternoon, with the ship suddenly quiet, a burial at sea. Louise Mack's first impressions of London were not of smoke but green leaves, clean streets, the absence of awnings, and the glory of the Turners at the National Gallery. 'Turner ought to have been born an Australian,' she wrote. 'In his pictures I see his craving for great distances. And there he would have satisfied himself. Turner in the Blue Mountains looking away up the Kanimbla Valley one winter sunset!'

Another visitor at this time was Nathan Spielvogel, a schoolteacher from Dimboola in Victoria, who wrote a series of letters from England and Europe to the *Dimboola Herald* and later published them as a book called *A Gumsucker On Tramp*. His strongest first impressions were of London's chimney pots, the tallness of the policemen, and the English reversal of Test cricket loyalty. 'Who won?' he asked a newsboy at Southampton. 'We won the h'ashes, Guv'ner,' replied the lad, though of course Australia had lost. Another newsvendor, when asked by Mr Spielvogel if he had any Australian newspapers, produced the *New York Herald* and insisted against all argument that it was Australian. 'My poor bleeding country!' wrote the tourist from Dimboola. Louise Mack was equally nettled by England's lack of knowledge about the distant continent which she carried around in her mind. 'Why should it ruffle me, this ignorance about us, eating our hearts out to come to her, calling her always "Home"? What does it matter? How could it well be otherwise? We are so far away. We have no way of attracting her attention over all those seas and oceans. Why should we want it? That is what puzzles us all when we are *here*.'

Nathan Spielvogel went happily back to Dimboola. 'I mounted my bike this morning and rode off,' he wrote after his first day back at school, 'up the old red winding road, through the long avenue of perfumed wattles, now all tenderly bending over under their burden of blossom, past the strip of nodding mallee bushes. The air was fresh and mellow. The sky was serenely blue. An old Jack sat on a dead limb and laughed merrily. Around the bend and past the little bridge, and there was the school on the hill, set in its little bower of gum trees. Ah! This is better than the Tower of London, Unter den Linden and the Vatican... London has its abbeys and museums; but it has its awful grinding misery. Berlin its palaces and galleries; but it has its militarism. Italy has its historic past; but also its filth and beggars. But here, the blue sky above, the spreading gums around, the innocence and the simple faith of my [pupils] – all these have no "but".' For thousands of Australian Britons, return to Victoria, Tasmania or Western Australia was not so simple. If they had come with any determination to try themselves against London, they were often detained there by either success or failure: the successful did not wish to leave, and the unsuccessful did not wish to arrive back in Australia as failures. In the foreword to her *Australians Who Count In London*, Mrs Leonard W. Matters said that Anglo-Australians took pride in following Henry Lawson's advice to his countrymen:

> Hold up your heads in London,
> Tread firm in London streets!

'And why?' asked Mrs Matters. 'Because they have the consciousness that they are accomplishing what they left their native country to do in London. And when one realises that in every section of society, art or industry, Australasians are taking the lead, this assurance will be understood.' Certainly there was no shortage of Australians who had entered the lists at the heart of the Empire and emerged victorious. The Australians who counted for most in London during the first decade of the century were the tempestuous Helen Porter Mitchell, better known as Madame Melba, idol of operatic audiences for the last twenty years; and Victor

Trumper, the young Apollo of Test cricket who had once scored 104 at Old Trafford before lunch, and during the summer of 1902 had scored 2500 runs against some of the finest bowlers England had ever produced.[3] Other Australians of renown in England were Annette Kellerman, 'the champion lady swimmer of the world'; the artists John Longstaff and Arthur Streeton, the sculptor Bertram Mackennal, and the composer Percy Grainger; the actor Oscar Asche and the singer Peter Dawson; the Regius Professor of Greek at Oxford, Gilbert Murray, and the anatomist and Egyptologist, Professor Grafton Elliot Smith; and the journalists Martin Donohoe, Chief Foreign Correspondent of the *Daily Chronicle*, A. G. Hales, foreign correspondent for the *Daily News*, and Dr G. E. Morrison, special correspondent of the *Times* in China.

But not all those who made the attempt managed to tread firm in London streets. In Louise Mack's novel there was a failed singer named Emmie – partly modelled on Amy Castles, the 'little Bendigonian songstress' who failed in her first attempt at Covent Garden. Melba did nothing to help the little Bendigonian – rather the contrary, in fact – but on subsequent visits Miss Castles did make her own mark in London. 'Why do we come here?' asked the fictional Emmie in a voice stifled with emotion. 'They don't want *us*. If we can push our way into a little slit they allow us to stay there perhaps, but not because they *want* us, only because we pushed. I'm sick of pushing. I'm sick of trying. I'm sick of agents. I think the musical profession is the most contemptible in the whole world. I'll be the bitter example. I'll go home and say, "I failed. Couldn't get on. Nobody wanted me. It wasn't the climate in my case. It was pure failure".'

'Em!'

'I'll be the first, the very first to fail. Everyone else who came back without a career was driven away by the climate.'

One of the most impressive failures, whose steadfast refusal to be daunted by sustained indifference amounted almost to a triumph in itself, was Reginald Carrington, a gawky young proof-reader's assistant on the Melbourne *Argus* who set out for London late in 1906, travelling steerage in the White Star steamer *Runic* via the Cape for £19. Soon after his arrival he managed to publish a *New Year's Greeting From Australia* in the weekly expatriate newspaper, *British Australasian*. It was a fair sample of Carrington's poetry, and a warning, though he failed to recognise it as such, of the insurmountable difficulties which lay between him and the

---

[3] During this period Australia's cricketers had a slight edge over England's. Of thirty-eight Tests played between 1900 and 1912, Australia won fifteen, England won fourteen, and nine were drawn.

literary career for which he yearned in London:

> In the distant sunny South,
> The Sun-God opens his mouth,
> Blowing a sweet perfume
> Over the wattle bloom,
> Over the gum-clad plain,
> Over the fleece and grain.

Many years later Reginald Carrington wrote *A True Story Of An Australian Journalist's Five Years' Search For Fame In Fleet Street*. The manuscript was never published, but he deposited it in Sydney's Mitchell Library, where it may be read today as a monument to Australian British tenacity. The book is written in the third person, but internal evidence leaves no doubt 'the poet' referred to throughout was Carrington himself. Occasionally the author seems to mock the poet, but the mockery is always gentle, and for the most part the tone of the book is a combination of sympathy and respectful wonder that anyone could persist against such overwhelming odds. We are told that the poet, who had grey-blue eyes and fair hair, had been dux of his class at the age of thirteen, but did no good thereafter when promoted to a higher class. On the voyage to London he shared his cabin for a while after Capetown with a reporter from the *Johannesburg Star* who slept on a scarlet pillow and put his false teeth in a glass of water under his bunk, and with nine rowdy miners who played cards and drank most of the time. One night the miners found themselves short of a glass, and spying one under the reporter's bunk threw his teeth away and used that. The poet moved to a vacant two-berth cabin and began writing a long poem called *The Quest*. As the *Runic* steamed north into tropical latitudes the sunsets became almost too beautiful for the poet to describe. The setting sun was a golden disc as big as a cartwheel, and it sank rapidly, sizzling the ocean all around. One evening, as he watched it sizzle, a butterfly appeared out of nowhere and settled on his coat.

In London, he found lodgings at Maida Vale with several other young Australians: Walter Kirby, Harold Cohen and a Miss Mueller, all of whom were singers; Thorold Waters, a journalist; and George Boyle, a composer. The winter was extremely cold. The snow outside reminded the poet of whipped white of egg, and his hair oil froze in its bottle. His funds amounted to only £12, so he needed a job. His board cost him 13s 6d a week; ale was a penny a glass, and whisky threepence a nip. 'This interminable city is the world's Mecca,' he wrote. 'Here all talent comes in its early years. Here is all poverty and all riches, all aristocracy, art, fashion and commerce. It is the centre of history and has been for a thousand years, and every street turning in its 120 square miles is noted for something or other or somebody or other from Boadicea to King Edward VII.' When down to his last eight shillings he secured, thanks to a reference from Alfred Deakin, a job addressing envelopes in the advertising department of the Orient Royal Mail Line for 30s per week. That night he closed his diary with the words 'Advance Australia.'

He kept a scrupulous account of his financial incomings and outgoings, and at the end of his five years in England he would be able to state that he had earned a total of £246 16s 6d, and spent £380 13s 6d. He had received a few small windfalls from Australia, and owed the sum of £96 17s to various creditors. When the envelope job at the Orient Line petered out, as most of the poet's jobs did fairly quickly, he moved to new lodgings for only 7s per week. His fare to the city was 2d, and lunch 7d. Dinner cost him only 4d: fish 2d, cocoa ½d, bread ½d, butter ½d, and a tip to the waitress ½d. In search of another job he called on Sir Gilbert Parker, a former associate editor of *The Sydney Morning Herald*, author of some twenty novels, and now MP for Gravesend in the House of Commons. When the poet told him how precarious his financial position had become, Sir Gilbert replied: 'A good deal often comes from humble beginnings.' He gave him a card to the Tariff Reform League, where he saw someone else who in turn passed him on to an oil magnate and former MP, Sir Harry Samuel. Next morning the poet called at the oil magnate's residence in Park Lane only to find that he was about to leave for the country. The magnate sent the poet to the National Union, where a Mr Goulding advised him that there was nothing offering at the moment. Next day the poet wrote forty applications for work, but nothing came of them either.

Desperate though his situation was becoming, the poet attended a lecture on Western Australia at the Royal Colonial Institute. Annoyed to hear the speaker advising those present against investment in Australia, he interjected to the effect that there were plenty of assets in Australia, and was gratified when subsequent speakers supported his remark and enlarged upon it. He also went to the Colonial Office during the 1907 Imperial Conference, and in one of the lobbies he shook hands with Alfred Deakin, who does not appear to have remembered him. At that time, he had enough money left to carry on for two more weeks. 'A peculiar feature of the attack of the poet on the battlements of London was that he invariably in making his calls for work chose the heads of the firms,' wrote Carrington in his thinly disguised journal. 'When he sent in a note to Mr Moberly Bell, manager of *The Times*, that gentleman granted him an interview, but when he learned all he wanted was some work he told him he would not have seen him had he known that. The poet however was not overawed. He left his testimonial and a cutting of a leader he wrote in Australia for a small paper. Bell later tore this up and when the poet asked for it back again the same day he could not give it. However he had a search made for the pieces, had them all carefully glued together, and sent it to him at his lodgings.'

The poet later attacked Printing House Square from another quarter, calling on the chief proprietor of *The Times*, Arthur Walter. Mr Walter very courteously took a lead pencil note of all that the poet said, but made no offer of employment. The search for work took him back to the Colonial Office, where he was interviewed without result by Winston Churchill's secretary, and to the Lagos Company, where he was offered a job at £190 a year on the Gold Coast. It was just as well he declined that offer, for a few days later he was taken on as a casual reporter by the *Daily Mail*. 'In this capacity,' wrote Carrington, 'he attended a lecture by Sir James Crichton Browne, a prize distribution by Princess Christian to long-service servant girls, a riot of hooligans at Shoreditch, and motor bus fatalities at Charing Cross. Next night he crashed. He was asked to cover a murder at Hoxton. Owing to lack of knowledge of bus routes, he took too long to get back with his story. This disclosed his lack of local knowledge and the news editor asked him to come back in two years.'

He wrote to the secretary of the Rhodes Scholarship Trust, Dr George Parkin, who replied that London was a great place for chances if one knew how to seize them. Unfortunately, however, Dr Parkin could not help the poet in any way. 'It seemed strange,' wrote Carrington, 'that here was a youth with all the Rhodes qualities – and yet he could not get the scholarship Rhodes offered. He had the daring, the spirit of adventure, the grit, the brains though undeveloped – but it was not to be.' Down to thirty shillings, the poet moved to even cheaper lodgings at Shepherd's Bush, which he shared with a Cuban, two Japanese, a Swede and an English commercial traveller. Sometimes he played chess with the Swede. He called at the War Office to inquire about obtaining a commission, only to be told he was too old, and in any case too short of funds. The uniform alone would have cost £80. He wrote to his father in Melbourne saying that he had superhuman difficulties to overcome without friends, experience or money. 'When a man takes on London single-handed,' he wrote, 'he fights a battle so tremendous that it is beyond the telling.'

In the nick of time he obtained a job with the *Tribune* initiating ideas for special pages to attract advertising and then preparing the pages for publication. His remuneration was £2 per week plus five per cent of all advertising revenue, and in a largely fruitless search for advertisers he visited Clacton, Great Yarmouth and Blackpool. The papers at this time were full of the plight of Sir Harry Maclean, Colonel of the Sultan of Morocco's bodyguard, who had been captured and held prisoner by brigands. The poet wrote to the managing editor of the *Tribune* suggesting that he be allowed to go to Morocco, get up an expedition and free Sir Harry; but the idea was not acted upon. He then asked for an increase of 30s per week, and when this was not forthcoming he resigned.

In 1908 the poet volunteered his services as Conservative parliamentary candidate for Peckham, but was not called for an interview. At about this time, however, he did earn £4 10s as a literary judge helping to select the best limerick from 40,000 entries in a newspaper competition. With part of this fee, he bought a box of chocolates for a barmaid named Tilly whose acquaintance he was then cultivating. He was also much impressed by the beauty of an actress named Kitty Montrose whom he met one evening while dining in Soho, but never saw again.

When the King and Crown Prince of Portugal were murdered, the poet offered to cover the story for the *Standard*, but it had already made other arrangements. He wrote to the Prime Minister, Arthur Balfour, suggesting that a new party might be formed from the Labor element in the tariff reform movement. Mr Balfour, who was a Conservative, replied that while he appreciated the suggestion he thought too many branches or sections of one party might be a source of weakness rather than strength. The poet also called on the editor of the *Spectator*, John St Loe Strachey, offering some of his verses. Mr Strachey told him that the verses, although not acceptable, showed promise. He asked the poet not to be discouraged. That was easier said than done. 'His dominating idea seems to have been "If I can last long enough I will get through",' wrote Carrington. 'It was a mistake. He never had the elementary knowledge of the business of journalism to live by it in London. It was only the poet's iron will which enabled him to hang on year after year.'

During one week in 1908 he was interviewed by sixty-four executives, without a single offer of employment. He was offered a job, on commission only, as canvasser for the Australian Mutual Provident Society, which sold life insurance in London; but he had to decline because he could not afford the fares. He wrote to Joseph Chamberlain suggesting the formation of an Imperial League (it is not clear from Carrington's manuscript how this would have differed from the British Empire League, which existed already, or the Imperial Federation League, which had gone into dissolution fifteen years before); he suggested to the Chancellor of the Exchequer, Lloyd George, that the British Government should assist the Australian State Governments to subsidise emigration; and he sent the *Daily Mail* some suggestions for increasing its circulation. He was writing a novel at the rate of 800 words a day, and his rent was now eleven weeks behind. He read Gray's *Elegy* in the original graveyard at Stoke Poges, and wrote an article about the experience for a journal called *TP*. The editor thanked him, but was unable to accept the article. In one week alone the poet left ten articles with ten different newspapers, all without result. His funds were down to 16s, but he managed to borrow £5 from an old friend of his father, a Mr Topham, who was thought to be a millionaire.

In June 1909 the *Evening News* took him on as assistant to its literary editor at £3 per week. This was the apogee of the poet's career in London. He reviewed some books, wrote a series of articles on London's hidden museums, and went down to interview villagers at Haslemere about their recollections of the late Poet Laureate, Alfred Lord Tennyson, the centenary of whose birth was imminent. The present Lord Tennyson, returned some five years from the Governor-Generalship of Australia, was absent from the family home, but a butler brought the poet a whisky and soda. His article was published, but it satisfied neither the poet nor his editor. 'The editor was not impressed with the article,' wrote Carrington, 'and rightly so, for it showed great lack of imagination and detail, and shortly afterwards the poet got his walking ticket, accompanied with a bonus of £5.' In keeping with his policy of going to the top, he applied for a job to George Cadbury the Chocolate King. Although nothing came of this, Mr Cadbury wrote back: 'I admire your pluck and energy.' The poet suggested to the Board of Trade that British manufactures should be exhibited abroad in a floating showroom, but the Board declined to discuss the matter with him. Other suggestions which he tried to promote with similar lack of success were a World Peace Club, an Anglo-German naval tour of the world, a Home Industries League and, for obvious reasons, a Colonial Labour Exchange. He faced the winter of 1909–10 with only £4 in hand. Mr Topham was away in Madeira.

In January 1910, while visiting the Albert Museum, the poet chanced to see a woman of unusual beauty. 'He thought this was a repetition of Dante and Beatrice among the iron turnings from Vienna, the old knives and forks and Japanese armoury,' wrote Carrington. 'It is a grand thing to have felt the same emotion as Dante must have experienced. He called several times afterwards at the Museum to see if he could see his dark beauty again, but it was not to be.' Next month, for the first time since his arrival in London three years before, he cabled to his father asking for a loan. He used a single code word, as arranged with his father before leaving Melbourne, which meant 'send money', but apparently his father had lost the code list, for there was no reply. Failure confronted him at every turn. Even Halley's Comet eluded him. He searched the skies each evening, but could not find it. In May 1910, after having applied unsuccessfully for 210 positions during the previous five months, he became a sub-editor at the Australian Press Association, cabling news to the Australian press from Fleet Street's morning newspapers. By that time he owed £106, including £30 to his landlady, which he now began to repay.

In 1911 the poet applied for and obtained a position with Centrale Press in Berlin, where he had to take down telephone messages from Paris, which were later translated into German and sent to newspapers throughout Germany. The only trouble was that his shorthand was considerably less than adequate. During his two months in Berlin he covered a boxing match between two American Negroes, and wrote a story for the Hearst newspapers about a Great Dane which purportedly could talk. The dog, which was being exhibited in music halls, was said to be able to enunciate *torten* (cakes) and several other words. The poet went to one of its performances and pronounced it genuine. One day, while strolling with his malacca cane in the Tiergarten, he saw Kaiser Wilhelm riding past with a suite of six generals. 'The Emperor saluted the poet as he raised his straw hat to him,' recorded Carrington. 'The poet afterwards said the Kaiser was so close to him that his horse's breath blew in his face.'

This German interlude came to an end when the poet was replaced by someone with better shorthand. Back in London he resumed his old regimen of job-hunting and suggestion-making, but by this time the continued rebuffs were more than even his iron will could endure. 'The poet had begun another novel,' wrote Carrington, 'but was generally meeting with keen setbacks from all London executives. His heart was still in Australia.' And so, after five years of unavailing struggle, he booked a passage to Melbourne on SS *Geelong*, gave away his malacca cane, paid the last debt to his landlady, and wrote a poem entitled *To England*:

> I gave her of my best
> And all that she gave me
> Was her Memory
> So let me once more give
> Who gave his best. May be
> What happened was the best
> For her and me.

'Surely under the circumstances some of the noblest lines in the language,' commented Carrington. 'The poet seems to have been popular on board the *Geelong*. He took a special delight in the children and presided at all their concerts and sport meetings. He also acted as treasurer for the ship's sporting committee. In his valedictory address to the passengers the Captain commended the efficient balance sheet the poet produced, and according to the poet's diary he hinted that a treasurer of such thoroughness might easily become treasurer in a larger sphere. It was a compliment the poet much appreciated. Before the *Geelong* reached Melbourne, the poet delivered a 50-minute address on Australia to some 200 steerage passengers. He answered questions, and received a hearty vote of thanks and three ringing cheers. This was the first time, so he wrote in his diary, that he had ever been cheered for anything.

Colonial Office

The British Empire used to be ruled, as one colonial politician of the 1860s put it, by a person named Rogers. In 1907 – when the Prime Minister of Australia, Alfred Deakin, joined the Prime Ministers of Canada, Newfoundland, New Zealand, Cape Colony, Natal and Transvaal at the Colonial Conference in London – the person in charge was named Hopwood. Like the remote but omnipotent Sir Frederic Rogers, Sir Francis Hopwood was Permanent Under-Secretary of State at the Colonial Office, an arm of the British Government which, together with the India Office, oversaw every corner of the Empire, from Mandalay to Melbourne. Federation had made surprisingly little difference to the Colonial Office's surveillance of Australian affairs. The Commonwealth was a self-governing colony, and the proper channel for any communication which it might wish to have with the British Government, or with any foreign government for that matter, was through the Governor-General and the Colonial Office. The bound volumes of Governors-General's despatches from the early years of Federation are plentifully sprinkled with initialled minutes, sometimes sarcastic but nearly always lucid and pertinent, by such persons as Hopwood and the Assistant Under-Secretaries, C. P. Lucas, H. B. Cox, R. L. Antrobus and H. W. Just.

Each of the four Assistant Under-Secretaries looked after his own share of the Empire. In 1907, Cox handled all business connected with North America and Australasia, Fiji and the Western Pacific, Mauritius, the Seychelles, Gibraltar, Malta and the Falkland Islands. The Colonial Office was heavy with talent but remarkably light in numbers. Its total establishment at Whitehall in 1907, from the Permanent Under-Secretary down through the Assistant Under-Secretaries and first class clerks to the third class messengers, amounted to only 120 people. Its budget for the year was a mere £54,050.

The urbane and scholarly men of the Colonial Office brought the air of an Oxford college or London club to their mahogany and leather-furnished offices at Whitehall. They were certainly impressive at close quarters, but at long distance they could often be infuriating. Deakin spoke of 'these charming men and their present inefficiency.' His principal grudge against the Colonial Office at that time was its deliberate and repeated failure to consult the Commonwealth about the future of the New Hebrides – a small enough matter for Britain, but one that had become almost an obsession with Australia. In its earliest months of existence, as we have already seen, the Commonwealth had tried un-successfully, for reasons of defence, to interest Britain in annexing the French island of Kerguelen. Its concern about the New Hebrides was deeper than that, though hardly more rational. The New Hebrides, a group of islands between Fiji and New Caledonia, was one of the few areas of land in the Pacific still unclaimed by a colonial power. Britain and France had jointly warned off other powers in 1888, but although they both exercised loose jurisdiction over their own nationals in the New Hebrides neither of them had made formal claim to the group. The only real interest in annexation – and that meant annexation by Britain – came from the Commonwealth of Australia. 'Australia is a country of vast distances,' wrote Edmund Barton in 1901, 'and in the eyes of Australians the [New Hebrides are] as near to them as the Channel Islands are to the inhabitants of Great Britain.' Even allowing for hyperbole, it was hard for anyone but an Australian to see how France's indeterminate part-interest in an archipelago about 2000 kilometres northeast of Brisbane could pose any greater threat to Australian security than her complete sovereignty over New Caledonia, less than 1400 kilometres from the Australian coast.

There was more to this affair than defence, though what more there was did little to strengthen Australia's case for British annexation. The Commonwealth wanted the status of the New Hebrides regularised so that British missionaries and planters could be adequately protected against native depredation, settlers could obtain proper title to their land, and Australia could benefit from the commercial opportunities which Burns Philp and Company seemed to discern there. National pride entered into it as well. Here was a project on which the Commonwealth could bring to bear its new external affairs power. The annexing would have to be done by Britain, of course, but in every other respect the New

Hebrides would be Australia's own contribution to the Empire. In August 1901 the Federal Cabinet authorised a French-speaking agent – a spy, in effect – to travel through the New Hebrides and report to the Prime Minister on conditions there. This agent, Nilson Le Couteur, reported that there were 146 British subjects in the New Hebrides: 77 missionaries and their families, and 69 planters and traders and their families. The New Hebrides question calling for most urgent action, he said, was not so much annexation as providing British settlers with the same recruiting and trading facilities as enjoyed by French settlers.

Australia nevertheless persisted in its futile advocacy of British annexation, arguing against the alternatives of Anglo-French partition and a joint protectorate. Britain, mainly through apprehension of growing German power, was then in the process of settling its differences with France. The Anglo-French Convention of 1904 left the New Hebrides question unresolved. Deakin brought the matter up again with the Colonial Office in 1906, unaware of how close it had moved by that time towards the *fait accompli* of a joint protectorate. 'The Australians who have never had to face any diplomatic difficulty seem to think we can treat France as if she were a Tonga or a Samoa,' wrote H. B. Cox at the Colonial Office. 'When the Premiers come over this subject is sure to crop up and a little plain speaking will do no harm.' As the person named Cox had foreseen, there was nothing Australia could do except complain about how the fact had been accomplished.

The meeting of colonial Prime Ministers at Whitehall in April and May 1907 was the fourth of its kind since 1887. Deakin, who as a young man had represented Victoria at the first Colonial Conference, made light of the institution twenty years later. 'If the British Constitution be undefinable,' he told a London audience in 1907, 'if it contain anomalies, what shall be said of our indefinable and anomalous Conference: a body called together from the ends of the earth consisting of Counsellors of the King, who may not tender His Majesty, directly or indirectly, any counsel; every member of it selected because he belongs to an executive, in order to constitute an assembly which has no executive power whatever – each of them qualified because he is a legislator, and all of them without a vestige of any power of legislation? As a result of these contradictions, what do we obtain? A parliamentary cabinet without revenue, without status, without equality of any kind, or any definite relation to our existing political organisations. . . That, surely, gives us an anomaly, even for the British Constitution, which can claim a high place among its many anomalies.' At most the Colonial Conference was a forum for the sorting out of Imperial detail, the recital of complaints and, more importantly, the discussion of ideas about the slowly changing organization of Empire.

In 1907 Deakin complained ineffectually about the 'casual and secret fashion' in which the Colonial Office had handled the New Hebrides matter; but he had considerably more than this to say in general about the Colonial Office's dealings with the self-governing colonies. What he took to London was nothing less than a plan to reform the Colonial Office along lines which would bring about closer imperial union. Deakin was an advocate of 'New Imperialism', the concept of giving wider power to self-governing colonies (which, of course, excluded India and the non-white Crown colonies) and putting them on a more even footing with Britain. He had been in touch with the Pollock Committee, and it was under the influence of this 'New Imperial' ginger group, chaired by Sir Frederick Pollock, Professor of Jurisprudence at Corpus Christi College, Oxford, that he had prepared a three-point proposal for the 1907 Conference: firstly, that an independent and permanent secretariat should be established to prepare agenda for Colonial Conferences; secondly, that the self-governing colonies should no longer communicate with the British Government through the Colonial Office, but with the British Prime Minister through the new permanent secretariat; and thirdly, that all business relating to the self-governing colonies should be separated from Crown colony business.

This was not the best of times to be proposing such a radical change, or to be arguing for imperial tariff preference, as Australia also intended doing. Sir Henry Campbell-Bannerman, whose Liberal Party had won a resounding victory over Balfour's Conservatives early in 1906, denied that his Ministry was 'a pack of Little Englanders . . . permeated by narrow, if not absolutely hostile views to the colonies'; yet the Liberals were obviously not as interested in imperial union as their predecessors had been (not that the Conservatives' interest had been much more than lukewarm), and where the Conservatives had been prepared to discuss imperial preference, the Liberals were firmly opposed to such a policy and the rise in British food prices which it would entail. The new Secretary of State for the Colonies was a former Viceroy of India, the somewhat vacillating Earl of Elgin and Kincardine. There was nothing dithery, however, about his young Parliamentary Under-Secretary, Winston Churchill, or about the newly promoted Permanent Under-Secretary of State, Sir Francis Hopwood. They would be more than a match for Deakin.

How modest the Prime Minister's entourage seems today! Deakin was accompanied to England by his wife, and joined there by the permanent head of his department, Atlee Hunt, and the Minister for Trade and Customs, Sir William Lyne. These three men were the entire Australian delegation. During the voyage to Naples, from where the Deakins completed their journey by train, the Prime Minister occupied himself by skipping and by reading the records of previous Colonial Conferences, a book by the orientalist Lafcadio Hearn, and Arthur Waite's *Studies In Mysticism*. The voyage was restful, but there was to be little rest for Deakin after he reached London. 'Woke up at Hotel Cecil,' he jotted in his diary on 9 April. 'Early – heavy post – The avalanche descends – callers and letters – Press 11 am – Lunch more calls – called Elgin – cards PM & others – dinner.'

Socially, Deakin's visit to London was a ritual progress through the upper reaches of Edwardian England: dinner at Buckingham Palace, lunch with Rudyard Kipling, dinner with Winston Churchill at the Ritz Hotel, a motor trip down to Flint Cottage at Box Hill to call on the old literary lion George Meredith, lunch with the Duke of Somerset, a garden party held by Lord and Lady Strathcona, and banquets at the 1900 Club, the Baltic Shipping Exchange, the Royal Colonial Institute and a Liberal group called the Eighty Club. The menu at this last function started with *Natives Royales*, which was nothing more exotic than oysters. Deakin responded for the guests with a short version of his familiar thesis that imperial enthusiasm was stronger at the periphery than at the centre. 'In every gathering that assembles [in Australia],' he said, '. . . . His Majesty the King is toasted with greater enthusiasm. Not because your sentiment of loyalty is one whit the less, but because the farther we are removed from the centre the more union means to us.'

The political side of Deakin's London sojourn was anything but a triumphal progress. His diary entry for 10 April read: '5 pm Informal meeting at C.O. begins – Battle with Elgin & C.O. begins.' Unknown to Deakin, however, the battle for Colonial Office reform was already lost. Churchill had 'captured' Canada's Prime Minister, the veteran Sir Wilfrid Laurier, who in any case had been predisposed to doubt the wisdom of Deakin's proposal. Although both were champions of colonial nationalism, Deakin and Laurier differed sharply on imperial union: Laurier, safe behind the shield of the United States, feared that a secretariat would endanger Canadian self-government; Deakin, whose only shield was the Empire, regarded closer imperial union as a source not of interference but of much-needed protection. Louis Botha, the former Boer General who was now Prime Minister of the newly self-governing Transvaal, had more to think about than the Colonial Office; but to the extent that he thought about the matter, he sided with Laurier. It was Elgin, Laurier and Botha against Deakin, Sir Joseph Ward (New Zealand) and Dr L. S. Jameson (leader of the abortive raid on the Transvaal before the Boer War, and now Prime Minister of Cape Colony), and it was plain to see which side would prevail.

Deakin's case was basically that the Colonial Office had too much work to do, and should therefore divest itself of the self-governing colonies, leaving them to communicate through a new secretariat with the British Prime Minister. 'I do not belittle the work of the Colonial Office – it is simply gigantic – but the Colonial Office finds it necessary to omit India,' he said on the third day of the Conference. 'It was recognized to be perfectly impossible for this Office to include the administration of that vast country with its enormous population. In the same way the Colonial Office must expect to see the self-governing communities out-grow its capacity for control, which is not capable of being indefinitely extended.' What he complained about was the Colonial Office's 'attitude of mind': 'a certain impenetrability; a certain remoteness, perhaps geo-graphically justified; a certain weariness of people much pressed with affairs, and greatly overburdened, whose natural desire is to say "Kindly postpone this; do not press that, do not trouble us; what does it matter? We have enough to do already; you are a self-governing community, why not manage to carry on without worrying us?"'

Lord Elgin, who chaired the Conference, told the delegates that he had informed his Prime Minister of the proposal, and had been asked to say for him that 'he does not see how the Prime Minister of this country could undertake the direction of the secretariat.' There would be some change in the channel of communication between the self-governing colonies and Britain, but only within the unchanging framework of the Colonial Office. 'I do not propose nothing,' said Elgin. 'I propose to do as much as I possibly can to meet the desire. It is quite true that this Office has grown considerably, and that the section of it which deals with responsible governments has not as yet been so clearly differentiated and defined as it may quite naturally seem reasonable now that it should be, but which everybody will understand was not at least as necessary in days gone by. . .We will endeavour . . . to so separate the departments of this Office, that you will have in the Office in the form which we shall present it to you, a distinct division dealing with the affairs of the responsibly governed Colonies. I will not say it will be exactly apart, because there is, and must be, at the head, at any rate, a connecting link between the several parts of any office, but there will be one division which you will feel will be concerned with the business of all the self-governing Colonies, and not directly with that of the Crown Colonies.' In closing, the chairman registered, 'in the most friendly manner possible', 'a little demur to the "attitude" which I think was the word which Mr Deakin attributes to us in this Office.'

> *Chairman*: I do not think if we were happy enough to have his assistance in the Office that he would find it [the attitude] really existed.
>
> *Mr Deakin*: I should become official too.
>
> *Chairman*: At any rate that shows that the attitude has some attraction, but I do hope that he will believe that we have no wish to be dictatorial or to be uncivil or anything of that sort in the correspondence we carry on with the Colonies.
>
> *Mr Deakin*: Too civil sometimes.

This rejoinder applied equally to the manner in which the Colonial Office responded to challenge: excessive civility combined with determination to concede as little as possible. A secretariat was set up within the Colonial Office, and before the year was out the Office was divided into three divisions, one of which was a Dominions department under Sir Charles Lucas. Henceforth all the self-governing colonies were to be known as Dominions, and the Colonial Conference as the Imperial Conference. The new names were slender but not altogether meaningless indications that the Empire was gradually changing; for several years to come, however, Australia would have little reason to think that its position *vis-a-vis* Great Britain, which was still to say the Colonial Office, had changed for the better. Lyne had made no progress with imperial preference (as Churchill put it, Britain 'would not give one farthing preference, on a single peppercorn'), and Deakin regarded the shuffling at the Colonial Office as no more than an ingenious game of musical chairs.[4] The secretariat proved to be ineffectual, and in Deakin's view the Dominions department continued to play the same sort of game as the Colonial Office had always played.

In 1908, for example, the Belgian Government invited *La Confédération Australienne* to attend a conference on family education at Brussels. Naturally the invitation went first to the Colonial Office, which forwarded it to each of the Australian State Governments, but not to the Commonwealth Government. Deakin protested to the Governor-General. 'If the practice of Australia speaking in foreign lands with six voices instead of one,' he wrote in September, 'were to be extended any further than is absolutely inevitable, it would be a distinct depreciation of the status of the Commonwealth, to some extent in derogation of one of the leading motives which inspired the Federal Union, in negotiations a certain cause

---

[4] For Deakin's dealings with the Admiralty about Australia's naval defence, see Chapter 7.

of friction, and in ultimate effect probably futile.' Sir Francis Hopwood, secure in the knowledge that Deakin's second term of office had recently come to an end, could afford to ignore this complaint. 'Our case on these papers is not a strong one,' read his minute on the Governor-General's despatch, 'and as we are rid of Mr Deakin for the time being I should put this by and run the risk of his successor asking for an official reply... *Prima facie* everything coming from a foreign country should go to the Commonwealth and the invitation in this case was addressed to them. On the other hand they take no part in exhibitions and apart from the pleasure of making themselves offensive the Commonwealth Government gets nothing by receiving or not receiving the invitations. I suppose, however, that we must try to get the Commonwealth to agree that invitations should go to them and also to the States.' There was nothing in subsequent despatches from the Governor-General to indicate that Deakin's successor, Andrew Fisher, ever asked for a reply. It would seem that the person named Hopwood had won again.

7

DEFENCE

White Ensign

WE COME NOW to a rite of passage inspired by the totems of sea, chrysanthemum and eagle: a national ceremony which neatly combined the Commonwealth's concern about naval defence, its fear of Japan, and its affinity with the American branch of the Anglo-Saxon race. The occasion was a visit to Sydney, Melbourne and Albany by sixteen United States warships during their voyage around the world in 1908. This fleet would have bypassed Australia but for the initiative of Alfred Deakin, who, breaking one of the prime commandments of colonial protocol, sent a timely invitation direct to Washington. And so it came to pass that, in the words of a topical song, Brother Jonathan visited 'the lonely Kangaroo, lonely by the old Pacific Sea.' 'We've got a big brother in America, Uncle Sam! Uncle Sam!/ The same old blood, the same old speech/ The same old songs are good enough for each. . .' The Colonial and Foreign Offices were furious, but for once Deakin had got the better of them. For reasons of its own, Australia would receive the American fleet; and the visit, which was to be described by *The Sydney Morning Herald* as 'the most impressive, certainly the most picturesque event in our short history' next to 'the inauguration of the Commonwealth itself', would impose interesting pressures upon the Australian-British relationship.

The sea totem had always loomed large in Australian mythology. It was too much to argue – as did the Australian-British romantic, C. E. W. Bean – that seamanship ran in the blood of Australians because they were descended from Danes, Jutes and Englishmen; but there was no denying the extent to which Australia depended for protection upon the power of the Royal Navy. Its own naval force, four colonial 'navies' which had come under unified Commonwealth control in 1901, was little more than a token defence for the nation's principal ports. At the coming of Federation, New South Wales, for example, possessed two torpedo boats and a naval brigade of 326 men. In a report to the Federal Government in September 1901 the Queensland naval commandant – Captain W. R.

Creswell, whose own naval force had consisted of two gunboats, one steel torpedo boat and a picket steam pinnace – warned that the future 'spectacle of some 5,000,000 Anglo-Australians . . . unable to prevent the burning of a cargo of wool in sight of Sydney Heads [would be] only the ordinary consequence of a policy of naval impotence.' By the time Captain Creswell was appointed Director of Commonwealth Naval Forces in 1904, those forces consisted of only two cruisers, two gunboats, five torpedo boats and two launches. No new ship had been provided in the last twenty years, and Creswell privately considered that only two of his lieutenants were fit for active service.

But of course there was always the Australia Station of the Royal Navy, the China Station, and all the other components of what Bean called 'the navy of navies, the great grey force, swift and silent, with which, though it be at the other end of the world, every navy must reckon; and with which no navy – no two navies – can reckon.' At that time, while the American Atlantic fleet was on its way around the world, Britain possessed almost fifty battleships; France, Germany and the United States had between twenty and thirty each; Japan had fifteen; and Russia and Italy each had twelve. Clearly Bean was not exaggerating. The continued presence of the Royal Navy in Australian waters had been guaranteed by a Naval Agreement of 1902, under which the Commonwealth paid a subsidy of £200,000 a year towards Britain's maintenance on the Australia Station of one armoured cruiser, six light cruisers, four sloops and a naval reserve of 25 officers and 700 men. This arrangement was cheap at the price (if Australia had bought itself a fleet of the same quality as Britain's in proportion to its own smaller population, the capital outlay for ships alone would have been £14,600,000), and Britain also undertook to help train a local naval militia; but reliance on the Royal Navy gave Australia little say in its own protection. Although Britain had agreed that the subsidized ships would not be moved out of the Pacific, could she be held to that promise in the sudden event of dire need in the northern hemisphere? As Deakin pointed out with almost paranoid generality, or perhaps merely with deliberate indiscrimination to hide a Japanese particularity, Australia was now within striking distance from no fewer than sixteen foreign naval stations: San Francisco, Mazatlan, Callao, Iquique, Hawaii, Tahiti, Samoa, New Caledonia, Yokohama, Port Arthur, Shanghai, Manila, Saigon, Bencoolen, Reunion and Tamative.

In 1905, during his second term as Prime Minister, Deakin advised the British Government that the 1902 Agreement was not popular in Australia. 'No Commonwealth patriotism is aroused while we merely supply funds that disappear in the general expenditure of the Admiralty,' he said. 'The Imperial sentiment languishes, too, since the squadron is rarely seen in most of our ports.' He submitted to the Admiralty a scheme for a flotilla of Australian destroyers, only to have it dismissed by the Committee of Imperial Defence in a report which confirmed his Government's gloomiest misgivings. The CID, a consultative body which advised the British Prime Minister on matters of imperial defence, described the possibility of an enemy raid on Australia as of 'secondary importance', and considered the flotilla proposal to be lacking in strategical justification. If ever warships of this kind could be justified, said the report, it would devolve upon the Admiralty to provide them, not upon Australia. The Admiralty also replied loftily to Deakin's criticism of the 1902 Agreement: 'My Lords are glad to find . . . that the paramount importance of the Navy to the whole British Empire is not questioned, and that the moral obligation of the Commonwealth to share in the general defence of the Empire is recognised.'

Captain Creswell, who had prepared the scheme for an Australian flotilla, and who in his annual reports was a persistent advocate of Australian self-reliance, regarded the Admiralty as a source of active opposition. 'It was an opposition,' he wrote in his memoirs, 'I have reason to know, such as only the Admiralty is capable of: an obstinate resistance of unhallowed tradition; and obduracy, inflexible and implacable, against which ordinary mortals beat their knuckles in vain. To the Admiralty was entrusted the gigantic task of defending the Empire, a task whose magnitude I should be the last to deny, and this responsibility it was prepared to shoulder, Atlas-like, unaided and alone. It neither desired nor would tolerate a family of infant navies overseas, and resolutely set its face against providing a nursery for the brats. Colonial control would have spelt dual control and dual control of the sea forces of the Empire was not to be thought of, for it seemed bound to lead straight to disaster.' Although a product of the Royal Navy himself, Creswell had spent as long in colonial naval service as he had in the employ of the Admiralty. During the 1870s he had taken part in the only forms of active naval service then available to a young officer anywhere in the Empire: the pursuit of pirate junks in Penang and the suppression of the slave trade around Zanzibar. In 1879, at the age of twenty-seven, he resigned from the Navy in order to try his luck as a pastoralist in the Northern Territory of South Australia. When his luck fell short of that Territory's stern demands, he accepted an appointment in 1893 as commandant of the South Australian naval force and captain of its 940-tonne steel cruiser, HMCS *Protector*. From there he moved in 1900 to command of the larger Queensland naval force, which in turn led him to Commonwealth command.

'Oh, Brown! He's a Colonial!'

'Oh, Jones! He's an Imperial!'

The chrysanthemum was a newer totem than the sea, but it complemented the other perfectly. Every expensive form of protection needs the justification of some possible danger, and after the Russo-Japanese war of 1904-5 the external danger perceived most clearly by Australia was the victorious Japanese navy. Australia's attitude towards Japan had altered slightly from the fear instilled by Japan's earlier military success against China (1894-5) to the reluctant 'friendship' enjoined by the Anglo-Japanese Alliance of 1902; but although certain appearances had to be kept up, fear of Britain's new ally became a permanent factor in Australia's national thinking after Admiral Togo's destruction of the Russian Baltic Fleet in the Straits of Tsushima. Three of Togo's battleships had visited Australia in 1903, and it had been something of a shock for many Australians to see the flagship on the Australia Station, HMS *Royal Arthur*, hoist the Japanese flag in honour of these visitors who would not have had the slightest chance of passing a dictation test in German or Swedish. At a military review held for them in Melbourne, the Victorian Government refused to let the Japanese Naval Brigade wear arms. 'The review was repeated at Sydney,' wrote Major-General Sir Edward Hutton, an English soldier who was then organising the Commonwealth's military forces, to a friend in Tokyo, 'where Tennyson took the law into his own hands assisted by the Admiral of our Navy and gave the requisite authority for the Japanese sailors to land armed to take part in the review.'

Lady Tennyson received a number of Japanese midshipmen at Federal Government House in Sydney, and was gratified to find that they were familiar with her late father-in-law's poetry. 'My father-in-law's portrait they beamed over, saying, "Lord Tennyson – Oh, we know 'Charge Of The Light Brigade'. Oh he taught in all our schools; we know him quite well, ha ha!" ' The 'English of the East', as they were called, inspired in Australia a recrudescence of Yellow Peril writing which included *Reaping The Whirlwind*, a play by F. R. C. Hopkins; *The Australian Crisis*, a novel by C. H. Kirmess; and several short stories in the magazine *Lone Hand*. As the curtain fell on *Reaping The Whirlwind*, the hero gasped: 'The Asiatics will enter this country without firing a shot. Oh! My God!' And if they did fire? After the siege of Port Arthur and the battle of Tsushima, no Australian could ever again dismiss the Japanese as 'little brown men.' Writing in the London *Spectator*, C. E. W. Bean depicted the Australian continent as being almost under siege. 'There are some three million whites in Australia inhabiting three million square miles,' he said. 'To the north, at its very gates, up to within a day's sail, are eight hundred million Orientals. . . Three men to hold [Australia] against every eight hundred – that is the quality of the danger.'

The struggle for a self-reliant, sea-going Australian navy continued after the set-back of 1906 with unremitting advocacy by Creswell and qualified approval by the Deakin Government. At the 1907 Imperial Conference, Deakin obtained what at first sight appeared to be acceptance of the proposition that Australia should maintain not only docks and installations but also some naval vessels under its own control; on closer scrutiny, however, it became obvious that the Admiralty would retain unity of control. Deakin also brought back to Melbourne an Admiralty proposal for additional Australian vessels – not the destroyers Creswell wanted, but nine submarines and six torpedo boats. Creswell regarded this proposal as inadequate, and the Government fell from office before being able to proceed with it.

In January 1908 Deakin had his brainwave about the American fleet, which was already on the South American leg of a year-long voyage around Cape Horn to Peru, California, Honolulu, Manila, Yokohama, Colombo, Port Said and Gibraltar. This 'Hurrah Party', as the Navy League Journal in Britain called it, was President Theodore Roosevelt's own idea, inspired by the Russian fleet's long cruise from the Baltic Sea to Tsushima. It was an expensive undertaking, of little operational value, intended partly to impress Japan and partly to advertise the United States abroad. Rear-Admiral Charles S. Sperry, who took command of the fleet when it left California, had sought to have his ships painted grey, like those of most other navies. President Roosevelt preferred the existing colour scheme of white with buff upperworks and funnels, and it was as the White Fleet that Sperry's battleships, almost all named after American States, captured public imagination around the world.

On 24 December 1907 Alfred Deakin despatched an invitation, via the American Consul-General in Melbourne, to the State Department in Washington. Two weeks later he also wrote to the American Ambassador in London, Whitelaw Reid, whom he had met while there for the Colonial Conference, seeking his good office in persuading the United States Government to accept the invitation. The invitation was worded ambiguously, but was construed by Washington as an invitation on behalf of the Commonwealth. Then, after a lapse of three more weeks, Deakin complied with Colonial decorum by asking the Governor-General, Lord Northcote, to ask the Colonial Office to ask the Foreign Office to extend an invitation to the State Department on Australia's behalf. As he well knew, both Office's would want to sink this invitation without trace; but whether they could now do so was a very different matter.

Northcote send a despatch on the subject by mail on 28 January, and by cable on 12 February. 'Yes, I suppose this is a demonstration for the delectation of Japan,' minuted one Colonial Office reader of the cable. 'It ought certainly to be discouraged from every point of view,' wrote another. After three days the cable was sent on for comment to the Foreign Office and the Admiralty. The Foreign Office replied testily on the 19th, and the Colonial Office was still waiting to hear from the Admiralty when, on 22 February, the *Washington Post* reported that the Secretary of State had accepted an invitation to the fleet from the Prime Minister of Australia. Consternation at the Colonial Office! Sir Charles Lucas, head of the new Dominions department, conferred with Sir Francis Hopwood and with the Secretary of State, Lord Elgin, and then contacted the Foreign Office. The Permanent Undersecretary, Sir Edward Grey, was of opinion that 'it would now be a mistake for HM's Government to approach the U.S. Government in the matter.' He also thought, reported Lucas, that 'Mr Deakin should be told that his action had been incorrect.'[1] Lucas was more cautious. 'Unless Sir E. Grey strongly presses the point,' he wrote, 'I think that it would be better not to criticize Mr Deakin over this matter. He may say that a week or ten days had gone without an answer to Lord Northcote's telegram, and accordingly he acted off his own bat.' What was to be done? At first the Colonial Office instructed Northcote to advise his Prime Minister that a further invitation 'would now seem to be superfluous', but within a few days HM's Government bit its lip and changed course completely. On 29 February the Foreign Office instructed the British Embassy in Washington to inform the United States Government of what it already knew – that 'the Government of the Commonwealth of Australia trust that it may be possible to instruct the U.S. fleet now visiting the Pacific to call at the principal Australian ports, where a most enthusiastic and cordial welcome would await them.' 'This invitation is most cordially endorsed by His Majesty's Government,' it said, 'and you should inform [the Secretary of State] of the satisfaction with which they would welcome an intimation that this invitation will be accepted.'

False though the second assurance may have been, there was no doubting the enthusiasm of the welcome which awaited the White Fleet as it steamed towards Sydney Harbour in August. The country was in the grip of what the newspapers called 'fleetitis'; indeed there were signs that

[1] Grey must still have had the White Fleet invitation in mind when he wrote two months later, in a private letter to Lady Helen Munro-Ferguson, whose husband was later to become Governor-General of Australia: 'I will come like a lamb on the 20th of May [to speak about the Empire to the Victoria League]. If I spoke my mind it would appear something like this: "Ladies and gentlemen of the Victoria League, I think there is too much tendency here to slobber over the Colonies, and they are too much given to spit at us. I except Canada from this criticism, but for Australia it might be put even stronger, etc. etc." I fear this wouldn't do.'

Australia had succumbed just as heavily as some of the world's larger nations to naval mania. It was a poor excuse for a nation which did not possess a Naval League; Russia referred to its 'holy fleet', and the Kaiser spoke of Germany's new battleships as his 'darlings'. In Australia there was an emotional, sensual tone to the naval lyricism with which the press regaled its readers. *The Sydney Morning Herald* sent its new feature writer, C. E. W. Bean, on board the flagship of the Australian squadron, HMS *Powerful*, to meet the American fleet in New Zealand. The experience was emotionally almost too much for him. The *Powerful*, he reported, was 'a great grey warhorse, brave and big and fast, and full of the gentleness of all big things', and its smoke was 'as black and soft as – as the coat of a Persian kitten.' Even naval guns evoked images of incongruous gentleness from Bean. 'A 7 in. gun is an ungainly pet,' he wrote. 'But the eyes of one [American sailor] grew very soft the other day as he slapped one fat barrel on the *Louisiana*. . . He fondled that cold steel contour as you might a woolly lamb.'

Any one of the American battleships could have blown *Powerful* out of the water, but Bean reminded his readers of the even greater power implicit in the ensign of the mighty navy to which *Powerful* belonged. 'There is a certain pure old cross of St George which the smallest grey gunboat carries about the world,' he wrote. 'I will tell you, Sir Politician, what that flag means to me, and I doubt not to hundreds of thousands besides. . . It stands for each and every one of these ideas – for generosity in sport and out of it, for a pure regard for women, a chivalrous marriage tie, a fair trial, a free speech, liberty of the subject and equality before the law, for every British principle of cleanliness in body and mind, in trade or politics, of kindness to animals, of fun and fair play. . .'

For once, however, the Stars and Stripes took precedence over the White Ensign and its heavy load of symbolism. On 20 August a crowd of 80,000 people stood on South Head, at the entrance to Sydney Harbour, straining to see down the coast through what remained of an early morning mist. The sun caught a white hull against the grey, and there was Admiral Sperry's flagship, USS *Connecticut*, followed moments later by more white blurs. As the last astern took definite form, and the *Connecticut* began to shape her course for the Heads, the last of the mist lifted and the sea turned bright blue as if in welcome to the big white and yellow ships which were so unlike those of the Royal Navy: *Connecticut, Kansas, Louisiana, Vermont, Georgia, Virginia, New Jersey*. . . Their bows slanted forward for ramming (a useless anachronism which reduced their maximum speed by five knots), and were adorned with shields, eagles and gold-painted curlicues of a kind which any of His Majesty's ships would have considered vulgar. Their crews, numbering 13,000 in all, were mostly young bluejackets and marines. The shore patrols wore buff leggings and carried long batons like Indian clubs. A sailor from the *Kentucky* threatened some Sydneysiders with a razor, and a Negro mess attendant from USS *Panther* took a knife to someone in Melbourne, but otherwise the shore patrols had little to worry about except deserters: 30 of them in Sydney and more than 300 in Melbourne. Brother Jonathan liked Australia, and Australia liked what it saw of him. The Roman Catholic citizens of Sydney tendered a banquet for more than 1000 of their co-religionists from the American fleet, and of course the Ulstermen of Sydney entertained Admiral Sperry's Ulstermen.

In Melbourne, Alfred Deakin – identified by one of the American journalists travelling with the fleet as 'the William J. Bryan of Australia' – addressed the naval visitors at a Parliamentary dinner. He spoke inevitably of Anglo-Saxon race patriotism, and referred obliquely to that unnatural treaty, the Anglo-Japanese Alliance. 'What more real and what more lasting – far beyond the treaties which are the outcome of temporary and devious policies – than a mutual understanding of real relationship, of kinship, of contact, of aim? All these you may well pass without haggling, bargaining and without bond, because they are better and brighter than the hopes which spring from the convention of a day which may perish in a year.' Admiral Sperry replied diplomatically, without referring to the undercurrent which he and some of his fellow voyagers discerned in Australia's welcome.

'What was that mighty undercurrent?' asked Franklin Matthews, a correspondent for the New York *Sun*. 'Want to know bluntly? Just this: It was Australia's way of telling Great Britain something extremely important, something . . . that she has had difficulty in telling the mother country about up to this time. It was that if England expects, as she has the right to expect, that [Australia] shall come to the assistance of the mother country when that country may be enfeebled . . . the mother country must take heed at this very moment of Australia's dread and Australia's aspirations. Australia's dread is the yellow peril, an influx of Orientals into this fair land. . . In short Australia meant by this welcome to the representative of a people who lately had shown signs of anti-Japanese feeling [in Hawaii and California] to tell Great Britain that Australia demands of the mother country the right to make Australia a white man's country and that she expects the mother country to accede to that demand, to the comfort and profit of both mother and daughter. . . If ever our old friend Vox Populi made himself heard in Australia it was when he kept shouting in the ears of the American visitors: "We want this kept a white man's country! We are determined to have it a white man's country! D'ye hear that, England, mother dear?" This dread of Oriental-ism is a present terror with the Australians, and with it is associated indissolubly Australia's aspiration to become before the end of this century the strong right arm of England.'

That was a partial summary of Australian motives, but Matthews should also have mentioned Deakin's hope that the White Fleet would further inspire the Australian people to acquire a navy of their own. If the visit offended Britain, that was too bad; but in no way did it signify any weakening of Australia's loyalty to the Empire. Three days before the American fleet left Albany for Manila, Lord Northcote's successor as Governor-General, Lord Dudley, cabled to the Colonial Office on behalf of the Commonwealth Government: 'Strong desire throughout Australia for visit British fleet calling each State capital it would receive most patriotic welcome. Very desirable that fleet should be impressive as possible in size and quality.' What would they think of next? 'Australia does not deserve a visit,' said one minute. 'I think personally,' wrote Lucas to his new Secretary of State, the Earl of Crewe, 'that it would be most unwise to send a British fleet at present. I was sorry enough that the American fleet went and was made so much of. It seemed to me to be a sort of hint to England that Australia had another string to her bow.' Lord Crewe agreed with Lucas that 'nothing could be less appropriate than to send a British fleet to Australia at once apparently as a sort of counterblast to the visit of the U.S. fleet.' 'This is an unlucky proposition,' he wrote, 'and they must have lost their heads.'

Four days later, to confound Whitehall even further, Dudley for-warded an invitation which his Australian Ministers wished Britain to convey on their behalf to President Roosevelt. Would the President con-sider a personal visit to Australia after his impending retirement? 'This is really very unworthy of the Australian Government,' read one of the minutes. 'To play off U.S. against us is not only foolish (for U.S. will not fight Japan for Australia), but is intended to be used to induce us to break our Japanese alliance.' 'We must send it on,' wrote Lucas, 'but it is a most objectionable message, and I cannot help thinking meant to be un-palatable to us.' As it turned out, Theodore Roosevelt preferred lionhunt-ing in Africa, and Australia saw neither ex-President nor the Royal Navy.

Determined though the Governments of Deakin and his Labor successor, Andrew Fisher, were about the establishment of an Australian navy, there were some Australians who felt that true Imperial loyalty required subsidisation of the Royal Navy rather than naval independence. Australian public feeling was deeply stirred in March 1909 by a debate in the British Parliament on the naval estimates, during which it was suggested that unless Britain ordered more dreadnoughts Germany's naval building program might soon fulfil the Kaiser's proclaimed ambition to 'wrest the Trident from Britain's grasp.' At that time the Royal Navy possessed only one of these superior battleships (HMS *Dreadnought*, 17,000 tonnes, 19 knots), with three more under construction at a cost of £1 million each. Germany was building seven. On 19 March the Melbourne *Age* suggested that Australia should 'provide Britain with the wherewithal to build a Dreadnought . . . whose possession by Britain in an hour of supreme need might determine the existence of the Empire . . .' and would 'show the world the splendour of Australia's loyalty.' The idea ignited like a powder train. Three days later, while a deputation of businessmen was asking the Lord Mayor of Melbourne to call a public meeting, the news arrived that New Zealand had offered Britain a battleship and was ready to give two if required. Next morning the *Age* contrasted this 'fine display of statesmanship and racial honour' with the 'sordid pettiness' of the Fisher Government's decision not to offer a dreadnought. The Fisher Government preferred its own 'steady, persistent and determined policy of Australian naval defence for the protection of Australia and for the assistance of the Empire in time of emergency.' It had adopted Creswell's scheme for twenty-four destroyers, and had ordered the first three vessels.

On the night of 25 March a crowded public meeting in Melbourne Town Hall passed a motion of utmost concern about the state of Britain's naval supremacy, but not without one Quixotic gesture of dissent. While the Rev Dr W. H. Fitchett, author of *Deeds That Won The Empire*, was seconding the motion, an unidentified young man walked on to the platform and announced his intention of discussing the other side of the question. He was shouted down, but later the Lord Mayor read out an amendment which, he said, the young man wished to move: 'That this meeting of citizens, desiring the progress of all humanity, and not the ascendancy of one race over another, places on record its opposition to the policy of imperial aggression – [Oh! Oh!] – and the antagonism it occasions, now being enacted by the States of Europe and America, and that attention be directed to the fact that in each nation certain powerful commercial and business interests – [laughter] – ship builders, merchants and army contractors, etc., are deriving immense profits in furnishing the equipment required to maintain the policy of aggression and encroachment.' The Lord Mayor then ruled the amendment out of order, and as the young man began to protest the organist struck up *Rule Britannia*. As one man, or almost one, the audience rose to its feet and roared out the refrain.

Fisher's Government stuck firmly to its guns against the dreadnought hysteria, but three months later was replaced by a 'fusion' Government which Deakin's Protectionists had formed with their erstwhile opponents, the Free Traders now led by the self-educated former coal worker and former Labor member, Joseph Cook. It was thus during Deakin's third prime ministership that the last obstacle to an Australian navy was removed. Although Deakin offered Britain an Australian dreadnought soon after taking office, as he had publicly undertaken to do, he found one month later that the Admiralty had decided, wonder of wonders, that the Dominions should be allowed to create fleet units of their own which would to some extent be under local control. This policy of interdependence, the joint product of concern about Britain's naval supremacy and concession to colonial opinion, swept the dreadnought offer away for all time. At an imperial defence conference in July 1909, the Admiralty proposed the creation of a Pacific fleet to which Britain, Australia, New Zealand and perhaps also Canada would contribute units. The Australian unit, paid for by the Commonwealth and manned as far as possible by Australians, would consist of at least one armoured cruiser, three light cruisers, six destroyers and three submarines.

While most of these vessels were being built in Britain during the next four years, the real meaning of Australia's naval 'independence' was finally settled. In 1911 the King granted the title of 'Royal Australian Navy', and at the Imperial Conference that year it was decided that ships of the Australian navy should fly the Australian flag on the jack-staff forward, and the White Ensign astern .[2] Australia would have preferred to see the seven-pointed star from its national flag on the White Ensign, but did not press the matter against the Admiralty's unwillingness to complicate the 'pure old cross of St George.' Naval 'independence' was much the same qualified concession as Federal 'independence' had been. His Majesty's Australian ships were to be exclusively controlled by the Commonwealth Government, but only so long as they were in Australian waters. In foreign ports they would take instructions from the British Government; and when, in time of war, they were put at the disposal of the Imperial Government, they would automatically become an integral part of the Royal Navy under Admiralty control. But at least Australia would have the sea-going navy for which the Deakin and Fisher governments had fought so strenuously.

[2] The Commonwealth Naval Board established in 1905 was now re-constituted with four members. Creswell, knighted and promoted to Rear-Admiral (later Vice-Admiral), was first naval member. By 1914 the Naval Board had under its control 3800 officers and men, of whom 850 were on loan from the Royal Navy.

In 1913 all Royal Navy establishments in Australia were transferred to the Commonwealth, and the British commander-in-chief, Australia Station, struck his flag in Melbourne. On 4 October, little more than five years after they had watched the White Fleet materialize out of morning mist, the people of Sydney welcomed the first ships of the Australian fleet: the battle cruiser HMAS *Australia*, the cruisers *Melbourne*, *Sydney* and *Encounter*, and the destroyers *Parramatta*, *Warrego* and *Yarra*. In his message of welcome the Prime Minister, Joseph Cook, expressed once again the familiar imperial-national dichotomy. 'May I stress for one moment the words "His Majesty's Australian Ships",' he said. 'The ships are none the less Australian because they are His Majesty's ships. They are none the less His Majesty's ships because they are Australian ships.'

It had been Fisher's ministry, enlivened by the driving force of W. M. Hughes, which carried this program to fulfilment. Deakin had left office for the last time in April 1910, and Cook had been Prime Minster for little more than three months. Although nine years of life were left to Deakin in 1910, including three more years in Parliament, he was already the conscious victim of as cruel a fate as ever awaited a man of his exceptional gifts. Ever since an illness which had been brought on by the strain of the Colonial Conference of 1907, he had periodically experienced failure of memory. Although his last term of office brought him great legislative satisfaction, it also involved the tension and misgiving of close association with former political enemies. 'Behind me sit the whole of my opponents since Federation,' he wrote to his sister in 1909 on the eve of taking office with the 'fusion' Ministry which followed Fisher's first term. Fisher and his fellow Labor men regarded the withdrawal of Protectionist support from their Party as rank betrayal by Deakin. 'I heard from this side of the House some mention of Judas,' said W. M. Hughes at the height of his vituperative power. 'I do not agree with that; it is not fair – to Judas, for whom there is this to be said, that he did not gag the man whom he betrayed, nor did he fail to hang himself afterwards.' The best that Deakin could manage in reply was: 'Two old jokes. Keep on repeating them.' By the end of the 'fusion' Ministry, Deakin's memory was troubling him severely. 'I am capable of repeating myself without knowing it at a few minutes interval,' he wrote, 'or of omitting it altogether under the belief that I have already used it. This is dreadful, but my gravest defects are those due to my qualities which are essentially those of the . . .'

Sometimes his entries petered out like that, as if in mid-sentence he had simply forgotten what he intended to write. By 1913 the full realisation of his plight left Deakin no alternative but resignation. 'Intellectual bankruptcy,' he wrote after leaving Parliament. 'I have begun to read and can enjoy old favourites but when I close the book they vanish still. I am helpless, poverty-stricken beyond all description and only now realise it to my horror.' All the reading of a lifetime – Sainte-Beuve, Meredith, the complete works of Wordsworth – gone beyond recall! A specialist spoke of 'hyperneurasthenia', but the modern diagnosis of Deakin's condition would probably have been cerebral arteriosclerosis. His final submission to this fate makes tragic reading. 'Except for the childish chatter accompanying everyday ordinary and meaningless observation,' he wrote, 'I am either speechless, irrelevant, confused or not infrequently all three together. I am without command of memory and almost without understanding. . . How long this will last, or into what gulfs it may plunge me is beyond my foresight. . . I have no suicidal tendencies though for a moment in wrath or despair I often feel capable of any sacrifice rather than prolong my miserably inept and useless existence. I am perfectly happy in home, wife, relatives and friends – happier than I can express, and am quite content with everything about me except myself – that self in its former character has vanished out of sight . . . it is as a hapless, helpless and almost hopeless child that I accept with more humility that I can express the exquisite love, kindness and sympathy which make my life happy and more than happy as long as I can forget myself and the utter wreckage that overwhelms my days.'

Slouch Hat

Although the Constitution mentioned naval defence before military, the Australian army came into being earlier, and with less travail, than His Majesty's Australian Navy. Its existence did not jeopardize imperial unity, as the Admiralty at first thought a navy would; the colonial defence forces, modest though they may have been, were at least more substantial than the colonial navies; and what better reason could there have been for pressing ahead with the amalgamation of those forces than the coincidence of Federation and Boer War? In March 1901 the Commonwealth Ministry of Defence took control of State military forces comprising 1544 permanent troops, 16,105 militia and 11,361 volunteers, a total of 29,010. The choice of someone to weld these separate forces into one army lay between three British officers: General Sir Reginald Pole-Carew, a friend of the Governor-General, Lord Hopetoun; General Sir Hector Macdonald, a Boer War hero who visited Australia in 1901; and Major-General Sir Edward Hutton, a fiery little Etonian who had been commandant of military forces in New South Wales and Canada, and had commanded

Australian troops in South Africa. Lord Hopetoun pressed strongly for the appointment of his friend 'Polly', but before any decision could be made General Pole-Carew let it be known that the proposed salary of £2,500 was not sufficient for him. Hopetoun cabled to the Secretary of State for Colonies that in his opinion Macdonald would be most unsuitable, and in December the appointment went to General Hutton.[3]

'Curly' Hutton, as he had been called since Eton, had placed on record his high opinion of Australian troops even before they had shown their mettle against the Boers. In a paper which he delivered to the Military Society at Aldershot in 1896, he said: 'If Australian soldiers, with their quick intelligence and strong individuality, fall into the hands of weak, ignorant and incapable officers, not only will indiscipline supervene but the very individuality I speak of will prompt the men themselves to take matters into their own hands. In this respect Australian soldiers are not dissimilar from the finest troops with whose deeds history has made us familiar, whether we take the Praetorian Guard of the Caesars, the Janissaries of the Caliphs, the Ironsides of Cromwell, or the Old Guard of Napoleon. No man, be he Cromwell or Napoleon, could *drive* Australian troops, but a strong and capable leader, no matter how strict, could *lead* an Australian army to emulate – aye, and surpass if need be – the finest and most heroic deeds recorded in the annals of British arms.'

No wonder Lord Hopetoun had remarked upon Hutton's 'inclination to oratory.' The General was an able administrator, however, and during his three years as Commonwealth commandant he created as sound a basis for future military expansion as he was permitted to by politicians innately suspicious of professional soldiers. Hutton's plan for the integration of colonial forces was resisted to some extent by local commanders and their friends in Federal Parliament, and his plan for an imperial reserve, to be called the Imperial Australian Force, was watered down in Cabinet and finally omitted altogether from the Defence Act of 1903. Like the good professional soldier that he was, Hutton was opposed to compulsory military training. He tried to inculcate a sense of professionalism by promoting two of his protégés, Major W. T. Bridges and Lt C. B. B. White, over the heads of part-time militia officers, and in that at least he was not disappointed.

The Defence Acts of 1903 and 1904 provided a legislative basis for a military system which would be voluntary during peace, voluntary during war involving the Empire, and compulsory only in the event of attack upon Australia. The Commonwealth was divided into military districts

---

[3] Hopetoun was right about 'Fighting Mac'. In 1903 General Macdonald blew his brains out in a Paris hotel while returning to Ceylon to face a court-martial.

corresponding roughly to the States, and the army was to consist of both permanent and citizen forces. The Commonwealth uniform was of khaki serge, with the type of felt slouch hat which had first been worn by the Victorian Mounted Rifles in 1885, and had been adopted five years later by the defence forces of all colonies. The word 'slouch' referred to the fact that one side of the brim was turned slightly down while the other side (the left side, leaving room to shoulder a rifle) was cocked up; in another sense, the word seemed to confirm part of General Hutton's assessment of the Australian soldier, the part about individuality and indiscipline. On the turned-up brim of his hat, the new Commonwealth soldier wore a badge which became known as the Rising Sun, but which in fact had been inspired by a trophy of bayonets in the main hall of General Hutton's Melbourne headquarters. The trophy consisted of Martini-Henri socket bayonets and cut-and-thrust bayonets arranged alternatively in a semi-circle radiating from a brass Crown. When the first battalion of the Australian Commonwealth Horse was being recruited for South Africa in 1902, Hutton cast around for a distinguishing Australian badge. He rejected kangaroo, emu and wattle as being not sufficiently warlike, and finally chose the bayonets.

Public discussion of Australian defence was concerned mainly with the introduction of some form of compulsory training. The Australian National Defence League, formed in 1905, campaigned strongly in its journal *The Call* for a military training scheme like Switzerland's, and the Australian Natives' Association advocated compulsion as the best way to 'defend our hearths and our homes and prevent the Eastern nations from settling on our continent.' Alfred Deakin returned from the 1907 Imperial Conference convinced that Australia should introduce compulsory training for all young men between the ages of 19 and 21, with a later extension of the scheme to boys between 12 and 18 and adults from 21 to 26. This policy was introduced with some modification on the see-saw of Deakin's and Fisher's successive Ministries. Before Deakin could introduce his Defence Bill of 1908, Fisher came to office with a more strenuous policy of compulsory training; and before *his* Bill was ready, Deakin was back in charge. During the 'fusion' Ministry, Parliament passed a modification of the 1908 Bill which terminated the voluntary system and provided compulsory training for junior cadets (12 to 14), senior cadets (14 to 18) and citizen forces (18 to 20).

Before this came into operation, however, the Commonwealth's military forces were inspected and reported upon, at the invitation of the Deakin-Cook Government, by the Empire's most famous soldier: Field-Marshal Viscount Kitchener of Khartoum, victor of the Sudan campaign and the Boer War, and lately re-organizer of the army in India. The public interest which attended Lord Kitchener's visit in January and February 1910 was a military equivalent of the 'fleetitis' which had been aroused by Admiral Sperry two years earlier. Kitchener was the perfect Imperial warrior, and when he spoke Australia stood respectfully to attention. ' "K" is not in the least like the fierce-looking individual who frowns from the grocer's picture calendars,' reported one journalist, 'or glares down – an ogre in scarlet – from the mantelpiece in the commercial room of the conventional country hotel.' Clad in grey and wearing a soft felt hat, Kitchener was 'for all the world like a well-to-do country gentleman' except for his famous cheekbones and eyes. 'Those eyes are really the most fearsome thing about him. A returned South African trooper once told me that when "K" turned his eyes upon a culprit it gave him the cold shivers. It is a cold, pitiless, unflinching, basilisk stare.'

'He was the greatest Englishman that had ever visited the country,' wrote an English officer who happened to be in Australia during Kitchener's tour. 'His personality and reputation appealed to the Australian people: they mobbed him wherever he went and fêted him to an alarming extent; every small town clamoured for a visit from him, and if he had accepted half the invitations he received he would have eaten about twenty square meals a day and made a corresponding number of speeches. In fact, for the time being, Australia went Kitchener mad. Every word he uttered, or didn't utter, was quoted and discussed, and his report was looked to with feverish interest. . .'

After visiting all States, Lord Kitchener in February 1910 submitted the Memorandum on which the Federal Government was counting 'for the purpose of formulating a scheme of defence which would enable us to hold this continent for ourselves and the Empire.' Measuring Australia's existing military defences against the apocalyptic demands of a war in which the whole strength of the Empire would have to be concentrated against a powerful enemy, and in which Australia might have to defend itself against invasion, Kitchener found their quantity and quality inadequate. He recommended the formation of a land force of 80,000 men – half to defend the cities and ports of Australia, and half to serve as a mobile striking force anywhere on the continent. He approved of the new compulsory training scheme, but recommended an extension of age to 25, and the division of the country into numerous military areas; he stressed the need for more railway lines, particularly between the eastern States and Western Australia; and for the training of permanent officers he urged the establishment of 'a Military College, similar in ideals, if not altogether in practice, to the Military College of West Point in America.'[4]

'The Government has appealed to Caesar,' said Deakin, 'and we shall be prepared to defer to Caesar's judgment.' An amending Act – passed under Fisher's second prime ministership, and proclaimed on 1 January 1911 – embodied most of Kitchener's recommendations. All young men, with some provision for exemption, were required to train for seven years, from the age of 18 to 25. The Commonwealth was divided into 224 training areas, and the annual training period between the ages of 18 and 20 was sixteen whole-day drills, of which eight were to be spent in a continuous camp. From the age of 20 to 25, the annual requirement was six days in camp. It sounded Spartan enough, but compulsion was not closely applied at first, and many eligible men managed to evade training.

On 27 June 1911 the Royal Military College of Australia was officially opened at Duntroon, the homestead of a sheep station within the site already chosen in the Yass-Canberra district of New South Wales for a permanent Federal capital.[5] Australia's representative on the Imperial General Staff in London, Colonel W. T. Bridges, inspected Sandhurst, West Point and Kingston, and on his return to Australia was appointed Commandant of the College with the rank of brigadier-general. Bridges was a lofty, bony man, rather gauche in personal manner and ruthless in professional style. He was best known at that time for the bluntness with which he had once told the Imperial General Staff: 'Your training manuals are as much use to the Australians as the cuneiform inscriptions on a Babylonian brick.' His first class at Duntroon consisted of thirty-two Australians and ten New Zealanders, and the course was to be four years long.

The Department of Defence had also intended to establish a military flying school in the Federal Capital Territory, but because the mountains there were regarded as too hazardous, the flying school opened in 1914 at Point Cook on the shore of Port Phillip Bay, Victoria. Senator George Pearce, the Labor Government's Minister for Defence, had come back from the 1911 Imperial Conference with a keen interest in the kind of military flying which he had seen in England and which he knew was being practised with equal enthusiasm in Germany. Aviation was still very much a novelty in Australia. The first powered aeroplane to leave Australian soil was a Wright biplane, which in 1909 at Victoria Park,

---

[4] It is not clear why Kitchener preferred the model of West Point to that of Sandhurst, but he was probably influenced by General Hutton's report of 1902, which – not surprisingly, in view of Hutton's service in Canada – mentioned West Point and the Royal Military College at Kingston, Ontario.

[5] For selection of the capital site, see Chapter 9.

Sydney, covered a distance of 100 metres in five seconds at an altitude of between 80 centimetres and 4½ metres. In the following year an Australian named John Duigan built an aircraft from his own design and flew it successfully at Spring Plains Station, Mia Mia, Victoria. The first Australian aerial mail was flown by a visiting French aviator, Monsieur M. Guillaux, from Melbourne to Sydney in July 1914.

In the same month, the flying school at Point Cook began tuition with two instructors and four mechanics from Britain, five Bristol box-kite biplanes and an initial intake of four student pilots. 'We flew only at dawn and at sunset, when there was no wind,' wrote one of the first graduates, Captain T. W. White, who married one of Alfred Deakin's daughters and later became Australian High Commissioner in London. 'Our labouring [Bristol], capable of only 45 miles per hour, was provided with no instruments other than a barometer, and lacked the enclosing fuselage and floor that give that feeling of security one experiences in a modern machine. The senses took the place of instruments. One's ears did duty as engine-counters; the rush of air in the face told whether the climb or glide was at the right angle. . .'

Early in 1914 the Inspector-General of Imperial Overseas Forces, General Sir Ian Hamilton, made an eleven-week tour of inspection of Australian military forces. This elegantly moustached Scot had once complimented the New South Wales Mounted Rifles on their success against the Boers at Diamond Hill; but although he still had some compliments to dispense, his report, submitted to the Commonwealth Government on 24 April 1914, carried something of a sting in its tail. He was not overly impressed by Australia's efficiency and discipline. While motoring past a Light Horse encampment one morning, for example, about half an hour after a tactical exercise had begun, he was aggrieved to notice 'lack of camp discipline and precision, and want of care of horse flesh.' 'Most of these men had not fallen in on parade,' he wrote, 'and their squadron had moved on without them. This was irregular, and although no reflection on the fighting value of the individuals, yet a reflection, certainly, on the war value of the unit.'

How would the Australian army, he asked himself, fare on the battlefield against an invading enemy? 'My own opinion is that, giving all due weight to the moral factor (i.e. that the men would be defending a country well worth defending and would be very angry); giving, I say, due weight to this factor, and to the advantage they would possess in knowing how to work over their own peculiar paddocks and bush, they would need to be in a majority of at least two to one to fight a pitched battle with picked regular troops from overseas on equal terms. Comparative lack of discipline and cohesion showing up strongly where large forces were involved – these are my reasons for allowing so large a margin of superiority to the invading forces.' Hamilton may have had a Japanese invading force in mind, for during the Russo-Japanese war he had been attached as an observer to the Japanese field army in Manchuria. But if so, he had picked the wrong foe. In the ordeal by fire which lay much closer ahead than was generally realized, Australian troops would be attacking rather than defending, and they would be doing so under conditions which few of them could possibly have expected. Before another year was out, almost to the day, General Hamilton would have personal cause to revise some of his opinions.

8

FISHER AND THE UNION JACKALS

IN SPITE OF its skirmishes with the Colonial Office and the Admiralty, and its gradual forging of national institutions, the Commonwealth of Australia was still fervently British in 1911, a year of elaborate imperial ceremony which included the coronation of George V, an Imperial Conference and a grand naval review at Spithead. Such fervour is hard to measure, but it could well have been that the flame of Australia's imperial loyalty, probably the brightest in the Empire, was then burning more strongly than at any time since Federation. 'Australia presents a paradox,' wrote Sir John Foster Fraser, the author of a widely read book of the time, *Australia: The Making Of A Nation.* 'There is a breezy, buoyant Imperial spirit. But the national spirit, as it is understood elsewhere, is practically non-existent – though one sees the green leaf sprouting. . . You drop from Imperialism to something like parochialism in Australia, with little of the real national spirit intervening – though it exists and must increase. . . At private luncheon and dinner parties the toast of "The King" is given. Semi-public gatherings rarely disperse without singing the National Anthem. There is more evidence of loyalty in Australia than I have ever met with in any other part of the King's dominions – not even excepting home. But it is loyalty to the Empire, not to Great Britain.'

The green leaf could be seen sprouting at a few political meetings. Jack Lang, for example, made a point of hanging the Australian flag instead of the Union Jack in front of his Labor platform table, and at meetings from 1910 onwards he used to lead his audience in singing a new version of an old song:

> If England were my place of birth
> I'd love her tranquil shore.
> If bonny Scotland were my home
> Her mountains I'd adore.
> But I confess that I'm content,
> I never wish to roam.
> Australia is my place of birth,
> Australia is my home.

Anti-Labor politicians, and some Labor politicians too, remained loyal to the Union Jack and often opened their meetings with the national anthem. Although the census of 1911 showed that in the previous three decades the native-born proportion of Australia's population had risen from 63 per cent to 83 per cent, an overwhelming 98 per cent of Australians was still either British-born or of British descent. All State Governments had been conducting assisted immigration schemes since 1906, and the annual intake of British migrants had risen in that period from about 20,000 to 80,000. This would not necessarily have strengthened Australia's filial regard for the British Isles; indeed it might temporarily have had the opposite effect. But as Foster and others had remarked, Australia's primary loyalty lay to the Empire rather than Britain: an Empire which comforted Australia against geographical and racial loneliness, and within whose friendly confines the young Commonwealth could feel rather more important a part of the world than in fact it really was. Australia's economic growth after 1906 enabled it to redeem some earlier loans from Britain, and to finance more development from its own resources. Although the proportion of British capital as distinct from local capital in Australian joint stock companies and public bonds had fallen from 73 per cent at the turn of the century to about 56 per cent in 1911, there was still some substance to – and some reason for Australian resentment about – the claim that British investors could call the Australian tune. 'The course of self respect,' wrote Richard Jebb in *Studies In Colonial Nationalism*, 'could not escape the pressure, subtle but unmistakable, with which the mortgagee knows how to check the independence of his victim. A whisper from the City, and Australian patriots sorrowfully weigh the prospects of the investment loan or the impending conversion against the behests of the national conscience.' But whatever resentment may have arisen from this, as from the inevitable frictions of 'New Chum' immigration, would have been directed towards Great Britain, not towards the Empire.

Even the Labor Federal Government – which must surely have resented whispers from the City, and which numbered some forthright critics of the imperial connection among its backbenchers – was no less loyal to the Empire, when the chips were down, than was the Opposition. The Prime Minister, Andrew Fisher, conducted himself more circumspectly at the Imperial Conference of 1911 than Deakin had done four years earlier. He gave the Colonial Office little trouble, and his concluding remarks were as loyal an address as His Majesty could have expected from any of his subjects. Only once, as we shall see later, did he step out of imperial character in London. Whatever the truth may have been about Fisher and the flag (there was some doubt about what really happened), he must have bitterly regretted the whole curious incident. Deservedly or not, the patriotic outrage of Australia fell upon him like a ton of bricks.

Although the Imperial Conference provided a useful stage for the acting out of imperial roles, it was not an occasion of great public interest. As the Federal Government did not announce its resolutions for the Conference of May and June 1911 until the last sitting day of Parliament in November 1910, there was little discussion of them. Senator Arthur Rae (Labor, NSW) regretted that Parliament was about to 'shut up shop for seven months in order that some people may go and act the goat in the Old Country.' In point of fact, Parliament was closing shop for ten months – a summer recess turned into a winter one as well by the sending of an Australian parliamentary delegation to attend what Deakin had called 'the greatest of our national gatherings' at Westminster Abbey. 'Kings come and kings go,' said Senator Rae, 'but what difference does it make to anyone? It does not matter whether there is a new king on the throne or an old one... We know, notwithstanding all the bunkum talked about loyalty, that it does not matter a snap of the fingers whether the king is crowned or not.'

One would never have guessed this from the Australian press coverage of the Coronation, or from the contingent of twenty-four Federal parliamentarians and their ladies seated in the Abbey. The *Age*'s report ran under no fewer than eight layers of headlines; 'THE CORONATION/ A MAGNIFICENT PAGEANT/ GREAT ARRAY OF ROYALTIES/ IMMENSE POPULAR ENTHUSIASM/ VAST CROWDS IN LONDON STREETS/ THE SCENE IN WESTMINSTER ABBEY/ SOLEMN AND STRIKING CEREMONIAL/ WORLD WIDE ACCLAMATIONS.' Fisher reluctantly wore Court dress, but only after removing the lace. At forty-eight he was a man of distinguished bearing but unassuming manner, straight and broad of back, with deepset brown eyes, a heavy dark moustache and a head of thick hair turned prematurely white. Like Deakin he had been offered an honorary Oxford degree, and like Deakin he had declined.[1] But there the similarity ended. Where Deakin fitted comfortably into a London which he knew of old, Fisher was ill at ease. He and the new Secretary of State for the Colonies, Lewis Harcourt, did not understand one another, and who could wonder at that?

Harcourt was generally unsympathetic to the aspirations of the Dominions, and when it had been suggested that his title should be changed to Secretary of State for Over Sea Dominions and Colonies, he replied waspishly that this would be rather like 'Mr Bug who became

---

[1] Deakin declined all offers of titles and honorary degrees, and was the only Australian prime minister to have refused a Privy Councillorship.

Norfolk-Howard.' He was described as 'the rather malicious Harcourt often seen with a faint half-mocking smile.' Fisher, on the other hand, was described by his secretary, and later head of the Prime Minister's Department, Malcolm Shepherd, as 'so essentially and frankly human that sometimes he reminded me of a big boy.' He had little sense of humour, but plenty of horse sense. His friends called him 'Andy', and even in the House of Representatives he used to address his colleagues by their Christian names. When his Minister for Trade and Customs, Frank Tudor, interjected during one of his speeches, Fisher's strong Scottish accent was heard to silence him with: 'Allow me Frank, Frank allow me!'

Fisher, who was born and raised in Ayrshire, left Scotland for Queensland at the age of 23. He had been a pit boy at 11, and a coal miner at 17; in Queensland he continued to work as a miner until his interest in industrial matters led him to trade union leadership and into the State and Federal Parliaments. He was the first prime minister to have an official motor car, but this was an unaccustomed luxury.[2] The written reminiscences of his daughter Peggy portrayed him as a solid, cautious, teetotal Presbyterian. 'Dad only smoked cigars and that rarely,' she wrote. 'He hated all bad language and did not swear or blaspheme. . . Dad disliked eiderdowns, feather beds and tea cosies. It worried him to see articles on the edge e.g. a cup and saucer on the edge of a shelf or table. . . Dad liked dishes stacked correctly e.g. he didn't like small, large, small plates in one pile.'

Before coming to Fisher's London visit, let us digress briefly to consider Australia's first Labor Ministry of 1904, in which Fisher had served as Minister for Trade and Customs. This Ministry, which lasted only four months, was unique among Labor ministries for two reasons. First, the Prime Minister, J. C. Watson, chose his own Cabinet without interference by Caucus. Second, he invited two men from outside the Labor Party to join his Cabinet. One of these men, C. C. Kingston of South Australia, declined the invitation for reasons of health; but the other – the radical member of Deakin's Protectionist group, H. B. Higgins – accepted. His legal experience was invaluable, for the Federal Labor Party's only barrister at that time, W. M. Hughes, had not been at the Bar for long. Higgins became Attorney-General, and Hughes the Minister for External Affairs. Senator Dawson took Defence, and E. L. Batchelor, a former Adelaide schoolteacher, took Home Affairs.

The Labor Government of twenty-four members faced a composite parliamentary force which was more than twice its own size but sharply

---

[2] Deakin had been content to walk or use the tram. He also rode a bicycle, and during his second term as Prime Minister received a police summons for cycling on a footpath.

divided. Watson's only hope of survival lay in keeping Deakin and the Free Trade leader, George Reid, at arm's length; to this end his party decided against nailing its colours to the mast, and went quietly. 'The situation has a distinctively comical side,' wrote the Governor-General, Lord Northcote, to the British Prime Minister, A. J. Balfour. 'Labour Ministers' words are a mixture of honey and butter – no extreme measures – bow to the will of the House – take into consideration etc – in short all the orthodox phrases of the most respectable of administrations.' Watson indicated his intention of legislating for a permanent Federal capital, a High Commissioner in London, and the construction of a trans-continental railway to Western Australia; but no amount of honey and butter could keep his Government in office long enough to introduce these measures.

The crisis came over an Arbitration Bill which would have granted a substantial degree of preference to trade-unionists. When this provision was defeated for the second time, Watson tendered his resignation to the Governor-General and asked for a double dissolution of Parliament. Instead Northcote called upon Reid, who was able to govern for almost a year with support from Deakin and some of his followers, and with four Protectionists sitting in his Cabinet. Lord Northcote also passed this titbit to Balfour. 'There is an intensely comic element in the whole situation,' he wrote. 'The Prime Minister is Free Trade, the Treasurer and Minister for Customs are ardent Protectionists, and so on. Hitherto half the Cabinet have spent their political lives in denouncing the other moiety.' Balfour professed to be more tolerant about colonial manoeuvrings. 'My personal belief,' he told Northcote, 'is that the Australasians will prove themselves to be possessed of the Anglo-Saxon gift of "muddling through".' Watson, who was still only 37 years old but had never much cared for the limelight, retired from politics and went gold-dredging in South Africa. The party leadership went to Fisher.

Fisher's principal demand, or rather request, at the 1911 Imperial Conference was for greater consultation of the Dominions by Britain. He did not, however, go as far in this direction as the Prime Minister of New Zealand, Sir Joseph Ward, who advanced several suggestions for change in the Imperial structure. Ward's ideas came from the Round Table Movement, which had taken over the Imperial unity campaign from the Pollock Committee; but the ineptitude with which he presented his case ensured its rejection. Great Britain, as Ward hardly needed to remind his fellow prime ministers, could legally commit the Dominions to war without consulting them in any way. He proposed that this legal authority should be transferred to an Imperial Parliament of Defence in which the United Kingdom, Canada, Australia, South Africa, New Zealand and

Newfoundland would be represented on a population basis. Laurier of Canada considered this idea 'absolutely impracticable', and spoke instead about the need for 'Imperial unity based upon local autonomy'; General Botha, Prime Minister of the Union of South Africa (which had been formed the year before by the Cape Colony, Transvaal, Natal and the Orange River Colony), spoke in much the same vein, adding privately that he had 'never heard of a more idiotic proposal'; and Fisher did not think it was 'a practical scheme at the present moment.'

In any case, there had never been much chance of the proposal being adopted at the expense of Britain's final arbitrary power. The British Prime Minister, Herbert Asquith, who chaired the conference, told the Dominions bluntly that an Imperial Parliament would impair the authority of the British Government in such matters as the conduct of foreign policy, the conclusion of treaties and the declaration of war. While Britain bore most of the Empire's defence burden, it would have to retain supremacy in the Imperial relationship, and that was that. In the atmosphere of hostility created by Ward's initial clumsiness, he had little chance of succeeding with a proposal for reconstitution of the Colonial Office. He would probably have failed again anyway, for the Colonial Office was armed to the teeth with memoranda on all possible aspects of attack by the Dominions.

The Colonial Office was as determined as ever to retain power, and even more condescending than usual about the Dominions' capabilities. On one occasion Harcourt remarked that it would 'never do to *say* we are too good for them, and they are not good enough for us', but that was apparently what he believed. One of his senior officials, Sir Henry Lambert, said in 1911 that Australia's Department of External Affairs could not even translate an ordinary letter in French correctly, and that generally the Dominions had 'very few men who would be any use whatever on . . . committees.' 'Yes – we must of course consult the Doms and carry them with us as far as we possibly can,' wrote Lambert. 'But it is no use offering to do so always or pretending that we will. . . This [conference] will be, like the Indians, an occasion for some frank speaking – without reporters of course. . . As long as we pay for fleets, armies and diplomatic services we, and only we, can have the ultimate responsibility for large questions of foreign policy such as are involved in the Convention of London.'

After hearing Harcourt's defence of the *status quo*, the Prime Ministers dropped the subject of Colonial Office reform; and after the Foreign Office had defended its negotiation of the Convention of London, they went quietly on that too. The Declaration of London, as it was more often called, was an attempt to reconcile by mutual agreement the conflicting international legal principles held by various nations. Some of its critics in the Dominions held that the Declaration, still unratified, embodied principles of maritime law which might be to the Empire's disadvantage – might even restrict the operation of the British and Dominions' navies in time of war. Fisher used this fear as an opportunity to argue rather cautiously for closer consultation. 'Hitherto the Dominions have not, as far as my knowledge goes, been consulted prior to negotiations being entered into by the Mother Country with other countries, as regards treaties or anything that led up to a treaty or a declaration of this kind. I hold strongly to the view – with great deference to the opinions of His Majesty's Ministers in the United Kingdom – that that is a weak link in the chain of our common interests.' The Minister for External Affairs, E. L. Batchelor, spoke more vigorously about Britain's failure to consult Australia on the Declaration. 'Had we been independent,' he said, 'of course we would have been consulted. The first intimation we got was from the [Parliamentary] Blue Book after it had been fixed up. That is the first intimation we had that there was any such proposal which necessarily would affect us considerably – the Blue Book – after the whole matter had been fixed up.'

The permanent head of the Foreign Office, Sir Edward Grey, was not perturbed. 'Just as . . . one individual Minister sometimes has to act to take responsibility without consulting the Cabinet,' he told the Prime Ministers, 'and the Prime Minister has to act without consulting the Cabinet on some things from the nature of the case when there is not time, so the Home Government when the conference is going on would have to deal with the points without being able to consult the Dominions, simply because it is not physically possible to do so.' Sir Edward, as we have already seen, believed there was 'too much tendency to slobber over the Colonies.' At this Imperial Conference, however, he treated them to an unprecedented exposition of Britain's foreign policy. With 'sad eagle eyes', as someone once described them, Sir Edward gazed out over the world and told the Prime Ministers exactly – well, not quite exactly – what he saw.

This briefing took place at a meeting of the Committee of Imperial Defence, which the Prime Ministers were allowed to attend as a special mark of esteem. Never before had that august advisory body – which included the Secretary of State for War, the First Lord of the Admiralty, Lord Kitchener and Sir Ian Hamilton – admitted outsiders to its deliberations. The whole performance was designed as consolation for the sternness with which Britain had clung to her final arbitrary powers: the Dominion Prime Ministers were to feel that for once they had been taken fully into Britain's confidence, and that was exactly how they did respond.

A large part of Sir Edward's briefing was devoted to the Anglo-Japanese Alliance, which the Foreign Office wished to renew before it expired in 1915. He assured the Dominions that Japan would not use the Alliance as a lever to loosen their immigration policies, and reminded them that only the friendly presence of the Japanese fleet in the Pacific permitted Britain to concentrate the Royal Navy in the Mediterranean and the North Sea against a potential European foe. Despite the absence of any immediate danger in Europe, there was always the possibility of some power or group of powers pursuing what Sir Edward called 'the Napoleonic policy.'

'That would be a policy on the part of the strongest power in Europe,' he said, 'or of the strongest group of powers in Europe, of first of all separating the other powers outside their own group from each other, taking them in detail, crushing them singly if need be, and forcing each into the orbit of the policy of the strongest power, or of the strongest group of powers. Now, if any policy of that sort was pursued by any power, it could only be pursued by the strongest power, or strongest group of powers in Europe at the moment. The moment it was pursued, the moment the weakest powers in Europe were assailed, either by diplomacy or force, one by one they would appeal to us to help them. I may say at once we are not committed by entanglements which tie our hands. Our hands are free, and I have nothing to disclose to our being bound by any alliances, which is not known to all the world at the present time.'

Fisher, Batchelor and the third Australian delegate – Senator George Pearce, Minister for Defence – came away from this meeting convinced that a European war was inevitable and determined to press ahead with Australia's defence program as quickly as possible. Fisher was particularly impressed by the meeting. 'Hitherto we have been negotiating with the Government of the United Kingdom at the portals of the household,' he said in his concluding address. 'You have thought it wise to take the representatives of the Dominions into the inner counsels of the nation, and frankly discuss with them the affairs of the Empire as they affect each and all of us. Time alone will discover what that means. I am optimistic. I think no greater step has ever been taken, or can be taken, by any responsible advisers of the King. . .' Fisher's optimism was misplaced. For all Sir Edward Grey's apparent frankness, he managed not to reveal the Anglo-French conversations of 1906, which both France and Russia regarded as tantamount to a British commitment to side with France in the event of any attack upon her by Germany. This made nonsense of Grey's assurance that Britain had no entanglements in Europe. David

Lloyd George, who was Chancellor of the Exchequer in 1911, wrote many years later that the information withheld by Grey on that occasion was more important than that which he imparted. Lloyd George himself knew nothing of the Anglo-French conversations until the Agadir crisis of July 1911.

This international crisis – in which Germany and France almost came to blows over Germany's sending of a gunboat to the port of Agadir on the Atlantic coast of Morocco, presumably with the intention of eventually establishing a naval base there – began only eleven days after Fisher's expression of optimism about imperial consultation in the future. Australian shipping routes, as one speaker pointed out later in the Federal Parliament, would have been set at risk by the establishment of a German naval base in Morocco; yet at no time did Britain consult Australia, or any of the Dominions, about Agadir. So much for Dominion optimism!

As far as the Australian public was concerned, Fisher's most controversial action in London, indeed his only controversial action there, had nothing to do with the Imperial Conference. It arose from an interview which he gave over breakfast, shortly before his departure for Australia, to W. T. Stead, an elderly English publisher-journalist who was sometimes billed as the world's greatest interviewer. Stead had interviewed the Czar of Russia and the German Kaiser, and soon after his meeting with Fisher he went to Constantinople for an interview with the Sultan of Turkey. His interview with Fisher was published in his own magazine, *Review of Reviews*, while the Prime Minister's ship was crossing the Arabian Sea, but the news soon caught up with Fisher by radio. It is not clear how much of the interview reached the ship, but it was enough for a meeting of passengers to send a letter to Fisher in his cabin asking for an explanation. Fisher replied that the radio report was an exaggeration, but the passengers nonetheless asked one of their fellows, the Mayor of Adelaide, to chair a meeting of protest. He declined. At Colombo Fisher saw a full report of the interview, and declared it a 'grotesque misrepresentation.'

What Stead had quoted Fisher as saying was this: 'Don't talk of the Empire. We are not an empire. No end of mischief has arisen through the use of that word. We are a very loose association of five nations, each independent, each willing, for a time, to remain in fraternal co-operative union with Great Britain, and with each other; but only on condition that if at any time, or through any cause, we decide to terminate that connection, no one can say us nay. We are independent, self-governing communities, untrammelled by laws, treaties or constitutions. We are free to take our own course in our own interests without anyone preventing us. There is no necessity to say that we will or will not take part in England's wars.

We recognize that our territory is subject to attack by England's enemy, and if we were threatened we would have to decide whether to defend ourselves, or, if we thought that the war was unjust and England's enemy in the right, we should haul down the Union Jack, hoist our own flag and start on our own.'

This was not very different from Sir Wilfrid Laurier's declaration, made with impunity eleven years earlier, that 'in future Canada shall be at liberty to act or not to act, to interfere or not to interfere, to do just as she pleases', or really much stronger than some of Laurier's quite recent assertions of Canadian autonomy. But Australia was not Canada, and when cable reports of the Stead interview appeared in the Australian press on 24 July every imperial loyalist took offence. The Governor of Victoria, Sir John Fuller, was addressing an assembly of the Salvation Army in Melbourne Town Hall that day, and when he had occasion to mention 'the British Empire' he added with marked emphasis '*and we are an Empire.*' The *Argus* reported next morning that no sooner had the last syllable of this remark been uttered than 'the great audience rose as if on the crest of a wave of enthusiasm, and found vent for its feelings in a wave of cheering.'

In Adelaide the Superintendent of Public Buildings – Owen Smyth, who was also founder of the South Australian branch of the Royal Society of St George, was addressing senior members of the League of Empire. 'I hope the Prime Minister did not make the statement,' he said, 'and believe that he did not, as it is not in keeping with the fine Imperialistic utterances previously made by him in the motherland. But if the day ever comes when any man could so act as to dishonour our flag and lower it before the enemy, I hope it will be my inestimable privilege to pistol that man with my own hand.' This was greeted by prolonged applause.

Had the Prime Minister been correctly reported or not? Fisher's defenders pointed out that Stead was 'a Little Englander of the narrowest and most crabbed kind' who might well have attributed separatist remarks to Fisher for political purposes. It was also recalled that two years ago, claiming to have communicated with the spirit world through a medium, Stead had enlarged his journalistic repertoire by interviewing the ghost of W. E. Gladstone. In Colombo, Fisher said that Stead's interview with him had lasted only seven minutes, and that the expression 'Haul down the Union Jack' had never entered his mind. 'To keep the flag flying is my ambition, with all its traditions,' he said. 'Nor have I harboured any idea that Australia should break away from the Empire.' Stead, on his return to London from Turkey, emphatically defended the accuracy of his report. He had taken no notes, for that was not his practice when conducting interviews; but his recollection of the brief conversation with Fisher was perfectly clear, and he had written the report at once. He had sent a printer's proof to Fisher before the Prime Minister left London, and when this was not returned he took silence to mean consent.

After his return to Australia in August, Fisher spoke more fully about the interview. He took particular exception to two phrases: 'loose association', which should have been 'close association'; and the remark about hauling down the Union Jack and raising Australia's own flag, which he said was entirely an emanation from Mr Stead. He did not deny having received a proof of the interview, but said that he had been obliged by pressure of work to leave such matters to his secretary. As for Australia's conduct in any future war, Fisher's considered position was this: 'I say at once that if the Empire is at war the Commonwealth *de facto* is at war. I do say, however, that the autonomy of the Dominions is complete, that their autonomy is such that it is for the Dominion parliaments to say how far they will actively participate in any war, and how they will dispose their forces.'

Constitutionally correct though this position undoubtedly was, the Melbourne *Argus* found it a 'wretchedly insufficient' statement of Australia's position in the Empire. Imperial unity, said the *Argus*, was even stronger now than when the Boer War began. 'It is preposterous,' it said, 'that such a stand-off attitude should be published to the world as the attitude which Australia will adopt in a moment of emergency for the Empire. The Parliament of the Commonwealth, should the perils of war arise, will not be found hanging back and whittling down its Imperialism to this or that fine limit.' The *Age* felt that Australia could not 'be in the Empire and out of it', and *The Sydney Morning Herald* welcomed Fisher's repudiation of an interview which had given an entirely false picture of Australia. 'There can be no doubt,' said the *Herald*, 'that the position taken up by the Prime Minister of Canada has justified of late the snappings of that curious anti-imperial minority which is ready to seize on any favouring detail of empire politics, and worry it into undeserved prominence. Thus with Sir Wilfrid Laurier appreciably lukewarm in this and that question of imperial interest, it has not been difficult either for a South African newspaper, or the Little Englanders of London, to launch a theory of Dominion independence and justify it by the trend of Canadian development. In that way, no doubt, has it come to pass that Australia has been projected as another Dominion breaking free of the trammels of Empire.'

What may have been trammels to some were to the majority of Australians more like a harness: a harness both for working in unison with others and for deflecting slings and arrows. When the Labor Premier of New South Wales, William Holman, asked for notice of an Opposition question as to whether he would send a cable to London dissociating New South Wales from the Stead interview, the questioner shook his fist at the Government benches and shouted: 'You won't haul down the Union Jack, at any rate!' When most Australians spoke of the flag, they meant the Union Jack. It was not unlike the feathered spear on the sacred ground of the Aranda at initiation time – an object of veneration, and a source of comfort. It too could ease the pain of separation for those who embraced it. Among the few organs of opinion which had not yet embraced the flagpole were the Brisbane *Worker* and the *Bulletin*, neither of which found anything to complain about in the Stead interview, even if it may have been partly fabrication. 'All the Jingoes in this Commonwealth are furtively kicking themselves for the way they fell in over the Fisher canard,' said the *Worker*. 'But, come now – was the idea involved (of Australian independence) so insane a notion after all explanations are made? There are a not inconsiderable number of *us* who, even if the sentiments attributed to Fisher were facts instead of fakements, would still not consider him a fit subject to have a writ *de lunatico inquirendo* issued against him by Attorney-General Hughes.'

'Andrew Fisher has the whole tribe of Union Jackals snapping at his heels,' said the *Bulletin* in one of its most cogent editorial expressions of nationalism. 'Talking to Stead – and he might easily have got a better ear to pour his ideas into – he seems to have said that 'the Empire' wasn't really one Empire but a loose bunch of five Dominions; and – repeating what Laurier, of Canada, said the other day, and what S'Africa would say any day of any week – he added that the children, being adults, would want to know what a row was about before taking part in it. Given a just quarrel, Mother could rely upon the children for support; given an unjust quarrel, the children might take a hand, or they might not. If they believed that the quarrel was so unjust that help was impossible, then Fisher recognised that the only alternative would be to go their own way under their own flag. The crowd that yells "My country right or wrong", distorting both Fisher's argument and Fisher's conclusion, demands Andrew's scalp, though, if it told the truth, it would say that it isn't so much concerned about getting Fisher's scalp as it is about getting a knife into the Labor Party's back. It knows well that once the cry of "Disloyalty!" is set going in earnest thousands of usually sane citizens become demented; and this political pack would just as soon have the vote of a mad citizen as a sane one. In the circumstances, and before the insanity spreads, it will be as well for citizens to ask themselves a question or two.

For instance: 'Which is my "mother country"? Is it Australia, or is it some other bit of the earth? If it is Australia, isn't that country ever going to have a mind of its own? If it had a population of 50,000,000 would it still be bound to follow blindly wherever the other might lead – even if it should lead into another Opium War? And is it any more righteous for 5,000,000 to follow blindly than it would be for 50,000,000?

'Also, if the Mother Dominion can rely absolutely upon the children joining in her quarrels, whether they understand anything about those quarrels or not, what earthly reason is there for the mother to take the youngsters' opinion? Australia, presumably, wants to have her interests considered; but why should they be considered if Australia is "in the bag"?'

These were hard questions to answer rationally, and why should most Australians even have tried when there were so many irrational but satisfying answers ready to hand? The most satisfying answer – and one that was not altogether irrational, for it involved some calculation of self-interest as well as jingoism – was not 'My country right or wrong' but 'The Empire right or wrong.' Australia depended upon the British Empire, and when next that Empire went to war Australia would have neither time nor inclination for much consideration of its response. The Commonwealth would respond instinctively, and that would go not only for the Union Jackals but for Andrew Fisher, the *Worker* and, after a while, for the *Bulletin* too.

9

THE VIEW FROM CAPITAL HILL

Canberra

ON WEDNESDAY MORNING, 12 March 1913, a cavalcade of forty
motor cars, followed by buses, lorries, four-horse drags, sulkies, wagon-
ettes, sociables, bicycles and mounted horsemen, set out from Queanbeyan
railway station in the uplands of southern New South Wales to attend the
laying of commencement stones at the site of Australia's permanent federal
capital. It was a fine autumn day, and the journey would take only half
an hour or so. The cars, packed with politicians and their wives, public
servants, judges and churchmen, soon crossed the unmarked boundary of
the Federal Capital Territory (later Australian Capital Territory), an
area of 2300 square kilometres which had been vested in the Commonwealth on 1 January 1911, ten years to the day after the inauguration of
the Commonwealth itself.[1] Keeping to the southern side of the Molonglo
River – which, on its way to the Murrumbidgee, crossed a grassy plain
upon which the capital city was to be built – the cars and carriages followed
a red streak of dusty road towards a bushy eminence recently designated
as Capital Hill. The limestone plains, as they were sometimes called, were
no longer quite the same as when their first settlers had arrived almost a
century before, but they had not changed very much either. The
Aboriginal name for the district – spelt Canberry by the first white land-
holder, but later evolving through Kembery and Kamberra to a generally
accepted Canberra – was said to have meant either 'woman's breasts'
(presumably inspired by the twin peaks of Mt Ainslie and Mt Majura) or
'meeting place'.[2]

To this brown-grey valley the Commonwealth had come after years

[1] Under the Commonwealth Seat of Government Acceptance Act (1909), the NSW
Government agreed to transfer to the Commonwealth not only the area near Queanbeyan
but also 5 square kilometres at Jervis Bay, about 120 kilometres to the east, to serve as a
Federal port, and another 932 hectares at Jervis Bay for defence purposes. The Federal
Government was also given water rights for the F.C.T., and the right to build and maintain
a railway line to Jervis Bay. The railway was never built.

[2] Although the second meaning was almost too apposite to be true, early Aboriginal word
lists from the region included *kaamberra* (woman's breasts) and *nganbirra* (meeting place).

of indecision about the site for a capital to replace Melbourne. There was never much doubt that the permanent seat of government would be somewhere in the oldest and most populous State, New South Wales; but at the constitutional convention of 1897 there was considerable opposition to a New South Wales demand that the choice should be Sydney. Sir Edward Braddon of Tasmania sardonically proposed 'some suitable place in Tasmania', Sir George Turner (Victoria) suggested in the same spirit his own electorate of St Kilda, and Sir Josiah Symon (South Australia) spoke up rather more seriously for Mt Gambier in his home State. Section 125 of the Constitution stated that the Commonwealth seat of government should be determined by the Federal Parliament within the State of New South Wales, and distant not less than 160 kilometres from Sydney. A NSW Royal Commission in 1899 had reported in favour of the Bombala-Eden district of the far south coast, with Orange (central west) and Yass (southern inland) sharing equal second place; after Federation, however, it became apparent that the new Parliament would not be content merely to accept whatever site New South Wales might offer.

Federal Members of Parliament inspected many sites in 1902, and on one of these tours – to Lake George, southwest of Yass – some of the travellers were favourably impressed by the Canberra plain. A Federal Royal Commission was set up in 1903 to examine the merits of Albury (strongly favoured by Victorian M.P.s because it could not have been any closer to Melbourne yet still in New South Wales), Tumut in southern New South Wales, Orange, Armidale on the northern heights of the Dividing Range, Bombala, Lake George and Dalgety in the Snowy Mountains. It recommended the first three, in that order of preference, but added a rider that Dalgety would be less costly to resume than any of the other sites. When Parliament debated this report, the House of Representatives voted for Tumut, and the Senate for Bombala. In August 1904 both Houses agreed on a Seat of Government Act for Dalgety, but not for long. One of the speakers, Senator Pearce, said that Dalgety's 'flowing streams and well-grassed lands' were far superior to either Lake George, 'a morass of filthy yellow mud', or Canberra, where 'the skeletons of stock that had died of starvation were to be found in every direction.' Despite this grossly unfair description, the opinion of Federal and State NSW parliamentarians gradually swung over to a site described as Yass-Canberra. Both Watson and Reid spoke strongly in its favour, and after some disagreement between the Federal and NSW Governments about transfering the Dalgety site, Parliament decided instead upon Yass-Canberra. As the Senate had confirmed the choice of Yass-Canberra while Dalgety was still the officially enacted site, that Act had to be repealed before Parliament could set the seal on its change of mind. When the Colonial Office heard about this, one of its officials wrote on the Governor-General's despatch: 'This is a comic muddle.'

And so in the autumn of 1913, out across the plains of kangaroo grass, past occasional clumps of red gum and yellow box, past whistling parrots and mournful currawongs, went the Prime Minister of the Commonwealth, Andrew Fisher, in black frock coat and tall top hat; his Minister for Home Affairs, King O'Malley, who was responsible for the new capital; the Attorney-General, W. M. Hughes; the first Labor Premier of NSW, James McGovern; the First Naval Member of the Commonwealth Naval Board, Rear Admiral Sir William Creswell; Major-General G. M. Kirkpatrick, the imperial officer who was then Inspector-General of the Commonwealth Military Forces; the Governor of the newly created Commonwealth Bank, Denison Miller; and altogether a crowd of some 5000. Griffith and Barton were absent because of High Court commitments, Deakin had left Parliament by that time, and Reid was now Australian High Commissioner in London. Most of the guests had reached their tiered seats on Camp Hill, a northern spur of Capital Hill, by 10.30 am, but the Governor-General, Lord Denman, was not expected to arrive for another hour. One can still see this microcosm of the Commonwealth on a cine film taken that morning: a guard of honour from the Royal Military College at Duntroon, only five kilometres away; Fisher, standing in solemn confab with some of his ministers; Hughes breaking into the circle like a talkative, joking gnome; and lesser dignitaries sitting in the grandstand, talking, thinking, or merely looking out over the wide valley floor to the blue Brindabella Range in the west, and a few isolated mountains to the north.

What else was there to see? The *Bulletin* had called these plains 'a handful of hovels in a howling wilderness', but an oil painting of the scene by Penleigh Boyd in 1913 gave the lie to that. Certainly the district was only sparsely settled. The population of the entire F.C.T. in 1913 was 1714 people, 1762 horses, 8412 cattle and 224,764 sheep. Boyd's painting, which now hangs in Parliament House, shows an open landscape of considerable beauty, with scattered homesteads, the solitary spire of St John's Anglican church, and a backdrop of mountain ranges as wild as any on the continent. To the city folk in their seats on Capital Hill, the distant Brindabellas were a reminder of the vast and lonely bush so easily forgotten inside the four walls of a Federal Parliament or suburban home. While the capital cities had been enlarging their share of the Australian population from 35 per cent in 1901 to 38 per cent in 1911, the elemental sovereignty of the bush had been little impaired by the incursion of roads and railway lines. The Australian bush was not hostile; merely indifferent. A man could lose himself in its immensity and never be heard of again. At about this time, C. E. W. Bean was describing such a fate in one of his books, *On The Wool Track*. 'Nothing appalling or horrible rushed upon these men,' he wrote. 'Only there happened – nothing. There might have been a pool of cool water beneath any one of those tree clumps; only – there was not. It might have rained any time; only – it did not. There might have been a fence of a house just over the next rise; only – there was not. They lay down with the birds hopping from branch to branch above them and the bright sky peeping down at them. No one came. Nothing happened. That was all.'

From Capital Hill the waiting guests could see the ancient gum-clad slopes of Black Mountain, and down below on the valley floor a new presence – the administrative offices of the Federal departments of Works and Home Affairs. These offices were visible reminders of an expanding Commonwealth: a Commonwealth whose public service had grown from 1408 employees early in 1901, and an expenditure of £3,565,840 in 1901–2, to comparable figures of more than 35,000 and £9 million in 1913. The Federal machine had accelerated at a rate which few of its founding mechanics had envisaged. The Commonwealth's exercise of its legislative powers proved more time-consuming and dynamic a process than had been expected from the limited nature of those powers. One thing led to another, particularly in matters of immigration and defence, and Federal politicians showed a taste for power which should not really have come as much of a surprise to anyone acquainted with human nature. 'A new political animal, the federal politician, manipulated the machine,' wrote Dr Ronald Norris, with a nice Darwinian turn of phrase, in his book *The Emergent Commonwealth*. 'These creatures, originally descended from the colonial variety, quickly adapted to the new environment and evolved into a distinct alien species. They were not unambitious, and desired to survive and thrive. They herded together and hunted in packs or parties, their quarry votes, their weapons popular policies. They competed for attention, support and power with each other and with their rival species. Colonial politicians drew up the Constitution. Federal politicians put it into effect. They discovered that the makers had fashioned not a sealed compact but a Pandora's box.'

In the field of industrial legislation the Commonwealth had taken initiatives which, although overruled by the High Court, were nonetheless having considerable social and economic consequences. In 1908 the Federal Government had provided a modest old age pension in place of similar schemes in NSW, Victoria and Queensland, and as the first scheme of its kind in the other States. The Commonwealth's spending power had been restricted by the Constitution's insistence that the Commonwealth should manage on its own quarter-share of customs and excise duties for a minimum of ten years, paying the residue to the States. It could have raised additional revenue by following the States into the field of income tax, but politically the time for that was not yet ripe. When the one-quarter requirement expired at the end of 1910, the Commonwealth negotiated in its place a more flexible arrangement under which it paid to the States an annual grant per head of population.

Thanks to the duty-free common market between the States, Australia was now more unified economically than it had been when Federation began. The Federal Government had founded a Commonwealth Bank, as we shall see later, and the Treasury had instituted its own note issue in place of the multifarious notes formerly issued by private banks. It had replaced the separate States' postage stamps with a uniform Australian penny post anywhere within the Commonwealth, and had started to build a transcontinental railway between South Australia and Western Australia. Australia had a nation-wide military defence system, and would soon take possession of its own naval fleet. The Commonwealth of Australia was now as much a reality in the public consciousness as were the new administrative offices on the Canberra plain. The Federal idea had had its ups and downs, and relations between Commonwealth and States were often strained; but whatever additional stresses the future might hold, the Commonwealth was undoubtedly there to stay. Nine years earlier, the Speaker of Federal Parliament, E. G. Blackmore, had expressed strong pessimism about Federation in a letter to the British Ambassador in Washington, James Bryce. 'There is no doubt that, outside the Labor Party, Australia is disappointed with Federation,' he wrote, 'and if the subject could be referred to a referendum it would be hopelessly rejected... The fact is Australia is too big, and the distances from the seat of government are too great for any but professional politicians. I am sorry and disappointed for I believed that Federation would raise the whole tone of politics, and that we might be able to say of the Parliament *Largior hic campes* etc ["The horizon was a larger one and the men rose to it"]. But I am afraid it is the same old gang on another shelf.' Another observer of that time, Lord Northcote, had more confidence in Federation. 'It is, temporarily, unpopular,' he told the British Prime Minister, Balfour, in 1904, 'but the history of the United States shows similar features; and the country recognises the *fait accompli* ... the bulk of the people accept it as inevitable, as we did, say with Gladstone's Irish Land Act of 1881; and won't seek to undo it. . . . Of course it is a pity that the Federal Parliament should be more radical than the State Parliaments, and the Federal Senate more radical than the House of Representatives; but such is life.'

Now, in 1913, one of Northcote's successors, Lord Denman, rode in state across the Canberra plains towards the waiting crowd on Capital Hill. He wore epaulettes and a plumed cocked hat, and sat his horse with the ease to be expected of a Sandhurst graduate and accomplished steeple-chase rider. Behind him rode two aides-de-camp in the uniform and bear-skins of the Coldstream Guards, and behind them an escort of Australian cavalry with pennants flying. There had been some uncertainty in the official mind as to whether the Union Jack or the Australian flag should have precedence on this occasion, but the difficulty was resolved by flying both flags in front of the site upon which the Governor-General, the Prime Minister and King O'Malley were each to lay a foundation stone for a commencement column which was to have contained stones from all the Dominions, but which in fact was never completed. After the three stones had been winched on to their beds of mortar, the crowd sang 'All People That On Earth Do Dwell', a fanfare of trumpets sounded, and precisely at midday Lady Denman, wearing a long green and white dress and a hat trimmed with ostrich feathers, opened a gold cigarette case to find which name Cabinet had chosen for the new city.

'I name the capital of Australia, Canberra,' she said (pronouncing the name 'Can'bra', as was to become customary usage), and a 21-gun artillery salute roared out over the plains and hills of the Capital Territory. Although the choice of name came as no great surprise, the possibilities had been almost infinite. Several parliamentarians were known to have favoured Canberra; but Fisher had preferred Myola; Sir George Reid, Pacifica; Hugh Mahon, Radiance; and Austin Chapman, Austral. Myola, which was said to be another Aboriginal word meaning 'meeting place,' seemed likely to prevail because of Fisher's support until the press pointed out how closely it resembled an anagram of 'O'Malley'. O'Malley himself claimed to prefer Shakespeare. Other Aboriginal names canvassed in the press were Kooringa, Warroon and Kalima. 'I am at a loss to understand the craze so many persons have for an aboriginal name for our Federal city,' wrote one reader of the *Argus*, 'particularly as we all know that a few years hence the language or rather gibberish of the aboriginal shall be no more.' He preferred Regina.[3]

[3] The list of suggested names prepared for submission to Cabinet provides an interesting guide to the aberrations of public taste. There were some nationalist suggestions (Australoo, Australetta, Australamooloo, Kangemu, Emuroo, Austral-Eden, Wattle City, Homestead and Waratah), personal ones (Dampier, Deakinburg, Banksborough, Phillipton, Bartons-burgh, Parkeston, Wentworth and Melba), abstract ones (Federalia, Democratia, Newera,

At luncheon in a marquee below Capital Hill, Lord Denman congratulated Cabinet on having avoided such names as Sydmeladperbrisho, and expressed the belief that 'Canberra' would 'commend itself to the good sense of the country.' King O'Malley spoke in his usual bombastic style, and Billy Hughes remembered to mention the vanished people who had first inhabited the Federal Capital Territory. 'We are here as visible signs of a continent,' he said. 'The people are incapable of nourishing abstract ideals. They must have a symbol. Here we have a symbol of nationality. . . The first historic event in the history of the Commonwealth we are engaged in today without the slightest trace of that race we have banished from the face of the earth. We must not be too proud lest we should, too, in time disappear.'

At the time of this stone-laying ceremony, the commencement column was intended to stand eventually in the centre of a grand avenue 400 metres wide. This had not been the original intention, and in any case the intention would soon change again. The planning of Canberra was an even more labyrinthine process than the choice of site. In May 1912 King O'Malley, as Minister for Home Affairs, endorsed a majority decision by two out of three judges who had failed to agree upon the winner of a world-wide competition conducted by the Federal Government to select a design for the new capital city. The first prize of £1750 went to a 36-year-old Chicago architect and one-time colleague of Frank Lloyd Wright, Walter Burley Griffin. Griffin's design was well received professionally, but politically it was thought by some to be too extravagant. In response to this criticism, O'Malley referred the design to an interdepartmental board under the chairmanship of Colonel David Miller, permanent head of the Department of Home Affairs and resident administrator of the Federal Capital Territory. This board found no merit in any of the entries, and recommended instead a design of its own inexpert concoction. O'Malley, to his discredit, gave Miller permission to proceed accordingly.

It was this departmental plan which Lord Denman inaugurated on Capital Hill. Griffin – usually a mild though determined man, but now understandably enraged by the change of plan – offered to come to Australia. The Cook Government, which had succeeded Fisher's second ministry only three months after the ceremony on Capital Hill, also

Concordia, Labora, Altruista and Utopia), composite ones (Phambs [the initials of all State capital cities], Bhamps and Meladneyperbane), and White Australian ones (Alba [white], Albinalia, Albania and Aryan City). But the most numerous suggestions were those inspired by the imperial or British connection: Imperialia, New London, Britangleburg, Britalia, Britonia, Britaustral, Georgius, Georgetown, Georgemary, Kingsland, Royalton, Britanspire, Victoria Cross and Empire City.

received strong criticism of the departmental plan from British and Australian architects. Cook suspended the plan and invited Griffin to visit Canberra and confer with the Board. Griffin arrived in August 1913, and was immediately captivated by the site which until then he had known only through a topographical model, cycloramic paintings and contour maps. 'The morning and evening lights at Canberra are wonderful,' he said. 'The shadows of the clouds and the mists as they cross the mountains are very beautiful indeed. It is a grand site for a city . . . Australians do not paint their country as they should. They give it a sombre appearance both in literature and in art, but what I have seen of it is anything but sombre. It is gloriously green. The gum tree instead of being one continual monotony has strongly appealed to me. It is a poet's tree, and ought to have a more dignified name. Gum tree! It does not fit it at all.'

Two months after his arrival, the new Minister for Home Affairs, W. H. Kelly, abolished the departmental board and appointed Griffin as Federal Capital Director of Design and Construction for three years. His design, which was again *the* design, placed the functions of executive government, recreation, civil education and military education along two axes: a land axis, containing government buildings, running from Mt Ainslie in the north to Capital Hill in the south; and a water axis, running from Black Mountain in the west along a series of formal waterways. There was to be a recreational casino near Mt Ainslie, a Capitol for national archives and ceremonies on Capital Hill, a parliament house below Capital Hill, and a university below Black Mountain. The axes would not be thoroughfares, but garden frontages for buildings. There would be a park of pink flora behind the Mt Ainslie casino, a yellow park on Black Mountain to serve as a backdrop for the university, and a white park behind the Capitol. Griffin's design was strongly symmetrical, with a complex system of radial and concentric circular street patterns.

Griffin found the going with Canberra extremely difficult, for Colonel Miller and his allies in the Department of Works had not forgiven him for their humbling in 1913. They found a friend in W. O. Archibald, the Minister for Home Affairs in Fisher's third ministry, and it was not until O'Malley received this portfolio again in 1915 that Griffin was able to prevail against their deliberate obstruction. O'Malley, to his credit this time, supported Griffin in and out of Parliament in what had developed into a vicious feud. In May 1917 O'Malley had this brush in Parliament with his predecessor, Archibald, who for other reasons was not to remain much longer in the Labor Party:

Mr O'Malley [to Archibald]: You left the office in chaos.

Mr Archibald: Show where the chaos was. It may be chaos in the opinion of American bounders; and I must say it is remarkable to see the honourable gentleman eating out of the hands of Yankees, as he is today.

Mr O'Malley: You were a good stagger-juice buster!

Mr Archibald: There is an obvious innuendo behind that interjection. The Minister cannot be a man, and he never has been a man since he came to the Australian continent.

Mr O'Malley: You are not a man; you were born a wombat.

In 1916 Cabinet renewed Griffin's appointment for another three years, and appointed a Royal Commissioner, Wilfred Blacket, to inquire into various matters concerning the Departments of Home Affairs and Works, and Griffin. Blacket came to the conclusion that 'there was in the Department [of Home Affairs] a combination, including Archibald and certain officers, hostile to Griffin and to his design for the Capital City'; 'that necessary information and assistance were withheld from Griffin, and his powers . . . usurped by certain officers'; and that 'Archibald and members of the Department Board endeavoured to set aside [Griffin's] design and to substitute the Board's own design.'

Griffin persevered with his work until his second term of engagement expired in 1919. In this time he issued a final plan of the city and environs, prepared the conditions of a design competition for Parliament House,[4] and began construction of some of the main avenues and the planting of forest reserves and parks. In 1920 Cabinet decided that Griffin was lacking in some of the qualities (including willingness to compromise) which it considered would be required to carry the work forward in a practical and economical way. The Prime Minister, who by that time was W. M. Hughes, informed Griffin that his appointment would not be renewed and that authority would instead be vested in a committee. Griffin declined to serve on this committee. 'The issue which is in fact the essence of the matter,' he wrote in a final letter to Hughes, 'is that the design and construction of the city is not to be vested in the committee, which is to have no executive power, but is to be transferred from me to the Works Department, which has, on the evidence on oath in open court before a Royal Commission . . . been adjudged to have been consistently hostile to myself, my plan and my procedure.'

Griffin's fears for the future of the project were only partly justified. Although his design was modified considerably over the next half-century, sufficient of it remained intact for Walter Burley Griffin to be rightly

---

[4] The completed building was opened on 9 May 1927. It was not until then that the Victorian Parliament was able to return to its building in Melbourne which had housed Federal Parliament since 1901.

acclaimed as the creator of Canberra. One of his planning successors – the Capital Territory Director of Planning (1958–67), Peter Harrison – said in 1975: 'I think it is fair to say that the simple grandeur of Griffin's conception for the central areas of Canberra remains as good an expression of "national capitalism" as anything that has been done this century. It is less pompous and much more human than Brasilia for example. The most remarkable thing about his plan is how, largely through Griffin's own efforts, it impressed itself on Sir Littleton Groom, who as Attorney-General had his street pattern formally gazetted. . . The gazettal had the important proviso that it could not be varied without the variation being tabled in both Houses of Parliament and open to a motion of disallowance. Although Canberra has grown far beyond the 75,000 population provided for in Griffin's plan (it reached 75,000 in 1964, the year the lake was completed), the procedure for variation of the gazettal plan is still followed.'

The Transcontinental Railway

Almost two thousand kilometres away from Canberra, far behind the cliffs of the Great Australian Bight, was another limestone plain – as different from the comely Molonglo valley as a lizard or a scorpion from a fat Merino lamb. Like some huge tabletop raised uniformly above sea level this plain ran flat and hot, unsettled and almost completely waterless, for 560 kilometres in South Australia and Western Australia. One of its earliest explorers had called it the Nullarbor Plain, for there were no trees to be seen from one horizon to the next, only low blue bush and a greenish-brown saltbush. There was water here all right, but nearly all of it was deep beneath the ground. The Nullarbor's limestone was not an occasional picturesque outcrop like Canberra's; it existed everywhere, and was as porous as a sieve. What little rain fell on the Nullarbor kept on falling, or rather seeping, down through the foundations of the plain to form lakes and rivers in vast underground caves. Sometimes after generous rain there would come a short season of grass and flowers, but for the most part life was represented on the Nullarbor only by stunted bush and such expert survivors as the dingo, the bustard and the lizard.

Across this plain, and other regions scarcely more hospitable, the Commonwealth was building the first of its major public works, a 1692-kilometre-long transcontinental railway. One month before the ceremony on Capital Hill, Andrew Fisher had turned a sod of desert soil at Kalgoorlie in Western Australia, and five months before that Lord Denman had performed a similar ceremony at Port Augusta in South Australia. After Lord Denman's turning of the sod, three rockets were fired into the sky to release parachutes containing a Union Jack, an Australian flag and an American flag. This had been the idea of King O'Malley, whose flamboyant presence attracted more attention in Port Augusta than even the Governor-General. 'The fascinated people of Port Augusta would not have been surprised to hear of anything he had done, or intended doing,' reported the *Age*. 'He looked as though he might be about to turn the first sod of a railway to Mars.' Kalgoorlie seemed almost as far away as that. It was one thing to survey the route, which camel teams had done in 1912, dragging heavy chains through the bush to mark the right of way; but quite another to lay the track. Colonel Egerton Warburton, who had visited the Nullarbor in 1860, reported that 'to traverse it would be dangerous; to occupy it impossible.'

Would a railway really be worth such trouble? For the 320,000 people of Western Australia, the answer was certainly yes. Although the Constitution had not mentioned a transcontinental railway, eastern Federalists had assured Western Australia that such a line would be built. 'Federation must at no very distant date result in the connection of east and west by rail,' said Charles Kingston, the former Premier of South Australia, to Sir John Forrest, the Premier of Western Australia who in his youth had taken five months to ride from Perth to Adelaide around the edge of the Bight. 'This would be an Australian work worthy of undertaking by the Federal authority on behalf of the nation.' This sentiment had been embodied in the official policies of every Federal Ministry since 1901, but years of procrastination came first.

The only substantial argument against the Transcontinental Railway was that Commonwealth funds derived from all States should not be used for the almost exclusive benefit of one State, Western Australia. Why should Queensland and Tasmania, even New South Wales and Victoria, help to pay for a railway that would be of little if any economic benefit to them? One good reason was to help hold the Federation together, and another was defence. Australia's first military commandant, General Hutton, had advised the Federal Government that a western rail link would have 'unquestionable value' for defence, and Lord Kitchener had repeated this advice in his memorandum on Australian defence. Most opposition to the proposal came from the Senate in its capacity as guardian of the States' rights against Commonwealth expansion. Labor's control of Parliament ensured the passage of the Kalgoorlie to Port Augusta Railway Act in 1911, but every Senator from Queensland voted against it.

Starting from Kalgoorlie and Port Augusta, construction gangs worked steadily towards the Nullarbor, scraping out the right of way with horse-drawn scoops, and dropping sleepers and rails on to the road-bed from two huge Roberts track-layers which King O'Malley had imported from Chicago. As the track-layers moved ahead of their flat cars and steam engines, another gang followed behind adjusting the fishplates, screwing up bolts and driving 'dogs' into the sleepers to hold the rails in place at a gauge of four feet eight and a half inches (1.4351 m).[5] The longest distance they ever covered in a year was 712 kilometres, and the longest in a single day was 3.66 kilometres. The labour force consisted of 3500 men and 750 horses and camels. Navvies were paid 10s, and later 12s 6d per day; senior camel drivers, £5 5s for a seven-day week. As the track moved out into the desert, supply trains carried the equivalent of whole towns to the railheads. They brought water for the men and animals, and for their own locomotives, whose boiler tubes could no more tolerate the calcium chloride of bore water than human tubes could.

The men lived in tents or rough shanties, and were harried by dust and flies and by extremes of temperature. Thermometer readings of 46 degrees Celsius were not uncommon in summer, and in winter the nights were bitterly cold. Sanitation was haphazard to begin with, and consequently the camps produced more than 120 cases of typhoid fever. Hard liquor was officially banned. The effect of this was not to reduce the consumption of alcohol but merely to raise its price; in some camps whisky sold for £5 a bottle. One of the few diversions after work was the gambling game of two-up. At one Saturday session an expert player named 'Clarence the Sport' won £360 by the judicious selection of heads and tails.

In its five years of construction, at a cost of £5,800,000, the Trans-continental Railway used 140,000 tonnes of rail and 2,500,000 sleepers. About one-third of the rails were manufactured from Australian iron ore, coal and limestone at the Broken Hill Proprietary's new steel works in Newcastle. The sleepers were cut from either jarrah or karri logs, and the relative merits of these Western Australian timbers became one of the railway's two most controversial issues. Jarrah, which grew in privately owned forests, was naturally resistant to white ants and dry rot; karri, an inferior timber in its natural state, was said to be the equal of jarrah after treatment in a mixture of molasses and arsenic. King O'Malley, who had

[5] This gauge had been adopted largely on the recommendation of the engineer-in-chief of the Commonwealth Railways construction branch, Henry Deane, who favoured it over South Australia's five feet three inches (1.6 m) and Western Australia's three feet six inches (1.07 m) because a conference of engineers-in-chief of State railways had chosen it as the future standard rail gauge for Australia.

ministerial responsibility for the railway, ordered karri because the Labor Government in Western Australia wanted to use this timber in new State-owned sawmills. A censure motion in the House of Representatives about the use of karri sleepers led to the establishment of a select committee of inquiry and a Royal Commission, and the Royal Commission presented two reports: one favouring karri, the other jarrah. Both were right, for the two timbers survived the rigours of the Nullarbor Plain equally well. The other controversial issue concerned the railway's labour force. Should the job be done by day labour under control of railway executive staff, as the Labor Government had decided, or should it be let out to private contractors? The Cook Government was expected to call tenders for contract work when it took office in June 1913, but it did not do so, and day labour continued until the end.

The end came on 17 October 1917 near Ooldea on a 479-kilometre stretch of straight line. As the morning passed, the gangs from east and west drew closer and closer until the last rails were laid end to end and the last dogs driven home. The men sang 'Hard Times Come No More' and had the rest of the day off. The engineer in charge sent the following prosaic telegram to his superiors at Port Augusta: 'Rails linked today, Wednesday, 1.45 pm SA Time at 620 miles 58 chains 50.5 links. October 17, 1917.' It was not for engineers to turn historic phrases on such occasions. That privilege belonged to the Federal Treasurer, and Emperor of the West, Sir John Forrest: 'From today east and west are indissolubly joined together by bands of steel, and the result must be increased prosperity and happiness for the Australian people. Improved means of communication will, I believe, create a broader and nobler national life, while closer union will, I feel sure, mean a wider sympathy with our kinsmen in the "old land", and with the British people throughout the world.' One advantage of the Transcontinental Railway was a shortening of the mail time between the Eastern States and Britain by two days.

On 22 October Sir John and Lady Forrest were among the official passengers on the first Transcontinental express to leave Port Augusta for Kalgoorlie. The journey took seventy-two hours, twelve hours of which were spent in delays for one reason or another en route. There had been good rain that winter, and in places the desert ground was covered with wildflowers. When the locomotive stopped to cool its axle-box at the edge of the Nullarbor, many of the passengers stepped down to pick everlasting daisies. 'The everlastings were particularly fine and large, white, pink and yellow,' wrote Lady Forrest. 'We had about half an hour to play about and the scene was very pretty and animated – one great impromptu garden party, everybody rushing about picking flowers or taking snap-shots'.

The Commonwealth Bank

Nothing made the Australian public more aware of Federation than the Commonwealth's own note issue and its own bank. The two might well have been combined in one institution from the beginning, for in 1905 the Federal Labor Party had adopted as one of its objectives 'a Commonwealth Bank of deposit and issue'; but by the time Fisher's second Labor Government established a Commonwealth Bank of Australia in July 1912, it had already placed the note issue in the hands of the Treasury. This temporary separation of powers was lost upon most Australians, to whom the note issue of eight denominations, from ten shillings to £100, and the new bank were both tokens of a growing Commonwealth.

For some years after Federation, Australia had continued to use British coins and bank-notes of great variety issued by a multitude of privately owned banks. At the 1907 Colonial Conference the British Chancellor of the Exchequer, Herbert Asquith, said grandly to the Australian Prime Minister, Alfred Deakin: 'If you like to coin for yourselves we can offer you that.' But the Commonwealth, dismayed by the cost of establishing its own mint, paid the Royal Mint in London to strike four silver denominations for it in 1910. The Treasurer, Sir John Forrest, told Deakin that he thought the reverse side of these coins should carry the words 'Rex Imperator' because they sounded 'more Imperial' than 'King and Emperor'. 'Agree as to sound,' replied Deakin, 'but English gives the sense to all, and it is something to distinguish our coins from those of Canada. For practical purposes, keep to your own tongue.' The Royal Mint seems to have had the last word, however, for when the Commonwealth's first silver coins went into circulation their lettering, on the obverse around King Edward's head, was even more cryptic than Forrest had proposed: 'EDWARDVS VII D:G:BRITT:OMN:REX F:D:IND:IMP'. On the reverse was the Commonwealth's first coat-of-arms, which will be described in a later section of this chapter. The British coins already in circulation continued as legal tender, but thenceforth were withdrawn by the British Government at the rate of £100,000 a year.

There was profit for the Australian Government in issuing its own coins, and greater profit still in the issue of notes. The effect of a note issue was to provide an interest-free loan from the public to the extent of 75 per cent of an issue, for under the Australian Notes Acts of 1910–11 only 25 per cent of the issue had to be backed by gold reserve. The Commonwealth took over Australia's paper currency by imposing a prohibitive tax upon the sixteen varieties of note then in circulation by private banks, thus driving them out of existence, and circulating its own issue in their place. The Treasury overprinted private bank notes ('Fisher's flimsies', as they were called) and put them into circulation until its own notes were printed in 1913. On 1 May 1913 the Governor-General's young daughter, the Honourable Judith Denman, pulled a lever at the King's Warehouse in Melbourne to impress the number 000001 in red ink on the first permanent ten-shilling note. This note, basically blue and rainbowed in lime green and orange, carried on its back a picture of Victoria's Goulburn Weir. The note was not popular because the British half-sovereign was still in circulation, and in any case it was sometimes confused with the £10 note. The Governor-General and his son numbered the next two notes, and the visiting English author Sir Rider Haggard pulled 000004.

The Constitution had given the Commonwealth power not only to issue paper money but also to consolidate the public debts of the States and to make laws on banking. From 1901 onwards, all Federal governments had expressed the intention of exercising one or more of these powers; but it was not until a Labor Government gained control of both Houses of Parliament for the first time, under Fisher's leadership, that both the note issue and the banking powers were exercised. The Labor Party's banking objective of 1905 was defined more fully at the party's Federal Conference in 1908, where King O'Malley spoke with his usual showmanship of a Commonwealth bank which would consolidate the State debts and carry on its deposit business through the nation's post offices. O'Malley's scheme was favourably received, and the conference endorsed the objective of a Commonwealth Bank of issue, deposit, exchange and reserve. King O'Malley also delivered a five-hour banking speech to the House of Representatives in the following year. As he seldom lost an opportunity to talk on this subject, and as he lived to the putative age of ninety-five (his birthday was just as uncertain as his birthplace), it is not surprising that the gilt-spurred Brahmapootra rooster came to be regarded by many Australians as founder of the Commonwealth Bank. This honour was not deserved. The heroic battle for the bank which O'Malley was later said to have fought in Caucus against opposition from Fisher and Hughes never really took place. The motion to establish the bank was introduced into Caucus as a Cabinet recommendation by Fisher himself.[6]

---

[6] In a paper entitled *King O'Malley: Founder or Fraud?*, Robin Gollan of the Department of History, Institute of Advanced Studies, Australian National University, came to the following conclusion: 'O'Malley was clearly not the founder of the Commonwealth Bank. On the other hand by his advocacy within the labour movement he popularized the idea of a bank. In a negative sense he did something to shape the bank established by Fisher, because Fisher was at pains to establish a conservative type of bank which would allay the fears of the business community aroused by O'Malley's advocacy.'

The Commonwealth Bank was established as a savings and trading bank in competition with the existing private banks. Its first Governor, appointed by the Government and responsible to Parliament as his board of directors, was Denison (later Sir Denison) Miller, a middle-aged Australian-born banker who had been assistant to the general manager of the Bank of New South Wales. Miller's name had been suggested to Fisher by the chairman of the Associated Banks in Victoria, C. W. Wren, after the governorship had been offered to and declined by the general managers of two private banks. The Commonwealth Bank opened for savings business in July 1912, with agencies at money order post offices, and for general banking in January 1913. Fisher and Miller set the foundation stones for a head office building at the corner of Pitt and Moore Streets (later to become Martin Place), Sydney, in May 1913, and a London office opened for savings and general business in the same year. The new Treasurer, Sir John Forrest, was worried that English banks might resent intrusion. Miller assured him, however, that 'there is no fear of anything the Commonwealth Bank does in London looking like competition with the London banks and great financial institutions, as they are working in perfect harmony with one another.'[7]

This was more than could be said of the Commonwealth Bank's relationship with Australia's private banks and State savings banks, to all of which it was an active competitor. It was not, however, the central bank which O'Malley had argued ought to be 'a financial reservoir of indestructible power', controlling the note issue, holding the gold reserves of all other banks, and sustaining credit in time of economic crisis by rediscounting those banks' securities. Instead, the Commonwealth Bank of Australia began life as what a leading member of the Opposition called 'O'Malley pasteurised': a trading bank which differed from its competitors only in acting as banker to the Federal Government, in being supported by Government guarantee instead of by shareholders, and in operating a

---

[7] To avoid any appearance of unseemly competition, there was no official opening of the London office. The Australian presence in London asserted itself lustily on 24 July 1913, however, when George V laid a foundation stone for a building over which, in the words of the High Commissioner, Sir George Reid, 'the flag of the Southern Cross and the Union Jack would fly proudly.' At the conclusion of this ceremony, reported the *Daily Express*, the Australians present 'burst into their strange echoing cooees.' At Reid's suggestion, the pompous new structure between the Strand and the Aldwych was called Australia House. The permanent head of the Department of External Affairs, Atlee Hunt, summed it up well in a letter to the Australian secretary in London, Captain Muirhead Collins: 'I cannot tell you how disappointed I am with the plans of the London offices. The architects don't seem to me to have risen to the occasion at all. Everything internal seems to have been sacrificed to an attempt at grandeur which in my judgment might have been equally well achieved without the sacrifice of utility . . . It is all taken up with that great doorway and wall at the eastern end . . . Perhaps the secret of the whole thing is the desire of the Australian artists to have a big space on which to erect their masses of sculpture.'

savings bank department. Sir Denison Miller once said that he would like to see the Commonwealth Bank become 'like the Bank of England.' He lived to see it take over control of the note issue in 1920, but its final transformation into a central bank did not take place until 1945.

Territories

For such an earnest advocate of Empire, the Commonwealth of Australia was slow to take up its own colonial responsibilities. The Australian colonies had persuaded Britain, against her better judgment, to annexe southeastern New Guinea as a buffer against the German colony in that island; and after Federation the Commonwealth had argued strongly, but without avail, for British annexation of the New Hebrides to forestall any possible threat from France. Yet the Commonwealth was in no hurry to shoulder two inherited burdens: the former colony of British New Guinea, which Britain unloaded upon Australia as soon as she could, and the Northern Territory of South Australia.

At the time of Federation the Australian Empire consisted only of three distant and tiny possessions – Norfolk Island, 1440 kilometres east of Brisbane, and administered by the Governor of New South Wales; Lord Howe Island, 560 kilometres east of Port Macquarie, but included within the boundaries of New South Wales by a statute of 1855; and Macquarie Island, a rocky, storm-swept dependency of Tasmania 1440 kilometres southeast of that island State.[8] This Lilliputian empire was enlarged considerably in March 1902 by the Commonwealth's acceptance of responsibility for British New Guinea. The Commonwealth could hardly have done otherwise, for Britain had not wanted this primitive and unprofitable colony in the first place; but another four years were to pass before Commonwealth legislation was proclaimed under which Australia could take practical charge of the colony, which was renamed Papua. During this interregnum, Australia provided £20,000 per year to meet the cost of administration, but the task of administering the colony, insofar as it was administered at all, remained in the hands of the British New Guinea service, a motley staff of about fifty men. In 1903 the Lieutenant-Governor, Sir George Le Hunte, departed from Port Moresby for a more salubrious vice-regal post in Adelaide. His successor, as Acting Administrator, committed suicide; and *his* successor – an English former resident magistrate, Captain F. R. Barton – took office in 1904. Barton was

[8] In 1913 Norfolk Island was surrendered by NSW and accepted by the Commonwealth. The other two islands are still administered by NSW and Tasmania respectively.

strongly influenced by the Colony's drunken but formidable Treasurer, David Ballantine, and was closely observed in all his official shortcomings by the new Chief Judicial Officer, the Australian-born Hubert Murray.

Murray, whose brother Gilbert was Regius Professor of Greek at Oxford, had accepted his judicial post at Port Moresby to escape the tedium of an unsuccessful legal career in Sydney. It was to Murray that the Prime Minister of Australia, Alfred Deakin, appealed for an objective assessment of the situation in Port Moresby when he was considering what course the Commonwealth should take there. Murray's reply, sixty hand-written foolscap pages, was far from objective; but it undoubtedly helped to clarify Deakin's attitude. There were two factions in the snarling, back-biting little community of Port Moresby. 'One, the Colonial Office men, thought that destiny was fulfilled if British New Guinea never became more than a glorified curiosity shop and an extensive and expensive ethnological museum,' wrote Murray. The other party welcomed Australian sentiment and development, and disliked the 'policy of retard'. The Colonial Office group was hostile to white settlement; the Australians would have welcomed it, and Murray agreed with them.

Not surprisingly, the Federal Government appointed a Royal Commission 'into the present conditions, including the method of government, of the Territory of Papua, and the best means for their improvement.' The Papua Act introduced in 1903 was not enacted until November 1905, and not proclaimed until September 1906. In that month a three-man Royal Commission arrived in Port Moresby to begin its inquiry. Murray's evidence had the effects of advocating a policy of dual responsibility (responsibility to the native inhabitants, but responsibility also to European settlers), and of damning Captain Barton and the rest of the British faction for neglecting the second of these. The Commission's report in 1907 might almost have been written by Judge Murray. It said that 'the hour [had] struck for the commencement of a vigorous forward policy' as far as white settlement was concerned, and that the Administrator should 'put behind him most of the late Crown Colony traditions.' It could not 'in justice to the Commonwealth or to Papua, recommend [Captain Barton's] permanent retention in his present office.' The Government decided that Barton should take twelve months' leave and then retire (he later became First Minister of Zanzibar), and that in the meantime Murray should act as Administrator. Deakin assured Murray that when the time came to appoint a permanent Lieutenant-Governor the post would be his – and so it came to pass, in November 1908. Under Sir Hubert Murray's sternly paternal hand for the next thirty-one years the Territory of Papua made steady but painfully slow progress within the limits of the meagre resources available to it. The Commonwealth paid little, and cared even less.

In 1911 another territory, the Northern Territory of South Australia, came under the direct control of the Federal Government. This area of 1,356,124 square kilometres – about 17 per cent of the entire continent, extending from the Simpson Desert and Alice Springs north to Arnhem Land and the town of Palmerston on the shore of the Timor Sea – had become part of the Commonwealth of Australia in 1901 'by the name of the State of South Australia.' South Australia, finding the sprawling territory little more than a costly burden despite its gold and pastoral industries, took advantage of Section 122 of the Commonwealth Constitution, which provided that Federal Parliament could make laws for the government of any territory surrendered by any State and accepted by the Commonwealth. South Australia passed a Northern Territory Surrender Act in 1907, but the Federal Parliament did not pass a complementary Northern Territory Acceptance Act and a Northern Territory (Administration) Act until 1910. The formal transfer took place on 1 January 1911, the same day as the Commonwealth received the Federal Capital Territory from New South Wales. The Commonwealth agreed to purchase an existing railway from Port Augusta to Oodnadatta, and to complete this line through Central Australia to Pine Creek, the end of a line which ran 233 kilometres south from Palmerston.[9] The name of Palmerston was changed to Darwin (Palmerston's harbour had been named Port Darwin by its discoverer, the captain of HMS *Beagle*, in honour of his passenger on an earlier cruise, the naturalist Charles Darwin); and the Professor of Veterinary Pathology at the University of Melbourne, Dr John Gilruth, was appointed Administrator of the Territory.

The year 1911 was a turning point in Australia's official treatment of its Aborigines – not merely because the Commonwealth, in accepting the Northern Territory, had for the first time acquired some responsibility for Aboriginal welfare, but also because public opinion was at last pressing for better treatment of the country's Aborigines. The Constitution had reserved to the States the right to make laws affecting their own Aborigines, but now that the Commonwealth also had Aborigines to think about (an estimated 20,000 full-bloods and several hundred half-castes in the Northern Territory) the question arose as to whether it should assume wider responsibilities in that field. In 1911 a Melbourne conference of members of the Australia and New Zealand Association for the Advance-

[9] All the Commonwealth ever did towards completing this line was to extend the northern spur 242 kilometres further south to Larrimah, and extend the southern line from Oodnadatta to Alice Springs.

ment of Science, members of the Linnean Society, church leaders and politicians recommended that the Commonwealth should establish new Aboriginal reserves and set up a Government department to deal with Aboriginal affairs. By that time every State except Tasmania (which had solved its Aboriginal problem in the bluntest conceivable way) had enacted legislation to protect and restrict Aborigines. South Australia, for example, passed a Northern Territory Aboriginals Act in preparation for the transfer to the Commonwealth. This Act, later incorporated in a Commonwealth Aboriginals Ordinance gazetted in 1912, established an Aboriginal Department under a Chief Protector and made provision for the declaration of reserves. The Chief Protector could take any Aboriginal or half-caste into his custody, and his staff and the police were empowered to make arrests without warrant for breaches of the Ordinance. Marriage between Aborigines and non-Aborigines could take place only with permission from the Minister for External Affairs.

That such Draconian regulations as these should have represented a turning point for the better was a measure of the harshness with which Australia had been accustomed to treat its Aborigines. The transcript of evidence before a 1905 Western Australian Royal Commission on the condition of Aborigines gave a vivid impression of the cruelty and degradation which were endemic at that time in northern Australia. Octavius Burt, the Comptroller-General of Prisons, was asked about the use of neck chains in Western Australian prisons:

> Are neck chains used in prisons? – Yes.
> Are these chains used continuously during the whole length of the sentence? – Yes.
> Kindly let us know what is your authority for the use of them? – There is no legal authority. I can only say it is one of those things so universally adopted that it is never questioned. The practice has been in vogue for about 30 years or more I believe.
> Are neck chains ever used for Europeans? – Not that I know of.

The weights of these chains were recorded as follows: 'Roebourne gaol, from 2 lbs 12 oz to 5 lbs 14 oz; Broome, 2 lbs 2 oz; Wyndham, 5 lbs 4 oz with Yale lock and everything complete.' Another witness, a stockman named Matthew Langtree from the Ord River, was asked about the treatment of Aborigines on cattle and sheep stations:

> Do any of the drovers and carriers take women away with them from this place? – Yes; they do.
> With the knowledge of the telegraph master? – Yes.
> What is the reason for taking these girls? – To help get wood and water, and other reasons best guessed.

187

Having knocked about the country as you have, what is your opinion as to alleged cruelty of station managers to blacks? – As regards the Fitzroy district, I consider that it is a disgrace. From what I have seen there, in the majority of cases women are employed. The 'boss' has his own fancy woman, and the overseer has from eight to ten to choose from. I have seen not one but several whipped at night for allowing sheep to wander or because they did not muster the sheep in the paddocks. I saw this at the Quanbung Station.

What is the name of the manager there? – Rose.

Has he got a fancy woman? – Yes.

What is her name? – I think it is Judy.

Where are the husbands of these women? – In the majority of cases there are no native men there.

What has become of them? – They may have been shot down years ago.

Even the most sympathetically disposed Australians were influenced in their approach to Aborigines by the kind of racism which existed quite respectably side by side with patriotism and imperialism. To be proud of one's country was to be proud of one's race; and if the Anglo-Saxons stood at the top of the racial scale, as most Australians believed, a people so dissimilar as the Aborigines must surely be at the very bottom – even lower than Asiatics.

At a ceremony of transfer outside the Administrator's residency on 2 January 1911, the white citizens of Darwin prevented the use of a Commonwealth flag which had been made by a local firm of Chinese tailors. Here was a grotesque example of what C. E. W. Bean referred to as 'the Eastern Question.' 'The Eastern Question has been in the world long enough in all conscience,' he wrote, 'that men should not dismiss it off hand in two words as 'colour prejudice'. If so, it has been a prejudice over which I suppose more men have fought and died than in any known cause. It has torn the east from the west since before the birth of history. . . This antipathy of the Australian to his coloured neighbours is not merely similar to the Eastern Question. It is the Eastern Question. The Australian is fighting the coloured nations of the East today in the same cause in which Themistocles fought with Xerxes, Pompey with Mithridates, Richard of the Lion Heart with the Saracens, and Charles Martel with the Moors.'

No one illustrated this kind of racism better than Professor W. Baldwin Spencer, the Melbourne biologist and anthropologist who had studied the tribes of Central Australia in 1901, and who in 1912 became Chief Protector of Aboriginals in the Northern Territory. Spencer almost certainly possessed more understanding of the Aborigines' spiritual life than any other Australian of his time. He respected that part of their culture, yet he was also capable of writing about the Aborigines as if they were sub-human. In a Federal Handbook prepared for the 1914 meeting of the British Association for the Advancement of Science, held in Australia, he wrote: 'It is probable that, with the exception of one or two isolated groups, [the Aborigines] represent the most backward race extant and, in many respects, reveal to us the conditions under which the early ancestors of the present human races existed.' Soon after his arrival in Darwin he tried unsuccessfully to secure the release from gaol of a young Aboriginal who had been sentenced to life imprisonment for murdering another Aboriginal at the instigation of a white man. 'If I can get him off I shall take him as my own "boy",' he wrote. 'He is a fine fellow and I should like to have him with me when I go up country. . . His physique is splendid and when once you get a native like this he will do anything for you. It is just like having a splendid watch dog.'

On Empire Day Spencer accompanied the Administrator and his wife to a bizarre ceremony in a flag-bedecked tent at which Mrs Gilruth distributed annual blankets to the natives. 'It was quite interesting,' he wrote, 'and she much enjoyed it but of course the natives were all clothed or partly so. Each of them got a blanket, stick of tobacco and box of matches. . . I was much amused after it was over when one old man came along trailing his blanket in the dust in the middle of the road. When we asked him what he was doing it for he said "Me been plenty make him thick fellow." The blankets certainly were rather on the thin side but the idea of thickening them with dust was rather original.'

Much of the Chief Protector's attention was occupied by the iniquity, as he saw it, of the Territory's 1500 Orientals (mainly Chinese) and by the racial affront of its 300 half-castes. 'The Chinese are a great curse here,' he wrote after a visit to Darwin's Chinatown. 'They get hold of the natives and give them opium and sundry vile concoctions that they call whisky. We are going to make it a penal offence for a Chinese to have a native on his premises. It will be a considerable surprise to the heathen Chinee and to the natives.'

The Territory's half-castes were usually the children of an Aboriginal mother and a European, Chinese, Japanese or Malay father. 'One thing is certain,' wrote the Chief Protector in his annual report, 'and that is that the white population as a whole will never mix with half-castes. . . No half-caste children should be allowed to remain in any native camp, but they should all be withdrawn and placed on stations. So far as practicable, this plan is now being adopted. In some cases, when the child is very young, it must of necessity be accompanied by its mother, and in other cases, even though it may seem cruel to separate the mother and child, it is better to do so, when the mother is living, as is usually the case, in a native camp.' At the end of his 12-month term of appointment, Professor Spencer returned to his Chair at the University of Melbourne. It is doubtful that he was greatly missed by either the Aborigines, the half-castes or the heathen Chinee.

Symbols

In retrospect the Commonwealth's choice of symbols with which to identify itself seems to have been obvious, indeed almost inevitable. For a national flag, how could anyone have ignored the Union Jack and the Southern Cross? The Union Jack went without saying, of course, and the Southern Cross peculiar to antipodean skies had already been incorporated in the Victorian colonial badge and in the only two 19th century Australian flags of any note: the blue silk banner hoisted by insurgent miners at Eureka Stockade, and the white ensign of the Federation movement. When a competition was held for a Commonwealth flag in 1901 the majority of the 30,000 entries included the Southern Cross, and the prize had to be divided among no fewer than five competitors with the same design.[10]

On 3 September the winning flag was flown for the first time from the Exhibition Building in Melbourne. It was a blue ensign with the Union Jack in the top left quarter; a large six-pointed white star below the centre of the cross of St George in the Union Jack, representing the six States of the Commonwealth; and in the fly five stars of nine, eight, seven, six and five points respectively, representing the Southern Cross. Before being officially gazetted in February 1903, the flag was altered slightly for the sake of neatness: four of the Southern Cross stars were given seven points and the fifth star five. The only other change ever made was in 1908 when, at the Deakin Government's request, the King agreed that a seventh point should be added to the large Commonwealth star, thus bringing it into conformity with a similar star on the Commonwealth's recently acquired coat-of-arms. The seventh point was to represent the Territory of Papua and any other territories which the Commonwealth might acquire in future.

In conjunction with the flag competition, designs had also been called for the great seal of the Commonwealth of Australia with which,

[10] The winners were Mrs A. Dorrington of Perth, E. J. Nuttall of Melbourne, Leslie Hawkins of Sydney, Ivor Evans of Melbourne, and William Stevens of Auckland, New Zealand.

according to his letters patent, the Governor-General was required to seal all public instruments in the Sovereign's name. The winners of this competition were two well-known magazine artists: D. H. Souter (whose design of Kipling's Young Queen on horseback was chosen for the obverse) and Blamire Young (the arms of Great Britain and Ireland surrounded by the badges of the Australian States and surmounted by the royal crown). At the Colonial Office's suggestion, however, it was decided that impressing a single design upon documents would be more convenient than attaching a two-sided wax seal. Young's design was chosen for this purpose, but was modified on heraldic advice from Britain and in accordance with a request by South Australia that it should be represented by a piping shrike (a black-backed magpie) rather than by its previous badge which showed, improbably, the robed figure of Britannia giving succour to an Aboriginal. The other State badges, arranged from right to left alternately, in order of State population at the time of federation, were lion, stars and cross of St George (NSW), southern cross and crown (Victoria), moline cross and crown (Queensland), black swan dexter (W.A.) and lion passant (Tasmania).

Until this seal arrived from England, Lord Hopetoun and Lord Tennyson used their personal seals. The modified Blamire Young seal arrived in 1904, and remained in use for many years with only minor changes to its design. In 1936 the South Australian device was altered a second time to a rising sun, taken from the State's new coat of arms; the moline cross by which Queensland had been incorrectly represented was altered to the State's official badge, a Maltese cross; and, more esoteric still, the Western Australian swan, which had been swimming incorrectly to the viewer's left, became 'naiant to the sinister', or swimming to the badge's left and viewer's right. In 1973 a great seal of completely new design came into use. It bore the Australian coat of arms (to be described later in this chapter), and around its edge, in place of the longer and more obscure royal styles and titles previously in use, were the words 'Elizabeth The Second Queen of Australia.'

Another design competition was held in 1911 for the Commonwealth's first postage stamp. Commonwealth postcards had already appeared in April 1911 bearing a printed stamp with a portrait of George V between two Ionic columns, but the first adhesive stamp was not issued until 1912. The competition was won by Herman Altmann of St Kilda (George V, flanked by kangaroo and emu beneath the six State badges), but a Labor Government which took office in October 1911 was not satisfied with this. The new Postmaster-General, C. W. Frazer, asked Blamire Young to prepare some deisgns which were typically Australian in character. Mr

The *Sydney Mail*'s verdict on Australia's first postage stamp.
Miss Australia: 'It's awful; I am utterly disgusted with it'.

Frazer's ideas of art and nationalism were primitive to say the least. 'If a picturesque stamp can be provided in which an outline of Australia is a feature,' he told the artist, 'I am certainly favourably inclined towards it.'

All of Blamire Young's submissions are believed to have shown scenes within an outline of the Australian continent, but none came up to Mr Frazer's expectations. One of them, showing two kangaroos inside the map, did resemble an earlier departmental design with only one kangaroo. Out of this combination emerged an anonymous, presumably departmental design which siatsfied Mr Fraser, but hardly anyone else. It showed a single red kangaroo and a tuft of grass inside the map of Australia, with the words *Australia* and *Postage* above and *One Penny* below. When proofs were made public in April 1912, the *Argus* affected to mistake the tuft of grass for a rabbit. 'The public will doubtless be gratified to learn,' it said, 'that Mr Frazer is not depressed by the chorus of derision with which his new postage stamp has been greeted. Why, indeed, should he be depressed? It is no new thing for a great and original work of art to be received with scorn on its first appearance. . . It is decidedly unpleasant to be reminded every time we attach a stamp to a letter that Australia is represented all over the world by a grotesque artistic ineptitude.' Mr Frazer was not entirely impervious to criticism. He ordered that the tuft of grass be removed.

In the search for philatelic and heraldic symbols, it was difficult to ignore the continent's two largest and most dignified faunal species (except, of course, for the entirely inappropriate saltwater crocodile): the kangaroo and emu. Their claims in this regard had been recognised as early as 1805, when a settler at Richmond, NSW, John Bowman, celebrated Britain's victory at Trafalgar by flying a white satin banner emblazoned with a shield of rose, thistle and shamrock supported by a dexter emu and sinister kangaroo. The emu and kangaroo had appeared on a £1 note issued by the Bank of New South Wales during the 1830s, and on various other bank-notes later in the 19th century.

The only alternative means of support was the British lion, and that was indeed a strong possibility. The Commonwealth might have chosen the lion and kangaroo had these two supporters not been appropriated by New South Wales in the arms granted to it in 1906. The New South Wales Government had originally wanted the emu and kangaroo, but was deterred by the knowledge that a former Governor of both New South Wales and Cape Colony, Lord Rosmead, had earlier been granted the ostrich (armorially indistinguishable from the emu) and kangaroo. The Commonwealth, when it began thinking about a coat of arms in the same year, had no such qualms. After preliminary discussions with the College of Arms, the Commonwealth secretary in London, Captain Collins, asked the College to prepare a tentative design which the Prime Minister, Alfred Deakin, could inspect while attending the Colonial Conference in 1907. The College's design was later modified at the Government's request by a Melbourne heraldry enthusiast, E. Wilson Dobbs. The Garter King of Arms in turn altered the Dobbs version, and in 1908 Deakin asked the Governor-General to ask the Secretary of State for Colonies to ask the College of Arms to make still more changes.

The finished article was to have, dexter (on the viewer's left), a kangaroo and, sinister, an emu, each holding, with two paws and one claw, a red, white and blue shield containing the cross of St George, five silver stars representing the Southern Cross, and six chevron escutcheons representing the States, though not carrying the State badges. Above the shield was a seven-pointed gold star on a blue and white wreath, and beneath it a compartment of grass and a scroll bearing the motto *Advance Australia*. In his letter to the Governor-General, Deakin explained that the colours of the shield had been chosen 'to preserve the traditional red, white and blue of the British flag.' This coat of arms was granted to the Commonwealth by royal warrant on 7 May 1908.

If this was the best that the College of Arms could do, it was not good enough. Apart from the supporters, it had little Australian character, and even the supporters' posture seemed unnatural. According to some complaints after the arms made their first appearance on Commonwealth stationery, the kangaroo's tail had an ungainly twist and the emu's right leg was raised as if the shield was a football and the bird was about to kick for goal. In 1911 the Fisher Government sent a brand-new design to the Colonial Office for the King's approval. At the Commonwealth's request the NSW Government Printer – Mr W. A. Gullick, another amateur king of arms and author of *Arms of New South Wales* – had prepared four designs. One of these, which Gullick strongly recommended, used lion and kangaroo as supporters of a shield containing five stars inside a Union Jack. In another, which he did not single out for praise, the lion and kangaroo supported a shield containing the six State badges.

The design sent to London consisted of this badge-bearing shield supported by kangaroo and emu in more naturalistic stance. The kangaroo's tail was flat, and the emu stood with both feet firmly on the ground. Fisher personally disliked the existing motto (he used to say that Australia *had* advanced), and in the amended version it was abbreviated to *Australia*. Two sprays of wattle were substituted for the grass upon which the supporters stood, and the wreath beneath the seven-pointed star became blue and gold. The Federal Government accepted advice from the College of Arms that the shield should be placed within an ermine bordure, thus uniting the separate badges in a single heraldic device; but otherwise it insisted upon having the coat of arms it wanted. The arms were granted by a second royal warrant on 19 September 1912. There was some heraldic carping about the new design, but to most latter-day observers it seemed a distinct improvement over its red, white and blue predecessor.

10

HIS EXCELLENCY

IN THE CONVENTIONAL FORMS of official correspondence, the Prime Minister of Australia was the Governor-General's most obedient servant. Barton used to present his humble duty to His Excellency, and even Fisher signed himself as having 'the honour to be, My Lord, Your Excellency's most obedient servant.' There was constitutional excuse for this courtly self-abasement, for on the face of it His Excellency, usually an earl or a baron, could command both honour and obedience. Under the Constitution, this representative of the British Sovereign in the Commonwealth had power to summon or prorogue meetings of Parliament, and to dissolve either the House of Representatives or the House and Senate simultaneously; to appoint and dismiss Prime Ministers;[1] to give or withhold the Royal Assent without which a bill passed by parliament could not become law, to recommend the amendment of such bills, and when in doubt to reserve bills for the Sovereign's pleasure. The letters patent constituting his office empowered the Governor-General to remove or suspend any Commonwealth officer, and 'instructions passed under the Royal Sign Manual and Signet' required him to send back to the Sovereign, with explanatory notes, copies of all Australian legislation. The Governor-General was in effect Australia's own constitutional monarch; but as in any constitutional monarchy, his power was far from absolute. Legally he could exercise his powers to summon, prorogue and dissolve Parliament at his own discretion; by convention, however, he almost always exercised them on the advice of his Prime Minister. When he did act on his own initiative he had to act carefully, for he could offend Parliament only at his own peril.

Take, for example, the case of a Prime Minister unable to govern because a minority group on which he depended had withdrawn its support. He would probably advise the Governor-General to dissolve one or both Houses of Parliament in the hope of regaining a workable majority at the ensuing election. His Excellency would not be bound to accept this advice, but would certainly need to be sure of his own political judgment

[1] For Sir John Kerr's exercise of the power of dismissal, see afterword.

in ignoring it. He could instead dismiss the Prime Minister and appoint another in his place. If the new Prime Minister commanded sufficient support in the lower House, the Governor-General would be seen to have acted wisely; if not, a hostile House of Representatives would show its displeasure by passing a vote of no confidence in the Government or failing to pass a money bill. The Governor-General would probably then be obliged to look for a third Prime Minister (perhaps even the first one again), or to grant the second Prime Minister a double dissolution. His authority might well be diminished in the eyes of Parliament, and – horror of horrors for all Governors-General – his 'most obedient, humble servant', the Secretary of State for Colonies, would probably ask him for an explanation.[2]

In his exercise of Assent, Amendment and Reserve powers, the Governor-General also needed sound political judgment. By giving Assent on the Sovereign's behalf to a Bill which adversely affected Britain's interests, he would incur the displeasure of Whitehall (although in theory the mistake could still be rectified, for the Constitution empowered the Sovereign to disallow any Australian law within one year from the Governor-General's Assent), and by withholding Assent from such a Bill he ran the risk of causing a Prime Minister to tender his resignation on the embarrassing issue of imperial interference in Commonwealth affairs. In his dealings with two obedient servants, one of whom was really his master, and the other of whom could sometimes turn master, the Governor-General was a prime embodiment of the two loyalties which characterized the Australian-British relationship. These imperial and national loyalties were no more mutually exclusive in a bemedalled vice-regal breast than in the average Australian; they existed side by side, but could make life rather difficult at times.

One writer has described the Governor-General's two roles as those of local constitutional monarch and imperial diplomat.[3] In his first capacity, the Governor-General symbolized the executive power of the

---

[2] The third Governor-General of the Commonwealth, Lord Northcote, refused a dissolution of the House of Representatives to the Labor Prime Minister, J. C. Watson, in August 1904. Parliament was then only eight months old. Labor had 24 seats, Free Trade 24, and Protectionists 27. Northcote commissioned Reid (Free Trade) to form a ministry, but in June 1905 Reid was also obliged to ask for a dissolution. Northcote again refused, and commissioned Deakin (Protectionist) to form a ministry. In June 1909 Northcote's successor, Lord Dudley, refused to grant Labor a dissolution of the House of Representatives. Labor then held 27 seats, Free Trade 32, and Protectionists 15. Dudley commissioned Deakin to form a Protectionist-Free Trade coalition ministry, but at the next election, in April 1910, the Deakin-Cook coalition was defeated and Fisher's Labor ministry was returned to office.

[3] C. Cunneen, *The Role Of The Governor-General In Australia 1901–1927*, Ph.D. thesis, Australian National University.

Commonwealth on behalf of the Sovereign, in whom that power was vested by the Constitution. He performed rituals, signed documents and was sometimes required to make difficult decisions which kept the machinery of government in motion. His presence was also a comforting reminder of Australia's membership in the British Empire. In his second capacity the Governor-General guarded imperial interests in Australia. He thus owed loyalty to his Secretary of State at home, and to his ministers in Melbourne who relied upon him to present their viewpoints sympathetically in London. As long as His Excellency was adequately endowed with experience and wisdom, the institution worked satisfactorily. But not all Governors-General possessed these qualities.

The six vice-regal incumbents during the first two decades of Federation were of two kinds: those who had been politicians, and those who had not. Two of them with long experience in the House of Commons – Lord Northcote (Governor-General, 1904–1908) and Sir Ronald Munro-Ferguson (1914–20) – were far and away the most successful appointments from both the British and Australian points of view. The other four owed their appointments largely to Whitehall's belief that private wealth was a desirable qualification for vice-regal service, and that aristocratic birth was a guarantee of political acumen and impartiality. Lord Tennyson (1903–4) was a moderately successful stopgap; Lord Hopetoun (1901–3), for all his personal popularity, was a tragic failure; and under Lord Dudley (1908–11) and Lord Denman (1911–14), for various reasons, the position of Governor-General suffered what the Colonial Office could only describe as 'an extraordinary deterioration.'

Although the Commonwealth Government was consulted about the selection of the Governor-General, the final choice was made by the Sovereign on the advice of British ministers. The first choice, as we have seen already, was the fragile but endearing 7th Earl of Hopetoun, who got off to a bad start by asking the wrong man (Sir William Lyne) to form the Commonwealth's first ministry, and then having to send for the right one (Edmund Barton). This was not his only mistake, for in Lord Hopetoun's case blue blood was no guarantee of either acumen or impartiality. His second blunder was to give the appearance early in 1902 of siding with the Barton ministry on the politically divisive issue of whether or not Australia should send another military contingent to the war in South Africa. The Government was inclined to wait in case reinforcements proved to be unnecessary, and Lord Hopetoun agreed. 'We were not of the opinion that the moment was a favourable one to ask the Australian people to make further sacrifices unless we had the assurance of the Imperial Government that such sacrifices were necessary and desirable,' he said at the annual luncheon of the Australian Natives' Association. 'We may have been right, we may have been wrong, in taking up this position. We believed we were right, we still believe we were right.' At the earliest opportunity the Leader of the Opposition, George Reid, who had been present at the luncheon, submitted a motion to Parliament rebuking the Governor-General for justifying the conduct of ministers and for expressing his own opinion about their delay in offering a Commonwealth contingent. 'I am bound to consider,' wrote the contrite Governor-General, when reporting the matter to the Colonial Office, 'that I have been guilty of an error of judgment.'

His greatest error, however, was in failing to appreciate how low Australia's threshold of tolerance was for vice-regal expenditure. Australians expected the Governor-General to keep up appearances, with even a certain amount of splendour; but they did not relish the spending of public money for such a purpose. The Governor-General's salary was fixed by the Constitution at £10,000 per annum. This was the same as the Governor-General of Canada received; but whereas Canada also provided a generous travelling and entertaining allowance (in 1900–1, £17,137 on top of the basic £10,000), the Australian Constitution provided for salary alone. It was clear to the Prime Minister that some further provision should be made, not only because of the strain imposed upon the vice-regal purse by the inaugural celebrations of 1901, but also to meet the continuing cost of maintaining two Government Houses – one in Melbourne, and one in Sydney. In March 1901 Barton promised the Governor-General that he would ask Parliament for another £8000 per annum. Had he been able to make this request during the euphoric inaugural months, it might have been granted. Instead he allowed fifteen months to pass before putting the matter to Parliament. By that time the cheering had long since died away, and the champagne was flat and sour. Parliament reimbursed the Governor-General for expenses connected with the visit by the Duke and Duchess of Cornwall and York for the opening of Parliament, but that was all. His Excellency – believing that he was required to conduct himself with almost the same pomp as an Indian viceroy, entertaining lavishly and maintaining the costly equipage of carriages, horses, postilions and outriders which he had brought with him from Britain – had already spent £15,000 of his own money over and above the official salary and reimbursement by Parliament. He was rich enough to stand such a loss, but he naturally resented it, and was dismayed at the prospect of continuing in office without permanent allowance. 'No allowance whatever will be given,' he cabled to the Colonial Office on 5 May 1902. 'On a salary of £10,000 per annum I am expected to pay a staff, visit various States, paying all travelling expenses excepting railway, occupy two great Government Houses, paying lights, fuel, stationery, telegrams, postage other than official, dispense hospitality, maintain dignity of office. . . The position is impossible. After grave consideration I think you had better recall me after the Coronation [of Edward VII].'

On the following day Lord and Lady Hopetoun arrived at Government House, Adelaide, to spend a week with the Tennysons. As senior State Governor, the gruff Lord Tennyson held a dormant commission to administer the Government of the Commonwealth during any absence by the Governor-General, and on 9 May he learned from Lord Hopetoun that this commission would soon become active. 'Hopetoun tells me that he has resigned,' he recorded in his diary, 'and that if he had been in Australia the last three years as I have been, he would not have attempted to do several things that he has done – and that I knew more about Australia as it is than he did. An astonishing confession!' On the day the Hopetouns returned to Melbourne, Lord Tennyson wrote to the Secretary of State for Colonies, Joseph Chamberlain. He did not hesitate, in this and in subsequent letters, to dwell upon Lord Hopetoun's failings and parade his own qualifications. 'May I earnestly report to you,' he wrote to Chamberlain, 'that, if Lord Hopetoun resigns, my government and other governments hope that someone who has had political experience and is well-versed in public affairs may be sent out to take the helm as soon as possible. I consider it my duty to write this to you, for the position of affairs is grave and ministers of the various States are of opinion that the outlook especially in the financial world is very serious. . . The Commonwealth do not want their Governor-General to keep up a great deal of State.'

This last assertion came rather strangely from a man who only three months before had written to Lord Hopetoun suggesting that 'on Coronation Day you should hold a small but magnificent "durbah" which might be repeated every year if found successful.' The extravagance in which Lord Tennyson had thus attempted to encourage Lord Hopetoun was something of a household joke at Government House in Adelaide. Writing to her mother in England, Lady Tennyson recounted a conversation between her six-year-old son Harold and Lord Tennyson's private secretary, Lord Richard Plantagenet Nevill. 'Harold was very funny the other morning,' she wrote. 'He came in saying when we were at breakfast – "Oh, Collins (the staff clerk, a delightful Irishman, the comfort of our lives and devoted to Harold) says I owe him £100 for his services and I can't pay that." "Well, you tell him," said Lord R, "that he is like the GG and wants too much" – "Yes and," added Harold, "that he better resign" – evidently having grasped the whole of the situation.'

In another letter to Chamberlain on 10 June, Tennyson wrote: 'Personally I much regret Lord Hopetoun's going, and I wish that I could have helped him in his administration. He wrote me a very kind letter the other day in which he said "Had it been my good fortune to spend a week in your company 12 or 14 months ago I tell you frankly I should have been better equipped for my business than I have been during my sojourn here." I hope that I shall be able to carry on the work that he has begun. The post is not at present to be envied, nor is it one that I have ever thought of occupying. But I shall enjoy trying to pull affairs together, and to show that – with a fair knowledge of Australia – it is perfectly possible to keep up the position with sufficient dignity on the salary of £10,000 and the extra £2000 or £3000 that I have always spent in South Australia out of my own pocket,' It was not surprising that five months later the Colonial Office offered the Governor-Generalship to this temporary but self-confident replacement. He accepted the post, but only for one year. 'I cannot stay longer,' he cabled, 'because of boys education.'

The handling of the delicate and embarrassing situation created by Lord Hopetoun's recall fell to Alfred Deakin, who was Acting Prime Minister during Barton's absence at the Coronation. Hopetoun behaved with great dignity; but although he made no reproach, his sense of injury was plain to everyone. On 1 June he wrote to Barton in London, telling him that 'the inevitable row over my prostrate body was finished and done with.' 'The only criticism upon me,' he wrote, 'has been that I have spent my own money too freely on other people. That is not a bad character is it? Again I repeat that I have no complaint to make against anyone. I know the Government did what seemed wise at the time in deferring the introduction of the measure, though with that wisdom which comes to us all *after* the event one is tempted to wonder whether it might not after all have been better to have had the thing settled once and for all one way or the other 12 months ago. I have not yet read the Senate debate but I am told that with the exception of one or two hasty sentences from Senator McGregor (which I can afford to disregard) it was in equally good taste.'[3]

[3] Blind Senator Gregor McGregor (Labor, South Australia) said that when Lord Hopetoun 'found that Australia was not prepared to go to this lavish expenditure, he should not, like any pettish individual, have thrown up his job.' 'Look at the difficulty Mr Chamberlain will find in selecting somebody else to take Lord Hopetoun's place!' he added facetiously. 'The nobility in England will go on strike! They will say – "Lord Hopetoun has not been treated liberally enough by the Commonwealth of Australia, and we are not going to blackleg on him."' The Senator went on to say that if the aristocracy did withdraw its labour he would have no hesitation in supporting a recommendation to the Secretary of State for Colonies for the appointment of Senator F. T. Sargood, Senator W. A. Zeal, Senator S. Fraser or Senator J. C. Stewart. It would be another 29 years, however, before an Australian (Sir Isaac Isaacs) was suggested and accepted for the post of Governor-General.

Lord Hopetoun, who was created Marquess of Linlithgow soon after his return to Britain, remained on friendly terms with Barton, who had been as much to blame for the allowance calamity as Hopetoun himself, and with Deakin. In October 1902 he wrote to Barton from Scotland, still using Government House note paper but signing the letter with his new name 'Linlithgow.' He was in bad heath, as usual, and undergoing a severe course of massage and electricity. When Deakin went to England for the 1907 Colonial Conference, he was met at Dover by the Commonwealth's ever-charming first Governor-General. That was their last meeting, for Linlithgow died in the following year.

The first long-term Governor-General, Lord Northcote, was a model of acumen and decorum. He became very friendly with Deakin, but was scrupulously impartial during the political crises brought about during his five years of office by the fact that none of Australia's three Federal parties commanded a majority in Parliament. Northcote, the second son of an Earl, had been raised to the peerage himself in recognition of his political and public service – first as a member of the House of Commons for nineteen years, and later as a creditable Governor of Bombay. He was a short man with a bushy moustache, and possessed great resources of political shrewdness. '[His] tactful, patient friendliness and modesty,' wrote Deakin, 'had given him not only knowledge but power among politicians and over the much wider area in which he was trusted and warmly liked.' Although the Governor-Generalship became more important as a channel of communication during Northcote's term, it was also for all practical purposes shorn of its discretionary power to reserve the Royal Assent. In this evolutionary change, Lord Northcote sided with his Australian ministers against the Colonial Office. In 1906 the Indian Government protested about certain amendments to the Immigration Restriction Act, and asked London to see that Royal Assent was withheld. When the Australian Government protested in turn, the Colonial Office persuaded India not to press its objection. Again in 1907 the Colonial Office suggested to Northcote that he should consider reserving a Judiciary Bill which would effectively put a stop to the practice of appealing to the Privy Council direct from State Supreme Courts in Constitutional cases involving the limits *inter se* of the powers of the Commonwealth and States. This would leave the High Court with exclusive power to decide such cases or, if it wished, to grant permission for an appeal to the Privy Council; no longer would *inter se* cases be able to reach the Privy Council by the back door. With the intention of helping rather than hindering, the Colonial Office raised the possibility of reserving assent until a relevant case had been decided in Britain. Deakin, who felt that the Assent power was an anachronistic restraint on Australian independence, was in no mood to tolerate even helpful interference. He protested strongly to London, and Northcote, fearful that Cabinet might resign over the issue, delayed his decision until the Colonial Office had withdrawn from the situation. No Governor-General ever came closer than this to using the discretionary Assent power.

When the time came for Northcote to leave Australia, he offered to discuss the complexities of Federal politics with his successor – William Humble Ward, the 2nd Earl of Dudley. The handsome, arrogant, 41-year-old Lord Dudley brushed Northcote's offer aside, however, and went on to become the worst Governor-General of this period. Dudley had come into his title, and into an immense income flowing from the ownership of iron and coal resources near Birmingham, soon after leaving Eton. At the age of eighteen he bought himself a superbly fitted schooner – the *Marchesa*, complete with captain and crew of twenty-seven – and embarked with three friends on a leisurely voyage around the world. The 40-metre schooner had a Nordenfeldt gun on its bow, and the cabin at its stern was furnished with Japanese silk panelling, green velvet seats, suits of armour, a piano and a harmonium. By the time the *Marchesa* reached Australia by way of Brazil, Patagonia, Juan Fernandez Island, Tahiti and the Marquesas, the floor and walls of its after-cabin were covered with the skins and horns of animals shot by the adventurers on every wild coast that had taken their fancy.

The young earl joined the Prince of Wales set, and in due course was appointed Lord-Lieutenant of Ireland. His marriage to Rachel Gurney, who was described by Lady Randolph Churchill as the most beautiful woman of her generation, was one of the great social events of 1891; but by the time the Dudleys reached Melbourne in 1908, they were badly estranged from one another. They were ripe subjects for gossip, and the scandalous innuendoes which justly or unjustly came to be directed at the Governor-General eventually brought his office into considerable disrepute. 'Sir,' wrote John Norton in an open letter to Lord Dudley on the front page of his paper *Truth* in September 1910, '—— The Time has come when you should explain yourself, or export yourself to the place whence you came. Why? Because you are being made the subject of scandalous stories, more or less mendacious, as I do believe, but, nevertheless, of such a shocking nature as to call for your categorical contradiction, or for your condign condemnation at the hands of the citizens of the Commonwealth. You are being credited with playing pornic pranks with matrons and maids, which would seem to designate you as a devil of a Don Juan – in short, a sort of salacious satyr.' In his most odious vein of alliterative prurience, Norton reminded the hapless recipient of his letter that 'two papers in Sydney, and two in Melbourne, have published statements respecting your alleged illicit intercourse with other men's wives' and said that he had been 'paying court to the chorus girls now displaying their bulging busts and beefy buttocks, and luxurious legs and marvellous agilities, at the Criterion Theatre in Sydney.' 'Rumour goes so far as to say that you have even motored down to Narrabeen with one of these singing sirens, dancing demoiselles, or saltatory sylphs; not, of course, in your official capacity, or under your official title, but simply as plain Mr William Humble Ward.'

Lord Dudley laughed off this gossip in a brief public statement, and denied a rumour that he would soon be returning to England; but in fact the end was only nine months away. At his last official levee, the unhappy Governor-General treated a totally unsympathetic Alfred Deakin, who was then Leader of the Opposition, to a catalogue of the weakness and incapacity of the current Labor Ministry. '[He] did not mention,' wrote Deakin, 'that his project of circumnavigating Australia in a fine vessel of war at the expense of the Commonwealth was steadily delayed and finally negatived on the ground of its cost by his Ministers. He had welcomed their coming into office, expecting to get much more from them than he had from us. . . He was openly fuming and pacing up and down his room, quite forgetting the exhibition of himself he was making. . . Dudley also expressed a very poor opinion of his successor Denman who he rightly described as pleasantly casual narrow ineffective and likely to have little influence on either our politics or politicians. He bitterly protested that there were no real opportunities for a Governor-General. My opinion was that he had no idea how distasteful his methods were to the public men on both sides and indeed the Commonwealth generally . . .'

The 37-year-old 3rd Baron Denman had been Lord-in-Waiting to the King, and Captain of the Honourable Corps of Gentlemen at Arms. He was not in the best of health (he suffered from asthma and hay fever, and was allergic to wattle), and not very experienced politically. He left little mark on the office, but at least he enjoyed good relations with Fisher's Ministry, and steered clear of personal blunders. The one incident which harmed the Governor-Generalship during Denman's term was no fault of his. This was a dispute between the New South Wales and Commonwealth Governments over Government House, Sydney. With the coming of Federation Sydney's Government House, near the Botanic Gardens on the western side of Farm Cove, had been leased to the Commonwealth for use by the Governor-General whenever he visited the city. Shortly before Lord Denman's arrival in 1911, the New South Wales

Government had informed the Commonwealth that when the lease expired in 1912 it would resume the property for public use. In effect the Labor Government of New South Wales – through the agency of its strong-minded Attorney-General and later Premier, W. A. Holman – evicted the Governor-General. In 1912 Lord Denman was sometimes reduced to staying in his railway carriage when he visited Sydney. The *Daily Telegraph* found the State Government's action 'boorish and shabby', and *The Sydney Morning Herald* thought it 'a wanton act of disloyalty.' Denman himself said that the dispute 'tended seriously to impair the prestige and position of the Governor-General.'

The stables at Government House were turned into a conservatorium of music, but legal action taken by a citizens' committee obliged the State Government to refrain from its original intention of converting the rest of the property into a hospital, library or museum of arts. Government House itself remained empty while litigation to determine whether the eviction was constitutionally valid made its way slowly through the Supreme Court, the High Court and eventually the Privy Council. In 1915 the Judicial Committee of the Privy Council held that the State Government could use the house and grounds for any purpose it thought fit – a view which had earlier been taken by the High Court in contradiction of a New South Wales Supreme Court ruling. The Governor of New South Wales, Sir Gerald Strickland, moved into Government House in October 1915 (since Federation, the Governors of New South Wales had resided at 'Cranbrook', Rose Bay), and at about the same time the Commonwealth obtained possession of Admiralty House, Kirribilli, as a permanent Sydney residence for the Governor-General.

By that time, Lord Denman had been replaced by a very different kind of Governor-General, Sir Ronald Craufurd Munro-Ferguson. This tall, dignified Scotsman (he reminded some people of Sir Walter Scott) could not have been appointed at a better time, for not only did the Governor-Generalship need shoring up in public estimation but Australia was on the verge of a cataclysmic experience which would impose strains of a new kind upon the Australian-British relationship. Sir Ronald Munro-Ferguson brought to the office of Governor-General a sagacity and oaklike reliability which would be equal to those strains and would prove of great value to his Australian ministers in a time of unprecedented crisis.

The sort of disapproval expressed in Federal Parliament over Lord Hopetoun's expenditure also manifested itself at a State level during the Commonwealth's first decade. In 1904 Queensland reduced the salary of its Governor from £5000 to £3000, and other States talked of making do with Australian Lieutenant-Governors. The Governor of Queensland, Lord Chelmsford, incurred criticism in 1907 by appearing to side with a conservative Opposition against a liberal Government, and in 1908 the Western Australian Government notified the Colonial Office of its wish to appoint the State's Governor. A similar motion in South Australia passed easily through the lower house but was rejected by the Legislative Council; the views of both houses were then conveyed to the Colonial Office, without discernible result.

The Australian Worker criticized vice-regal institutions on aesthetic as well as economic and political grounds. Lord Hopetoun's outriders and postilions, 'dressed like Dresden china dolls, with their rouged cheeks and their powdered wigs, belonged to the stage of comic opera', and Lord Dudley looked ludicrous in his Court dress. 'Our sturdy, strenuous work-a-day life,' said an editorial in 1908, 'has nothing whatever in common with this feudal finery, this "Peter Pan" make-believe laboriously carried down the stream of the centuries from a wicked, cruel and, happily, dead past. . . The Order of the Red Button or the Peacock's Feather is not a jot or tittle more ludicrous than the Order of the Garter, the Bath, the Golden Fleece or the Black Eagle. The Court of King Edward or Kaiser Wilhelm is as constructively idiotic as that of the Brother of the Sun and Moon or the Mikado, and the totems of a Red Indian constitute heraldry quite as essentially respectable as that presided over by the Garter King-at-Arms.'

The conservative daily press did not cavil at finery or heraldry, however, and by the time Sir Ronald Munro-Ferguson arrived in May 1914 its support for the office of Governor-General, strengthened no doubt by a steady deterioration of Anglo-German relations, was fairly typical of public opinion. 'The representative of the King and of the race,' said *The Sydney Morning Herald*, 'and the racial ideals and traditions, the great institutions and the splendid history which the King symbolizes, has, as a matter of course, the goodwill of every shade of Australian opinion. . . Whenever the day comes when real trouble threatens, trouble from outside – why then, for better or for worse, in victory or in disaster, whether it means eventual success or absolute irremediable ruin, through cloud or sunshine, or rain, or snow, or whatever the future holds, until that trouble is through, we are in it with the rest of our race.'

The new Governor-General was a political veteran of thirty years in the House of Commons. After graduating from Sandhurst and serving in the Grenadier Guards, he represented the Scottish constituency of Leith Burghs as a Liberal MP, and for a time was private secretary to Lord Rosebery, the Liberal Imperialist president of the Imperial Federation League. In his first three months as Governor-General, Sir Ronald encountered two rather thorny problems. One was Joseph Cook's request for a double dissolution of Parliament, against the wishes of the Labor Opposition, and the other was the strange behaviour of the Governor of New South Wales, Sir Gerald Strickland, who held a dormant commission to act in Sir Ronald's absence. Sir Ronald granted Cook's request for a double dissolution – a decision later applauded as constitutionally correct and politically wise – and at the consequent election Fisher's Labor Government was returned to power. The problem of Sir Gerald Strickland was more complicated. Strickland was vain, ambitious and, in Munro-Ferguson's careful judgment, not altogether stable. 'To see him open Parliament was a joy,' wrote Mrs Ada Holman. 'He was dressed up so beautifully, and was evidently so happy in the limelight.' When announcing the Governor's presence for the opening ceremony, the Clerk of the Legislative Assembly used to recite all his titles and honours, including 'Count della Catena', which earned His Excellency the nickname of 'Delicatessen.' On his first visit to New South Wales, the Governor-General heard from the former conservative Premier, Sir Charles Wade, that Sir Gerald had consulted him about the propriety of his being sworn in as Governor-General immediately after Lord Denman's departure from the Commonwealth and a few hours before Sir Ronald's arrival. 'Sir Gerald is so obsessed by petty personal ambition,' reported Sir Ronald to the Colonial Office, 'that one is sometimes tempted to think that in spite of his ability he is not perfectly sane on certain points. . . The whole of the ability and influence of the Governor are enlisted on the side of making things difficult for the Federal Government and, knowing that he is distrusted by the leading members of Mr Cook's administration, I think it my duty to record my view officially that it would be dangerous at any rate in time of war were he to become Governor-General.'

Although finding Strickland an agreeable guest at Government House, Munro-Ferguson regarded him as 'a submarine working under water, his course marked by the bubbles which rise to the surface.' The analogy was probably suggested by two Royal Navy submarines, AE1 and AE2, which had reached Sydney in May. Both came to grief early in the war, and in due course so did Sir Gerald Strickland. Sir Ronald recommended that, in the event of his own demise, the recently appointed Governor of Victoria, Sir Arthur Stanley, should be sworn in as Governor-General. The Colonial Office agreed with him about Sir Gerald ('If Sir G. Strickland would resign on getting a peerage,' read one minute on the Governor-General's despatch, 'I would recommend making him a Duke forthwith'), but pointed out that Sir Gerald could not be prevented from using his dormant commission unless the commission were revoked. There was no need for such precaution, as it turned out, for Sir Ronald continued in office for more than six years, and Sir Gerald, after losing a constitutional joust with the Holman Government, was censured by the Colonial Office and recalled in 1917. For most of his term, Sir Ronald Munro-Ferguson was intimately involved in the Commonwealth's slow and painful progression through its next rite of passage – an ordeal by fire. His involvement, as we shall see in the next chapter, began at the very beginning of that ordeal.

11

GALLIPOLI

ON THE BLAZING midsummer afternoon of 1 July 1914, three days after a Serbian terrorist had murdered the Austrian Archduke Franz Ferdinand and his wife at Sarajevo, Norman Brookes of Australia played the tennis champion of Germany, Otto Froitzheim, in the final match of the men's singles competition on the centre court at Wimbledon. It is unlikely that the dying echoes of those shots which had been heard around the world so recently were audible at the All England Lawn Tennis and Croquet Club. Even if waves of sound or concern still quivered faintly in the summer air, they would have been overwhelmed at Wimbledon by the detonations of hand-stitched ball against sheep-gut strings, and by salvos of applause from more than 6000 spectators. The outcome of this match for the King George Cup, apparently so clear at first, was in fact acutely uncertain for the last three sets. Brookes, a slim left-hander with a powerful service and volley, took the first two sets 6–2 and 6–1. Froitzheim, a much bigger man, had been unnerved by his opponent's left-hand drive and aggressive approach to the net; but in the third set, with the score 5–4 against him, he began lobbing over Brookes, forcing him to the back line, and eventually won 7–5. The same tactics worked again in the fourth set, for Brookes, despite the protection of the cloth cap which he habitually wore on court, seemed to be wilting in the afternoon heat of 30 degrees Celsius in the shade. Froitzheim won 6–4, taking five games in a row, two of them off his opponent's service from thirty-love.

At the end of this set some of Brookes's supporters opened a bottle of champagne for him, but he took only one sip. The news of Froitzheim's miraculous recovery had drawn another thousand or so spectators from the tea lawns to the centre court, and they were not disappointed in their expectation of a close finish. The last set — which went to the fourteenth game, leaving Brookes victorious at 8–6 — was a struggle all the way, with the Australian always just in front. Froitzheim won his opponent's service once, but Brookes did the same to him next game. Each seemed to be seeing the other's cards,' reported the *Times* next morning, 'and the amount of court they covered recalled Mr Kipling's lines:

'Kangaroo bounded away, his back legs working like pistons –
Bounded from morning till dark, twenty-five feet at a bound.
Yellow-Dog Dingo lay like a yellow cloud in the distance –
Much too busy to bark. My! but they covered the ground '

It was through such feats as this, and little else, that Australians occasionally enjoyed the heady pleasure of international acclaim both inside and outside the Empire. Norman Brookes – the Australian Achilles or the Australian Invader, as the British and American sports writers called him – and Anthony Wilding had won or retained the Davis Cup four times since 1907, when they first defeated the British Isles; and in the challenge round of August 1914 this Australian-New Zealand partnership defeated the United States for the third time. In Test cricket, Australia and Britain had each won the Ashes four times since 1901, and in rugby league there was little to choose between British and Australian scores. The Australian rower George Towns had won the World Sculling Championship four times since 1901, and the swimmer Fanny Durack won the 100 metres women's freestyle at the Olympic Games in 1912.

If an Achilles in white flannel could do as much for national self-esteem as Norman Brookes or Victor Trumper, how much more could an Achilles in khaki do? War was a powerfully attractive means of asserting national identity. The Boer War had given Australia a tantalising taste of such satisfaction – a mere sip of champagne between sets – and by 1914 there were many Australians who, as C. E. W. Bean wrote later, 'half consciously longed for the day when their untried people would be pitted against the fighters of other nations.' Australia expected war some day, and had begun preparing for it; but few if any Australians realised, when their Achilles beat Germany's Hector at Wimbledon, just how close they were to a conflict which would not only satisfy their thirst for war but positively satiate it. During the next four years Australia, with a population of only 4,875,325, would raise 416,809 military personnel, of whom 331,781 took the field in battle, 59,342 were killed or died of wounds, and 152,171 were wounded. Its sense of nationhood would be enhanced by defeat and victory, but the magnitude and inequity of the ordeal would also cause deep rifts within Australian society.

The Australian Government – preoccupied in July by an election campaign, and kept in the dark as always by the Colonial Office – did not appreciate the full significance of the drift towards war. On 23 July Austria served an ultimatum on Serbia, which it held responsible for the assassinations at Sarajevo; on 25 July Germany urged Austria to declare war on Serbia, and Serbia reacted by mobilizing; on 29 July Austria invaded Serbia, the British fleet went to its war stations in the North Sea, and the first official warning to Australia that war was imminent was cabled by the imperial Government to the Governor-General, Sir Ronald Munro-Ferguson, who happened then to be in Sydney. The cipher message, which reached the Governor-General's office in Macquarie Street at 3 pm on 30 July was intended to read: 'See preface defence scheme. Adopt precautionary stage. Names of powers will be communicated later if necessary.' This was a prearranged signal that war was probable, and an instruction to implement certain preliminary steps in a defence procedure which had been laid down by the Committee of Imperial Defence in 1907; but through an error in deciphering, which seemed to symbolize the clumsiness with which Australia went to war, the code word for 'adopt' was rendered as 'adoption.' The Minister for Defence, Senator E. D. Millen, who was the only senior Minister in Sydney, assumed that the message was merely an answer to someone's request for information. However, it had gone to all parts of the Empire. By 10.30 pm the Naval Board in Melbourne, having heard of the instruction from the British admiral on the China Station, had implemented the prearranged naval measures. Senator Millen was unwilling to do the same for the army without consulting the Prime Minister, Joseph Cook, who was temporarily out of reach on the campaign trail in Victoria. On 30 July Russia mobilized; on 31 July Austria followed suit; on 1 August Germany declared war on Russia, and France mobilized; and on 2 August Germany invaded Luxembourg. Not until that day did Senator Millen – with moral support from the Attorney-General, Sir William Irvine, newly arrived in Sydney from Queensland – put Australia's military forces on alert.

The Governor-General had already used his own initiative on 31 July by sending the following telegram, in cipher, to the Prime Minister: 'Would it not be well, in view of latest news from Europe, that ministers should meet in order that imperial Government may know what support to expect from Australia?' Cook was in Ballarat, without a code book; he was not able to read the Governor-General's message until the following day, but then called a Cabinet meeting in Melbourne for 3 August. Both he and the leader of the Labor Opposition, Andrew Fisher, who was also campaigning in Victoria, had already made their positions identically clear. On the night of 31 July, Cook told a meeting at Horsham: 'Whatever happens, Australia is a part of the Empire to the full. Remember that when the Empire is at war, so is Australia at war.' At Colac, Fisher used much the same words as H. B. Higgins had used during the Boer War, though without any of Higgins's prevarication: 'Should the worst happen after everything has been done that honour will permit, Australians will stand beside [the mother country] to help and defend her to our last man and our last shilling.' This might also have reminded Mr Justice Higgins of his warning to Parliament in 1902 that automatic loyalty would commit Australia to the principle that she must aid the British Government 'in all wars with her young lives . . . although she has no voice in the negotiations which precede war, and is not to be consulted in regard to its expediency or necessity.' Many years later W. M. Hughes was to recall how such events came to pass in August 1914. 'The Dominions,' he wrote, 'after clamouring through many years for the right to be informed, now found themselves without a moment's notice swept into a savage struggle arising, technically at all events, out of a treaty of which not one out of every ten thousand had ever heard, and about the terms of which none of the Dominions had been consulted, a treaty made indeed before any of them were Dominions at all.'

Australia had no legal right to declare war, or even to remain neutral in the face of an imperial declaration. All that the Commonwealth could decide for itself was the extent to which it would participate in a war declared by Britain. That extent was the sole topic of discussion at the meeting of Federal Cabinet on 3 August, the day Germany declared war on France and Britain warned Germany not to violate Belgian neutrality. After the Cabinet meeting two cables were sent to London: one offering to place the Australian fleet under Admiralty control and to despatch an expeditionary force of 20,000 men, and the other asking 'if any official communication could be made stating the present position in Europe as to a state of war or peace.' At 1.45 pm Greenwich Mean Time on 4 August, the day Germany invaded Belgium, the Colonial Office thanked the Australian Government for its prompt offers of assistance. As to the state of war or peace, it said only: 'Will telegraph later.' By the time that message was despatched, Britain had issued an ultimatum to Germany over the invasion of Belgium. The ultimatum expired at 11 pm London time and the British Empire was then automatically at war with Germany. This news reached the Governor-General at 12.30 pm Melbourne Time on Wednesday 5 August. Fifteen minutes later the Prime Minister told a press conference: 'I have received the following despatch from the Imperial Government – War has broken out with Germany.'

Australia's response was predictable; indeed the Governor-General had predicted it with a fair degree of accuracy the day before when he cabled to the Secretary of State for Colonies: 'There is indescribable enthusiasm and entire unanimity throughout Australia in support of all that tends to provide for the security of the Empire in war.' What did it matter that Australians had not been consulted when they endorsed so ardently the course of action decided for them? The Governor of New South Wales, Sir Gerald Strickland, speaking at a banquet held in Sydney for High Court and Supreme Court judges on the night of 5 August, compared the occasion to 'revelry by night' on the eve of Waterloo. In Melbourne on the same night several hundred men and boys marched along Collins Street behind Union Jacks, then joined a larrikin crowd of some 2000 which rioted until dispersed by mounted troopers.

The prevailing emotions in Australia during the next few months were sheer excitement and a surge of tribal loyalty. 'If Great Britain goes to her Armageddon, we will go with her,' said Sir John Forrest. 'Very exciting news,' wrote Ida Dawson, a governess at Euralah Station near Collarenebri, NSW. 'Germany has declared war against England, and our first Fleet has put to sea. . . Today was so lovely that we felt we couldn't stay in the house, so I made sweet scones, and the girls cut sandwiches etc and we went "up the drain" for a picnic. Took reading and needlework with us, as those were the afternoon's lessons.' On the other side of the world, and the other side of the war, another Australian governess, 28-year-old Hilda Freeman, was teaching English to the children of Baron von Klinggraeff in the north German province of Mecklinburg-Strelitz when the war began. 'I always knew that I loved Australia,' she recorded in her diary before being repatriated to England, 'but every day I realise more clearly that the love of Empire is an integral part of my being. . . I felt that if I chose to consider myself non-British I would be taken back into confidence [by the Klinggraeffs]. Something had happened evidently to the public feelings regarding Britain's Dominions. They seemed to be considered non-combatants. "Now we will see what Australia will do," said Dorchen exultantly. "She will not uphold England." "Australia is British, Dorchen," I answered shortly. I felt that I was putting myself out from their sympathy, but I couldn't help that.'

Not everyone was excited, of course. On the night of 5 August a young man, Martin Boyd, later to become a sensitive literary chronicler of middle-class British-Australian society, went to *The Mikado* at Her Majesty's Theatre in Melbourne. 'I was immeasurably depressed,' he wrote later. 'Everyone seemed to think some glorious picnic had begun, and one which was made more enjoyable by the ingredient of moral indignation. My adolescent belief that I should have to go and fight if England were attacked by Germany had been overlain by my Shavianism, my aesthetic preoccupations, and all my optimism for the brave new world. It was difficult to drag it up from under these things. Two other Australian disciples of G. B. Shaw – Vance and Nettie Palmer, both 29, and both at the start of distinguished literary careers – were spending their honeymoon in a stone cottage beside the sea at Trégastel, in Brittany, when war was declared. Nettie, who was the niece of Mr Justice Higgins, wrote to her mother in June saying that Vance was writing a serial for an American newspaper syndicate and that summer had begun at last. 'The sun is hot and high, long after seven o'clock in the evening: and you can feel the crops stiffening and ripening in the heat.' On 1 August Vance came back from the village square asking if Nettie had heard all the noise. 'He said there were groups in the square clustered excitedly round the baker and one or two other men. The baker's a fine, fair man who makes great primitive good bread in a primitive way. It seems that he and several other men have to go to the war. That means, of course, that they are mobilizing the reserves.'

In September the Palmers returned to London, where Nettie thrashed out the rights and wrongs of the war in regular correspondence with her brother, Esmonde Higgins, who was then a prefect at Scotch College in Melbourne but nonetheless a confirmed socialist like his sister. In each letter they used different, nonsensical forms of address such as 'Glorp', 'Blibb' or 'Glonk'. In October Esmonde complained that the Palmers 'apparently approve of the Allies.' 'Finding Christian and Bernard O'Dowd and lots of decent people had become violently anti-Germany or else flag-waggers, I did my honest best to see if I could be either, but I couldn't, since, although the German war lords and Bismarck are damn rotten, their rottenness cannot make me sympathetic with hypocritical, capitalistic cows like Asquith or mock-Socialist time-servers like Fisher, or with Imperialism or capitalism or militarism. . . You brought me up a socialist, thank you Gug, but I am not going to be an anti-Socialist even though you are.'

'Glorpie Dear,' replied Nettie, '. . . I'll grant you that capitalism is as bad in France as anywhere, but this war is not an act of capitalism, so far as France at least is concerned. . . England is another matter. With regard to that I'll send you a long pamphlet of Shaw's that Vance read aloud to me last night. . . With regard to England as Perfidious Albion I'm afraid he's right, although, now that the war has begun, I feel that fighting it through is the only way to finish it. . . I feel that we must face realities, and that talking against war now is like talking against a thunderstorm when you're in it. I don't understand you quite, Blinkie dear. You're trying hard to be an internationalist, aren't you, so that's what makes you react against popular sentiment and seem like a pro-German for the time.'

In another letter, Nettie wrote: 'Oh, Blinkie, it's a little bit ghastly to read in the Australian papers about Australia's certainty that "England *will* be pleased with *us*": and then to read the English papers with their total neglect of the subject, beyond an occasional cable that forces its way in – such as that the loyal residents of Heidelberg, Victoria, intend changing the name of their suburb. . . They say the *Bulletin* has turned "patriotic": is that so? It's the only Australian paper that is well known over here, and its anti-Japan policy makes me wonder if it has really accepted this war as a whole.' While Australia's daily press was indeed unanimous in its loyal support of the war, the *Bulletin* was still a bit inclined to wish a plague on both houses, but by 1915 it too had fallen into line with the majority. 'It is one of those Imperial death-struggles which occur but once in centuries,' the *Bulletin* concluded, 'the sort of war that Carthage waged – and lost. It is peculiarly our war.' The main trade union papers had immediately, though not without some reluctance, accepted the necessity of Australian involvement. 'Australia is as much a part of the British Empire as England is,' said the *Worker* in Brisbane, 'and while we remain so any attempt to evade responsibilities under present conditions would not only be courting eventual disaster as a people, but would be altogether unworthy of us.' The *Australian Worker* in Sydney thought that Australia had to protect itself, but hoped 'no wave of jingo madness will sweep over the land, unbalancing the judgment of its leaders, and inciting its population to wild measures.'

Edmund Dwyer-Gray, editor of the labour *Daily Post* in Hobart, and an Irishman to boot, said: 'Our people love the Empire and would come down to their shirt-sleeves to save it.' Irish-Australian opinion, which was to change sharply as the war proceeded, at first seemed as solidly pro-war as the majority Anglo-Saxon opinion. A spokesman for the Melbourne Celtic Club said that its members were prepared during the present crisis to set aside their campaigning for Home Rule in Ireland, and at a public meeting in Melbourne Town Hall on 6 August John Gavan Duffy, a former state parliamentarian who said he was speaking as an Irish Catholic Nationalist, asserted that the Irish Nationalists of Australia were 'ready, eager and willing to stand shoulder by shoulder, knee by knee, fighting the battle of the great Empire to which they belonged.' The only direct and uncompromising opposition to the war came from the revolutionary Industrial Workers of the World and from certain other isolated spirits on the far left of the Australian labour movement. 'Workers of the world, unite!' said the IWW journal, *Direct Action*. 'Don't become hired murderers. Don't join the Army or Navy. Answer the declaration of war with the call for a general strike. Don't go to Hell in order to give piratical, plutocratic parasites a bigger slice of Heaven.'

But the workers of Australia did enlist, and in proportionately greater number than might have been expected. Forty-three per cent of the 54,000 men who enlisted during the first five months of the war were trade-unionists, a figure well above the percentage of adult Australian males who were unionists. In one other respect the Army did not accurately reflect Australia's demographic pattern: it included no Aboriginals. Successive Defence Acts had exempted from military training 'those who are not substantially of European origin or descent', and if any part-Aboriginals gained admission to the army they must have been more white than black. The task of organizing the first volunteer contingent of 20,000 was entrusted to Major-General W. T. Bridges, who had recently left his position as founding commandant of the Royal Military College, Duntroon, to become Inspector-General of the Australian Military Forces. Bridges created the contingent, devised a name for it (the Australian Imperial Force, perhaps inspired by General Hutton's still-born 'Imperial Australian Force,), and for a short time was its first commander in the field.

'*Are U Satisfied To Remain A Loafer In Australia?*' asked a slogan of the time. From every part of the continent the answer was 'No', and men converged upon recruiting offices to join the AIF. One group of volunteers called the Kangaroos marched from Wagga Wagga to Sydney, a distance of 560 kilometres, growing from 88 to 230 on the way. In the Western Australian pearling town of Broome, a 22-year-old shell-opener named Snowy Howe was drinking in the Continental Hotel when a telegram was posted up announcing the outbreak of war. The pearling fleet had come to port so that its Japanese divers could celebrate Kigensetsu, the festival of the Emperor's birthday. Howe, a lively young New South Welshman with fair hair and bright blue eyes, was drinking with Richie Richardson and Barney Winter, both of whom were in the naval reserve, and nearby at the bar were two German pearlers, Tony Albrecht, who had recently found a pearl worth £2000, and Harry Ripon. The telegram landed in this convivial company like an exploding shell. As soon as the Germans read it they left without a word, went to the bank, drew £2000 in gold, boarded Albrecht's lugger, and as soon as it floated with the incoming tide set sail for the Dutch East Indies. Richardson and Winter went straight to the post office, where they sent a telegram to naval headquarters in Melbourne asking for instructions; Howe walked to the steamer office and booked a passage for the next day to Fremantle and the AIF.

At Wyong, NSW, early in 1915, a 20-year-old baker named Jack Tarrant started his delivery run at midnight so that he could catch the early morning train to Sydney and enlist. 'You could call it adventure,' he said sixty years later, 'and it was loyalty too. Everyone was King and Queen, and everyone was enlisting,' Jack was not sure that he would be accepted, for although he had done a bit of blacksmithing and could use his fists, he was only 158 centimetres tall. 'You're not high enough to pick strawberries,' said the sergeant at Victoria Barracks, but marked him down as 164 centimetres.[1] Within a few days Jack Tarrant was wearing the boots, knee britches, puttees, dull-buttoned khaki tunic and slouch hat of the AIF.

As a result of the defence expansion which had taken place since 1911, Government factories in Victoria were now producing military clothing, harness and cordite, and the Lithgow Small Arms Factory was producing its first Mark III Lee Enfield .303 rifles at the rate of 2000 per month. This supply of rifles was not sufficient for the initial intake of recruits, but the shortage was soon made up with British weapons. Australia's annual defence expenditure had risen from £1,535,405 in 1910 (13s 6d per head of population) to £4,752,300 (19s per head) in 1913, but from 1914 onwards the country had to find astronomically higher sums. In doing so, the Commonwealth ran deeply into debt; but it also tapped new sources of revenue which would continue to nourish Commonwealth growth in peace as well as war.[2]

The first shot fired by Australia in what was to become known as the Great War came on the afternoon of 5 August from Fort Nepean at the entrance to Port Phillip Bay, Melbourne. It went across the bows of a German steamer, *Pfalz*, which was making for the open sea; was heard by many people in Melbourne; and had the desired effect of halting the *Pfalz* without further ado. The first Australian to be killed in action was Able Seaman W. G. V. Williams, a former employee of Melbourne City Council, who was shot on 11 September 1914 while advancing on a German wireless station at Bitapaka, 31 miles from Rabaul on the island of Neupommern, or New Britain as it had been known earlier and would soon be

[1] The minimum height for the AIF, originally 168 cm, had been reduced to 163 cm by the end of 1914, and it gradually fell to 152 cm by 1917.

[2] The Fisher Government, which came to office in September 1914, had hoped to finance Australia's military activities during 1914-15 from revenue alone. This proved impossible, and in 1915 the Government obtained an initial loan of £18 million from Britain. As the war went on, the Commonwealth borrowed heavily from the Australian public (£250,172,440 in seven war loans), expanded the note issue six times over, and imposed one tax after another. In the first year of the war it increased a land tax which it had introduced four years earlier, and imposed a succession duty on all estates valued at more than £1000; in 1915-16 it began levying income tax, a form of taxation which had hitherto been the exclusive domain of the States; in 1916-17 it imposed an entertainment tax; and in 1917-18 a wartime profits tax. Robert Garran, who as head of the Attorney-General's Department supervised the drafting of the Income Tax Assessment Act, later described it proudly as 'a thing of beauty and simplicity that would not have shamed Wordsworth or T. S. Eliot.'

known again. On 6 August the British Government had asked Australia, 'as a great and urgent imperial service', to help destroy German wireless stations which would otherwise be of great value to several German warships which were believed to be cruising in the Pacific. These stations were at Yap in the Caroline Islands, north of the equator; on the island of Nauru, northeast of the Solomon Islands; and on Neupommern.

While General Bridges was forming the AIF, the new Chief of the General Staff, Colonel J. G. Legge, organised a smaller contingent of 2000 volunteers, known as the Australian Naval and Military Expeditionary Force. On 19 August this hastily assembled force sailed from Sydney with the objective not only of destroying the Bitapaka wireless station but also occupying the German colonies of New Guinea and Nauru. The station at Yap had already been disabled by the Royal Navy, and on 9 September Nauru was dealt with similarly by HMAS *Sydney*. During the next four weeks the ANMEF captured Bitapaka with the loss of six dead and four wounded, accepted the German surrender, and occupied Nauru. The Caroline and Marshall Islands were occupied by Japan, which had declared war on Germany on 23 August.

This Asian ally, about whose enlistment many Australians were no happier than the *Bulletin*, sent its cruiser *Ibuki* to help escort a convoy of thirty-eight Australian and New Zealand troopships which left King George's Sound, the harbour of Albany in Western Australia, on 1 November 1914. The *Ibuki*, which took the starboard station, was far more powerful than either HMAS *Sydney* (port) or HMAS *Melbourne* (rear); and more galling still, it could outgun and outrun HMS *Minotaur*, the Royal Navy escort leader steaming proudly ahead of the convoy. This convoy, bound across the Indian Ocean for the Suez Canal and England, carried the 1st Division of the AIF (12,000 men, consisting of one infantry brigade each from NSW and Victoria and a third made up of troops from the other four States, a regiment of light horse, three brigades of artillery with thirty-six horse-drawn field guns, three companies of engineers and three field ambulances), the 1st Australian Light Horse Brigade (226 men, consisting of one regiment each from NSW and Queensland and a third from South Australia and Tasmania combined), and two New Zealand brigades, one of infantry and one of mounted rifles.

The convoy faced two possible dangers: the German light cruisers *Königsberg* and *Emden*, both of which were thought to be in the Indian Ocean. On 9 November, while passing near Cocos Island, the naval escort heard Cocos wireless station signalling, 'Strange warship approaching', and shortly afterwards 'SOS'. The *Ibuki* had to be restrained from racing to the kill. For the sake of imperial pride (that was to say, *British* imperial pride) the hunt was assigned to HMAS *Sydney*, whose speed and armament were superior to those of either *Königsberg* or *Emden*. The quarry turned out to be the *Emden*. With its heavier and longer ranged guns, the *Sydney* – after rashly venturing close enough to be hit, and paying the price of four dead, twelve wounded and slight structural damage – was able to stand off at a safe distance and tear the *Emden* apart so effectively that the Captain ran her aground on one of the Cocos reefs. After chasing and sinking the *Emden*'s collier, *Sydney* returned to the reef, and, because its stricken prey was still flying the German ensign, opened fire again without parley, killing 20 more Germans without a shot in reply and bringing the *Emden's* casualty list to 134 dead and 65 wounded.

It was a victory. Sir Henry Newbolt did his best to give it the *Drake's Drum* treatment, but ruined his attempt with the memorable couplet: 'Their hearts were hot, and, as they shot/ They sang like kangaroos.' The fact of the matter was that Cocos had been a somewhat one-sided encounter; and so had Bitapaka. If the Germans had been able to resist on equal terms in New Guinea, and if the landing had developed into a prolonged and bloody campaign, New Guinea might have provided the font for Australia's military baptism. As it was, that baptism still lay five months ahead, and its font was called Gallipoli. Because winter quarters for the Australians and New Zealanders were not yet ready in England, the Secretary of State for War, Lord Kitchener, decided that the Dominions contingent, instead of training on Salisbury Plain for probable service in France, should disembark in Egypt and train there. When the Australians heard of this change in plan soon after the convoy left Aden, many of them thought they discerned significance in the fact that Turkey had recently entered the war on Germany's side; and they were right.

In Egypt the Dominion troops came under the command of Brigadier-General W. R. Birdwood, a dapper little British cavalryman who formed them into the Australia and New Zealand Army Corps. While ANZAC (the acronym used by Birdwood's staff as a telegraphic address) trained in the desert outside Cairo, the British Government was contemplating, with a mixture of fascination and misgiving, a grandiose plan of action against Turkey. This plan – supported obsessively by the young First Lord of the Admiralty, Winston Chruchill, who according to one of his contemporaries had 'the courage of Satan (*and some of his other attributes*!!)' – was to force the Dardanelles, the narrow strait leading from the Aegean Sea into the Sea of Marmara, capture Constantinople and open a route to assist Russia. When naval bombardment in February and March 1915 did not silence the Turkish forts which guarded the Dardanelles, it was decided that a Mediterranean Expeditionary Force under the command of Sir Ian Hamilton should attempt to occupy the narrow strip of land forming the northwestern side of the Dardanelles, a peninsula called Gallipoli. The British 29th Division would land near Cape Helles, at the tip of the peninsula, and Birdwood's Australian and New Zealand Army Corps would land at a cove 21 kilometres to the north, about three kilometres north of a promontory called Gaba Tepe ('Rough Hill'). When Birdwood was asked to choose a name for the northern landing place, he suggested 'Anzac Cove'.

No more appropriate ground could have been chosen for what was to be, in the estimation of many Australians, a climactic ceremony of national initiation. This part of the Aegean world was hallowed by many extraordinary events from the mythic and historic past – events which admittedly may have been outside the ken or interest of many of the young men who were now approaching that ground, but whose symbolism would not be lost upon Australia when the time came to incorporate 'Gallipoli' into the national lexicon. The Dardanelles were in fact the Hellespont, once sailed by Jason and the Argonauts, swum by Leander to visit Hero, and spanned with a bridge of boats by Xerxes on his way to invade Greece. Only sixteen kilometres south of this strait stood the ruins of Troy, where Achilles had slain the Trojan champion Hector, and from whose shore Ulysses embarked upon his odyssey.

From Egypt Hamilton's invasion force sailed early in April to the Greek island of Lemnos, 100 kilometres from Gallipoli. At that time of year the peninsula is a place of astringent, incandescent beauty. Its eroded hillsides and scrub-clad ridges rise luminously above the cornflower sea, their gullies aglow with yellow mustard flowers and marguerites, and fragrant with thyme. On the Dardenelles side are valleys green with barley and yellow with flowering sesame. This beauty does not last long in the withering heat of summer. The flowers die, the hills become parched, and the sea wind spreads a shroud of dust over the peninsula.

Thoughts of approaching death came to Sir Ian Hamilton on his ship at Lemnos when he received the news on 23 April that the poet Rupert Brooke had died of blood poisoning and been buried on the island of Skyros; or perhaps they came to him only in retrospect. In his *Gallipoli Diary* – expanded from notes made at the time, and published after the war – Hamilton wrote: 'Death! He is fed up with the old and sick – only the flower of the flock will serve him now, for God has started a celestial spring cleaning, and our star is to be scrubbed bright with the blood of our bravest... Our star burns dim as a corpse light: the huge black chasm of space closes in: if only by blood ... ?' The General, who had inspected and found fault with Australia's armed forces only the year before, rather fancied himself as a man of letters; it would have been better for the Australian and New Zealand Army Corps if he had followed that career to the exclusion of any other. In the words of Snowy Howe, who had given up pearling to come to Gallipoli, no general ever nearly won so many battles as Sir Ian Hamilton. At the age of 62, he was a slender, charming man whose career, distinguished though it was, had not quite kept pace with those of such brother officers as French, Wilson and Haig. His left hand was shrivelled and virtually paralysed as the result of a wound received at Majuba Hill in the first South African war.

The first landings on Gallipoli took place at 4.30 am on Sunday, 25 April. In the north, a covering force of 4000 men of the 1st Australian Division was to land in three successive waves at Anzac Cove, fan out and upwards to take Chunuk Bair and Scrubby Knoll, two heights in the Sari Bair Range, and the promontory of Gaba Tepe, thus preparing the way for a rapid thrust by following ANZAC forces across the five-mile-wide peninsula to the town of Maidos on the Dardanelles. The plan was simple enough, but it went disastrously wrong. For reasons which have never been satisfactorily explained, many of the forty-eight small boats in which the first wave of the covering force was towed from warships towards the Turkish coast were cast off by their naval pinnaces not at Anzac Cove, where the going inland was relatively easy, but further north, near Ari Burnu ('Bee Point', named after wild bees hiving in a wind-eroded cliff which the Australians named the Sphinx), where the hinterland was almost impossibly steep. 'Tell the Colonel,' yelled a naval officer leading one of the tows, 'that the damn fools have landed us a mile too far north!'

The Turks had seen the tows coming, and bullets were hitting the water and striking sparks from the shingle as the men waded ashore. Private 'Combo' Smith of the 11th Battalion, sitting beside Snowy Howe in one of the first tows to land north of Ari Burnu, was reminded of a sergeant who had likened the sound of bullets to a flight of small birds overhead. As they rowed through the pre-dawn darkness, hearing the bullets around them, Smith muttered: 'Just like little birds, ain't they, Snow!' On the shore near Ari Burnu, with Turkish machine gun and rifle fire coming from the hills, another soldier asked an officer: 'What are we to do next, sir?' 'I don't know, I'm sure,' replied the officer. 'Everything is in a terrible muddle.' It remained so all day long. The day was one of desperate but unco-ordinated effort, temporary achievement and ultimate failure.

By 6 am 4000 Anzacs had landed, and the Turks confronting them probably numbered no more than 700. The unfortunates who had landed around Ari Burnu clambered up through steep holly scrub, leaving their wounded there, while the luckier Australians made quicker progress inland. 'They did not look bigger than ants,' wrote Hamilton, who at 5.30 am was watching the Anzac advance from HMS *Queen Elizabeth*. 'God, one would think, cannot see them at all or He would put a stop to this sort of panorama, and yet, it would be a pity if He missed it; for these fellows have been worth the making. They are not charging up into this Sari Bair range for money or by compulsion. They fight for love – all the way from the Southern Cross for love of the old country and of liberty. Wave after wave of the little ants press up and disappear. We lose sight of them the moment they lie down. Bravo! every man on our great ship longs to be with them.' By 8 am some of these men had reached Scrubby Knoll, from which they could see the Dardanelles gleaming in the morning light barely three miles away. By 2 pm 12,000 Anzacs were ashore, opposed by no more than 4000 Turks, but the Turks were winning. Like the Anzacs they were dressed in khaki; some of them wore cloth caps, and star and crescent belts. The course of the day may well have been decided shortly before 10 am when Mustafa Kemal – the commander of the 19th Turkish Division, destined later to become the first President of post-Ottoman Turkey – rode to the top of Chunuk Bair with only a few aides and found it still unoccupied by the invaders, who at that stage were thought by many Turks to be Greeks. Realising the crucial importance of this height, Kemal rode forward with his aides to meet some Turkish troops who were retreating before two groups of Australians led by Captains E. W. Tulloch and J. P. Lalor. Kemal later wrote his own account of what followed. 'I said to the men who were running away, "You cannot run away from the enemy." "We have got no ammunition," they said. "If you haven't got any ammunition you have your bayonets," I said, and shouting to them, I made them fix their bayonets and lie down on the ground.' At the same time Kemal sent an orderly back to hasten the arrival of the 57th Regiment, which he knew to be advancing on Chunuk Bair. 'When the men fixed their bayonets,' he wrote, 'and lay down on the ground the enemy also lay down. The moment of time that we gained was this one.'

For some of the desperate fighting which raged all afternoon on the heights around and below Chunuk Bair, the Australians were led by Captain Lalor, a professional soldier who more than anyone else that day personified Achilles. Not only was he a grandson of the Peter Lalor who had led the goldminers' revolt at Eureka Stockade in 1854, but his own career had been more warlike than his father's. He enlisted as a boy in the

Royal Navy and later deserted, served in the French Foreign Legion, and fought in a South American revolution before joining Australia's permanent army. During his first and only day on Gallipoli he wore a family sword, the hilt of which was wrapped in khaki cloth. The Turks later reported having seen an Australian officer with sword in hand, but before the afternoon Lalor was dead.[3] He had plenty of company on the slopes of the Sari Bair range. Both sides were reinforced during the morning and early afternoon (the Turks, by Kemal's entire 19th Division), and one particular height, Baby 700, changed hands no fewer than five times. In a general counterattack about 4.30 pm, the Turks took Baby 700 again and, with cries of 'Allah!', drove the Australians and New Zealanders in disorganized groups back towards the coast. This first day, like the eight-month-long campaign which lay ahead, was a defeat for the Allies. Admittedly ANZAC had landed 16,000 men, but its casualties exceeded 2000; Anzac Cove was a chaos of supplies, reinforcements and wounded; and worst of all, the assault had lost its initial impetus. 'How we longed for nightfall!' wrote one of the first Anzacs. 'How we prayed for this ghastly day to end!'

Colonel John Monash, a civil engineer and militia officer from Melbourne who commanded the 4th Australian Infantry Brigade which formed part of the following force that first day, brought with him – to stimulate the interest of his men in British military traditions, he said – a copy of the Rev. Dr W.H. Fitchett's *Deeds That Won The Empire*. The Gallipoli campaign lacked only one of the qualities that went to make such deeds, though admittedly rather a vital one: the quality of success. But in all other respects – courage, suffering and persistence – Gallipoli was as much the stuff of legend as Albuera on another peninsula, or the Heights of Abraham at Quebec. The summer came, the flowers died, and the dust blew everywhere. The flies spread dysentry from dugout to dug-out, and a man was as likely to be killed out of the firing line as in it. 'A few days ago,' wrote Lt Mervyn Higgins to his father, Mr Justice Higgins, 'Major Scott . . . was walking back to his dugout after breakfast, when a shell blew him to bits.' Private Herbert Parry, who had been court-martialled for incitement to mutiny after the debacle at Wilmansrust in the Boer War, was asleep when a Turkish shell landed squarely in his dugout. His father, who had described him as 'a true Briton' during the Wilmansrust affair, eventually received a letter from the 6th Battalion

[3] Lalor's sword was said to have been picked up by Lance-Corporal Harry Freame, one of the very few Anzacs who was not impeccably European (he was half Japanese), but dropped again and captured by the Turks. Snowy Howe, who was in the thick of that day's fighting, told a different story. 'My mate Clive De Mole picked up Lalor's sword,' he said in 1975, 'brought it back to the beach and gave it to a naval officer.'

padre: 'May your sense of present loss be tempered by the assurance of future and permanent gain when all wars and partings shall be o'er.'

The first class of cadets at Duntroon, many of whom had formed a guard of honour at the Canberra commencement ceremony in 1913, was graduated for active service before completing its fourth and final year. Of these twenty-seven Australians and eight New Zealanders, five Australians and two New Zealanders were killed on Gallipoli. Their average age was 20. Their former commandant and the first commander of the 1st Australian Division under Birdwood, General Bridges, was himself hit in the thigh by a Turkish sniper's bullet while walking up from Anzac Cove to the headquarters of the 1st Light Horse Brigade in Monash Valley only three weeks after the landing. The bullet severed an artery, and three days later the General was dead. Soon after Bridges's death, Sir Ian Hamilton's secretary, Lt-Colonel S. H. Pollen, visited Anzac Cove with the novelist, Captain Compton Mackenzie. Later, in his *Gallipoli Memories*, Mackenzie was to present the Anzacs in a light to which neither they nor their fellow countrymen would take exception. Decribing Pollen's encounter with three Australians ('not one of whom was less than six feet four inches tall'), Mackenzie managed to convey the qualities of mordant humour and egalitarian independence verging on insubordination which came to be associated with the Australian soldier:

> Pollen, who had a soft, somewhat ecclesiastical voice, was saying: 'Have you chaps heard that they're giving General Bridges a posthumous KCMG?'[4]
>
> 'Have they?' one of the giants replied. Well, that won't do him much good where he is now, will it, mate?'
>
> Poor Pollen, who was longing to be sympathetic and not to mind the way these Australians would stare at his red tabs without saluting, walked on a little depressed by the reception of his effort at making conversation, perhaps on the very spot where General Bridges had been mortally wounded. He looked carefully at the ground when he met the next lot, whereupon they all gave him an elaborate salute, and then because he had looked up too late to acknowledge it one of them turned to the others and said: 'I suppose that's what they call breeding.'
>
> They really were rather difficult; and so, no doubt, was Achilles.

To replace General Bridges the Commonwealth Government nominated the Chief of the Australian General Staff, Major-General J. G. Legge. Knowing that Legge was unpopular with his fellow officers, the Governor-General at first queried his appointment, then signed it. Two of the brigade commanders who would be serving under Legge, Colonel Monash and Colonel James McCay, talked of resigning because of the

[4] Bridges was in fact gazetted KCB the day before he died.

appointment; they would have preferred to continue under a British general who had taken Bridges's place temporarily. Hamilton, who had little confidence in Dominion staff officers, reacted to Legge's appointment with characteristic elitism. 'A commander of men,' he wrote to Sir Ronald Munro-Ferguson, '[is] not created so much by education as by birth. . . It takes a long time to manufacture a true military character and frame of mind.' Even Bridges, he wrote, 'fine character, brave soldier as he was . . . would not have been big enough to command a Corps.' The Australian Government considered, however, that it was 'expedient that an Australian officer should command the First Australian Division', and Legge held the position for several months until he formed the 2nd Division in Egypt and took it to Gallipoli. At this time General Birdwood was given command of the entire Australian Imperial Force, a position which he continued to hold for almost three more years.

After weeks of stalemate, followed by a determined but ultimately ineffectual offensive during August, the Dardanelles Committee, which was in charge of the campaign, resigned itself to the inevitability of replacing Hamilton and evacuating the peninsula. In taking the first of these decisions the Committee was influenced by a remarkable letter written to the Prime Minister of Australia by a young Australian journalist, K. A. (later Sir Keith) Murdoch. While travelling through the Middle East on his way to represent a group of Australian newspapers in London, Murdoch obtained Hamilton's permission to visit Gallipoli. After a brief visit to Anzac in early September, he returned to Hamilton's headquarters on the island of Imbros, where he met, among other war correspondents, Ellis Ashmead-Bartlett of the London *Daily Telegraph*. Ashmead-Bartlett, who had covered the campaign from its beginning, was by now thoroughly disillusioned about the prospect of success and was frustrated by the military censorship which prevented him from writing freely about what he had come to regard as a débâcle. Convinced by Ashmead-Bartlett that any prolongation of the campaign into winter would lead only to further disaster, Murdoch agreed to take with him to London an uncensored despatch by the *Daily Telegraph* correspondent. This was a clear violation of the undertaking given by all war correspondents, including Murdoch, to work only under censorship. Someone – either a fellow journalist, or one of the batmen on Imbros – informed Hamilton, and when Murdoch reached Marseilles he was arrested by a military escort and released only after he surrendered Ashmead-Bartlett's despatch.

As soon as he arrived in London, Murdoch wrote an 8,000-word personal letter to the Australian Prime Minister, Andrew Fisher, recounting everything he could remember from the confiscated despatch and from his own conversation with Ashmead-Bartlett. He made no secret of this, and allowed a copy of the letter to reach Britain's Minister of Munitions, Lloyd George, who had been openly critical of the Gallipoli campaign. At Lloyd George's suggestion, Murdoch also sent a copy to the British Prime Minister, Herbert Asquith. The letter, which was not made public until the 1960s, was a remarkable hodgepodge of fact, error and prejudice; but it carried enough weight to convince its readers, Asquith no less than Fisher, that affairs on Gallipoli had gone terribly astray. It also provided an interesting picture of British-Australian frictions in a deteriorating military situation.

Murdoch had visited Gallipoli soon after the crucial August offensive in which Anzac troops tried to seize 'the waist of the peninsula', the rugged Sari Bari range. In support of this main thrust, they also suffered very heavy casualties in diversionary attacks at Lone Pine and the Nek. Murdoch's letter described these August operations as 'a costly and bloody fiasco'. The whole Gallipoli campaign, he said, had been 'a series of disastrous underestimations, and I think our Australian generals are right when they say that, had any one of these been luckily so un-English a thing as an overestimation, we should have been through to Constantinople at much less cost than we have paid for our slender perch on the cliffs of the peninsula.'

He portrayed the Australians on Gallipoli as exhausted but still tenacious; the new British reinforcements, which had landed at Suvla Bay in support of the Sari Bair offensive, were thoroughly unreliable; and the British general staff, from Hamilton down, was incompetent and complacent. 'I could pour into your ears so much truth about the grandeur of our Australian army,' he wrote to Fisher, 'and the wonderful affection of these fine young soldiers for each other and their homeland, that your Australianism would become a more powerful sentiment than before. It is stirring to see them, magnificent manhood, swinging their fine limbs as they walk about Anzac. They have the noble faces of men who have endured. Oh, if you could picture Anzac as I have seen it, you would find that to be an Australian is the greatest privilege the world has to offer.' Although weakened by illness and overworked through lack of reinforcements, their fighting spirit was represented as a standing rebuke to what Murdoch described as 'the toy soldiers of Suvla.' 'Our men have found it impossible to form a high opinion of the British K men [products of the recruitment scheme introduced by Asquith's War Minister, Lord Kitchener] and territorials. They are merely a lot of child-like youths without strength to endure or brains to improve their conditions. I do not like to dictate this sentence, even for your eyes, but the fact is that after the first day at Suvla an order had to be issued to officers to shoot without mercy any soldiers who lagged or loitered in an advance.'

For the red-capped general staff, Murdoch's Anzacs had nothing but contempt. 'Sedition is talked round every tin of bully beef on the peninsula,' he wrote, 'and it is only loyalty that holds the forces together. Every returning troopship, every section of the lines of communications, is full of the same talk. I like General Hamilton, and found him exceedingly kindly . . . but as a strategist he has completely failed. Undoubtedly the essential and first step to restore the morale of the shaken forces is to recall him. . . The continuous and ghastly bungling over the Dardanelles enterprise was to be expected from such a General Staff as the British Army possesses, so far as I have seen it. The conceit and self-complacency of the red feather men are equalled only by their incapacity. . . What can you expect of men who have never worked seriously, who have lived for their appearance and for social distinction and self-satisfaction, and who are now called on to conduct a gigantic war? Kitchener has a terrible task in getting pure work out of these men, whose motives can never be pure, for they are unchangeably selfish. I want to say frankly that it is my opinion, and that without exception of Australian officers, appointments to the General Staff are made from motives of friendship and social influence. Australians now loathe and detest any Englishmen wearing red.'

Murdoch's letter was useful and timely ammunition for the London critics of Lord Kitchener and Gallipoli. Without consulting Kitchener or Hamilton, Asquith had the letter printed as a State Paper and circulated to members of the Committee of Imperial Defence. Hamilton was replaced in October and his successor, Lt-Gen Sir Charles Monro, immediately recommended evacuation. At Hamilton's request in November, the Committee of Imperial Defence circulated his detailed and dignified reply to Murdoch's charges; but his reputation was by then blighted beyond recovery. He summed up Murdoch's 'sweeping generalities' in words once used by Lord Derby: 'No gentleman would have said it, and no gentleman will believe it.' Although he would never want for admirers who continued to defend his name, Hamilton was never again trusted with command. Admittedly he had been unfortunate in some of his subordinates at Gallipoli, but his critics claimed that with more ruthlessness and closer personal supervision Hamilton could have compensated for that. Perhaps the fairest judgment on him came from the campaign's official British historian, Captain C. F. Aspinall-Oglander. 'The enthusiasm, self-confidence and personal courage demanded of the military commander-in-chief he possessed in full measure. But he lacked the iron will and dominating personality of a truly great commander. . . He left too much to his subordinates and hesitated to override their plans, even when in his opinion they were missing opportunities.'

The evacuation of Anzac, Suvla Bay and Cape Helles was the most successful single operation of the campaign. It was conducted by night, without arousing Turkish suspicion, and – confounding Hamilton's pessimistic prediction of a 50 per cent casualty rate – almost without loss of life. Birdwood, who said at first that he would rather die than leave the peninsula, was told by one Australian, with a nod towards a nearby burial ground: 'I hope *they* won't hear us going down the deres [gullies]'. There were many thousand left to hear what little sound was made by the Anzacs' muffled boots, for 7600 Australians and 2500 New Zealanders had been killed or mortally wounded in the campaign. The Allies, including British, Indian and French troops, probably suffered about 265,000 casualties, 46,000 of whom were killed or died of wounds or disease. The Turks, whose records were less carefully kept, acknowledged 86,700 dead and 164,000 wounded and sick. It seems likely, however, that the combined total of casualties on both sides exceeded half a million.

One of the last Australians to leave Anzac Cove on the night of 19 December 1915 was Colonel Monash. The feelings which he observed and recorded that night were feelings of relief rather than regret. 'The strain being over,' he wrote, 'the reaction came in wild and hilarious greetings, mutual felicitations and hearty handshakes all round. The steamer got under way for Lemnos, and the sights and sounds of Gallipoli dropped back into the past.' Into the past, but not out of mind. Australians who had been on Gallipoli (from 1917 they were distinguished by a brass 'A' for 'Anzac' on their shoulder patches), and Australians who had been there only vicariously, would long continue to assay the meaning of that experience; but most of the themes which were to be expounded and refined on successive Anzac Days were already discernible at the first ceremonies of this kind on 25 April 1916.

The first Anzac Day was an occasion for pride, the commemoration of self-sacrifice, and national self-assessment. The Chief Justice of Tasmania, Sir Herbert Nicholls, claimed that the Anzacs had performed a feat 'the like of which man had never adventured before.' What then, it might have been asked, had the Turks performed? Such vainglory as Sir Herbert's could almost be excused, for after all the Australians had won nine Victoria Crosses at Gallipoli.[5] The new Prime Minister, William Morris Hughes, was in London for the first Anzac Day, and in his address to Australian troops at the Hotel Cecil he spoke almost as wildly as the

[5] The distribution of these awards was curiously uneven. Seven of the Gallipoli VC's were awarded for valour at Lone Pine, and all but one of these were dated 9 August 1915.

Tasmanian Chief Justice. 'As a military operation the Anzacs had achieved the impossible,' he said. 'It was a feat of arms almost unparalleled in the history of war; yet it was but the beginning of a campaign in which such feats were daily done.' Self-sacrifice was a saving grace which softened the ugliness of those terrible months, and somehow compensated for failure. 'Since it has evoked this pure and noble spirit,' said the Prime Minister, 'who shall say that this dreadful war is wholly an evil? Into a world saturated with a lust of material things, which had elevated self into a deity, which had made wealth the standard of greatness, comes the sweet purifying breath of self-sacrifice.' Yet failure was not really any disqualification for the purpose which Gallipoli would serve; on the contrary, it may well have been essential. Australians had not evolved many legends to reflect and glorify aspects of their collective identity; but those they valued most – Lalor at Eureka, Burke and Wills at Cooper Creek, Kelly at Glenrowan – were all concerned with men who had taken their chances against great odds, and failed. Did Australian self-esteem perhaps contain a core of self-pity?

Some celebrants on the first Anzac Day were less concerned with the qualities displayed at Gallipoli than with the effect of that campaign on the world's opinion of Australia and on Australia's opinion of itself. At its most primitive level, this meant the unabashed enjoyment of acclaim. 'Soldiers,' said the Prime Minister at the Hotel Cecil, 'your deeds have won you a place in the Temple of the Immortals. The world has hailed you as heroes. Your comrades of the British Army have claimed you as brothers in arms, and the citizens of the Empire are proud to call you kinsmen.'[6] As other writers and speakers observed, however, the effects of Gallipoli were wider and more complex than mere acclaim and gratification. The performance of Australians in a world arena, in unison with but clearly distinct from British troops, was seen as a rite of passage which confirmed national confidence and incorporated Australia into a community even larger than the Empire. The frequent allusions on 25 April 1916 to adulthood, blood and fire were strangely reminiscent of the initiation ceremony which Spencer and Gillen had watched in central Australia on 25 April 1901. The Hobart *Mercury* said that at Gallipoli Australia had 'taken up the duties of manhood', and undergone a 'baptism of fire' which admitted it to the 'full family circle of British peoples.' *The*

---

[6] In 1916 the Anzac Day issue of *The School Paper* in Queensland gave its Class I and Class II readers much the same assurance of international praise:

    'Nev-er be-fore has a hard-er task been giv-en to sol-diers than that of this now fam-ous land-ing.

    All the coun-tries which are friends of the Al-lies soon rang with praise for the brave Aus-tra-li-ans and New Zea-land-ers too.'

Sydney Morning Herald thought that Anzac Day would 'go down to posterity as the day in which Australia cast on one side the ideas and ideals of adolescence, and assumed the more serious responsibilities of man's estate.' Even such an imperial-minded paper as the *Mercury* now spoke of the national consciousness within Australia's imperial identity. Australia, it wrote, had become a 'blood brotherhood in the best sense' with 'Australian rights, Australian liberties ... [and] Australian responsibilities.' 'It cannot be too definitely known and realised that we are fighting our own battles in the War, not merely rendering filial and chivalrous assistance to a distressed Motherland.'

In Sydney the Roman Catholic *Freeman's Journal* found evidence of new national self-confidence. '[Before Gallipoli],' it wrote, 'we were Australian in name, and we had a flag, but we had been taught by our politicians not to trust ourselves – we were constantly admonished by our daily journals to remember that we were nothing better than a joint in the tail of a great Empire ... Anzac Day has changed all that. The Australian flag has been brought from the garret and has been hoisted on a lofty tower in the full sight of its own people. No matter how the war may end – and it can only end one way – we are at last a nation, with one heart, one soul and one thrilling aspiration ... there runs through the Commonwealth a lifting spirit such as it never knew before.' But perhaps the most considered view of Gallipoli came from the NSW Director of Education, Peter Board. In a paper which he read to the Australian adult nationhood: 'She became an active partner in a worldwide Empire,' he said. 'If there is one day of the year more than another on which it is fitting to celebrate an Australian Empire Day it is 25th April. For on 25th April 1915 Australia first took up the responsibilities of Empire by the active participation of her sons in the defence of the Empire against an enemy that had willed her humiliation. 'On 25th April 1915.' he said, 'Australia passed beyond a partnership resting on the mere sentiments of kinship into a partnership of national sacrifice in the interests of an Imperial cause, and in resistance to an Empire's enemy. On 25 April history and Australia's history were fused, and fused at white heat. Never again can the history of this continent of ours stand detached from World history. Its voice must be heard in the Councils of the Empire, because its men and its women have striven and fought and died in an Empire struggle.'

Few Australians then realised how much fighting and dying still had to be endured. The torment of the final Aranda initiation ceremony, in which young adults were made by their elders to lie upon a bough-covered fire, was as nothing compared to the ordeal which lay ahead of many Gallipoli veterans and reinforcements from Australia. When the Anzacs returned from Gallipoli to Egypt, many of them met Norman Brookes, the 1914 Achilles of Wimbledon. Although kept out of the army by a duodenal ulcer, Brookes was now Commissioner for the Australian Red Cross Society in Cairo. His German opponent of the previous year, Otto Froitzheim, had been interned in England; and his Davis Cup partner, Tony Wilding, had been killed when a German shell landed on the roof of his dugout in France. That was where the AIF would be going next: to France, where the green boughs were laid out on fires, and smoking.

POZIERES

WHEN AUSTRALIA'S official war correspondent, C. E. W. Bean, first saw the village of Pozières, or rather the part of Picardy in which that village could once have been seen, he was reminded of a dry creek bed in central Australia. In midsummer Pozières should have been a tidy, fragrant collection of houses, orchards and barns about eight kilometres from the town of Albert in northern France. The orchards should have been heavy with stone fruit, the gardens should have been in flower, and the fields on all sides of the village should have been carrying crops of wheat and vegetables – for this was the ripe, verdurous condition of some parts of Picardy. Only a few kilometres south of Pozières the narrow Somme River made its way to the sea between low grassy banks and tremulous poplar trees, past villages whose gardens were in flower and wheatfields already being harvested. 'The harvest looks as if it had been a bountiful one,' wrote an Australian army nurse, Sister Alice Kitchen, who travelled through this countryside at about the same time as Bean. 'The yellow white was being cut and stooked everywhere.'

How different was the scene at Pozières, where another kind of harvest had lately been taken in. 'Imagine a gigantic ash heap,' wrote Bean, 'a place where dust and rubbish have been cast for years outside some dry, derelict, God-forsaken up-country township. Imagine some broken-down creek bed in the driest of our dry central Australian districts, abandoned for a generation to the goats, in which the hens have been scratching as long as men can remember. Then take away the hens and the goats and all traces of any living or moving thing. You must not even leave a spider. Put here, in evidence of some old tumbled roof, a few roof beams and tiles sticking edgeways from the ground, and the low faded ochre stump of the windmill peeping over the top of the hill, and there you have Pozières.'

In this pulverized waste the AIF underwent its worst ordeal of the war. It suffered almost as many casualties here in less than seven weeks as it had in the full thirty-four weeks at Gallipoli. No bombardments of that terrible artillery war were as prolonged, and few as intensive, as those which fell upon the Australians at Pozières, churning and re-churning the flat, wire-strung terrain as far as anyone could see. Men who had served on the

Peninsula said it was a picnic compared to this. 'How we do think of home and laugh at the pettiness of our little daily annoyances!' wrote one man. 'We could not sleep, we remember, because of the creaking of the pantry door, or the noise of the tramcars, or the kids playing around and making a row. Well, we can't sleep now because – six shells are bursting around here every minute, and you can't get much sleep between them; guns are belching out shells, with a most thunderous clap each time; the ground is shaking with each little explosion; I am wet, and the ground on which I rest is wet; my feet are cold, in fact I'm all cold with my two skimp blankets; I am covered with cold, clotted sweat, and sometimes my person is foul; I am hungry, I am annoyed because of the absurdity of war; I see no chance of anything better for tomorrow, or the day after, or the year after.'

By the time the AIF began reaching France in March 1916 the Allied and German armies had been locked in more or less unchanging position for the best part of eighteen months, grinding on each other like two jaws extending 800 kilometres from the North Sea to Switzerland. The greater part of this front, southeast from the Somme and southward to the Swiss border, was held for the Allies by French armies; north of the Somme it was held by four British armies to within a few kilometres of the coast, where the Belgians took over. By July the Anzac forces, which had doubled their strength in recent months, numbered 90,000 in France, another 90,000 in England and 25,000 (the Mounted Division) in the Middle East. The infantry consisted of I Anzac Corps (the 1st and 2nd Divisions of the AIF and one New Zealand Division, under General Birdwood) and II Anzac Corps (the new 4th and 5th Australian Divisions, under another British commander, Major-General Sir Alexander Godley). Birdwood's Corps left Egypt first, going to Marseilles and then north by train and route march to a relatively quiet section of the British front near Armentières.

There were many differences from Gallipoli. In France the Australians were issued with British steel helmets and box respirators for use during gas attack; they were equipped with trench mortars, and for the first time they saw aeroplanes flying regularly overhead. The enemy on the ground was less visible than at Gallipoli – a grey uniformed figure in spiked black helmet, glimpsed briefly through a telescope while crossing from one parapet to another – yet obviously he was a more calculating, formidable adversary. The accuracy with which German shells found farmhouses in which Australians were billeted was a painful lesson to the Australians that their movements were being carefully watched by German spotters. In any case, the Germans belonged to a race in whose fortitude and competence the Australian people had long held a vested interest. As if to make this point explicit, one of the Anzac Corps's first adversaries in the field was the Saxon Division.

The apprenticeship of I Anzac Corps on the 'nursery front' was curtailed by an Allied offensive on the Somme, which began on 1 July. This drive by British and French armies was intended to break the enemy line and take some of the German pressure off the French fortress of Verdun on the southeastern front. If a wide enough breach could be made, a Reserve Army under General Sir Hubert Gough would try to push through and 'roll up' the German line to the north. The breach made in the first attack was not wide enough for any rolling up operation, and a second attempt in mid-July foundered on stubborn German resistance at Pozières, an advance post protecting the German stronghold of Thiepval further north. Lacking the resources to press consistently right along the Somme front, the British Commander-in-Chief, Sir Douglas Haig, continued to attack strongly in the south, where his 4th Army had had some success, and ordered Gough's Reserve Army facing Thiepval to maintain 'a steady, mechanical, step-by-step advance.'

What Haig meant by this was that the Reserve Army, strengthened by the addition of I Anzac Corps, should keep the Germans busy in that sector until the arrival of the New Army then being formed in Britain enabled the Allies to launch a more general offensive. It was to do so by repeatedly making shallow attacks on a narrow front. When the 4th Army delivered its next blow on the southern sector, there would be another attack on Pozières, this time by the 1st Division of the AIF. So far the German garrison in that wilderness had survived four British infantry attacks and a bombardment which had reduced the village to heaps of rubble. This time there was to be no mistake: before the attack, the ruins of Pozières and the old German lines on slightly higher ground beyond the village were bombarded relentlessly for several days. The noise of bombardments on this front was at times so great that it could be heard in England.

On the eve of the attack General Haig visited Gough's headquarters to make sure, as he recorded in his diary, that the Australians had been given only a simple task. 'This is the first time,' he wrote, 'that they will be taking part in a serious offensive on a big scale against the German forces.'[1] The taking of Pozières was indeed relatively straightforward, but

[1] It would not, however, be the first time they had faced German troops. On 19 July and 20 July the newly arrived 5th Division of II Anzac Corps took part in an attack on Fromelles, in the Armentières sector, intended to prevent German forces being transferred from there to the Somme. This feint cost the 5th Division 5533 casualties.

the further the Australians advanced beyond the village the harder their task became. 'Our movements are timed to the second with artillery,' wrote Lance-Corporal Arthur Foxcroft, a bush worker from Gilgandra who took part in the advance on 23 July. '12.15 am over 15 hundred of our guns concentrated on Pozières, licking the ground from our barb wire through the village and back to Huns heavy batteries. 12.30 am Fix bayonets and over you go lads, could not hear guns for excitement. Sky one blaze from fire from guns. I had helmet dented by shrapnel just as I jumped into No Man's Land. . . The lads walked across 600 yards at right angles to main road in middle of village, our pre-arranged objective, as though going to a cricket match. Our artillery prevented huns from coming out of their burrows. Met a few huns in shell holes on way over demoralised by intensity of our bombardment, and settled them. Reached objective, and dug ourselves in.'

The only failure by the Australians that day was in the OG (Old German) lines about 400 metres out along the Pozières–Bapaume road, where a slight crest rose above the rest of the countryside. On the 'crest', if it could be called that, for in the distance it seemed no more than a few feet higher than the village, stood the splintered stump of what had once been a windmill. The 1st Division captured part of the OG lines; but on the extreme right, where the windmill had once creaked as it gound the wheat of Pozières, the advancing Australians were not able to locate the German machine-gunners and bomb fighters who were known to be concealed somewhere in that desert of barbed wire, decaying corpses and scarified earth.

Such failure could be overlooked, for the taking of Pozières had been the Allies' only success during the offensive of 23 July. The penalty for success was bombardment, and for the next three days the 1st Division was subject to continuous shelling by a large part of the German artillery in the Thievpal sector. By 27 July, when the 2nd Division relieved it, the 1st Division had suffered more than 5000 casualties. A sergeant who watched the survivors coming out into a rest area wrote: 'They looked like men who had been in Hell . . . drawn and haggard and so dazed that they appeared to be walking in a dream and their eyes looked glassey and starey.' Hardly less affecting was the sight of men going into the lines knowing that they were more likely to die than live. 'I saw a battallion of 1000 men going up to go in,' wrote Private M. Burrows of Sydney, 'and within half an hour there was only 300 left . . . everywhere you would look you could see pieces of men dead and moaning. It was terrible I will never forget. . .'

In the early minutes of 29 July, assault battalions from the 2nd

Division set out from their trenches to try to take the OG lines. The ground they had to cover was pitted with craters, strung with barbed wire which had survived the bombardments, and swept by storms of machine-gun fire. Some Australians managed to reach the OG lines, but were soon driven out by hand-thrown bombs and machine-gun fire. The night attack was an almost complete failure, and it cost the 2nd Division 3500 casualties. One of the officers with the 23rd Battalion was Lieutenant Alec Raws, who made his first appearance in this narrative as captain of the 1st XI at Prince Alfred College, Adelaide, in 1901. At Speech Day that year Alec Raws had heard Lord Tennyson assure the boys of Prince Alfred that one day they would win even greater victories than Wellington at Waterloo. Did he recall that old jingo's confident prediction as he walked back from the OG lines?

Raws was a journalist. He worked on the Adelaide *Register* and *Advertiser*, the Perth *Daily News*, and finally the Melbourne *Argus*, where he was chief parliamentary reporter from 1907 until his enlistment in 1915. Despite his success at cricket and tennis (he was captain of the St Kilda Tennis Club in Melbourne), Raws was at first rejected for military service because of his small physique. But like Jack Tarrant from Wyong, who was also out between Pozières and the OG lines that night, he found the recruiting office more amenable in 1915. Raws was a wry, reluctant soldier who could express himself with more style and candour than most of his comrades. His letters from France, written mainly to his relatives and friends in Melbourne (he was not married), are among the most memorable of that genre. 'Tomorrow I shall be in the midst of it all,' he wrote in July. 'There is something humorous in the situation, when I actually come to it. John Alexander Raws, who cannot tread upon a worm; who has never struck another human being except in fun; who cannot read of the bravery of others at the front without tears welling to his eyes; who cannot think of blood and mangled bodies without bodily sickness – this man, I, go forth tomorrow to kill and maim, murder and ravage. It is funny.'

Alec Raws had welcomed his posting to the 23rd Battalion on the eve of the 2nd Division's attack, for he knew that his younger brother, Goldy, a Gallipoli veteran, was there already. The two were not destined to meet, however, for Goldy disappeared without trace during the night attack of 29 July. After helping to search for his brother in No Man's Land without success, Alec wrote: 'I lost, in three days, my brother and my two best friends, and in all six out of seven of all my officer friends who went into the scrap – all killed. Not one was buried, and some died in great agony. It was impossible to help the wounded at all in some sections. . . The dead were everywhere. There had been no burying in the sector I was in for a week before we went there.'

Jack Tarrant of the 20th Battalion was unable to return from the OG attack before being stranded by daylight, so he took shelter with four others in a crater. The sky was clear, and shells burst overhead all day. In the course of the day three of Tarrant's companions were hit by shrapnel. As soon as night came again, he crawled back to his trench for help. 'Who the hell are you?' called a voice.

'Twentieth!'

'There's no 20th out there!'

'There was!'

The Commander-in-Chief made known his displeasure at the 2nd Division's failure. 'From several reports,' he wrote on 29 July, 'I think the cause was due to want of thorough preparation. After lunch I visited HQ Reserve Army and impressed on Gough and his GSO that they must supervise more closely the plans of the Anzac Corps. Some of their Divisional Generals are so ignorant and (like many Colonials) so conceited, that they cannot be trusted to work out unaided the plans of attack.' Later, at Anzac headquarters, Haig said to Birdwood and his chief of staff, General C. B. B. White: 'You're not fighting Bashi-bazouks now! This is serious, scientific war and you are up against the most scientific and most military nation in Europe.' This likening of Gallipoli's defenders to 19th century Turkish irregulars must have stung Birdwood and his Australian advisers. Although General Legge's preparation for the 2nd Division attack had not been without fault, Haig's detailed criticism of it was almost entirely inaccurate. When the lecture ended, General White – ignoring a warning head-shake from one of Haig's staff – defended the 2nd Division point by point. Haig heard him through, doubtless reflecting to himself about Colonial conceit, and then said, fatherly hand on White's shoulder: 'I dare say you are right, young man!'

At Legge's request, the 2nd Division was permitted to attack the OG lines again rather than be withdrawn after failure. This was a privilege which Alec Raws and others like him could well have done without. 'We are lousy, stinking, ragged, unshaven, sleepless,' he wrote to a friend on 4 August, the day the second attack was launched. 'I have one puttee, a dead man's helmet, another dead man's gas protector, a dead man's bayonet. My tunic is rotten with other men's blood, and partly splattered with a comrade's brains. It is horrible, but why should you people at home not know? Several of my friends are raving mad. I met three officers out in No Man's Land the other night, all rambling and mad.'

If anything was worse than the uproar and confusion of a night attack over featureless terrain, it was the task of digging jumping-off trenches at night while under bombardment. The men who dug these trenches, from which attacking troops would later begin their advance, were sometimes buried as they worked, dug out and buried again. Raws went out with one of the entrenching parties which excavated a jumping-off line for the night of 4 August. They went forward through communication trenches, under bombardment all the way, and for some time in No Man's Land they were unable to find the appointed site. 'I would gladly have shot myself,' wrote Raws, 'for I had not the slightest idea where our lines or the enemy's were, and the shells were coming at us from, it seemed, three directions. As a matter of fact that was right. Well, we lay down terror-stricken along a bank. The shelling was awful. I took a long drink of neat whisky and went up and down the bank trying to find a man who could tell where we were. Eventually I found one. . .

'Our leader was shot before we arrived, and the strain had sent two other officers mad. I and another new officer took charge and dug the trench. We were being shot at all the time, and I knew that if we did not finish the job before daylight a new assault planned for the next night would fail. It was awful, but we had to drive the men by every possible means. And dig ourselves. The wounded and killed had to be thrown to one side. I refused to let any sound man help a wounded man. The sound men had to dig. Many men went mad. Just before daybreak, an engineer officer out there, who was hopelessly rattled, ordered us to go. The trench was not finished. I took it on myself to insist on the men staying, saying that any man who stopped digging would be shot. We dug on and finished amid a tornado of bursting shells. All the time the enemy flares were making the whole area as light as day. We got away as best we could. I was again in the rear going back, and again we were cut off and lost. I was buried twice and thrown down several times – buried with dead and dying. The ground was covered with bodies in all stages of decay and mutilation, and I would, after struggling free from the earth, pick up a body by me to try to lift him out with me, and find him a decayed corpse. I pulled a head off . . .'

On the night of 4 August the Windmill crest and the OG lines running along that height were taken by the Australians, and securely reinforced. The 2nd Division could have pushed further east, but General Gough's orders were to advance from the Pozières plateau, as this elevated position was rather grandiosely called, northward on a narrow front to Mouquet Farm and on behind Thiepval. The consequence of having taken Pozières plateau was a bombardment of unprecedented intensity on 6 August, for the further the Australians pushed their salient into German lines, the more they were surrounded by German artillery. As Alec Raws had observed, the shells sometimes came from three directions. The 'methodical, step-by-step' attack on Mouquet Farm by the relieving 4th Division was even more exposed to German fire – from the front, flank and rear. Food, water and stores had to be carried northward through constantly shelled ridge trenches, and then over two undulations whose crests were visible to the Germans and barraged by them at every sign of movement. The gains seemed absurdly inadequate compared to the price paid for them in human life. On 22 August the 2nd Division relieved the 4th and renewed the attack on Mouquet Farm with stronger forces. It was not until late September, however, that a wider advance by the Reserve Army succeeded in taking both Mouquet Farm and Thiepval.

Lt Raws, who went back to Pozières with the 2nd Division, had written from a rest area to his brother-in-law: 'You always told me I would stick it all right, and I did, but I'd give anything to be out of it for good. All of us would. I saw strong men who had been through Gallipoli sobbing and trembling as with ague – men who had never turned a hair before. The fact that it was all so new to me probably helped enormously.' To his brother in Melbourne, however, he confided that he had lately experienced fainting spells – 'fortunately only one in public, and then among strange officers.' 'I was terribly glad I was never even threatened with anything of the sort during those ten days in the line,' he wrote. 'The first I ever had was quite unexpected – the night before, in an adjoining village. None of this for father of course. . . Before going in to this next affair, at the same dreadful spot, I want to tell you, so that it may be on record, that I honestly believe Goldy and many other officers were murdered on the night you know of, through the incompetence, callousness and personal vanity of those high in authority. I realise the seriousness of what I say, but I am so bitter, and the facts are so palpable, that it must be said. Please be very discreet with this letter – unless I should go under.' He did go under. On his second day in the line, he and three others were killed instantly by an exploding German shell; there were no marks on Raws's body, so he must have died from concussion. He was buried nearby, under the usual wooden cross. After the Germans came back through Picardy in March 1918, and the earth was turned over again, the whereabouts of the graves of men like Alec Raws were anyone's guess. In words later to be inscribed upon the unidentified headstones at a military cemetery near Pozières, they were 'Known Only To God'.

Pozières was a darker version of Gallipoli. For all its anguish, the 1915 campaign had left Australians with a feeling of national fulfilment; Pozières left in its wake only disenchantment and resentment. The casualty lists of August and September 1916 turned war into murder, and Achilles into Cain. The months of September drew to a sombre close with a list of 1718 casualties on the 25th, 1796 on the 26th, 1837 on the 29th, and 1597 on the 30th. *The Sydney Morning Herald* of 30 September contained 141 Roll of Honour advertisements. Many of these were trite though doubtless comforting expressions of British-Australian loyalty: 'Your death has made us sad, dear Jack,/ We are sorrowed by your fall;/ But you died a British soldier,/ 'Tis the grandest death of all.' Others expressed only raw, disconsolate grief: 'Oh Ted, Ted.' As we shall see in the next chapter, the casualty lists from Pozières formed a funereal prelude to a referendum on conscription for overseas military service – emphasising the need for reinforcements, but at the same time helping to tip the vote against compulsion. Who in good conscience could vote to send someone else to another Pozières?

In less than seven weeks at Pozières the AIF had lost 6842 dead and 17,513 wounded or gassed. The effects of this could be seen not only in the referendum but in two attitudes within the AIF: one was a narrower concept of duty, and the other a new degree of bitterness towards the British high command. The most severe penalty for indiscipline in the AIF, repatriation in disgrace, lost much of its deterrent power after Pozières, and wounds were welcomed as much as they had once been feared. 'Poor wounded devils you meet on the stretchers are laughing with glee,' wrote Alec Raws. 'One cannot blame them. They are getting out of this.' Sapper Ernest de Mouncy of Perth had this to say: 'In civilian life the thought of a broken limb would be something awful, but it's very common in the lines to hear the men wish for a loss of an arm or leg and if a fellow gets his leg or arm shattered he is looked on by his mates as a very lucky beggar and they congratulate him and regret it is not themselves who got it.'

The effect of Pozières on Australian-British relations was assessed some years later by C. E. W. Bean in the third volume of the *Official History of Australia In The War of 1914–18*. Bean, who was an editorial and feature writer on *The Sydney Morning Herald* when the war began, had been appointed official correspondent with the first expeditionary force on the understanding that he would eventually write the official war history. He landed at Anzac Cove on 25 April, and was wounded later in the campaign. He was a tall, rather thin man of thirty-seven, freckled, with yellowish-red hair, glasses and an accent which owed everything to his English education and nothing to his Australian birth. The AIF could not have found a more tireless, devoted chronicler. Bean revered the idealised Australian as a reincarnation of the 16th Century Briton, and this reverence he now focussed with unswerving clarity upon the AIF. He took immense trouble, and no little risk, and by the end of the war had filled no fewer than 226 notebooks. His history was microscopic in its attention to detail (Gallipoli alone filled 1635 pages, and Pozières another 445), but it was not very critical.

Bean held the view that as official historian he could write nothing in conflict with official military reports; his strictures upon the British staff at Pozières, carefully phrased though they were, stood out conspicuously against a background of habitual reticence. 'Some of the more thoughtful soldiers wondered (and could not be blamed for wondering) whether any sufficient object was being gained by this excessive strain and loss,' he wrote. 'The prevailing tactics – repeated shallow advances on narrow fronts – were dreaded and detested. . . Although most Australian soldiers were optimists, and many were opposed on principle to voicing – or even harboring – grievances, it is not surprising if the effect on some intelligent men was a bitter conviction that they were being uselessly sacrificed . . .

'The author of the "piecemeal" policy between July 23rd and September 15th was . . . the Commander-in-Chief; but the actual steps by which that policy was carried out Haig left, as was his wont, almost unconditionally in the hands of Gough; his own control barely went beyond the emission of a few general maxims. . . The Australian troops, who learned to hate the reiteration of attacks on narrow fronts, not unfairly attributed to him the responsibility, and their aversion from serving under him, which became pronounced in the following year, dated from this time. . . To throw the several parts of an Army Corps, brigade after brigade, in a series of battering-ram blows twenty times in succession against one of the strongest points in the enemy's defence . . . may certainly be described as "methodical", but the claim that it was economic is entirely unjustified. In spite of the British preponderance in the air and in artillery, the repeated assaults from the Pozières salient were . . . almost inevitably more expensive to the attacker than to the defender.'

In 1917 one Australian officer, Major Garnet Adcock, wrote in a letter home to Victoria: 'Everyone here is "fed up" of the war, but not with the Hun. The British staff, British methods and British bungling have sickened us.' Although the AIF remained willing to fight, its morale was undoubtedly soured by some of the demands made by British generals and by the failure of some of the British units on Australian flanks. By 1918 the Australians had become so free with criticism that the War Office felt compelled to ask the Commonwealth Government to keep out of Australian newspapers the 'scurrilous and unfair allusions to the conduct of United Kingdom troops' which censors had noticed in soldiers' letters. The Australians themselves were not above reproach on the score of indiscipline. Their reputation in this regard prompted Haig to write: 'I am sorry to say that the Australians are not nearly as efficient [as the Canadians]. I put this down to Birdwood, who, instead of facing the problem, has gone in for the easier way of saying everything is perfect and making himself as popular as possible. We have had to separate the Australians into Convalescent Camps of their own, because they were giving so much trouble when along with our men and put such revolutionary ideas into their heads.' According to Haig's diary, the Australians had nine men per thousand in prison compared with only 1.6 per thousand among the Canadian, New Zealand and South African forces, and one per thousand in the British Army. 'This is greatly due to the fact,' he wrote, 'that the Australian Government refuses to allow capital punishment to be awarded to any Australians.'[2]

Resentment immediately after Pozières was heightened by a belief that newly raised British forces were being withheld from active service while Australians continued to fight in France. As the first battle of the Somme ended indecisively in November 1916, the Australian journalist Keith Murdoch wrote to the Secretary of State for Colonies, Bonar Law, about 'the sadness of heart of the men in the field.' 'They are quite ready to go on to the end,' he said, 'but it is tragic if we do not do everything possible to make them fit in mind and body and glad in heart. They were ready for anything – and very eager – after their rest in Egypt from December to March, and any brief spell would make them fully the old force again. Of course, the Australians ask no favours, and military necessities may make any rest impossible, but perhaps some allowance should be made for the special disadvantages our men are under – their long distance from home, the strangeness of climate and surroundings, and the fact that they have not seen their own people for two years and are not – like the British Army – fighting at their own back door. The real necessity of course is to increase the men's respect for Great Britain.'

At about the same time the Colonial Secretary received similar advice from the Australian Governor-General. 'It is understood by my Ministers,' cabled Sir Ronald Munro-Ferguson, 'that the Australian troops have been in France almost continuously and there is feeling that in the matter of leave these are not being fairly treated. It has been reported to Government that there is considerable discontent in Australian Imperial Force in

[2] Under Australia's Defence Act, the death penalty could be applied only to mutiny or desertion to, or treacherous dealings with, the enemy. It was not invoked at all during the war. By contrast, the British Army executed three of its own officers and 343 men between 1914 and 1919.

consequence of this impression particularly as it is believed, as result of information which has reached soldiers, that there are large numbers of troops raised in United Kingdom none of whom have been sent to front for active service though they have been organised for more than twelve months.'

There had been some Australian troops in Britain from 1915 onwards, either recovering from wounds received at Gallipoli, or training for service in France. Vance Palmer remembered later in his life how deeply and unexpectedly he was affected in 1915, while still wanting to regard the war as a European affair, by the sight of 'three lean, uniformed figures, in leggings and Australian hats, sauntering down Charing Cross Road.' In December 1916 Sister Alice Kitchen noticed how 'pale, sick and thin' the Australian soldiers looked in London. 'I suppose they are mostly convalescents,' she wrote. 'A great many invalids are about the streets wearing khaki overcoats with a blue band on their sleeves. What someone calls "the blue badge of courage." ' From that time onwards, however, the Australians in France could look forward to spending leave in England about once a year without the painful prerequisite of a wound.

'How often do you get leave to Australia?' one Anzac was asked in Britain. 'Once every war,' he replied, '– at the end of it.' Britain was the next best thing to Australia, but on closer acquaintance most Australian soldiers decided that it ran a pretty poor second. After watching the London crowds go by, Captain George Mitchell wrote home to South Australia: 'They all bore the hallmark of the Cog. Pale faced and undersized, they appeared quite passionless, these people who work year in and year out beyond the reach of sunshine and out of touch with nature.' Sapper de Mouncy was annoyed by 'the following legends . . . on notice boards in every field or paddock – "Private", "Out of Bounds", "Trespassers Will Be Prosecuted" etc. We would take no notice of these signs but walk anywhere our fancy took us.' The Australians seem to have enjoyed visiting the land of their forebears, which they had been taught to revere since childhood, but they were certainly not over-awed; on the contrary, their self-esteem not only survived the experience but positively throve on it. They continued to respect the imperial ideal, but each fault they found with Britain enhanced their pride in Australia. 'The Australian on leave in London was very proud of himself, and very proud of his country,' recalled Jack Tarrant, who took the opportunity while there of having his right arm tattooed with a skull and dagger, 'Death Before Dishonour' and a girl in a wine glass.

The Australians seem to have regarded themselves, and not without reason, as heaven's gift to English girls. They were glamourised by the

London press (one British war correspondent, Phillip Gibbs, wrote of 'these clean-cut Australian boys with the fine, steady, truth-telling eyes which look so straight even after a nerve-breaking ordeal of fire'), they were usually wearing new uniforms supplied by AIF headquarters in Horseferry Road, and their pay was three or four times greater than the British soldier's. On the debit side of English leave, the venereal disease rate was so high that General Birdwood asked the Colonial Office to introduce drastic health measures under the Defence of the Realm Act. 'We do what we can,' he wrote, 'in the way of having the men met on their arrival in London, accommodation arranged for them in extensive quarters . . . and I believe that the vast majority of men would remain reasonably free of disease, but for the molestation which I hear from all sides they receive from women in the streets of London. Unfortunately, as far as this particular aspect is concerned, our men are well paid, and very liberal handed with their money. Women have of course found this out long ago, and consequently will not leave them alone, as long as they have the power to get hold of them. I have had so many letters from the parents of my boys in Australia, writing so sadly and, indeed, indignantly on the subject, saying they are proud to give their sons to fight, and if need be to die, for the Empire, but they had not reckoned with *this*.'

The majority of Australians on leave in London simply enjoyed their popularity, without worrying unduly about *that*. 'The Aussie soldier is a very very popular chap indeed with the majority of the feminine portion of the English people,' wrote Sapper de Mouncy. 'That is easily accounted for they have made a fuss of the girls, practically brought them out of the old groove they have lived in so long. For instance a Tommy takes his donah for an evening outing he treats her to the 3d or 6d seats in the pictures or theatre, buys her peppermint lollies, has fish and chips for supper, takes a twopenny tube or penny bus or tram home. She was quite satisfied with this till the following happens. The same girl meets an Aussie a night or two after the above outing, first thing he does is to buy her the best box of chocolates he can get, pays for the best seats in the theatre or pictures expense being no object, she reclines back in plush seat of the dress circle or front stalls trying to make herself and people think she has been born to it and thinks of the difference between this and the 3d or 6d touch of the night or two before. She is then taken to one of the best places in town for supper amongst officers and ladies of all degrees, and at last when homeward bound nothing but a motor car is good enough for her. Tommy does not like us they have no chance, they cannot compete with the Aussie nor have they the assurance that our boys have.'

13

THE WAR IN AUSTRALIA

THE WAR on the home front was really a war among Australians. It was a war without bloodshed, unless one counts the Battle of Broken Hill,[1] or the minor injuries of public disorder; and a war without fear of external attack, unless one counts whales wrongly reported as German submarines, or flocks of migratory birds mistaken for aeroplanes. Yet war of a kind it was, with contention more widespread than at any previous time in Australian history, even in the worst sectarian and industrial upheavals of the 19th century. The nation was divided – not neatly into two camps, but into several overlapping ones which all drew their acrimony from the war against Germany. To start with, the families of men who had gone to the war, and perhaps even lost their lives, looked askance at those who had not volunteered. The working class was less enthusiastic about the war than the middle class, for it was the more severely affected by wartime wage freezes and rising prices. Many Labor politicians resented the extent to which the war effort had taken precedence over social reform, and in this they were at odds not only with the Liberal Opposition but with their own parliamentary leaders. Religious sectarianism could also be relied upon to set neighbour against neighbour. Despite their professed early intention of sinking Irish grievances in imperial loyalty, many Australian Catholics found it increasingly difficult to reconcile Britain's solicitude for the independence of small European nations with its denial of Home Rule to one small island in particular. Protestants, on the other hand, regarded agitation for 'Rome Rule' as almost treasonable.

[1] This extraordinary incident was the closest Australia came to armed conflict on its own soil during the war. On the morning of New Year's Day 1915 Mullah Abdullah, a butcher from Broken Hill, and Gool Mohammed, an ice-cream vendor, opened fire on a train carrying 1200 picnickers from Broken Hill to Silverton in open ore trucks. Lying on a bank near Gool Mohammed's cart, which was flying the Turkish flag, the two men poured rifle fire into the passing train, killing three passengers and wounding seven others. Police, soldiers and members of the Broken Hill rifle club made short work of the attackers, killing one and mortally wounding the other. The two men were not Turks, as their flag suggested, but natives of Afghanistan and northwestern India. Both were Mohammedans, however, and recognised the Sultan of Turkey as their religious leader. Beyond that, their motives remained a mystery.

Through all these various divisions, like an earth tremor running along fault lines, went the overriding issue of conscription, shaking friends apart, splitting the Labor Party, dividing the Roman Catholic Church, exacerbating class hatred, and widening the gap between returned soldiers and the men who stayed at home. The Commonwealth Government already had power to conscript for military service within Australia. Should it also seek power to conscript men for service overseas – which was to say, in the cauldron of France – or should it set civil liberty above the war effort and continue to reinforce the AIF solely by voluntary enlistment? Although there were more than two ways of looking at this, the question was susceptible of only two answers. For that reason, the various factions of the war in Australia may be assembled arbitrarily and somewhat loosely under two standards. Under the Union Jack, lustily singing the national anthem, were likely to be found imperialists or 'win-the-war' loyalists, conservatives, capitalists, militarists, donors of white feathers, the middle class, the daily press, Protestants, returned soldiers and of course conscriptionists.[2] Under the Australian flag, singing 'Advance Australia Fair', were nationalists, workers, the bulk of the Labor Party, pacifists, socialists and anarcho-syndicalists, arsonists, strikers, suffragettes, Irish Catholics and anti-conscriptionists. Some groups were represented under both flags, and to confuse the polarisation even further the win-the-war imperialists in Federal Parliament eventually called themselves Nationalists. The British-Australian duality survived the war in Australia, though not without some change of proportion. There was still room for the Lion beside the Kangaroo, but not as much room as before.

The Governor-General, Sir Ronald Munro-Ferguson, observed in December 1915 that Australia's loyalty to the Crown was 'almost unique in its touching simplicity.' His Excellency, who saw his main duty as facilitating the despatch of as many Australian soldiers as possible to the northern hemisphere, had good reason to be satisfied, for enlistment during the half-year just ending had averaged more than 18,000 men per month. Gallipoli had not slaked Australia's thirst for war, and the urge to volunteer was kept in a state of continual stimulation by recruiting campaigns, appeals to national pride, and sometimes even the threat of social ostracism. The hero of Mrs M. M. Phillips's novel *The White Feather* received one such threat at his club in Melbourne. 'He pulled out the

---

[2] Returned Soldiers' Associations sprang up in 1915 out of the returned soldiers' club rooms which had been provided by public subscription. Representatives of several such associations in Queensland, NSW, Victoria and Western Australia met in June 1916, and the first Federal Congress of the Returned Sailors' and Soldiers' Imperial League of Australia was held in Brisbane during September of that year.

paper, unfolded it, and the little white feather fell through his fingers to the floor. Unheeding, he let it lie there, as he stood with grey face and unseeing eyes. The revulsion of feeling made him swallow nervously as if he had difficulty in breathing. . . Some men passed, and looked at him curiously, and then at the little vicious emblem lying on the floor. In a few moments it had flashed through the club that Harper had received a white feather.'

Even the near-sighted poet and bush worker, Shaw Neilson, felt the subtle pressure of disapproval that he had not enlisted. When he went to an oculist for stronger glasses in 1916, the oculist said he could do nothing for him. 'In fact he seemed rather surprised to think that there was anything wrong with my eyes at all,' recalled Neilson. 'I could hardly make this out, but later on, when I got back and told [my brother] about it, he gave me an idea. He thought it possible that the doctor might have thought I was trying to dodge conscription. It was that very month October that the conscription poll was taken. . . To look upon me as a possible soldier was rather ridiculous. I was 44 years of age, and I had a very weak knee, and my eyes were almost useless at times; but one must remember that the war fever was very strong in Victoria in 1916. I can remember one man, a young clergyman about 25, a splendidly made fellow over 6 feet high, and as sound as a bell. He went round advising every young fellow to go to the war yet he never volunteered himself, not even as a chaplain. Such hypocrisy one cannot forget.'

There were some outright objectors to the war, but only a few. Professor G. A. Wood, who had fought so strenuously against Australia's participation in the Boer War, was not among the objectors this time. He was convinced by the published diplomatic documents which became available in Sydney two months after the outbreak of war that Britain's intervention in Europe had been just and necessary, and in 1915, at the age of fifty, he joined a volunteer group which undertook military training at the University of Sydney three afternoons each week. Another outspoken critic of the South African adventure, W. A. Holman, was now the Labor Premier of New South Wales, and a zealous supporter of the Universal Service League, which was advocating conscription for overseas military service if the voluntary impulse flagged. Among the League's members were the Anglican and Roman Catholic Archbishops of Sydney, Perth and Hobart.

Labor parliamentarians were already showing signs of disunity in their attitude towards the war. Frank Anstey, the radical Federal member for Bourke, withdrew temporarily from the Labor Party in June 1915 in protest against the Fisher Government's neglect of its domestic program;

he and his supporters argued that the working class would gain nothing from the war except the dubious honour of serving as cannon fodder. Although the strains of such dissension within the Federal parliamentary party contributed to the weary Andrew Fisher's retirement from Parliament in October 1915, and his appointment to succeed Sir George Reid as Australian High Commissioner in London, there was no falling off in the vigour with which the Government pursued the war effort under its new leader, 53-year-old William Morris Hughes.

Billy Hughes, who had been the principal force in each of Fisher's three Cabinets, shared with Alfred Deakin the political primacy of the first two decades of the Commonwealth. Both men became turncoats of a kind, willing to sit with former political opponents in order to keep hold of power. But in other respects they were utterly dissimilar. While Deakin was a man of peace who regarded war as 'the dread exception', Hughes was a fighter to the very marrow of his bones. He relished parliamentary combat, and when war came he exulted in that too. In action, Deakin's greatest fault was indecision. Hughes was autocratic by nature: he knew instinctively what to do, and if necessary he would lead Cabinet by the nose. Deakin was the essence of dignity, not leonine like Barton, but more the elegant, wary leopard; Hughes was an alley cat, scraggy, acute and resilient. At times he could be a charming and witty companion, but his more usual manner was cantankerous, mocking and bullying. If challenged in discussion, it was his habit to defer with mock courtesy. 'Let the orator speak!' he would snarl, and the orator would then do so at his peril. It is hardly surprising that in the course of his long political career Hughes managed to get through more than a hundred secretaries.

Deakin zealously guarded the privacy of his 'inner life'. Hughes was secretive, but for a very different reason. He trusted no one. 'He has all the arts of a crab,' wrote one of his greatest admirers, Sir Ronald Munro-Ferguson. 'When he does not wish to be drawn, he withdraws within the impenetrable shell of his designs, and very literally disappears into space, and apparently neither gets nor answers letters. . . Mr Hughes is a curious combination of candour and secretiveness. I find it hard to get hold of him at times, but when I do he often pours out his soul, though doubtless even then there are "reservations".' In stature he was small, narrow-shouldered and stooped, though strong-handed with big, bony knuckles; his face was pinched and seamed, and in the days when he wore a drooping dark moustache he looked almost Oriental. He had a rasping voice, but his enunciation was always meticulously clear. The Professor of Classics at Melbourne University once likened him to Demosthenes, and tried to prove the point by rendering one of the Prime Minister's wartime speeches into classical Greek. It is doubtful whether the attempt succeeded, for much of Hughes's strength as an orator lay in his theatrical pauses and the savagery of his invective. His accent preserved the harshness of working-class London, but also a slight intonation of Wales.

Billy Hughes was born in Pimlico, London. His parents were Welsh, and from the age of six to eleven, after the death of his mother, he lived with an aunt in Wales, at Llandudno and the village of Llansantffraid. After returning to London he received a good education at St Stephen's School, Westminster. Thus he was both English and Welsh when, at the age of twenty-two, he emigrated to Brisbane. Although inclined to poor health, he roughed it for several years in Australia, working successively as drover, boundary rider, fencer, seaman, supernumerary in a Shakespearean repertory company, locksmith, umbrella mender, journalist and bookseller. The worst turn he ever did himself was to spend a cold winter's night sleeping on the ground in a railway yard while taking some cattle by train from Nyngan to Orange. In this manner he caught a chill which developed into the deafness from which he never recovered. He was able to hear reasonably well, however, with the help of his Acousticon, consisting of a small battery box, which he set on the table in front of him, and a connected earphone which he held up to either ear or clipped over his head. Some pitches of voice he could hear clearly without the earphone; others sometime he affected not to hear, even with it.

Hughes's aggressive ambition took him up through the trade union movement to the NSW Legislative Assembly, and from there into Federal Parliament where he was destined eventually to serve as Attorney-General for eleven years, and Prime Minister for seven. There was no stopping him. *The Sydney Morning Herald*, misquoting Byron, called him 'that fiery particle', and the Governor-General wrote of his 'intellect, courage, skill . . . and hurricane force.' One of the best descriptions of Hughes in action appeared in a French magazine, *L'Illustration*, in 1916 while the Prime Minister was attending an Allied economic conference in Paris. 'One has to hear him in council. At first he sits doubled up and lets others do the talking. The partial deafness from which he suffers and which would have discouraged any less energetic spirit, compels him to make a prodigious effort of his whole being to follow the thread of the discourse. Already he has been forgotten by the other speakers. But suddenly he straightens out, darts forward his thin arms and the double trident of his extended fingers, and projects into the centre of the flabby discussion an incisive remark. It is not only his voice that carries – a distinct voice, a metallic voice that cuts across all the others. His first words con-

Billy Hughes makes a speech, drawn by Low for the *Bulletin*.

vince you that he is determined to push his thrust home, and that no obstacle will stop his indomitable will. One understands at once the ascendancy which this little Welshman – who resembles a black spider – had been able to obtain not only over audiences in Australia and Britain but over the oldest parliamentary hands in Europe.'

Hughes and the Prime Ministers of Canada and New Zealand had been invited to London in order to acquaint themselves more fully with the progress of the war. The other Prime Ministers were unable to go, however, and when Hughes arrived in February he found himself alone in the Imperial limelight – a situation that was anything but distasteful to him. In his own words, he carried a fiery cross: touring the country and at every opportunity delivering the old imperial message of common race and common destiny with new, pugnacious urgency. His British-Australian vigour contrasted sharply with the desiccated style of Britain's Liberal Prime Minister, Asquith, who in Hughes's estimation was too much Cicero and not enough Caesar. Hughes's judgment on Asquith revealed as much about himself as it did about the cultivated Englishman who was so patently failing to meet the stern demands of war. 'He had all the great virtues,' wrote Hughes, 'a fine and catholic taste in literature and a considerable experience of men. But life terrified him. He could bear to regard it from a library window. . . He was perhaps too perfectly civilized.'

When some of the London newspapers urged that Hughes should be included in the British Cabinet, Asquith obliged by asking Hughes to sit beside him at a few Cabinet meetings – not as an established practice, but by invitation each time. The cabled press reports of Hughes's forceful part in these proceedings inspired David Low's famous *Bulletin* cartoon, which showed the diminutive Australian Prime Minister ranting and pounding one end of the British Cabinet table while at the other end an apprehensive Asquith whispered to Lloyd George, who was to succeed him as Prime Minister before the year was out: 'David, talk to him in Welsh and pacify him!'[3]

When Hughes visited Australian troops in France they said jokingly that Andrew Fisher had finally sent Australia's last man. Admittedly

[3] Hughes's biographer, L. F. Fitzhardinge, said in 1975 he did not believe that Hughes spoke or understood more than a few words of Welsh. 'I could find no evidence that he ever used the language, and when he himself said of one altercation with LG "I spoke to him – well in Welsh" I am sure this was metaphorical.' On the other hand, Jack ('Snowy') Howe, the Gallipoli veteran who later became one of Hughes's longer lasting secretaries, said in 1975 that he heard Hughes speak Welsh at St David's Day ceremonies in Melbourne and Sydney. Howe maintained that Hughes had spoken Welsh while living with his aunt in Wales, and that he had to learn English all over again when he returned to London at the age of eleven.

Hughes did not cut a very soldierly figure, but he was deeply impressed by what he saw of the war and by the gravity with which the war was being viewed in Britain, where military conscription had been introduced in January. He also had a son in the AIF. 'I am sure you are right in saying a short rest at your beautiful château would have done me much good,' he wrote to General Birdwood towards the end of his stay in June, 'but unfortunately rest is for me a fleeting phantom that for ever eludes my grasp. But during this war one must keep going. My one regret is that I can do no more. How I wish I had been trained as a soldier!'

It was said later of Hughes that he came back from Britain a changed man; that he had been 'duchessed' into a militarism which ill became a Labor Prime Minister. Certainly he had been fêted (he met everyone from the King to Kitchener, was made a Privy Councillor, and received several honorary doctorates), but 'duchessed' was hardly the right word. Jack Lang, who had known Hughes in the Labor Leagues of NSW, and was soon to differ with him on the issue of conscription, believed that his 'militarization' was the natural response of a Briton seeing Britain at bay. 'He got carried away,' said Lang many years later. 'He was a first-class Labor man, but above all he was a Welshman. He fought for Wales. That's what changed him. He had no attachment for Australia like I had, but he had it for Wales. He had to decide for peace or war, and he decided for war.' With the substitution of Britain for Wales, and the acknowledgment that war was no difficult choice for such a fighter as Hughes, Lang's explanation will serve. Once Hughes had chosen, his autocratic nature suffered no impediment. If it was to be Hughes or the Labor Party which Hughes himself had done so much to create, then the party would have to go. It was as simple as that.

Hughes returned to Australia on 31 July, only two days after the 2nd Division's disastrous first attack at Pozières. Australia then had about 100,000 men in France; but if there were to be more battles like Pozières, and if monthly enlistments continued to follow their present trend, that figure was obviously going to fall. During the first quarter of 1916 voluntary enlistments had averaged 18,700 per month; since then the monthly figures had been 9876, 10,659, 6582 and 6170. To the disappointment of the Universal Service League and the daily newspapers, Hughes did not move immediately towards compulsion. He knew that any such move would give grave offence to the trade union movement,[4] and

---

[4] A manifesto issued by the Brisbane Trade Union Congress on 26 August ended with these words: 'If necessary, when the call comes, let the wheels of production stop rather than that the yoke of conscription be fastened upon you. Show the master class, despite what other countries may do, that the workers of Australia refuse to be crushed by the juggernaut of MILITARISM.'

would cause at least one member of his Cabinet (the Victorian Frank Tudor, Minister for Trade and Customs) to resign. What worried him even more than this was the difficulty of enacting conscription as New Zealand did successfully during August. With help from the Opposition there would be a clear majority in the House of Representatives, but in the Senate there would not be enough Opposition members to counteract those Labor Senators who would be certain to vote against conscription. The alternative was a referendum; even the most confirmed anti-conscriptionists in Caucus would hardly jib at putting the question to the people.

On 24 August the War Office cabled to Melbourne asking for urgent reinforcements to maintain Australia's five Divisions in France at full strength. It asked for 32,500 men during September, followed by 16,500 in each of the next three months. These figures were subsequently found to have been unnecessarily high, but at the time they were taken at face value. So far the voluntary enlistment for August had amounted to only 4144. How then could Australia answer Britain's call for help without conscription? On 30 August the Prime Minister announced the Government's decision to hold a referendum as soon as possible.

That did it. On 4 September Hughes was expelled from the NSW Labor League, and the splitting of the Labor Party had begun. Frank Tudor resigned from the Government on 14 September, the day on which Hughes moved the second reading of the Military Service Referendum Bill in the House of Representatives; and on 27 October, the day before the referendum was held, Tudor was followed by three more Ministers – W. G. Higgs (Treasurer), Senator Albert Gardiner (Vice-President of the Executive Council) and Senator E. J. Russell (Honorary Minister). In the last few days of the referendum campaign, Hughes had rashly attempted to introduce a provision whereby male voters who appeared to be between the ages of 21 and 35 could be asked by returning officers at the polling booths whether they were eligible for military service within the Commonwealth, and if so, whether they had reported to the military authorities. This proposed regulation was rejected on 25 October by a Melbourne meeting of the Executive Council chaired in the Governor-General's absence by the Vice-President, Senator Gardiner. Two days later the same regulation was presented to and passed by another meeting of the Excutive Council chaired in Sydney by the Governor-General and not attended by the three ministers who had earlier opposed the regulation as an offence against civil liberty. Within a few hours those three ministers had heard about this piece of Hughesian chicanery, and had resigned.

At midnight, only hours before the polling booths opened, Hughes telephoned Sir Ronald Munro-Ferguson at Admiralty House in Kirribilli and asked to see him immediately. The Governor-General crossed the harbour to Circular Quay, where he found a very worried Prime Minister waiting for him in a taxi. What should he do about the three resignations? 'The poor little man asked for advice and sympathy,' wrote Munro-Ferguson, 'saying he "had not a brain wave left".' With unabashed partiality, the Governor-General suggested that news of the resignations should be censored until after the referendum. Hughes hurried away to do this, but found that he was too late: the morning papers already contained the news. His melodramatic meeting at Circular Quay had not, however, been a waste of time. He now felt confident of the Governor-General's support in the political crisis rapidly developing within his party.

The issues raised during the referendum campaign included not only civil liberty and the morality of sending men to war, but also two inflammatory issues of long standing – religion and race. The press (with the exception of the Labor papers) and the Protestant churches (with the exception of a few individual clergymen) were solidly in favour of conscription. 'Compulsory service means order, method, strength and certainty,' said the *Bulletin* in its new martial tone of voice. 'Voluntaryism means the other thing – the dodge and the twist and the fumble and the stumble in the dark. This paper holds no brief for Hughes. It has little admiration for either his tongue or his judgment. But it does hold a brief for Australia. And the evidence it relies upon is the casualty lists which reveal the hole knocked into Australia's army, the presence of the German on thousands of square miles of conquered territory, and the indisputable fact that war – our war – is raging as no other war ever raged since killing became a public enterprise; and on that evidence it claims that it is the business of the Australian people to see the thing through – to play the game to their mates and their sons and their brothers right to the end.'

Themes of self-protection and mateship ran through most of the pro-conscription propaganda. In a Norman Lindsay poster, a wounded Anzac sounded a desperate bugle call for help as a horde of Huns advanced towards his trench. Another poster showed a spike-helmeted firing squad executing Australian farmers in front of a country water tank. 'Will you fight now or wait for THIS?' The Prime Minister himself invoked the obligations of mateship in a series of filmed referendum 'bullets' made for showing at cinemas. 'You would answer a cooee for help in the bush,' he said. 'The Anzacs are cooeeing. . . Are you going to scab on the Anzacs?' 'Every citizen must decide in which camp he must stand – for or against Australia, for or against Britain, for or against the Empire.' The Labor

Premier of New South Wales, Holman, and the former Prime Minister, Watson, both took their stand with Hughes. So did all previous Prime Ministers except Fisher. Hughes cabled Fisher at Australia House asking him to sign a joint 'Yes' appeal, but the High Commissioner, who had earlier warned the Labor Party about the probable divisive effect of conscription upon its own ranks, does not appear to have committed himself. Thus removed from the battle, Fisher served as a confidant for former political colleagues on both sides of the referendum. 'It is now apparent that there are elements in the Labor Party with which I have nothing in common, which in fact I hate and distrust,' wrote Hughes to Fisher on the eve of polling day. 'I am worn with the storm and stress of a conflict – the most severe, the most bitter Australia has ever known. But I keep on!' On the night before Hughes wrote this letter, an angry crowd shouted down the chairman of a pro-conscription meeting in a Roman Catholic school at Port Fairy (Victoria), gave 'Three cheers for the Kaiser', and attempted to put a buggy trace around the chairman's neck. There were shouts of 'Hang the ——', but the lights went out and the chairman escaped unharmed.

The 'Yes' campaign opened in Sydney Town Hall with speeches by the Prime Minister and the Lord Mayor, Alderman R. D. Meagher, whose imperial fervour belied his Irish name. 'While we stand proud in the reflected glory of the Anzacs,' said the Lord Mayor, 'with their ineffaceable deeds, with their fadeless glory, we will stand all the prouder amid that glory when we fill up the thinning ranks of the Anzacs. [Hear, hear] I am convinced, as a democrat, the Australian democracy will realise that her destiny is at hand. [Hear, hear] I am satisfied that . . . after October 28 the verdict will be such that Australia will have proved true to herself, true to the grand old Empire and true to the great cause of democracy. [Loud applause]' Not everyone applauded. Indeed someone dropped boxes of soldier ants (Antis?) among the crowd surging around the entrance to the Town Hall. A few people were bitten.

The Anti forces included a large majority of the political and industrial labour movement, and a considerable part of the Roman Catholic community. To the trade union press, the conscription campaign was yet another battle in the class war; its cartoons showed the conscriptionist as a bloated capitalist wearing a Union Jack in his top hat, and its editorials railed against Hughes as a 'tool of capitalism' and the 'pampered pet of Dukes'. Anti-conscription posters were emotionally and artistically every bit as lurid as those which said 'God bless dear Daddy who is fighting the Hun, and send him HELP!' One poster, entitled 'The Blood Vote', showed a Mephistophelean Hughes watching an obviously worried woman with her 'Yes' vote poised above the ballot box. ' "Why is your face so white, Mother?" ' began a poem beside this picture. ' "Why do you choke for breath?"/ "Oh, I have dreamt in the night, my son,/ That I doomed a man to death." ' In another poster a mother embraced her small sailor-suited son who was saying: 'Vote NO Mum. They'll take DAD next.' Although Hughes denied any intention of conscripting married men, or sole remaining sons, the Antis warned voters not to trust him. They also argued that Australia was already doing more than its fair share of the fighting. Canada, with a population of 7,200,000, had enlisted 308,000 men. On a proportional population basis, Australia would have been doing equally well to have enlisted 232,000 men; in fact it had enlisted 270,000.

The deceptively named Anti-Hun Society in Brisbane preferred heavy irony to the pathos of mothers and children. 'Workers, the Empire is in danger!' declared one of its posters. 'Hughes, the damned little Hun, says he will force you to fight for him. Before you make up your mind about going make sure how much of the Empire you own. Is it YOUR EMPIRE? ARE THEY YOUR MOTOR CARS? DO YOU DRAW THE BIG SHIPPING PROFITS? All that is expected of you is that you go into a trench and shoot at some poor unfortunate German who you have no quarrel with – and the chances are you will be blown to blazes, that is all that is expected of you. AND IF THAT AIN'T ENOUGH YOU MUST BE THE MOST ASTOUNDING HOG ON THE FACE OF THE EARTH. . . Let Hughes and his bloody Hunnish friends go to blazes before YOU put on the soldier's uniform. LISTEN: Every man who dons the khaki will be a scab on his mates, and when the chance comes he must be SHOT and that time will come as sure as Jesus is dead.'

The Brisbane *Worker* argued against conscription on grounds of civil liberty ('To apply military compulsion to these men, and deprive them of all control over their destinies . . . is to be guilty of the sin of Sacrilege against humanity') and economic development ('It would be like cutting open the veins of the country, and letting the vital stream gush forth till it expired of exhaustion'), and also on the old ground of racial purity. 'Vote "No" and guard against cheap black labour now landing,' said one referendum card. This was a reference to a shipload of Maltese men, mostly of military age, not exactly black, but indubitably about to land. There were only 98 of them – not 800, as at first claimed – but another 200 were also en route in another vessel. These unfortunate immigrants were not allowed to remain in White Australia, but were sent back to Malta at Commonwealth expense. Their untimely arrival was a sharp reminder, however, that if the country's veins were cut by conscription Australia's vital stream could be replenished with blood of lesser purity.[5]

Just as the Maltese immigrants breathed fire into the racial issue, so the memory of Easter Sunday in Dublin helped to keep sectarianism alive during the campaign. On 23 April 1916 Patrick Pearse and his supporters occupied several public buildings in Dublin, and began shooting British soldiers. They surrendered six days later, and in due course Pearse and thirteen others were executed by the British Army. Dr Daniel Mannix, the Coadjutor Archbishop of Melbourne, wept when he read the news of these executions. Archbishop James Duhig of Brisbane, who was born only a few miles away from Mannix's birthplace in County Cork, was 'dazed' by the news, but remained a vigorous recruiting campaigner and a strong advocate of conscription. The elderly and ailing Archbishop of Melbourne – Archbishop Carr, also Irish born – protested at the executions but did not join the conscription debate on either side. 'Conscription is purely a State matter,' he said. 'The Church neither advocates nor opposes it. She leaves it to her members to freely decide how they should vote.'

Archbishop Mannix decided to oppose conscription out of respect for moral principles, love for Ireland, distrust of British motives, and perhaps something rather less obvious as well. Although never involved in public controversy in Ireland, where he had been president of Maynooth College, and Professor of Theology, Dr Mannix had no sooner reached Melbourne in 1913 than he was delivering speeches on the vexed subject of State aid for Roman Catholic schools. And how he could speak! He was a tall, distinguished-looking man who swayed audiences not with rhetoric but with the uncompromising clarity of his thought and the directness of his words. It was said that Hughes's indiscriminate invective divided Australia more than was necessary during the referendum campaign. Dr Mannix also deepened sectarian divisions by his remorseless criticism of Britain and the Empire. After a particularly savage attack, and the backlash which inevitably followed, he was likely to open his next meeting, looking over two metres tall in his black top hat, by saying: 'I am unchanged and unrepentant.' And so he was. In the opinion of some Protestants, there was method in his controlled savagery. Professor J. L. Rentoul, a Presbyterian,

[5] Racial purity was also stressed in a different context by the pacifist and suffragette, Adela Pankhurst, whose meetings enlivened the referendum campaign. In *Put Up The Sword*, published by the Women's Peace Army, Melbourne, in 1915, she wrote: 'Every British man that dies in battle is a loss to the British race in the present and for the future.... A Basuto or a Hottentot can fight, but a civilized man should serve his country in a civilized way. Races fighting under the Union Jack include Britons, Sikhs, Punjabis, Somalis, Soudanese, Yoribas, Wagandas, Nubians, Swahilis and many other African tribes. So the Melbourne *Herald* told us in the year of grace 1914. Nice company for Christian men! A great achievement for the British nation!'

was not alone in seeing the Mannix style as 'part of a concerted campaign to shatter the central principle of the State-school system in Australia, and to obtain State-establishment for separatist Roman Catholic schools.' 'To effect any hope of such result,' said Professor Rentoul, 'it would seem there must be a stirring up of strong sectarian and racial feeling in the minds and hearts of [Dr Mannix's] co-religionists.' Shortly before the referendum campaign, Mannix was expressing sympathy with the Lutherans, who also maintained schools for the religious education of their children. With his usual fearless disregard of consequences, he warned that the anti-German bigots who were trying to close Lutheran schools would probably get around to suppressing Catholic ones as well.[6]

The question to be answered on 28 October was: 'Are you in favour of the Government having in this grave emergency the same compulsory powers over citizens in regard to requiring their military service, for the term of this war, outside the Commonwealth, as it now has in regard to military service within the Commonwealth?' To considerable surprise on both sides, the answer was 'No' by a slight majority of 72,476. Of the 2,247,590 votes cast, 1,160,033 were negative, 1,087,557 affirmative, and 61,013 informal. Victoria, Tasmania and Western Australia gave 'Yes' majorities; but NSW, Queensland and South Australia voted 'No'. The 'No' majority of 117,739 in NSW was decisive, and what may well have decided the outcome there was a heavy 'No' vote by primary producers who feared that conscription would leave them short of labour. The soldiers themselves returned a 'Yes' majority of about 10,000, but it was said that voting by men on active service in France had been three to one against compulsion. General Birdwood advanced several reasons for the high 'No' vote in France: strong objection to bringing more troops from Australia while the 3rd Division was still in Britain, reluctance of volunteers to serve beside conscripts, resentment over lack of leave, the fact that Australia had had no say in the declaration of war, and the fact that there was no self-contained Australian army.

The Governor-General, who had boasted in July that Australia would 'certainly raise another quarter of a million men at a pinch', was infuriated by the result. Forgetting his earlier remarks about Australia's touchingly simple loyalty to the Crown, he told the Colonial Secretary, Bonar Law:

[6] The 33,000 people of German birth in Australia, and the larger but uncertain number with more distant German antecedents, were subjected to prejudice during the war; but the total number of internees in Australia was only 6890. Anti-German feeling manifested itself at community level, and in the alteration of such place names as German Creek (Empire Vale), Mt Bismarck (Mt Kitchener) and Blumberg (Birdwood). The Australian-born Attorney-General of South Australia, Mr H. Homburg, resigned from office because of his ancestry, and a German-born member of the House of Representatives, Mr G. Dankel, refrained from standing for re-election in 1917.

'For the moment the anarchist and most ignorant section of society has shown itself more powerful than all the rest, and that in a community which is in the main the most irresponsible, self-confident and inexperienced in the Empire, or even perhaps outside of it.' The 'No' majority had closed the conscription debate for the time being, but it did nothing to halt the splitting of the Federal Labor Party. On 14 November Hughes and his supporters found themselves opposed in Caucus by a hostile majority which submitted a formal motion of no confidence in Hughes's leadership. While the debate was in progress, Hughes rose from his chair and said: 'Let all who support me follow me!' He was followed from the room by twenty-three members of Parliament, among whom were three other ministers: Senator George Pearce (Defence), J. A. Jensen (Navy) and William Webster (Postmaster-General). The forty-three members who had remained seated in the Caucus room then expelled Hughes from the party leadership, and elected Tudor in his place. Similar exoduses took place from the parliamentary Labor Parties of all States except Queensland, and in December a federal Labor conference finalized the split by expelling all members who had supported conscription or joined another party.

Hughes commanded the direct allegiance of only fourteen out of the seventy-five members of the House of Representatives, including himself, and eleven out of thirty-six Senators (he had gained one more parliamentary supporter after the Caucus meeting); but he knew that he would be supported by the Liberal Opposition in the lower house. When Hughes submitted his resignation to the Governor-General and asked to be recommissioned, Sir Ronald Munro-Ferguson sought and obtained a written assurance of co-operation from the Liberal Party, then granted Hughes's request. Hughes subsequently tried to extend the life of Parliament for the duration of the war, but the Senate, still under Labor control, blocked the move. For a short time there were two Labor parties in Federal Parliament: National Labor, as the Hughes faction was at first known, and the Australian Labor Party. In February 1917, National Labor merged with its Liberal supporters to form the National Party.

At a Federal election in May 1917 the Australian people showed that although marginally opposed to conscription they still supported the war. Hughes's 'win-the-war' Nationalist Party won forty-six seats in the House of Representatives (an increase of seven), leaving the ALP with only nineteen, and won all eighteen of the half-Senate vacancies. In both Houses the Nationalists received 54 per cent of the total vote, and the ALP 43 per cent. Again the rural community played an important part in the outcome. Having protected its labour supply at the referendum, it now reverted to its previous anti-Labor and pro-war voting habits. On the left, however, opposition to the war and dissatisfaction with economic and social conditions in Australia became more deeply entrenched. In June the NSW, Victorian, Queensland and South Australian branches of the ALP called for moves to secure a negotiated peace in Europe, and in July workers began laying down tools in what was to become the biggest industrial upheaval Australia had ever known. From first out to last back, this general strike lasted eighty-two days. It began at the NSW Government tramway workshops, where a job-record system had been introduced without union consultation. Suspecting that the object of the innovation was to make everyone measure up to the pace of the fastest, engineers at the workshops refused to use the new job cards and went on strike. The mood of tramwaymen, railwaymen and other workers was so militant that by early August 50,000 men had stopped work in NSW. The strike eventually involved 95,000 workers in transport, mining, maritime and other industries throughout Australia, causing the loss of 3,980,000 man-days.

'The enemies of Britain and her Allies have succeeded in plunging Australia into a general strike,' said the Nationalist Government in New South Wales. 'For the time being they have crippled our country's efforts to assist in the Great War. AT THE BACK OF THIS STRIKE LURK THE IWW AND THE EXPONENTS OF DIRECT ACTION. Without realising it, many Trade Unions have become the tools of Disloyalists and Revolutionaries.' Certainly the Industrial Workers of the World – the 'syn-*dic*-alists' whom Billy Hughes had once threatened to attack with 'the fer-*oc*-ity of a *Ben*-gal *ti*-ger' – were no figment of the Government's imagination; but it seems doubtful that the general strike was manipulated by such an extremist minority, or that the NSW Government was justified in contending that the unions were challenging its ability to rule. One labour historian, Ian Turner, has concluded that the strikes bore no marks of IWW leadership, and that unions went on strike not because their leaders so ordered but because the members so demanded.[7] The NSW Government was determined to prevail, and it did. It refused to abandon the job record system, and continued to insist upon preference for 'loyalists' after the strike. It sacked the strikers, and introduced strike-breaking volunteer labour. In September the unions surrendered unconditionally.

[7] In any case the IWW, which deliberately affronted orthodox Australian opinion with anti-British and anti-war statements and actions, had been largely suppressed after an outbreak of arson in Sydney in mid-1916. 'Far better to see Sydney melted to the ground than to see the men of Sydney taken away to be butchered for any body of infidels,' one IWW speaker, Peter Larkin, was alleged to have said. In September 1916 Larkin and eleven other

Just as the NSW Government had suspected syndicalist conspiracy, so the unions believed that the Government's hard line in the strike had been the prelude to a second referendum on conscription. This seems no more credible than the IWW conspiracy theory; on the contrary, the humbling of the unions would surely have been more likely to stiffen than weaken their opposition to another referendum – which was indeed in the offing. In February Britain had asked Australia about the possibility of raising sufficient troops for a sixth division, and in subsequent months the Allied position in Europe had been gravely weakened by the collapse of Russia after the revolution in March. Despite the most determined recruiting effort, monthly enlistments during the first half of 1917 averaged only 4500, and since then they had fallen steadily from 4155 in July to 3274 in August and 2460 in September. Canada had now followed Britain and New Zealand into conscription. Why not Australia as well? On 7 November Hughes announced that a second referendum would be held. This time the campaign reached new levels of vituperation and violence. The Antis maintained that the first referendum should have been accepted as final, while the 'Yes' campaigners argued that deterioration in the Allied war position made opposition to conscription more reprehensible than ever. Returned soldiers broke up 'No' meetings, and unionists did the same in reverse. At a 'No' meeting in Brighton, Victoria, the chairman called upon a returned soldier who had lost a leg at Gallipoli to speak against conscription. A uniformed AIF lieutenant then jumped to his feet and shouted: 'Let us have the national anthem first!' A number of soldiers, who formed about half the audience, jumped to their feet, lustily sang 'God Save The King', and gave three cheers for the Empire. As soon as the one-legged Anzac began to speak, he was assailed by jeers and cries of 'Waster'. 'I'm not a waster!' he yelled. 'I defy any soldier here to produce a better discharge than I have!' One of the uniformed men shouted 'What a poor specimen you are', and the meeting broke up in confusion. In Warwick, Queensland, the Prime Minister was mobbed by an angry crowd when he tried to address them on the railway platform. Someone threw two eggs at him, missing with one and splattering his hat with the other; a returned

---

IWW members were arrested and charged with treason – or rather with 'feloniously and wickedly' devising or intending 'to levy war against the King within His Majesty's domains.' The charges were concerned with actual and intended arson. All twelve defendants were found guilty: seven were sentenced to fifteen years in gaol (on appeal, two of these sentences were reduced to ten years), four others were sentenced to ten years, and one to five years. Allegations that some evidence against the accused had been fabricated were dismissed by one Royal Commission and subsequently upheld in part by another Royal Commission. Ten of the 'Sydney Twelve' – including Donald Grant, who later became a Labor Senator – were released after the second Royal Commission's finding in 1920. The remaining two were released in the following year.

soldier leapt at the egg-thrower, and from the ensuing disturbance the little Prime Minister emerged with dishevelled clothes and bleeding knuckles. As a result of the Warwick incident, the Hughes government established a´small Commonwealth police force, but this was not the origin of the present Commonwealth Police. The wartime force was disbanded in 1921, and another federal policy body, the Peace Officers, came into being four years later. In 1960 the Peace Officers and the Commonwealth Investigation Service (a security service which had been formed in 1911) became part of the present Commonwealth Police.

From the tragic isolation of his physical affliction, Alfred Deakin wrote a few lines in support of conscription – his last public statement on any subject. 'God in His wisdom has decreed that at this great crisis in our history my tongue must be silent, owing to my failing powers. He alone knows how I yearn, my fellow Australians, to help you to say that magic word which shall aid our gallant soldiers and save our civilization. My countrymen, be true to yourselves, to Australia, and to our great Empire. Let our voices thunder "Yes", and future generations shall arise and call us blessed. God save Australia, Alfred Deakin.' Not everyone was as simple and direct as Deakin; both sides exaggerated, and often distorted the issues involved. *The Antis' Creed*, distributed by the 'Yes' side, attributed to 'No' voters twenty-four beliefs such as the following: 'I believe that men at the front should be sacrificed. I believe it was right to sink the *Lusitania*. I believe in the IWW. I believe in Sinn Fein. I believe in the murder of women, and baby-killing. I believe that Nurse Cavell got her just deserts. . .'

Even the question to be answered on 20 December was said by the Antis to have been worded deceptively: 'Are you in favour of the proposal of the Commonwealth Government for reinforcing the Australian Imperial Forces overseas?' There was no mention of compulsion this time, and newspaper editorials spoke not of 'conscription' but 'reinforcement'. Archbishop Mannix, who was even more to the fore than at the first referendum, accused the Government of not having 'the ordinary honesty or even decency to put a fair, straight question.' Mannix had now succeeded the late Dr T. J. Carr as Archbishop of Melbourne. It is doubtful whether he would have been any the less outspoken without this added ecclesiastical authority, but the new see made him harder to silence than ever.

If England was so anxious about the protection of small nations, asked the Archbishop at one meeting, how was it that a certain small nation could not get justice from that power? There were people, including Mr Hughes, who said the war was for the economic domination of the world. If the war was entered into for that purpose, then it was an unjust cause. There was some reason for thinking that the time had come when Australia could get out of the war and make an honourable, just and lasting peace. If, however, the war had been entered into for unjust causes, it was likely to go on for a long time yet. At another meeting the Archbishop, unchanged and unrepentant, said that murder was murder, whether it was committed in Belgium or in Dublin, and the bloody stain could not be blotted out simply by covering it with the Union Jack. He conceded that some of his statements would be called seditious or disloyal; he was glad, however, that his loyalty to the Empire, such as it was, did not prevent him from being loyal in the first place to Australia, his adopted country, and to Ireland, the land of his birth.

Hughes was acutely conscious of the Home Rule issue, and tried unsuccessfully to mitigate its political effects in Australia. In August he raised the subject with the British Prime Minister, Lloyd George: 'Ireland: There is your plague spot – or one of them – if you like. And its effects are felt over here. . . The Irish question is at the bottom of all our difficulties in Australia. They – the Irish – have captured the political machinery of the labour organisations – assisted by the Syndicalists and IWW people. The church is secretly against recruiting. Its influence killed conscription. One of their archbishops – Mannix – is a Sinn Feiner – and I am trying to make up my mind whether I should prosecute him for statements hindering recruiting or deport him.' Britain was not prepared to soften its Irish policy for the sake of an Australian referendum; and despite Hughes's dark thoughts on the subject, he neither prosecuted nor deported his turbulent priest.

Vance and Nettie Palmer, who had returned to Melbourne from London in 1915, were devout anti-conscriptionists, as was Nettie's brother, Esmonde Higgins. Neither Vance nor Esmonde had yet enlisted, though Esmonde intended going as soon as his university exams were over; but another branch of the family had already suffered the loss of an only child.[8] Nettie's cousin, Mervyn Higgins – the son of Mr Justice H. B. Higgins – had been killed by a Turkish sniper in the Sinai desert. 'Isn't it ghastly about Mervyn?' wrote Nettie to her brother. 'It was five hours ago I heard the news and ever since then I have been almost howling. . . To think of those bonzer people Uncle H and Aunt M is just ghastly. I have never been so much cut up because of anyone's death.' When the second conscription campaign began, Vance Palmer went to work with the Antis in Queensland; Nettie stayed in Melbourne with her children and did some Anti

---

[8] Esmonde went into camp in January 1918, and Vance enlisted in March. Both were sent to England, but arrived too late for active service.

writing. Her diary that year preserved some of the flavour of a highly polarized society. 'Frances Berkman arrived by dinner-time, laden with fish & fruit & sweets &, in the end, conscriptionist arguments. The sectarian issue! One ¼ of the population, the Catholic, isn't represented at the war: so we need conscription to bring these eligibles forward. This from a Russian Jewess. She's brainy but a trifle rigid surely. . .

'Mother worried about voluntarism forcing all the men with consciences to go and leaving the others. . . Any suburban varsity friends of mine to whom I've written in hopes of anti-support return polite blanks. "I can't argue because I've had no practice. Not one of my friends or relatives is Anti," says Effie Merrilees. . . Letter from Christian [O'Dowd] telling of anti-conscription attempts and their exting·ishers in town. Refused the Town Hall for a meeting, refused publication of anything . . . *Thursday*. Polling day. Vance [who had returned from Queensland] walked in with me and we polled and got the mail. Elizabeth Lothian is "Yes" because she admires Professor Moore and because English people are taking the war seriously. Are there any Noes? There were some at the polling booth here, by the way. Shimmering hot day. *Friday*. Went into the PO and heard rumour that Noes were winning. Incredible.'

Incredible but true! This time the 'No' majority was greater than at the first referendum – 166,588, compared with 72,476. Victoria had swung from 'Yes' to 'No' by a small majority, and the three original 'No' States had remained negative, with NSW and Queensland showing slightly higher 'No' majorities than before. The national 'No' total was 1,181,747; 'Yes', 1,015,159. This ended the conscription debate, but not the Nationalist Government and not Billy Hughes's hold on the Prime Ministership. Before the referendum, Hughes had pledged that his government would not remain in office if it were denied the power to conscript. Early in January 1918 the Nationalist Party confirmed its confidence in Hughes's leadership by sixty-three votes to two, and decided that the Government should 'take whatever steps it deems advisable to give honourable effect to the pledge given to the people of Australia.' On 8 January Hughes tendered his resignation to the Governor-General and was asked to continue the administration until a new commission was issued. Hughes offered no advice as to who should be asked to succeed him. As the ALP leader, Frank Tudor, could not command a majority in either House, the Governor-General held conversations with several of Hughes's colleagues. One of these – Sir John Forrest, who had cast one of the two dissenting votes on the party's motion of confidence in Hughes – pressed his own claim to the Prime Ministership. This seemed a possible solution at first, but after testing the opinion of two other prominent Nationalists the Governor-General concluded that Forrest would not be able to form a Ministry. By evening Sir Ronald had decided that he was left with only one course of action: he sent for Hughes again and commissioned him to form a new administration. 'How these imported titled gentry do hate Labor,' said the Victorian *Labor Call*. A mass meeting of Labor supporters demanded a double dissolution and the recall of the Governor-General; but the matter was closed. Hughes had good reason to be grateful to his midnight comforter at Circular Quay. Shortly before he left Australia in April 1918 to attend an imperial conference in London, Hughes told Sir Ronald Munro-Ferguson: 'You have been in many a serious and trying crisis a great help to me. Many times I should have thrown up the sponge but for your advice, your sympathy and the feeling that you believed in me.' So much for vice-regal impartiality!

The war in Australia had produced a strange contradiction between acceptance of the war against Germany (as demonstrated by Hughes's electoral triumph) and rejection of conscription. But perhaps this was not so strange after all. If the Australian ethos was flexible enough to accommodate both imperial and national loyalties, why not pro-war and anti-conscription attitudes as well? In fact the two dualities were not unrelated. While the British half of public consciousness (or was it now less than half?) conceded the grim necessity of war, the Australian half (or was it more?) refused to compel participation in something which had started like a tennis match and turned into a slaughter. Australia's refusal to conscript has been variously interpreted as evidence of immaturity, selfishness, moral courage and independence. But whatever inspired the decision, who would say now that it was wrong?

14

HERCULES AND THE LION

Victory

WHEN W. M. HUGHES reached London in June 1918 to attend an Imperial Conference, the war looked as if it might grind on for another year or two. In fact it lasted only five more months; but this was long enough for the AIF to achieve its greatest success – not another stultifying exchange of slaughter, like Pozières and so many subsequent battles on the Western Front, but a plain and glorious victory which was hailed by one British general as 'the finest single feat of the war'. The laurels of Mont St Quentin were a welcome change from wreaths of blood red poppies, and they seemed all the greener for sitting upon the brow of an Australian rather than a British commander. By this time the five Australian infantry divisions in France were serving together in one corps under a Melbourne civil engineer, Lieut-General Sir John Monash.

Hughes had been trying to bring about this consolidation of the AIF since 1916. The British Commander-in-Chief, Sir Douglas Haig, had at first opposed the notion on grounds that a corps of five divisions would be unwieldy; but by late 1917 the Australian Government's lobbying for a distinct Australian corps was more than the British Government could withstand. 'I am having a great deal of trouble about [the Colonial Forces] at the present moment,' wrote the Secretary of State for War, Lord Derby, to Haig in November, 'especially with regard to the Australian Corps, and I am afraid, for various reasons, we must look upon them in the light in which they wish to be looked upon rather than the light in which we should wish to do so. They look upon themselves, not as part and parcel of the English Army but as Allies beside us and I see they are beginning to take the analogy of the Portuguese, not from the point of view of fighting but from the point of view of administration and self-control.'

The Australian Corps came into being on 1 January 1918 under the command of General Sir William Birdwood, the British officer who had commanded the ANZAC forces in their various roles since Gallipoli. The new corps was not the self-contained 'Australian Army' which the Commonwealth Government had been urging upon the War Office, but its numerical strength (about nine per cent of the combined British and Dominions combat forces on the Western Front) was at times greater than that of some Allied armies, and it remained the strongest corps in France. It was strong in quality as well as numbers. The Diggers may have had a reputation for lack of discipline and insubordination, but they were also acknowledged to be among the Allies' most effective shock troops.[1] The Australian Corps was not involved in the sudden reversal of March 1918, when a German offensive swept General Gough's 5th British Army back towards Amiens and seemed about to separate the British and French armies; but it was involved most creditably in the halting of this offensive and the saving of Amiens. In May the 'nationalization' of the Australian Corps was made complete when General Birdwood relinquished its command in order to re-establish the disgraced General Gough's 5th Army, of which the Australian Corps was still an administrative part. Although Birdwood thus retained administrative command of the AIF, the operational command of the Corps was the most important attainable in the Australian Army. Birdwood's preference for his successor in this coveted post lay between the Corps chief-of-staff, General C. B. B. White, and the 3rd Division's commander, General Monash. Monash was the senior officer, and was favourably known to Haig; White went as chief-of-staff to the 5th Army, and on 31 May, shortly before his fifty-third birthday, Monash took over the Australian Corps.

He was a most unlikely Australian commander: a Jew, a non-professional soldier, and the son of European parents. His parents, Louis and Bertha Monasch, came to Victoria from the Prussian part of Poland, and John Monasch, who was born soon after their arrival, grew up speaking German as well as English. One suspects that Monash, like Isaac Isaacs, was propelled and steered through his youth by a formidable mother. While Louis Monasch ran a business in Jerilderie, NSW, Bertha and her son lived in Melbourne so that the boy could go to Scotch College. He became dux of the school, went on to take a master's degree in civil engineering at Melbourne University, and also became a devoted peace-time soldier. Monash was a militia lieutenant in his early thirties during the Boer War, but for reasons unexplained he did not go to South Africa. Monash went into private engineering practice, specializing in the new technique of ferro-concrete, and was one of three original directors

---

[1] The term 'Digger', which came into general use in 1917, was an application of the Australian gold-digging and New Zealand gum-digging usages to trench-digging on the Western Front.

(another was David Mitchell, the father of Dame Nellie Melba) of the Monier Pipe Company. By 1914 he was president of the Victorian Institute of Engineers and part-time colonel of the 13th Infantry Brigade. He was a heavily built man of strong, swarthy appearance, and was passionately interested in the science of war.

Atypical of his countrymen though this pre-eminent Australian soldier may have been, he was deeply conscious of the national significance of his promotion to command of the Corps. He rode to his first Divisional Commanders' conference in Birdwood's former Rolls-Royce, flying the Australian flag on its bonnet, and every commander waiting for him at corps headquarters was a native-born Australian. 'My new command,' wrote Monash, 'comprises a total at present of 166,000 troops, and covers practically the whole Australian field army in France. . . For all practical purposes I am now the supreme Australian commander, and thus at long last the Australian nation has achieved its ambition of having its own Commander-in-Chief, a native-born Australian – for the first time in its history. My command is more than two and a half times the size of the British Army under the Duke of Wellington, or of the French Army under Napoleon Bonaparte, at the Battle of Waterloo. Moreover I have in the Army Corps an artillery which is more than six times as numerous and more than a hundred times as powerful as that commanded by the Duke of Wellington.'

Fortunately his pride was soundly based. Monash knew how to use the Corps, and he used it to excellent effect. His reputation already stood sufficiently high for him to be mentioned as a possible commander of the 5th Army, and who knew what might have followed from that? If the war had lasted long enough – so Australia's military folklore was later to assert – Monash might even have succeeded Haig as British Commander-in-Chief.[2] The former possibility was canvassed as part of an intrigue against Birdwood. 'Certain people strongly desire to displace Birdwood [from the 5th Army]', wrote Monash on 25 June. 'They fear the Australian public would resent his being got rid of unless another man, equally acceptable to the War Office, the AIF and the Australian Government can be found. No such man can be found other than myself. In order to induce me to accept such a position, they propose to try and win me with the offer of further promotion and, of course, increased status and emoluments. As they fear that I would decline these temptations, and as the only

[2] The main basis for this assertion was the following remark in the war memoirs of Haig's critic, Lloyd George: 'Since the war I have been told by men whose judgment I value that the only soldier thrown up by the war on the British side who possessed the necessary qualifications [to become Commander-in-Chief of the British armies in France] was a Dominion general. But I knew nothing of this at the time.'

excuse for getting rid of B. is that they wish to separate the functions of Corps Commander from those of GOC, AIF, their first problem is to displace me from the Corps. In order to bring this about they have started an attempt to attack my capacity to command the Corps, and are putting about propaganda that Brudenell White, being a permanent soldier, would be better fitted for this job. . . These proceedings are being undertaken in London, in order to bring pressure to bear upon Mr Hughes.'

Monash had no intention of leaving the Australian Corps until he had proved his ability as its commander. This he did at Hamel on 4 July, and at Mont St Quentin on 31 August. The assault on the village of Hamel, east of Amiens, by three Australian brigades and several American battalions was Monash's first operational task as corps commander, and its success greatly enhanced his standing with the British high command. On 12 August he was knighted in the field by King George V in the presence of 100 men from each of the five Australian divisions. As the Australian Corps moved east with the Allied counter offensive, the steady advance of the 3rd Australian Division north of the Somme permitted the 2nd Division to cross the river from the southern bank, thus enabling Monash to propose an attack on Mont St Quentin, a height overlooking the German stronghold of Péronne. The British high command altered the direction of the advance to conform with this plan, and told Monash to go ahead.

Mont St Quentin was ringed with trenches and wide belts of wire entanglement, and was garrisoned by one of the best divisions in the German army, the 2nd Prussian Guard; yet the initial attacking force consisted only of three battalions. Contrary to usual practice, these battalions were given an issue of rum before the action rather than after it. Yelling 'like a lot of bushrangers', as one of their officers said, they began their advance towards the summit at dawn. They met surprisingly little resistance, but took a great many German prisoners. 'It all happened like lightning,' said the Kaiser Alexander Regiment's history of the war, 'and before we had fired a shot we were taken unawares.' Sergeant Jack Tarrant, the little bread carter from Wyong who had been stranded in No Man's Land at Pozières, took thirty-six prisoners single-handedly. 'We came in the dark and didn't know where the German lines were,' he recalled later in life, 'but we could see flashes from their artillery and the light of their machine guns. When it got daylight a Corporal came up to me and said, "We're having hellish trouble up here with machine guns. They're holding us up." I went along the side of them. They reckon a snake's belly is nothing to what you can do when you're in trouble. I was always a believer in Mills bombs. I had one in each hand, a rifle on a sling, and two more bombs in my coat. When I was about 15 feet away I threw two bombs. Including the dead, there were over 20 of the coots. They were demoralised. I would have been the same if I was them.'

Sergeant Tarrant, who was awarded the Distinguished Conduct Medal for his work that morning, sent his prisoners back with the following message written proudly on a piece of brown paper from around a German parcel: '36 in this group. Captured by Jack Tarrant, B Company 20th Battalion.' The 5th Brigade, to which Tarrant's battalion belonged, captured the summit of Mont St Quentin, but was obliged to give it up during the afternoon. Next day (1 September) the summit was retaken and held, and by 2 September the moated town of Péronne was also firmly in Australian hands. Three weeks later the Solicitor-General of the Commonwealth, Sir Robert Garran, who had come to England with Hughes for the Imperial Conference, visited Mont St Quentin with a party of war correspondents. 'It had been cleaned up of course,' he wrote in his diary. 'but it still reeked when we were there. I don't know how it is done: it seems that the Australians have a superb confidence which gives them a moral ascendancy and makes the Boche a beaten man before the fight begins. Monash told me that General Rawlinson, Commander of the Fourth Army, told him, the night before, that it was absurd to attack Mont St Quentin with three battalions. Next morning, when Monash telephoned to him, "Well, we are there – on top of Mont St Quentin,' he snapped back, "I don't believe it." Later, when he had to believe it, he rang up and said, "Look here, Monash, do you know what you have done? You have altered the whole course of this —— war, that's all." '

In this mood of triumphant euphoria, the Australian Corps went on to take part in the climactic Allied offensive against the Hindenburg Line. Garran returned to London confident that the war was almost over, and so it was. On 11 November he recorded in his diary: 'At 10.15 I descended into the basement [of the Savoy Hotel] to get my hair cut, and on emerging a little before eleven was greeted by the sound of the first maroons and the sight of the first flags fluttering from windows in the Strand. In a few minutes, as if by magic, flags were everywhere, and everybody was in the street – cheering and singing with the pent-up exuberance of four years.' Garran hurried to Australia House, where he found a crowd of Anzacs with a brass band in possession of the concert hall; when a party of nurses and war girls arrived, the gathering turned into an impromptu concert and dance. Garran led off the dancing in an agile two-step with one of the Anzacs.

Sergeant Jack Tarrant, who had been on leave in England after Mont St Quentin, was returning to his battalion in France that very day. He was forming up with other Australians at Folkestone to march down to the ship when a woman dressed in black called from a balcony: 'Well, boys, the armistice has been officially signed this morning at 11 o'clock. The Canadians have taken Mons, and the war has almost finished where it started.' That was the kind of war it had been.

Peace

Just as Britain had committed the Empire to war without so much as a by-your-leave, now she had also agreed to the terms of armistice without consulting any of the Dominions. Not all the flags in the Strand nor exploding maroons could brighten Hughes's mood on Armistice Day, for he was still seething about the British Government's latest failure to consult him on matters of direct concern to Australia. His mood was all the darker because, until the last days of the war, he believed that Britain had been made to see the error of her uncommunicative ways. Hughes had come to London determined to raise the matter of communication at the Imperial Conference. He had not informed the Governor-General of his intention, but on his way across the Pacific had sent a cable to the Colonial Office, through the Governor of Fiji, requesting that the conference agenda be extended to include 'channels of communication between Britain and the self-governing Dominions.'

Sir Ronald Munro-Ferguson, scenting a challenge to the vice-regal network, conveyed his fears to the Colonial Office and enlisted the support of his fellow Governors-General in the other Dominions. But he was too late. Hughes had secured the Canadian vote in advance, and had not left the Colonial Office sufficient time to organise its usual stonewall defence. 'I think there is a tendency,' wrote the Colonial Secretary, Walter Long, to Munro-Ferguson on 3 July, 'though at present it is very undefined, to suggest alterations in the procedure between HMG and the Governments of the Dominions. This is, I think, natural enough: the war has thrown new and tremendous responsibilities upon the Oversea Prime Ministers and their colleagues: they have been brought into contact for the first time with the great realities of Government . . . and it is not to be wondered at in my judgment that all this should tend to make them feel that they must be treated rather more as representatives of Sister Nations than as the leaders of Colonies. There is one feeling – how deep it goes or how widely it extends I do not know – but it is there, and it is that the Prime Ministers of the Dominions should have a direct right of access on the part of their Governments to HMG. It is urged that the process of communicating through the Governor-General to the Prime Minister is one which causes a great deal of circumlocution and consequent delay, and I think, though I may be wrong, that there is a little feeling that it is not treating the Dominion Prime Ministers with sufficient respect or clothing them with sufficient dignity.'

The Imperial Conference passed a vague resolution calling for 'such a change in administrative arrangements and in the Channels of Communication between the United Kingdom and Dominions Governments as will bring them more directly in touch with each other.' On the broader question of Dominion status, the Imperial War Cabinet had made certain observations in 1917 which were to be considered further after the war. It had resolved unanimously that postwar readjustment of the constitutional relations of the component parts of the Empire should be based upon 'a full recognition of the Dominions as autonomous nations of an Imperial Commonwealth, and of India as an important part of the same, should recognize the right of the Dominions and India to an adequate voice in foreign policy and foreign relations, and should provide an effective arrangement for continuous consultation in all important matters of common Imperial concern. . . .' In light of these resolutions, and his own attendance at meetings of the Imperial War Cabinet, Hughes was understandably but mistakenly confident of his access to full information on the all-important subject which had caused him to prolong his stay in London – the terms of the armistice and peace. The Australian Government felt that it had a closer interest in the formulation of these terms than many other small Allied nations – not so much because of Australia's 60,000 war dead, though that was a useful rhetorical point, but because its national security would be affected for better or worse by the terms of settlement. For one thing, Australia felt that its security depended strategically upon continued possession of the Pacific territory which it had seized from Germany; for another, it was apprehensive about Japanese intentions.

Unknown to Hughes until 5 November, the Allied Supreme War Council decided at a conference which began at Versailles on 29 October to base the armistice on fourteen points which had been drawn up by President Wilson of the United States. Some of these points, impeccable though they seemed to the pure of heart like Woodrow Wilson, struck Hughes as being likely to violate Australian interests. 'My Cabinet,' he wrote to the British Prime Minister, Lloyd George, two days before the armistice was declared, 'has requested me to bring before you and the Imperial War Cabinet without delay their emphatic protest against the decisions made at the Versailles conference, and their deep regret that the Dominions were not consulted in regard thereto. They ask me to say they are both surprised and indignant that conditions of peace should have been decided without Australia being consulted; that in light of many definite assurances to contrary, embodied in Secretary of State despatches, and the reported utterances of British Ministers from time to time, they regard this as a painful and serious breach of faith.' The letter warned that Australia would not accept any interpretation of President Wilson's third point (removal, as far as possible, of economic barriers), which seemed likely to limit its right to determine its own tariffs, and said that the Supreme War Council's terms should have specified the right of Australia and New Zealand to retain the former German colonies in the southern Pacific, a right which might well conflict with Wilson's fifth point (impartial adjustment of colonial claims).

Lloyd George replied rather lamely by reminding Hughes of the distinction between the terms of an armistice, which had been decided at Versailles, and the terms of peace, which had yet to be settled at a conference in Paris. 'An armistice has often to be arranged in the shortest possible time,' he said, and there could be 'no certainty that all the belligerents would be consulted in reference thereto.' Hughes argued that the setting of armistice terms had been a preliminary and integral stage in the peace-making process, and he continued to depict Australia's exclusion from that stage as, in Garran's words, 'altogether inexcusable and damnable'. Hughes undoubtedly cultivated his umbrage, for he must have known that it would serve him well during the months of peace-making that lay ahead.

Before the peace treaty was signed, Hughes would have spent fifteen months away from Australia. The electorate did not seem to mind having an absentee Prime Minister. The Acting Prime Minister – the Treasurer, W. A. Watt, a former Liberal from Victoria – inspired confidence at home, and to most Australians it seemed only natural that the Prime Minister should be watching Australia's interests where they were being affected at this crucial time. The only discernible misgivings in Australia were those inspired by Hughes's nationalism, which some Ministers regarded as anti-British. Hughes was accompanied during his long stay in England and France by his second wife and baby daughter and a small but select entourage which included the Minister for Defence, Sir Joseph Cook; Cook's adviser, Lieut-Commander J. G. Latham (later Sir John Latham, Chief Justice of Australia); Sir Robert Garran who had been appointed Solicitor-General in order to relieve Hughes of his legal duties as Attorney-General; and Hughes's private secretary, Percy Deane. They had plenty to occupy them, even after the Imperial Conference and before the peace conference began. Hughes spent 'laborious and fretful days, going round and round like a clockwork mouse', persuading the War Office to grant Australian leave to the 1915 Anzacs in France, scrounging ships for troops and trade, selling Australian produce and metals, attending War Cabinet, flying to Paris and back for preliminary peace discussions, and above all keeping his Acousticon ear to the ground.

Occasionally there were unscheduled breaks from this clockwork round. On 17 September Hughes and his companions attended the funeral of Sir George Reid, the former Prime Minister and Australian High Commissioner who had finished his days as a member of the House of Commons. 'After service in the church,' wrote Garran, 'we motored out at a good pace to the cemetery at Putney Vale – a beautiful spot, where we left him.' Garran enjoyed good relations with Hughes, and on one occasion they went shopping together. Hughes wanted a signet ring which he could use as a personal seal when signing the peace treaty. After looking through various curio shops, he chose a ring bearing the device of Hercules killing the lion. 'This struck his fancy,' wrote Garran, 'and it was one of the few occasions on which I defied Hughes to his face, and the only occasion, I think, when I did so successfully. I said, "No, Mr Hughes, you are not in the least like Hercules, and your job is not killing the lion." It was hard to get his eyes away from this device, but eventually he found another, a representation of the three legs of Man, which is apparently a Welsh as well as a Manx device. So he agreed to that.'

Garran should have kept out of this decision, for it is easy to see why Hercules and the lion would have taken the Prime Minister's fancy. Billy Hughes was indeed a kind of Hercules, and although in the peace negotiations he was not trying to strangle the British lion he was certainly grappling with it. The first stage of this encounter was his fight for separate Australian representation at the Paris peace conference. On his previous visit to Britain in 1916, Hughes had learnt two important lessons: his talks with the Japanese Ambassador and the British Foreign Secretary, Sir Edward Grey, had convinced him then that Australia's national interests would come under challenge from Japan as soon as the war ended, and that in such an eventuality Britain could not be relied upon to defend Australian interests. As Hughes's biographer, L. F. Fitzhardinge, has pointed out, he was also made aware by the 1916 Allied Economic Conference of the danger of a common delegation in which Australia's voice might be submerged in a single British vote. According to Fitzhardinge, there was good reason to believe that from this time on the need for an independent Australian vote at the peace table was never far from Hughes's mind.

For several weeks after the armistice, Hughes, the Canadian Prime

Minister, Sir Robert Borden, and the South African Prime Minister, J. C. Smuts, lobbied for various forms of Dominions representation at the peace conference. Smuts suggested a Dominions panel from which an appropriate representative would be chosen at different times according to the subjects under discussion, and Borden would have been satisfied with one permanent Dominions representative, provided that representative was himself. Hughes, however, wanted separate and permanent representation for each Dominion. His own Cabinet was strangely alarmed by his pertinacity. 'Claim for representation of Dominions as Dominions, either at Versailles or Peace Conference, is not reasonable, and cannot be supported by the Cabinet,' cabled the Acting Prime Minister in late November. 'It is not proposed to ask Parliament to carry any resolutions claiming representation of Dominions as Dominions. We feel that it would be impossible to pass such a motion.' Ignoring this timidity, Hughes buckled down to his Herculean task with what Professor Fitzhardinge has called 'characteristic intransigent indirectness', and in the end he won. He ingratiated himself with the French Prime Minister, Georges Clemenceau, and pressed his case at every opportunity in England. It is easy to see why Smuts would have said to Borden at about this time: 'Hughes gets on Lloyd George's nerves.' President Wilson was at first strongly opposed to separate Dominions representation on the ground that it might lead some of the smaller nations to accuse the great powers of trying to pack the conference. Eventually he relented, and on 31 January the Supreme War Council, which by then was known as the Council of Ten, decided that the British Empire Delegation should include two delegates each for Canada, Australia and South Africa, one for New Zealand and two for India.

For the Commonwealth and its sister Dominions, this was the most important step towards autonomous nationhood. Not only would they be attending an international political assembly as separate entities (the only precedents for this had been at purely technical conferences), but they would also have dual status. At the proceedings which began in Paris during January, they were represented on the same footing as such powers as Belgium and Portugal. Admittedly they had no vote separate from that of the British Empire Delegation, but this was more than compensated for by the fact that their representatives could also serve as British delegates. The Paris peace conference was a confusing organism which inched its way towards a peace treaty on several different levels. Its business was transacted at separate delegation meetings by the five great powers and twenty-two smaller allies; in the Council of Ten (consisting of the heads of the five great powers and their foreign ministers), which determined what matters should be submitted to plenary conference; in the more selective Councils of Five, Four and Three; in the commissions and committees set up to draft various sections of the treaty; and in the plenary conference, whose proceedings, attended by all delegates, were nearly always pre-arranged and formal. Without full knowledge of what was happening in the councils and commissions where the real decisions were taken, Australia would have been as much on the outer – to use John Latham's simile – as Uruguay or Siam. But thanks to their membership of the British Empire Delegation, the two Australian delegates, Hughes and Cook, were always fully informed. 'Although technically the status of the Dominions and India was no higher than the status of the score of smaller nations which waited about with little information, and even less influence,' wrote Hughes, 'while the four or five great powers decided, in actual fact they were included in the deciding powers, for, by virtue of their membership of the British Delegation , they formulated the policy which their spokesman, the Prime Minister of the United Kingdom, advocated in the Council of Four. They were kept in touch with all that went on; they were able to express their views at every stage.'

The Australian delegates and their staff[3] lived and worked at the Hotel Majestic, one of four Paris hotels which housed the British Empire Delegation. Hughes thrived on the multi-national politicking which filled his days and nights in Paris. In the course of one day alone he conferred with representatives from China, Peru, Japan, America, Poland, Arabia, Czechoslovakia, Italy, Greece and Brazil. 'It would cheer you tremendously,' he wrote to Sir Ronald Munro-Ferguson in Melbourne, 'to hear me making jokes in English which, filtering through the joyous mentality of the French interpreters, ultimately make the Czechs and Arabs and Greeks laugh.' Hughes affected different people in different ways, but no one could ignore him. The Italian Prime Minister, Francesco Nitti, thought him 'a small-minded, insensitive, violent man', and Lord Robert Cecil, the Parliamentary Under-Secretary for Foreign Affairs, once called him 'that shrimp Hughes'. The American Ambassador to the Court of St James, Walter Hines Page, reported to President Wilson that Hughes was 'a somewhat narrow but very earnest and surely very convincing man, a free-and-easy and ready campaigner with a colonial breeziness which "takes" '; and Clemenceau, in his memoirs, referred to 'the noble delegate from Australia, with whom we had to talk through an electrophone, getting in return symphonies of good sense.'

[3] Among the advisers to Hughes and Cook were Garran; Latham; H.S. (later Sir Henry) Gullett; Lt F.W. (later Sir Frederick) Eggleston; the financier W.S. Robinson; and the journalist Keith Murdoch.

The indestructible 80-year-old 'Tiger' Clemenceau, sufficiently recovered from an assassin's bullet in the lung to preside over the conference, left vivid sketches of some of Hughes's British colleagues. Lloyd George was 'fresh and pink' with 'a bright two-fisted smile'; Arthur Balfour 'the most cultured, the most gracious, the most courteous of adamantine men'; and Bonar Law 'the prince of balance, who would have been a first-class Frenchman had he not been wholly British.' In the first of Hughes's labours at the peace conference – his struggle for the annexation of German New Guinea by Australia – he had to contend with these adamantine British delegates as well as with the righteously anti-colonial Americans. Australia and Japan were at one in their desire to obtain full sovereignty over the various colonies which they had seized from Germany – New Guinea and Nauru in Australia's case, and the Marshall and Caroline Islands north of the Equator in the case of Japan. They were united in this against President Wilson's strong desire to avoid any appearance of scrambling for spoils of war; but there the identity of interest ended.

Australia's deep-seated fear of Japan had been reinforced during the war, despite the latter's status as an ally, by Japan's rapid industrial growth and undisguised imperial ambition. Hughes could not argue against Japan's claim north of the Equator without weakening Australia's own case; but where the racial and commercial interests of the two countries conflicted, he was determined to give no ground. He saw nothing but danger in a proposal that the German Pacific territories should be administered by mandatory powers acting as trustees for the League of Nations, which would soon come into being. How could Australia be certain of receiving and retaining the mandate for New Guinea? If it did receive the mandate, would it be able to restrict Asian immigration into that territory as effectively as it could into its own continent? And would it have to accord Japan equality of commercial opportunity in the mandated territory?

At Hughes's urging, Lloyd George arranged for the Dominions prime ministers to present their views on colonial annexation to the Council of Ten. 'Bring your savages with you!' said Clemenceau grandly to the British Prime Minister. Smuts spoke on German South-West Africa, and W. F. Massey (New Zealand) on German Samoa; but the most ardent plea for annexation came from Hughes. The Pacific Islands encompassed Australia like fortresses, he said; and any strong power controlling New Guinea would control Australia. Certainly the rights of the indigenous population should be safeguarded, but these would be secure under Australian control, which would constitute a threat to no one. Back inside the British Empire Delegation, Hughes and Massey continued to argue for

unqualified control of trade and immigration in the face of growing cool-
ness on the part of British delegates. On 29 January a compromise was
evolved. Lieut-Commander Latham, who privately considered that
mandates would be in the best interests of both the Empire and Australia,
and Sir Maurice Hankey, secretary to the British Empire Delegation,
drafted a proposal for a special class of mandate. This would apply to
territories which, 'owing to the sparseness of their population, or their
small size, or their remoteness from the centres of civilisation, or their
geographical contiguity to the mandatory state . . . can best be administered
under the laws of the mandatory state as integral portions thereof.' The
mandatory state would be responsible to the League of Nations for the
welfare of the indigenous population.

Hughes was still suspicious; but, after a blunt warning from Lloyd
George that the Dominions would have to manage without British help
if they persisted in holding out for more than this compromise, he accepted
the proposal subject to the approval of his Government. At a Council of
Ten meeting that afternoon, Massey announced that New Zealand would
accept the compromise although it would have preferred annexation.
President Wilson then asked angrily whether New Zealand was presenting
an ultimatum. If it did not obtain the compromise, would it try to stop
the whole arrangement? Massey backed down, but Hughes, fiddling
theatrically with his Acousticon, said that he had not heard the question.
'Mr Hughes,' said Wilson, 'am I to understand that if the whole civilized
world asks Australia to agree to [an unqualified] mandate in respect of
these islands, Australia is prepared to defy the appeal of the whole civilized
world?' 'That's about the size of it, Mr President,' said Hughes. The
compromise was accepted provisionally, and later embodied in the 'C'
Mandate under which the former German colonies in the Pacific were
administered by Australia, New Zealand and Japan. It was less than Hughes
had wanted, but more than a less determined negotiator would have
obtained. In any case, the future would show that Australia's interests
were adequately protected by the compromise.

One British delegate observed that Hughes 'had the knack, possessed
by none other, of knocking [President Wilson] completely off his balance.'
The knack also proved useful in the second of Hughes's labours – his fight
against Japan's attempt to have embodied in the Covenant of the League
of Nations a clause which, in Hughes's estimation, would have endangered
the White Australia policy. The fight took place in the Commission,
chaired by President Wilson, which drew up the articles of the Covenant.
On 13 February Baron Makino of Japan moved that an article dealing
with religious toleration should include the following paragraph: 'The

equality of nations being a basic principle of the League of Nations, the High Contracting Powers agree to accord, as soon as possible, to all alien nationals of States members of the League, equal and just treatment in every respect, making no distinction either in law or in fact on account of their race or nationality.' Not on your life, said Hughes; such a high-minded clause would throw Australia open to indiscriminate immigration, and – as Sir Ronald Munro-Ferguson had remarked in 1915 – 'any relenting in the White Australia policy would bring any Government here to grief.'

When Baron Makino called on Hughes to discuss the racial paragraph, he said it was intolerable that Japanese should not be treated as the equals of Australians and other races. Hughes replied that Australia would have no objection to a declaration of racial equality provided it stated clearly 'that this did not confer any right to enter Australia – or any other country – except as and to the extent that its Government might determine.' Baron Makino said that Japan wanted no more than a recognition of the technical right of free entry, and that its people would not wish to exercise such a right. Unconvinced, Hughes delivered a gratuitous lecture on cultural differences: 'Your ideals, your institutions, your standards, are not ours. We do not say that ours are greater or better than yours; we only say they are different.' President Wilson's confidential adviser, Colonel E. M. House, noted in his diary on 27 March: '[The Japanese] are having no end of trouble with Hughes of Australia. He will not consent to anything in the way of satisfying Japan's desires. He threatens if anything is passed by [the Commission] he will bring it up at the plenary conference.' Early in April Baron Makino came back to Hughes with a shorter draft which had received the blessings of Wilson, Lloyd George, Smuts and Borden: 'The equality of nations being a basic principle of the League of Nations, the High Contracting Parties agree to endorse the principle of equal and just treatment to be accorded to all aliens, nationals of States members of the League.' Hughes refused to countenance that, or even a third and still shorter version: 'by the indorsement of the principle of the equality of nations and the just treatment of their nationals.' When Baron Makino proposed this final version in the Commission it was approved by eleven of the fifteen delegates, but President Wilson ruled from the chair that the motion had been lost because it was not unanimous. Only the British and Americans had refrained from supporting it. Hughes later claimed to have influenced Wilson's attitude by threatening, through Colonel House, to whip up a storm against Japanese immigration in newspapers on the west coast of the United States.

Successful though he had been at racial intolerance and colonial expansion, Hughes made little headway with another labour – the exaction of maximum war reparations from Germany. Maintaining that the Allies were entitled to reparation for the full cost of the war, and not just compensation for direct injury, Australia submitted a claim for £464 million: £364 million for war expenditure and £100 million for the capitalized value of pensions, repatriation and damage to property. Vain hopes! 'You have assured us that you cannot get better terms,' wrote Hughes to Lloyd George when it became clear that general war costs would not be paid. 'I much regret it, and hope even now that some way may be found of securing agreement for demanding reparation commensurate with the tremendous sacrifices made by the British Empire and her Allies.' Hughes asked that he be recorded as having dissented from the reparations decision, and in return he received the following tart reply from Lloyd George: 'I quite understand your attitude. It is a very well known one. It is generally called "heads I win, and tails you lose" which means that you get the full benefit from the arrangement we have painfully elaborated in compensation and especially in pensions, whereas your comrades in the Dominions, in Great Britain and in France get all the abuse.'

The most that Australia ever received in the way of war reparations was £5,571,720. By contrast, the direct cost of the war to Australia from 1914 to 1918 had been £376,993,052. Of that amount, £333,594,954 was actual expenditure by the Commonwealth on war services. This came mainly from war loans (£262,507,829) and to a lesser extent from revenue (£71,087,125). The rest of the total cost (£43,398,098) consisted of debts owed to Britain for payments made, services rendered and goods supplied to the Australian military forces. In one year alone, 1918–19, the war cost Australia £80,802,181 – or £3,214,181 more than Britain, with five times Australia's existing population, had spent in the three years of the Crimean War. Astronomical though the total cost of £376,993,052 seemed in 1919, it was only part of the ultimate cost of the war to which Australia had been so ready to contribute its last shilling. By the mid-1930s repatriation, pensions, war gratuities, interest and sinking fund charges had lifted the figure to £831,280,947.

The peace treaty was signed on Saturday afternoon, 28 June 1919, in the Galerie des Glaces at the Château de Versailles outside Paris. In the morning Hughes and Garran called on the President of France, M. Poincaré, and presented him with a painting by Will Ashton of the memorial to La Pérouse at Botany Bay. After lunch at the Hotel Majestic they and the other Australians motored out to Versailles along roads lined on both sides by steel-helmeted *poilus*, past *fleur-de-lis* fountains to the vast honey-coloured building from which Louis XVI and Marie Antoinette had once watched the approach of an ominous revolutionary mob. Up the marble staircase they went, past Gardes Républicains in gleaming cuirasses and helmets with drawn sabres at the salute, and into the Galerie des Glaces, a richly tapestried and chandeliered hall where each window was reflected in a corresponding mirror. Seated at tables covered with gold draperies were the Allied plenipotentiaries, guests and the world press. Clemenceau, looking small and yellow, took his seat below a Bourbon scroll proclaiming: 'Le Roy gouverne par lui-même.' As he looked around the hall Clemenceau noticed, sitting on a velvet-covered bench between two windows, 'three ghastly masks of the hellish tragedy, with eyes unsocketed, with twisted jaws, their faces ploughed with scars – three grievously wounded men, invited to the place of honour, a reminder of hideous torments heroically borne.'

In this hall half a century before, France had signed a humiliating treaty with Prussia. Now the humiliation was Germany's. As the German delegates were announced at the entrance of the hall, the Gardes Républicains sheathed their sabres with a resounding clash. 'Faites entrer les Allemands,' said Clemenceau, and in walked two circumspect German civilians, Dr Müller and Dr Bell. The Germans signed first, then the Americans, and at 3.18 pm Lloyd George led the British Empire Delegation to the signing table. The British Empire's only party to the treaty was His Majesty the King, signed for by Lloyd George and four other British Ministers, and by the Dominions delegates. Hughes and Cook, treating 'on the part of His Majesty the King in respect of the Commonwealth of Australia', signed between the Canadians and the South Africans.

The Australian delegation dined that night at the Hôtel Majestic, danced the two-step and fox-trot until the early hours of the morning, and then returned to London. A few days later they embarked for Australia on the *Friedrichsruhe*, a captured German steamer crowded with 1000 homebound Australian troops. The *Friedrichsruhe* had been named after Bismarck's country estate, and in its dining saloon was a bronze bas-relief of the Chancellor. Sir Robert Garran, whose *Song of the Commonwealth* had been published in *The Sydney Morning Herald* during the Federation festivities of January 1901, was inspired by this plaque to write a poem entitled *Who Are These?*

> Bismarck gazes down in wonder from his frame upon the wall
> Seeing sights and hearing noises that he can't make out at all;
> Who are these that dress like soldiers, but are lean instead of fat,
> And in place of pickelhaube wear a caballero hat?
> Why, they sing 'God Save The King', and pledge in water, not in wine.

And their talk is like the English mostly, but with two or three
Words my mother never taught me that are quite unknown to me.
Yet their home is not in England, for they say they're homeward bound,
And the *Friedrichsruhe* is nosing on and on, the wide world round.
Now, with alien flag, she bears an alien army o'er the sea,
And I look and wonder dumbly, darkly, vainly –Who are these?

Who were they, indeed? They were not the same men who had
embarked from Australia a few years before, bound happily for
Armageddon; nor were their kinsfolk in Australia quite the same. As the
heat of summer hardens a cicada newly emerged from dark years in the
ground, so the heat of war might be said to have hardened the Australian
sense of identity. The British/Australian duality was still discernible, but
not to the same pervasive extent as it had been in 1901. There were clearly
two kinds of Australians now, probably about equal in number, and not
easy to define. There were the British-Australians, unchanged in their
imperial loyalty, predominantly middle-class, Protestant, and politically
conservative; and there were those who in varying degrees had rejected,
outgrown, forgotten or simply never known the British inheritance. To
this second group, which might be called the Indigenous Australians,
belonged a large part of the working class, most Irish Catholics, the
children of European immigrants, the industrially militant and the
politically radical. The two groups had been at loggerheads during the
war – over conscription, the merits of the war, and the right to strike –
and relations could hardly be said to have improved with peace. As we
shall see in the next chapter, Australia was shaken during 1919 by outbreaks of political and industrial violence which further estranged the
British and Indigenous Australians.

In his first speech after returning to Australia, Hughes divided his
countrymen into two groups – those who had supported the war, and
those who had not. This was not the same as distinguishing between
British and Indigenous Australians; but the two sets of criteria had something in common, for the British Australians were more prominent in the
first of Hughes's categories than in the second, and it could be argued that
the reverse was true of the Indigenous Australians. 'There are in this
country sheep and goats,' said Hughes at a civic reception in Fremantle
Town Hall, '– those who have earned salvation, and those who have done
nothing. . . Those who have borne the heat and burden of the day, those
who in season and out of season endured, have fought, have sacrificed,
have died – to them has been given the right to say what shall be the
destiny of Australia. To them I shall look – and to those who sent them
out – their fathers, mothers, sisters, brothers and friends. . . But to those

who passed by on the other side, I say let them do what they will. But as far as I am concerned they need not look to me. There are some people in this country who speak of fighting, who are tired, so it seems, of government by the people and government by the free constitutional methods that we have earned after a thousand years of ceaseless effort. They say, so I have read in the wireless, that if Australia is not ready for Bolshevism or some other "ism" they must do a little blood shedding. Let them beware how they start that.'

15

LAND OF ECHOES

ALL THAT STILL had to be performed was the rite of homecoming, a rite which usually began at the docks of Southampton, Gravesend or Liverpool, and ended at a Town Hall or School of Arts on the other side of the world. Gold medals were awarded with due ceremony, the names of those who had gone to the war were inscribed on rolls of honour, and the names of those who had not returned were carved in stone below white marble statues or captured German guns. Australia had sent more troops to the Great War than even Britain herself had ever sent abroad before; when the last shot was fired, there were 270,000 Australians in Europe, Britain and the Middle East. Bringing these men and women home in 137 different ships, and in little more than a year, was as great an organisational feat as any victory of the war. The first returning troopship left England on 3 December 1918, and the last on 23 December 1919. By the first anniversary of the Armistice no fewer than 250,000 troops were already home in Australia.

Once the first excitement of homecoming had passed, Australia was often something of an anti-climax to these veterans. 'It seemed dead,' recalled Sergeant Jack Tarrant, who returned to Wyong late in 1919. 'We were coming back from cities, remember, and by the time I got to Sydney the glamour had died. I was expecting a bit of enthusiasm from the crowd, but no one noticed me. I can tell you I felt like catching another boat back to England.' It should have been obvious from his white kit bag, the brass 'A' on his colour patch, and the excitement of his mother and sister that Sergeant Tarrant was a newly returned Anzac, but at Central Station in Sydney a military policeman asked officiously: 'Got a pass, Digger?' That question rankled all the way down to the Hawkesbury River and up to Wyong. 'Fortunately,' said Tarrant many years later, 'a 3rd Division officer spoke to me on the train. That did more for me coming back than anything.'

The Australia to which Sergeant Tarrant and his comrades returned in 1919 may have fallen short of some expectations, but it was a bigger and in some ways better Australia than the one with which this narrative began on the first day of the 20th century. The population had grown from

3,766,000 to 5,435,000, and was still overwhelmingly British in racial origin; the Commonwealth was firmly established, though not as firmly as some centralists would have liked; and the economy was prospering, though not by any means to the fair advantage of all. The proportion of British-born Australians had fallen from 18 per cent to 12 per cent, but restrictive immigration laws had seen to it that genetic competition was negligible. The percentage of non-British, European-born Australians was only 1.26, compared with 1.98 in 1901, and the percentage of non-Europeans was 0.89. Among this small but unwelcome group of non-whites were 17,157 Chinese (compared with 29,907 in 1901), 2740 Japanese, 322 Javanese, 150 Afghans, 37 Arabs, 11 Persians and 6 American Indians. They were a threat to no one.

Although Federation had incurred a certain amount of unpopularity since 1901, it was now accepted as an accomplished fact. Admittedly the electorate was reluctant to widen the powers of Commonwealth Parliament (at a referendum in 1919 it refused for the third time to grant more extensive powers over trade, monopolies and industrial affairs), but before many more months had passed the High Court would strengthen the central power in ways already foreshadowed in some of Mr Justice Isaacs's dissenting judgments. The Commonwealth's revenue and expenditure had risen gradually from 1901 to 1914, and rapidly during the war. Once acquired, such budgetary habits were hard to change and the level of Government spending continued to rise. The Commonwealth's expenditure per head of population rose from £1 0s 7d in 1901 to £3 3s 5d in 1914 and £7 12s 1d in 1919. By 1921 it was £10 10s; 1922, £11 6s 1d; and 1925, £12 7s 4d. In 1914 the Commonwealth raised £16,587,906 in taxation compared with £6,304,836 raised by the States; and by 1919 these two figures had risen to £32,864,486 and £11,971,254 respectively. The cost of running Commonwealth ministerial departments had risen from £3,733,218 in 1901 to £15,458,776 in 1914 and £38,262,585 in 1919. The Commonwealth now had its own courts, its own bank, its own currency and postage stamps, its own flag and coat of arms, its own railways, its own colonial territories, and of course its own armed forces. The seat of government was still Melbourne, but although little work had yet been done in the Federal Capital Territory the Government had decided soon after the war ended that an early move to Canberra was desirable. As if bestowing war's benediction on the new capital, the official war historian, C. E. W. Bean, moved his staff and files into the homestead of Tuggeranong in the Capital Territory and began his monumental task of recording Australia's part in the war.

In this year of endings and beginnings, Walter Burley Griffin's contract expired and was extended by a few months in prelude to his permanent departure from the direction of design and construction in Canberra. In 1919 Sir Samuel Griffith retired as Chief Justice of the High Court, Vice-Admiral Sir William Creswell retired as first naval member of the Commonwealth Naval Board, and King O'Malley retired from politics. Alfred Deakin died in October that year, and one of his closest parliamentary colleagues, Sir Edmund Barton, had only three more months to live. Lord Forrest had died at sea in 1918 while travelling to take his seat in the House of Lords (he was buried at Sierra Leone, and later re-interred in his native Western Australia); and Sir George Reid, as we have seen, died during the same year in London.

Economically, Australia was in good fettle. The war had been a great economic stimulus, and there was not even much reason to worry about the wartime legacy of national debt; that could wait to be repaid by posterity. The last few seasons had been good, and because of the war there had been strong demand for Australian wool, wheat, metals and butter. The balance of trade had risen from £42,434,000 worth of imports and £49,696,000 worth of exports in 1901 to comparable figures of £98,697,000 and £148,565,000 in 1919. Australia had come to rely less on Britain for imports (34 per cent of total imports now came from Britain, compared with 62 per cent in 1901), but exported relatively more than ever to Britain and the rest of the Empire (80 per cent of Australian exports went to the Empire, including Britain, compared with 72 per cent in 1901). Wartime import restrictions led to more extensive local manufacture of such products as motor bodies, chemicals, paints and boots, and to the manufacture of many new products for the first time: fibro-cement, typewriter ribbons, carbon paper, ether, sheep and cattle dips, electrical batteries and machine tools. Industrial employment had increased from 429,000 in 1901 to 731,000 in 1919, and there had been corresponding changes in the structure of the work force as a whole. In 1901, 26 per cent of total breadwinners were engaged in industrial work: in 1919 the figure had risen to 31 per cent, while the next largest occupational category, primary industry, had shown a fall from 32 per cent to 25 per cent in the same period.

To those who drew their fair share of prosperity, Australia afforded new conveniences and new pleasures: the telephone was no longer the rarity it had been in 1901 (205,272 connections, compared with 24,577), motor cars were becoming commonplace (55,596, compared with 60), and cinema-going had become the nation's most popular pastime. By 1919 there were 862 cinemas throughout the Commonwealth, and attendances at such silent films as *Stella Maris* (Mary Pickford and Douglas Fairbanks),

The Immigrant (Charlie Chaplin) and *Rule Britannia* (British War Office films released for the first time) commanded an annual average of twenty-three attendances by every man, woman and child in the country. For those who could afford its pleasures, life was becoming easier and less regimented. There was a trend towards later marriages, family size was dwindling, the divorce rate was rising, and church attendances were falling. The average weekly working time for men had fallen from 48.6 hours in 1914 to 47.36 in 1919, while the figure for industrialized countries overseas still ranged between 50 and 72 hours.

The bright side of the economy was no comfort to the six per cent of the work force which was unemployed, nor to thousands of employees whose wages in real terms were lower than before the war. In 1919 the average weekly wage for men was £3 14s 11d, and for women £1 17s 1d; yet little more than twelve months later a Royal Commission on the basic wage would conclude that the bare minimum required to keep a husband, wife and three children at an acceptable standard was £5 16s. Poverty in the larger cities, and discontent over wages and conditions in such industrial centres as Townsville and Broken Hill, were irresistible challenges to those Australian critics of capitalism who had been deeply interested in the activities of the Bolsheviks in Russia, the Red Guards in Hungary and the Spartacists in Germany. 'The war of the rival imperialisms – Germanic and British – is at an end,' wrote the radical Labor MHR for Bourke, Frank Anstey, in a book entitled *Red Europe* (1919). 'Peace is declared, but peace is not in the world. . . Once more we see under every flag Two Nations – the Master Class and the Subject Masses. Ever the Master Class has treated the majority of its own race and blood as a foreign race. Only in time of war has it recognised the blood tie; only then has it sworn brotherhood. . . This Master Class of every land and brand has not even treated its own workers as cattle fit to be fattened for a profit. It has, wherever it has had the power, overworked and underfed them, and when it had no work it has turned them out to starve. . . In every land and clime and age the struggle of the masses has been not so much against the foreign intruder as against the internal degrader.'

In Australia, as in other lands, peace brought fierce conflicts of its own. A new strain of violence appeared in public altercation, sometimes pitting returned soldiers against 'Bolsheviks', militant trade unionists and larrikins. The daily press undoubtedly magnified the 'Bolshevik' threat; yet after allowing for such bias, and acknowledging that most Australian workers were not committed to anything like revolutionary class warfare, it remains true that 1919 was the strangest, most violent year the Commonwealth had ever known.

In a poem entitled *Echoes* (1918), Frank Wilmot saw his country 'drowned in echoes of reflected troubles.' Wilmot, a Melbourne bookseller with pacifist leanings, had not been to the war; but in this poem he tried with some success to see Australia through the eyes of a returned soldier:

> I have returned into a world of shadows,
> I have returned into a land of echoes,
> A thin-drawn filament of echoed impulses
> Smothers your gleaming spaces.
> Echoes of false, unworthy things
> That blast the older worlds I've loitered in
> Hide you from me,
> Hold you from me,
> Blast your green gullies,
> Cloud your arboured roads.
> For you I have struggled and sinned,
> Stood firmly against the lure of a comforting death,
> And now you are dying, betrayed,
> Bloodless, pale as a dream,
> Murmuring foreign ideas,
> Brooding on the Romanoffs, the Syndicates, the Boyne!
> Shuddering in echoes of ceaseless war and causeless revolution . . .

Resenting the foreign infection of Australia, Wilmot wrote: 'Speak in a voice of your own./ I do not understand what things you tell me/ With these strange lips and foreign tones;/ Is it not enough/ That your wharves are piled with alien merchandise –/ Must your young soul be flooded with foreign despairs?' An Australian voice, but which one: the voice with English overtones, used quite naturally by many Australians; or the rougher-textured indigenous one? Addressing Parliament in September 1919, W. M. Hughes made much of Australia's homogeneous Britishness. 'Do you realize', he asked, 'that, if you go in England from one county to another, men speak with a different accent; that if you go a few miles men speak with a different tongue? Yet you can go from Perth to Sydney, and from Hobart to Cape York, and find men speaking the same tongue in the same way. That cannot be said of any other Dominion in the Empire, except New Zealand, where, after all, it can be said only with reservations, because that country has a large population of Maoris. We are more British than the people of Great Britain, and we hold firmly to the great principle of the White Australia, because we know what we know.' Hughes was right about race, but not about accent. Australians spoke in two accents: the British or cultivated Australian accent, and the distinctive general Australian accent which had begun to develop from a basis of working-class London speech as early as the 1830s, and was distinguished from British Australian by its stronger diphthongs, less retracted vowels and slower tempo.

Thus there were literally two Australian voices, just as there were two flags and two loyalties, though the dualities did not necessarily correspond. Many Australians still owed allegiance to both lion and kangaroo, and when they paid respect to one they meant no disrespect to the other. Alfred Deakin was a proud native-born Australian, yet his coffin was draped with the Union Jack. There were also two wreaths upon the coffin: one of gum leaves, the other of imperial laurel. When the Federal Treasurer, W. A. Watt, paid tribute to Deakin at a funeral service in Queen's Hall, Parliament House, he said: 'He was a true Britisher of the finest type, proud of his race and proud of his line, and doubly seized of the fact that upon the fortunes of our Empire for weal or woe depended the fortunes of civilization.'

Discussing the character of Australia's population, the *Commonwealth Year Book* remarked in 1919 that it would probably not be possible to identify a distinct Australian type for another three or four generations. 'The Australian at present is little more than a transplanted Briton,' it said, 'with the essential characteristics of his British forebears, the desire for freedom from restraint, however, being perhaps somewhat accentuated.' Many British Australians, let alone the indigenous ones, would have disputed the truth of that statement. In an essay written in 1917 and published in 1920, the British-born historian G. A. Wood said that Australians were 'the most British people in the world, and more British now than ever before'; but he added that 'Australian ideas are the expression of a civilization and a temperament that have become distinct from the civilization and temperament of Britain.'

In other words, Australia did possess a voice of its own. Sometimes the accent was part-British, sometimes wholly Australian; and sometimes, as Wilmot complained, it was drowned out by echoes from elsewhere. One indigenous Australian, Vance Palmer, criticised imperialism for the way it made Australians think of themselves as being 'too far from the centre' to have any ideas or any art of their own. Writing in the Brisbane *Worker*, he quoted a Governor of Victoria who had once remarked that Melbourne would be all right 'if it were not so far from town.' 'Unfortunately he exactly voiced the sentiments of many native Australians who take more pride in being imitation-English than in being Australian. We have to give up the idea of being far from town, and Imperialism will not teach us to do so. We have to learn that the centre of every circle is one's own country, whether it is Australia, England or Madagascar. There is nothing jingoistic in this sentiment, any more than there is anything egotistic in the feeling of one's own personal identity. . . What literature, what art, what ideas ever came from people that looked abroad for its "centre"? The first step towards healthy national existence is to throw off [our] second-hand clothing. But the tendency of Imperialism, whatever its exponents may say, is all the other way. Australia must not be bound more closely to the Empire; she is too tightly bound already.'

Certainly the Australian arts were no great testimonial for the aesthetic side of imperialism. Most of Australia's best painters had been drawn physically as well as spiritually to the centre – to London or Paris – leaving behind them a provincial vacuum. Tom Roberts, Arthur Streeton, Charles Conder and George Lambert were all absent from Australia for the greater part of the first two decades of the century. Back at the remote circumference, Norman Lindsay indulged himself with what one critic has described as 'a pantomine world of cavaliers, troubadours, Greek gods, courtiers, imps, panthers and magi'; and of course with gaudy, fleshy women. Only the gum-trees of Hans Heysen and a few other landscape painters could be said to have represented a genuine national vision; and for all of Heysen's undoubted skill, that was not saying very much.

The level of literary achievement during the first two decades of the century was not much higher. *Such Is Life*, written by Joseph Furphy ('Tom Collins') during the 1890s but not published until 1903, was an idiosyncratic swag of anti-romantic bush lore, social comment, anti-British attitudes and anything else that happened to come into Furphy's self-educated, ironic mind. The temper of the book was democratic and its bias offensively Australian, as Furphy himself proclaimed, and its style was in places quite unreadable. Later in the century *Such Is Life* came to be regarded as the most original and impressive book of its day: a work of great if unfulfilled ambition, a sort of indigenous *Tristram Shandy* or poor man's *Moby Dick*. What else from the writing of that period is still valued? C. J. Dennis's *The Songs Of A Sentimental Bloke* and *The Moods of Ginger Mick*, Steele Rudd's *On Our Selection*, Louis Stone's *Jonah* (a novel about Sydney larrikins), and Miles Franklin's *My Brilliant Career* all seem either farcical or superficial. Perhaps the only real survivors are the last short stories of Henry Lawson, the first novels of Henry Handel Richardson (particularly *Australia Felix*, the first part of her Anglo-Australian trilogy *The Fortunes Of Richard Mahony*) and some of Shaw Neilson's simple, luminous poems.

Neilson spent most of his life as a manual bush labourer, yet he made hardly any poetic use of that harsh experience. His poems were universal, and if sometimes they seemed to resemble French symbolism he was not aware of it; Neilson's voice was always his own, never an echo of someone else's. The same could not be said of other poets who were usually detached from their Australian surroundings. Christopher Brennan, an academic who wrote densely and floridly within a framework of European thought, consciously echoed the French symbolist Mallarmé; but his tortuous, interminable poetic wanderings had nothing in common with Neilson's innocent lyrics. Hugh McCrae made no poetic use of Australia, and in his anxiety to avoid the mundane concerns of poetic nationalism he echoed the voices of Greek gods, centaurs and fauns, mediaeval knights and Elizabethan pirates. Even such an earnest patriot as Bernard O'Dowd was apt to invoke exotic deities. Although he shared Wilmot's uneasiness about external influences, O'Dowd saw nothing incongruous in crowding his nationalist poem *The Bush* with such names as Zeus, Pan, Leda, Oison, and even Quetzalcoatl. He did, however, want Australia eventually to compose its own mythology, to resist the 'alien breezes' which he sometimes heard 'above the music of the Bush's breath . . . drowning her oracles to very death.' 'Exotic battle-cries the silence mar,/ Seductive perfumes drive the gum-scent far.'

'Alien breezes' and 'poisonous winds' bearing 'exotic battle-cries' and 'echoes of reflected troubles'. In 1919 many Australians could have expressed those accordant images in one new and alien word: Bolshevism. 'What is Bolshevism?' asked the Melbourne *Argus* in March 1919. 'By this time even the most incredulous and the most indifferent are beginning to realize that there is some new, strange force bursting out in Central Europe and trying to spread among the nations. So even the thoughtless are beginning to ask: What does it mean? How strong is it? Will it spread? They are looking on it as a kind of epidemic or plague which is both infectious and contagious, and may have an "explosive" outbreak in any community.' The epidemic analogy would have evoked strong emotional response, for since January Australia had been in the grip of a most virulent infection from abroad – a pandemic strain of pneumonic influenza which was thought to have arisen in either the United States or Asia, to have been introduced to Europe in 1918 by either American troops or Chinese labourers, and to Australia by homecoming soldiers. During 1919 it caused the death of almost 12,000 Australians, mostly young adults and the middle-aged. While this poisonous wind was at its height between February and July many hotels, schools, churches, theatres and race courses were obliged to close. Quarantine camps were established at State borders, and people wore face masks in public.

Bolshevism was not as infectious as influenza; but its symptoms were widely diagnosed, and sometimes other manifestations – industrial militancy, the discontent of returned soldiers, and mere larrikin behaviour – were mistaken for those symptoms. Red flags and street mobs did not in fact portend the establishment of an Australian dictatorship by Soviets; but sometimes, particularly in Queensland, they looked rather as if they might. The illusion was strengthened in Brisbane by the presence in that city of a number of pro-Bolshevik Russians who had emigrated to Australia after the revolution of 1905.[1] On Sunday 23 March 1919 the Brisbane Industrial Council staged a demonstration against the continued operation of the War Precautions Act. One regulation under this Act, proclaimed in September 1918, prohibited the public exhibition of red flags. The police had given permission for a protest march, but only on condition that red flags were not displayed. The 400 marchers came mainly from the Australian Socialist League, the Industrial Union Propaganda and Education League (consisting mainly of former IWW members) and the Russian Workers' Association. They had no intention of abiding by the police stipulation, and after a quiet start many of them unfurled red flags. They were stopped by mounted police, and after some scuffling several men were arrested. At 7.30 pm an impromptu meeting attended by a large number of returned soldiers, both in and out of uniform, decided to march on the Russian Workers' Association. There were cries of 'Come on, Diggers!' and 'Down with the Bolsheviks!', and three shots were fired from the Russian building as the crowd approached it. The police arrived, and the Diggers dispersed.

On Monday night a crowd of returned soldiers and others, estimated at 8000 by the *Brisbane Courier*, marched on the Russian building again with an Australian flag at their head. 'Let's dig them out!' they shouted. 'The whole crowd will have to be wiped out!' This time they were stopped by a line of police with fixed bayonets. Revolvers were fired by both sides, a mounted trooper was shot twice in the back, and the Police Commissioner was wounded in the shoulder when forced back on to the bayonet of one of his own men. Altogether nineteen men were injured. Next evening a 'loyalist demonstration' passed a resolution urging Queensland's Labor Government to intern or deport all Bolshevik Russians and their sympathisers. As the crowd sang the national anthem one of the soldiers on the platform pointed angrily at a man who had not removed his hat. 'Scarcely had the last word of the hymn been finished,' reported the *Courier* next morning, 'before half a dozen soldiers had grabbed the offender, and his hat was torn off his head. They intended to

[1] The number of Russian-born persons in Australia rose from 2881 in 1901 to 4456 at the 1911 census. The 1921 census showed a figure of 4138.

LION AND KANGAROO

The Bulletin

Registered at the General Post Office, Sydney, N.S.W., Australia, for Transmission by Post as a Newspaper.

THURSDAY, MARCH 27, 1919.

Price 6d.

THE KING IS DEAD—LONG LIVE THE KING!

make him sing the anthem all by himself, but in a moment there was a wild rush, and an angry crowd of probably 2000 persons surged in upon the scene. A dozen police constables or more crushed to the centre of the disturbance, and the packed mass of humanity swayed backwards and forwards across the street. The man who had refused to raise his hat was forced against the wall of the Albert Hotel, and a hundred voices roared: "Make him sing it." "Sing it, man, sing it," roared a police inspector, who hoped by that means to pacify the crowd, and he followed this up by shouting, "Give him a chance and let him sing." The man steadied himself for a moment, and ducked his head as if to break through, but a fist planked fairly in the face, with an uppercut, brought him back to the wall. Then he sang, or tried to sing. A thousand voices took up the cry, 'It's all right, boys, he sang it.' The crowd then besieged the office of the Labor *Daily Standard*, broke all its windows and fired a few revolver shots.

A second loyalist demonstration on 28 March was addressed by the president of the Queensland branch of the Returned Soldiers' and Sailors' Imperial League, a Gallipoli veteran named Pearce Douglas. Ex-Private Douglas repudiated a suggestion that the meeting had any political overtones, saying that returned men were concerned only with rooting out anarchy, Bolshevism and IWWism which, unless stopped forthwith, would lead to bloody revolution. The soldiers had fought for Australia on the battlefields, he said, and they were ready now to fight the scum, the sore on society, that dared to preach disloyalty in Brisbane; such disloyalty was a microbe that would have to be cut out before it grew into a dangerous cancer. Two days later a body of 1750 returned soldiers assembled outside Parliament House to demonstrate, so it was said, that they were a disciplined body of men and not the kind of rabble which had threatened Brisbane's Russians and the *Daily Standard*. They were led by Major A. G. Bolingbroke, DSO, a light horseman from the Middle East campaign who was described by the *Courier* as 'young, tall and stalwart, and bearing the indelible scar of battle.'[2] Addressing these expectant ranks, Pearce Douglas hinted at the prospect of eventual action. 'He knew that some of them expected direct action [reported the *Courier*], but if they waited – and there was always a lull before a storm – unless steps were taken by the Federal and State Governments to root out and deport, shoot or do something with the anarchists – Voices: Yes, shoot them [Laughter and cheers].' Major Bolingbroke read out a telegram which he had received from Western Australia. 'Well done,' it said. 'Clean out the

---

[2] During the Bolshevik scare the *Courier* excelled even its own reputation for bias. Most of its extensive reports of the red flag Court proceedings were published under the headline: 'Uprooting Bolshevism.'

stables, and then come west and clean up here.'

Although Douglas and Bolingbroke undoubtedly spoke for a large number of returned soldiers, they did not speak for them all. One of the arrested red flag carriers, George Taylor, was a returned man too. 'I am a Socialist,' he told the Court which sentenced him and his co-defendants to six months in prison, 'and I believe in the Socialist state. I carried the red flag because I believe it is the flag of the working class, and symbolic of the ideals which I hold. I entered into that demonstration because I considered the War Precautions Act to be a violation of the British Constitution and the rights of free citizenship, granted by the Magna Carta, and accepted by the peoples of the British Empire. I would further like to ask why the red flag is banned in Australia and allowed to fly in Great Britain.' In another statement to the Court, 19-year-old Gus Orance said: 'I carried the red flag in the procession because I believe the red flag is the flag of the working class, to which I belong. . . First of all I want to say that this unlawful Act was brought to bear upon the workers of Australia by that terrifying and horrifying insect known as Billy Hughes for the specific purpose of squashing the working class movement. But alas! Like all other terrifying insects, or parasites, he failed miserably. I feel sure that the psychological moment for the overthrow of this rotten system of capitalism is about at hand.'

On any objective reading, it would seem that most of the violence in Brisbane had come from anti-Bolshevik demonstrators. The situation was rather different in Fremantle during early May and in Townsville during late June. In Fremantle returned soldiers who had formerly worked on the waterfront joined forces with striking members of the Lumpers' Union to confront the strike-breaking National Workers' Union. Barricades were erected in the streets, the Riot Act was read, and police used bayonets and revolvers. In one waterfront battle twenty-six police and six lumpers were injured, one lumper receiving a bayonet wound which eventually proved fatal. On another occasion a launch carrying the Premier of Western Australia, Hal Colebatch, was bombarded with blue metal and scrap iron as it passed under Fremantle's two bridges. After five days of rioting, the Western Australian Government withdrew non-union labour.

The trouble at Townsville occurred during an eleven-week strike at the Ross River and Alligator Creek meat works, the second strike of its kind within the year. Townsville, an isolated tropical community of 25,000, was as militant a union town as any in Australia. Many of the meatworkers were active members of the IWW. Their union, the Australasian Meat Industry Employees' Union, had campaigned fiercely against conscription, leaving a residue of more than usual communal rancour; and its long struggle against the meat companies for union preference had been hard fought on both sides. At public meetings under Townsville's Tree of Knowledge, the air was heavy with talk of class warfare and the Bolshevik example. One address was entitled 'The Foundation Of The Soviet Republic Of Australia.'

The second strike at the meat works was over the continued employment of 'loyalists', including a number of returned soldiers who had 'scabbed' during the union's earlier unsuccessful strike. On the afternoon of Sunday 29 June police arrested two men who, according to information received, were the ringleaders of a conspiracy to attack the Ross River works. The men were Mick Kelly, president of the Townsville Industrial Council, and Pierce Carney, a spokesman for the shop committees at Ross River and Alligator Creek. After a noisy meeting that night under the Tree of Knowledge (a great Indian almond outside the post office), a crowd of about 1000 advanced on the police lock-up singing 'The Red Flag' and chanting 'We want Kelly and Carney!' The effective police strength in Townsville had been reduced by the influenza epidemic, and only thirteen police were on duty at the lock-up when the mob arrived. The police fired one rifle shot and five revolver shots, and at least twenty shots were fired from the crowd. Nine people were wounded, but none fatally. Gradually the crowd dispersed, and Kelly and Carney stayed in gaol.

Next day a crowd of men and youths invaded two stores which stocked firearms. They looted ninety-one rifles, then walked up the main street taking occasional pot shots at pigeons. 'Stand aside Missus,' said one of them to a woman. 'We are going to shoot the police.' But no one was shot. Frightening though the Townsville trouble must have seemed, it was mostly talk and posturing. Eighty more police arrived in the town, and during the next few weeks the tension gradually subsided. The ringleader of the rifle-looting – John Chapman, a 60-year-old fitter at the Townsville railway works, and one-time editor of the Charters Towers *Eagle* – was sentenced to three years' hard labour, but was released after four months.

Strikes and civil disorder flared, subsided and flared again throughout the period of Australia's adjustment to peace. Rising prices and relatively stable employment were an open invitation to direct action for higher wages and better conditions, and so widely was this invitation accepted that more working time was lost in 1919 than in 1917, the year of the general strike. The metal miners at Broken Hill, who had won a 44-hour working week during the war, went on strike in May for a 30-hour week and a minimum wage of £1 a day. The strike lasted eighteen months, and was concluded on terms that fell far short of the men's original demands. The seamen had more success with a four-month-long strike which Mr Justice Higgins attributed to 'the teachings of overseas theorists.'

Civil disorder could not be explained as facilely as that. Among its causes were the restlessness of returned soldiers; the larrikin element which had long existed in Australia's larger cities (in 1919 rival 'pushes' were still fighting pitched battles in Melbourne's inner suburbs); and, as we have seen, the echoes of reflected troubles from abroad. Even some of the Peace Day processions held throughout Australia on Saturday 19 July were affected by such disturbing influences. At Queenstown in Tasmania a group of returned soldiers exchanged blows with some 'Bolsheviks', wrestled a red flag from them and set fire to it. Bendigo's procession was about to set off behind the Mayor and his fellow councillors when some returned men claimed the right to lead. The civic party withdrew, and the soldiers took their place. In Townsville the trade unions sullenly refused to have anything to do with Peace Day.

Melbourne's procession went off without incident, but there was trouble in the offing. The procession consisted principally of 7000 soldiers, sailors and returned men, and ninety motor cars carrying sick and wounded. Five Avro and Sopwith fighters performed spiral nose dives over the city. At 11 am the procession halted: flags dipped in salute to the dead, and at the saluting base outside Parliament House a bugler sounded the Last Post. After the procession came a certain amount of unruliness. Theatres were invaded, trams were captured and derailed, and there was an attempt to rush the Town Hall, where police were holding disturbers of the peace. More disturbances were to come.

On Sunday night, at about 8 pm, a crowd of fifty or sixty uniformed soldiers and sailors, carrying a naval ensign, tried unsuccessfully to force the gates of Victoria Barracks. They brawled with the sentries, and one of their number, Private James O'Connor, was fatally wounded by a revolver bullet fired by one of his companions in the crowd. When mounted police arrived, the insurgents fled into the nearby domain, where they were pursued and in some cases bloodily subdued by police armed with batons. The *Age* reported next morning that the ringleaders had been heard saying their objective was to force the armoury in the barracks, but it was later stated officially that the crowd had been trying to reach the quarters of the civil police, which were also inside Victoria Barracks.

Relations between returned soldiers and the police were severely strained. Soldiers complained that they were harassed without provocation, and the police maintained that they were provoked more than enough. 'I have been to the front fighting German mongrels like you,' said one Digger to Senior Constable John Scanlon during the disturbances of Saturday night. 'You are worse than —— Germans.' Scanlon, who became a focal point for soldier-police antipathies, was alleged to have said for his part: 'You are one of those khaki ——s who have been looking for trouble all day', and 'Knock those khaki lot down first!' On Monday afternoon a crowd estimated variously at between 2000 and 10,000 – mainly uniformed and discharged soldiers, but others as well – marched to Treasury Gardens, where the Victorian Cabinet was meeting. Their leaders rode in a buggy behind four soldiers and sailors with a large Union Jack. As rain was falling when they reached the Government Offices, many of the marchers took shelter boisterously inside the building.

About 200 of them burst into the office of the National Party Premier, H. S. W. Lawson, and heard their spokesman, Captain G. A. Burkett, read the Premier a list of demands: police not to use batons on soldiers, Constable Scanlon to be dismissed (far from being dismissed, he ended his career as a Superintendent), soldiers arrested at the weekend to be released from custody, and all fines imposed in connection with those disturbances to be remitted. The Premier then addressed the main body of the crowd from the roof of a portico in front of the building. When he mentioned arrangements for bail, the crowd roared with anger. One of the soldiers on the portico roof approached the Premier with a large stone and yelled to the crowd: 'Shall I down him?' As the Chief Secretary – Major Matthew Baird, a returned man himself – began to speak, the Premier stepped hastily inside. Seeing him disappear, some of the crowd ran into the building, raced up the stairs and cornered him in the board room of the Lands Department. They broke the legs off chairs, and scattered papers and books. Someone threw a wooden ink-stand at the Premier, opening a five-centimetre gash in the side of his head and soaking his collar with blood. The whole extraordinary incident lasted about an hour. Three hundred foot police and twenty mounted troopers eventually cleared the building and restored order outside, but not before some of them had been pelted with stones taken from the rockeries of Treasury Gardens. That night 6000 people surrounded Russell Street police station, where the prisoners of the weekend were still being held, and bombarded it with road metal. The police responded with a baton charge, and fourteen people were injured.

How could the heroes of yesterday be involved in such disgraceful behaviour? 'There is no gap wider than that between the gallant charges of Gallipoli, Villers-Bretonneux or Pozières and the surging of a howling, stone-throwing mob through the public offices of Melbourne,' declared the *Age.* 'The one represents the sublimity of public service and manly courage; the other is worthy only of the "red-raggers" or those who seek their country's downfall rather than its safety.' The *Argus* exonerated the returned men, and placed the blame squarely on non-military shoulders. 'There can be no doubt,' it said, 'that the excesses in which the affair ended were largely due to the action of hoodlums and revolutionists who inflamed the minds of the soldiers, and urged them on to violence and destruction.'

The world was closing in upon Australia, 'smothering its gleaming spaces', as Frank Wilmot put it, 'with a thin-drawn filament of echoed impulses.' As 1919 drew to an end, Wilmot's imagery was matched perfectly by two Rolls-Royce Eagle VIII aeroplane engines which droned their way across the world from London to Darwin, and then from Darwin to Melbourne, covering the Australian continent with a symbolic veil of echoed and re-echoed sound waves. The first echoed impulses from Britain, received in Sydney on 22 September 1918, had formed a morse code message from the absent Prime Minister, Billy Hughes: 'I have just returned from a visit to the battlefields – where the glorious valour and dash of the Australian troops saved Amiens and forced back the legions of the enemy – filled with greater admiration than ever for these glorious men . . .' While in Paris for the peace conference Hughes announced that the Australian Government would offer a prize of £10,000 for the forging of another imperial link, the first flight by an Australian-manned aeroplane or seaplane from Great Britain to Australia in 720 consecutive hours, or 30 days.

Not only had the competitors to be of Australian nationality, but the aircraft had to be entirely constructed within the British Empire. Although ineligible on both these counts, Etienne Poulet and Jean Benoist took off from an airfield near Paris on 12 October 1919 in an attempt to steal Australia's thunder. Their Caudron G4 had reached Albania when, on 21 October, the first Australian crew (Captain G. C. Matthews and Sergeant-Mechanic T. D. Kay) left Hounslow aerodrome, London, in a two-seater, single-engined Sopwith Wallaby. This plane was somewhere in Germany, and the French Caudron somewhere over India, when on 12 November another competitor left Hounslow, a two-engined Vickers Vimy with a crew of four: Captain Ross Smith (pilot), a 26-year-old South Australian who had served both as an unmounted light horseman at Gallipoli and a highly decorated pilot with the Australian Flying Corps in the Middle East; his 28-year-old brother, Lt Keith Smith (navigator), who had been a Royal Air Force instructor; and two Australian Flying Corps mechanics, Sergeant James Bennett, 25, from Melbourne, and

Sergeant Walter Shiers, 28, from Sydney. Ross Smith was superbly qualified for the task he was undertaking. He was a most resourceful pilot, fair-haired, sharp-featured, equable in temperament and heroic by impulse. 'I'll be all right,' he wrote to his mother on the eve of going to Gallipoli four years before. 'An Australian with my blood is good enough for any six Turks. Patriotism is a wonderful thing, isn't it? Here are hundreds of men as happy as kings because they are going to face bullets, and I bet that half of them couldn't tell you what started this war. But it's that wonderful fighting spirit in them that is crying out for adventure and danger more than anything else.'

As an observer and pilot with No 1 Squadron of the Australian Flying Corps, he was awarded the Military Cross and bar, and the Distinguished Flying Cross with two bars. The last of these bars he won in Palestine by grounding a German two-seater, apparently intact, then landing beside it and forcing the occupants to stand aside while he set alight to it with a Very pistol. His ability to land on rough ground served Smith well on the way from England to Australia. He also had the advantage of having surveyed most of the route – from Cairo to Calcutta by air (he had flown Major-General Sir W. G. Salmond, commanding officer of the Royal Air Force in the Middle East, to Calcutta on a tour of inspection late in 1918), and from Calcutta to Burma, the Federated Malay States and the Dutch East Indies by sea (he accompanied an AFC expedition surveying possible air routes to Australia).

For his own homecoming flight, Smith chose a Vickers Vimy long-range bomber similar to the one which had been used by Sir John Alcock for his trans-Atlantic flight five months previously, but supplemented with an additional petrol tank. Its two wings had a span of twenty-two metres, and its total weight when loaded was six and a half tonnes. The fabric-covered Vimy had two open cabins – open, that is, to wind and rain – and the two Rolls-Royce engines between its strutted, taut-wired wings were on a level with the crew. It carried enough petrol for thirteen hours' cruising at 130 kilometres per hour, emergency rations of tinned meat and biscuits, 400 air mail letters, and a copy of the London *Times* for the Governor-General of Australia; but no wireless. Its distinctive lettering, G-EAOU, was interpreted by the crew to mean 'God 'elp all of us!'

From the snow-covered aerodrome at Hounslow the Vimy headed south over what Smith later, in his book *14,000 Miles Through The Air*, referred to as 'old England, the land of our fathers.' He could see waves lashing white against the cliffs at Folkestone and breaking all the way across the channel, but once the Vimy reached France a snowstorm forced it to climb above cloud into the Arctic cold of 2700 metres. Even at this altitude the Vimy still encountered towering barriers of snow cloud. The three and a half hour flight from Hounslow to Lyons was one of the worst laps of the journey: the fliers lost almost all feeling in their hands and legs, and because their goggles iced over they sometimes had to look ahead with unprotected eyes through a 150-kilometre per hour blast of snow. 'This sort of flying is a rotten game,' noted Ross Smith in his cockpit diary. 'The cold is hell, and I am a silly ass for having ever embarked on the flight.' On each side of him a 360 horse-power Rolls-Royce engine roared away with unfaltering precision. 'I regarded those engines with envy,' he said in his book. 'They had nice hot water circulating around them, and well, indeed, they might be happy. It seemed anomalous, too, that those engines needed water flowing around their cylinders to keep them cool, while we were sitting just a few feet away semi-frozen.'

For most of its flight to Australia the Vimy flew at a comfortable altitude of between 1200 and 1500 metres. It landed successfully at each port of call, but sometimes took off again with only the barest margin of safety. At Calcutta, when the plane was only a few metres off the ground and heading straight for a line of trees, one of its propeller blades struck a hawk. No damage seemed to have been done, the trees were safely cleared, and the Vimy soared out across the Bay of Bengal to Akyab, Burma. Smith and his companions were greeted at Akyab by Poulet and Benoist, but they quickly left the Frenchmen behind on the next leg of the journey, to Rangoon. (Poulet reached Burma, but had to withdraw from the race there because of engine trouble. The only other plane then in transit, the Sopwith Wallaby, had still progressed no further than Austria.) Taking off from Rangoon racecourse, the Vimy cleared a fence with no more than thirty centimetres to spare. Its next hazard was at Sourabaya, Java, where – with only five days left in which to reach Darwin in time for the prize – it sank up to the axles in mud. After much digging, and the laying of a bamboo pathway, the Vimy was hauled back to firm ground by 200 coolies. On the morning of 10 December it took off from Atamboea, Timor, on the last seven-hour lap across the Arafura Sea to Australia. 'I opened up the engines,' wrote Smith, 'and just managed to scrape out of [Atamboea]. Scrape is exactly the word, for the branch tops of a gum-tree rasped along the bottom of the machine as we rose. It was indeed one of the closest shaves of the trip.' At 11.48 am Keith Smith pointed ahead to the distant smoke-plume of HMAS *Sydney*, which the Australian Government had sent to patrol the flight path. At 2.06 pm the fliers sighted the Australian coast, and at 3.40 pm they touched down safely before a cheering crowd at Darwin's Fanny Bay aerodrome. They had travelled 11,060 miles from England in 135 hours' flying time, and had won the prize with 52 hours to spare.[3]

Smith and his companions were formally welcomed to Darwin by the Mayor, a hairdresser named Robert Toupien. Darwin had been one of Australia's most turbulent communities during this year of turbulence, and Mr Toupien had been right in the thick of it. As Ross Smith remarked jokingly in his reply to the Mayor, one of the last sounds he heard in London had been newsboys crying: 'Revolution In Australia!' Under the headline 'An Australian Soviet; Government Officials Expelled', the *Times* had reported that a deputation of trade unionists led by the Mayor had insisted, under threats of riot and rebellion, that the Northern Territory's three most senior Government officials leave Darwin on the first available steamer, which happened to be leaving the next morning. This expulsion of the Director of the Territory, H. E. Carey, the Government Secretary, R. J. Evans, and the chief judicial officer, Judge D. J. D. Bevan, had followed a similar departure by the Administrator of the Northern Territory, Dr J. A. Gilruth. On the earlier occasion the *Northern Territory Times and Gazette* had remarked: 'It behoves us to say unto (Dr Gilruth) as one man, "Get thee hence, thou Scottish bawbee-chaser, and darken this land no more!"'

'Why did you leave Darwin?' asked a Royal Commissioner who was inquiring into the Darwin disturbances while the Vickers Vimy was there. Dr Gilruth replied: 'I was obliged to. I was told that if I did not there would be a revolution.'

'Did you think there would have been one?'

'I did.'

'Do you think there is any real element of Bolshevism other than is found in other Australian ports?'

'I certainly think there is a very strong element.'

'It is a question of nationality?'

'I think the foreigners, especially the Greeks and Russians, are more inclined that way.'

'What about the British population?'

'A member of the Advisory Council ended a speech with "Long live the revolution", and used to say that the only solution was a Soviet Government.'

---

[3] The only other competitor to reach Darwin was a De Havilland 9 flown by Lieutenants R. J. Parer and J. C. McIntosh. Its journey took 207 consecutive days, compared with the Vimy's 28 days. The Sopwith Wallaby, which was in Yugoslavia when the Vimy landed at Darwin, crashed on Bali in April 1920. Its crew survived, and so did the crew of a Blackburn Kangaroo which crashed while landing in Crete. Only two other crews started in the race, and they were killed when their planes crashed in England and in the Mediterranean.

The main grievances felt by the Northern Territory's 4657 white citizens, and particularly by members of the Australian Workers' Union, were the imposition of income tax without parliamentary representation; the high cost of food and drink, especially beer; and certain allegations of improper collaboration between Government officials and the British meat firm, Vestey Brothers. The Royal Commissioner eventually reported that Dr Gilruth, Judge Bevan and other officials had failed to exercise their powers with firmness, common sense and justice; and criticized the Commonwealth Parliament for not having granted full citizens' rights to the people of the Northern Territory. Darwin's citizens had no vote at the Federal election on 13 December, and there is no record that the crew of the Vimy voted either.[4]

The Vimy took off early that morning on its way south to the Federal capital, Melbourne. Ross Smith intended to follow the Overland Telegraph as far as Newcastle Waters, then turn southeast towards the west Queensland town of Cloncurry. After four hours of very turbulent flying over a shimmering mid-summer landscape of scrub and termite mounds, he detected valve trouble in the starboard engine. He landed on a dry swamp called Warlock Ponds, where Shiers was able to repair the engine, but before the plane could take off again the crew had to pass a night of torment by mosquitoes.

Next morning the Vimy's engines went echoing over the land of the Warramunga, one of the northern tribes visited by Spencer and Gillen in 1901. Somewhere on that speckled yellow landscape was a human skull which the Warramunga, in a burial ceremony observed by Spencer, had secreted in a hole scooped out of a termite mound, soon to be cemented over by the ants. Further to the south on this summer's day in 1919 were the Aranda, whose initiation ceremonies Spencer had recorded so faithfully. The last nineteen years had not been as kind to the Aranda as to the Commonwealth from which they and other Aboriginal groups were in so many ways excluded. The Lutheran mission at Hermannsburg had done its best for them, effecting about 150 baptisms and 15 confirmations since 1901; but these well-meaning Germans could hardly be said to have fulfilled the ambition of their motto from Isaiah 35: 'The desert shall rejoice and blossom as the rose.' For every one of the Aranda who may

---

[4] Hughes's Nationalist Government was returned to office at this election, but with a reduced majority – 21–15 in the Senate, compared with 25–11 previously, and in the House of Representatives 37 seats compared with 49 in the previous parliament. In the House of Representatives the Nationalists now had to contend with 26 Labor members and 11 members representing rural electorates. In January 1920 these rural members formed the Australian Country Party which, although it had little in common with the ALP, was not as well-disposed to Hughes as it would be later to other non-Labor leaders.

have seen the glory of the Lord and the excellency of our God, there were perhaps ten who saw nothing but their own world being emptied of totems and *quabaras*. Nineteen hundred and five was a good year for Christianity at Hermannsburg, with fourteen baptisms, but 1907 saw the expulsion of some Aranda Christians for 'participation in heathen enjoyments.' In 1919 the Aranda were smitten by the influenza epidemic. There were fifty-three deaths at Hermannsburg in six weeks, and an unknown number among those of the Aranda who were still living in the bush.

According to official estimates, the Aboriginal population of the Northern Territory had fallen from 23,363 in 1901 to 17,973 in 1919 (or rather at the 1921 census), and the figures for the Commonwealth as a whole had fallen from 67,000 to 60,000. In 1919 the Commonwealth's mixed-blood Aboriginal population numbered about 11,500. Although public opinion was at last becoming concerned about the Aborigines, there was little ground for satisfaction in the Northern Territory. In 1919 the Protector of Aboriginals reported that he was still having trouble with Europeans regarding the treatment and payment of Aborigines. Half-caste girls made useful domestics, he said, and some had been taken as far as Adelaide under agreement with their employers. The killing of Aborigines by the Northern Territory police, which was to become the subject of public controversy in a few years' time, was still condoned as an unavoidable part of police work. In 1918 a stockman was speared while repairing a stockyard on Auvergne Station. During the investigation of this crime, the police shot seven Aborigines.

On the advice of Professor (by now Sir Baldwin) Spencer, the Northern Territory Administration was preparing to enlarge considerably the areas of land gazetted as Aboriginal reserves. There were, said Spencer, only two alternatives: 'either to allow the Aborigines to wander about as outcasts, some of them doubtless working for the settlers but all of them practically dependent for their existence on promiscuous charity, or to establish a reserve for them under proper control.' In 1920 – 'to provide a sanctuary for the native population, or, in other words, mitigate the apparent harshness of the decision that all native lands shall become Crown lands' – the extent of Aboriginal reserves in the Northern Territory was increased from 6032 square kilometres to 85,200 square kilometres, including 5180 square kilometres in Arnhem Land and 56,656 square kilometres in the southwest corner of the Territory. The latter was combined with reserves in South Australia and Western Australia to form the Central Australian Reserve. These were well-intended, inexpensive gestures. They might have had more beneficial effect if sufficient Government funds had permitted the following of rational policies in the use of reserves. In 1920 the Northern Territory and Western Australia each spent less than £10,000 on Aboriginal affairs.

After turning away from the Overland Telegraph at Newcastle Waters, the crew of the Vimy had to look out for two patches of scrub meeting in the form of a V. They had been told by stockmen in Darwin that a few kilometres beyond this landmark they would see a rough bush road leading towards Cloncurry. They found the road without difficulty, but about an hour later were alarmed by a loud crack from the port propeller. One of the propeller's four wooden blades, no doubt weakened by the collision with a hawk at Calcutta, had cracked from tip to boss. Ross Smith shut off both engines and glided to a landing about thirty kilometres from Anthony's Lagoon homestead. Soon afterwards the fliers were joined by two motor cars containing a party of men who were sinking a sub-artesian bore. From this unexpected quarter they obtained food and a sheet of galvanised iron with which Sergeant Bennett performed a miracle of workmanship on the split propeller. With a penknife he carved bits of wood from a piece of packing case to replace splinters lost from the damaged propeller blade. He then glued the split portion together, bound it with narrow strips of galvanised iron, fastened the strips to the blade with screws from the Vimy's floorboards, covered the whole blade with fabric, and painted it. Finally he treated the opposite blade in the same way to prevent vibration. All this was done in a shade temperature of 50 degrees Celsius.

On went the Vimy with its mended propeller – over Camooweal, just across the Queensland border; down at Cloncurry, where the fliers were entertained at a smoke concert; down at Longreach, there the Smith brothers heard that the King had made them Knights Commanders of the Most Excellent Order of the British Empire;[5] over Barcaldine, where people were waiting in the streets to see them pass; and on 23 December down at Charleville, where the Vimy was to remain for seven weeks. The fliers took off again briefly on Christmas morning, but while still climbing to cruising altitude they heard a loud explosion from the port engine and saw a flash of fire. Sir Ross Smith switched off the engine and made a forced landing near Charleville. Not only had the engine been damaged when its propellor split, but it was showing signs of metal fatigue. The engine was sent by rail to the railway workshops at Ipswich, and came back weeks later with several new parts and a new propellor made of Queensland maple.

[5] Sergeants Bennett and Shiers had to be satisfied with equal quarter shares of the £10,000 prize, bars to their Air Force Medals, and eventual promotion to Lieutenant in the AIF Reserve of Officers.

When the Vimy left Charleville on 12 February 1920 it carried as a passenger the former official photographer to the AIF, Captain Frank Hurley. During its triumphal progress to Sydney and Melbourne, Hurley took aerial photographs of Bourke, a poignantly small patchwork of urban streets in the gleaming spaces of western New South Wales; Lithgow, with its smoking ironworks; and Katoomba, a bush-encircled town beside the railway line running across the Blue Mountains and down to Sydney. As the Vimy passed over Katoomba on the morning of 14 February a telephone call was made to Sydney, where an Australian flag was promptly broken out from the GPO tower. This was a signal for people to begin mounting rooftops all over the city which had staged the Commonwealth's biggest inaugural procession on the first day of federation nineteen years before. Flying over the escarpment of the Blue Mountains, the Vimy crossed the Nepean River, named after an 18th century English civil servant, and passed south of Windsor and Richmond. Over Penrith, named after a town in the English county of Cumberland, the Vimy was met by three smaller aeroplanes. Looking, as one journalist wrote, 'like gnats around a hawk', all four machines then flew low over the city of Sydney before landing.

Hurley's photographs of the inner city showed crowds of people gazing up from the rooftops and the Botanic Gardens, and dozens of motor cars in the streets. A ferry was crossing from North Sydney to the southern shore, where the Harbour Bridge was to be opened twelve years later, and two British passenger steamers were tied up at Circular Quay; but in contrast to that first day of Federation, nowhere was the mast of a sailing ship to be seen. A Manly ferry was leaving Sydney Cove, and at Manly and Bondi beaches the figures of a few late summer bathers could be seen in the surf. On 23 February the Vimy and its crew took off from Richmond aerodrome with two passengers – Captain Hurley again, and the begoggled Premier of New South Wales, W. A. Holman, who was travelling to an election meeting at Cootamundra. They flew over the inner city once more, down the harbour, and past South Head to the sea. As the Vimy turned south its crew would have been able to see South Head Cemetery where Sir Edmund Barton, the principal Australian actor in the British-Australian ritual of New Year's Day 1901, had been laid to rest under a grey granite cross only six weeks before.

After following the coastline south for an hour, and passing over Wollongong, the Vimy turned inland as far as Goulburn and then south again to the Federal Capital Territory. At Canberra the fliers saw only a few workmen's tents. Sir Ross and Sir Keith Smith did not realize that they had reached the Capital Territory until, over Duntroon, they saw

Australia's white-uniformed military cadets standing in the shape of the letters 'R' and 'K'. There was not much else to see at Canberra, even on the ground. So far the Commonwealth had spent only £989,600 on its new capital, and this amount included £254,869 on water supply, £75,550 on electric light mains and plant, £82,000 on bridges and roads, £124,000 on buildings and repairs – and £20,000 on the destruction of rabbits.

After delivering the Premier to Cootamundra, and staying there overnight, the crew of the Vimy took off for Albury, expecting to reach Melbourne later the same day; but they were lucky ever to have reached Melbourne at all. A defect in the oil feed of the port engine obliged Sir Ross to make no fewer than three forced landings in less than fifty kilometres: one in a field of wheat stubble near Cootamundra, another on a racecourse at The Rock, and a third for the night near Henty. When taking off from the wheat field, one of the plane's wings brushed the branches of a gum tree, but was not damaged. As the mechanics were unable to repair the engine at Henty, the Vimy flew the remaining 300 kilometres to Melbourne on its starboard engine alone. On the morning of 25 February, it reached the capital; flew over Exhibition Building, where the Duke of Cornwall and York had opened the first Federal Parliament in May 1901, and over Parliament House, down the steps of which Alfred Deakin's coffin had been carried only four months ago; and finally, 175 flying hours out from London, landed at Point Cook flying school. At a reception in Parliament House later that day the fliers were accorded a British-Australian welcome of the kind which had changed little during the last nineteen years. It was noticeable, in this 20th year of Federation, that paeans for young Australian heroes included just as many imperial allusions as did elegies for dead Australian statesmen.

Deakin had been eulogized as 'a true Britisher of the finest type, proud of his race and proud of his line', and on Barton's death it was said that 'the Empire in general, and the High Court in particular, [had] sustained a great loss in the death of a noted Imperialist, statesman and judge.' Australia still took second place to the Empire at times of triumph as well as bereavement. The Governor-General, Sir Ronald Munro-Ferguson, rejoiced at 'the skill, endurance, courage and capacity of four men of the British race', and the Prime Minister described the two new knights and their non-commissioned equerries as 'Empire builders'. 'They have bridged the last distance that separates us from England,' said Hughes. 'They have added fresh laurels to the name of Australia. They have shown us a way to bring the further outposts of Empire in touch with one another.'

For the Vimy's small consignment of aerial mail, the Postmaster-General's Department issued a commemorative stamp showing maps of the British Isles and Australia side by side and roughly equal in scale. Was this how the Commonwealth thought of itself in relation to its distant progenitor – no longer second best, but demonstrably equal? 'Daughter no more but Sister,' Kipling had said at the start of the century. In terms of quality if not quantity, Australia could now accept that compliment without blushing; the transplanted Britons of the southern hemisphere could remind themselves that they had sent a greater army to France than those of either Napoleon or the Duke of Wellington, and that their scars of battle were at least as honourable as anyone else's. Australia's combined casualties in the Great War had been 65 per cent of its total embarcations; New Zealand's were 59 per cent, Canada's 50 per cent, and Britain's 51 per cent.

The war had tempered the loyalty of Australians to Britain in two senses of that word: in some cases it had hardened the imperial consciousness; in others it had moderated that consciousness, even replaced it, with a new awareness of nationalism. As the Secretary of State for War had said, Australians had begun to take the analogy of the Portuguese. If Portugal could administer its own armed forces during the war, why not Australia? And if Portugal and Belgium could attend the peace conference as separate entities, why not Australia too? Gradually during its first two decades the Commonwealth had arrived at a new understanding with Britain. The Governor-General's discretionary power to reserve Assent had become virtually a dead letter, and the Colonial Office had become more respectful – though Britain, of course, retained its supremacy in the imperial relationship.

To most Australians in 1919, this seemed a proper relationship, but not one which would continue indefinitely. The last rites of passage had taught the initiate that when his own interests were at stake he could and should go his own way. In the last few years Australia had invited the United States fleet to visit its ports, launched a navy of its own, refused conscription, demanded its own army corps, and insisted upon representing itself at the peace conference. In that international forum, Australia had fended for itself even to the extent of defying world opinion.

Thus the initiate had taken his first occasional steps outside the British Empire into the world at large. He would continue by choice to dwell within that smaller, familiar sphere – obeying its antique rules, and sometimes helping to change them – but would do so only as long as it suited him. As one commentator had observed on the first Anzac Day, Australian history and world history had been fused at white heat, and never again could the two be considered separately. The Commonwealth of Australia was still a dominion of the Empire, but its true fealty was now both narrower and wider than that. Australia's first obligation was to itself, but it knew also that it was part of the world.

POSTSCRIPT

Without attempting to be exhaustive, I would like to tie some loose ends together, and mention a few sequels to my narrative. Although the first two decades of the Commonwealth were nicely self-contained – starting with the turn of the century and the death of an old Queen, and closing with the eruption and subsidence of war – the interplay of British and Australian sentiment has continued *diminuendo* to this day. And although some of the young Commonwealth's most conspicuous public figures had died by the end of its second decade, others lived on for a year or two, a decade or two – and even, in the case of Archbishop Mannix and others, for another three or four decades.

Obsequies

The most heroic and universally admired Australian of 1920, Sir Ross Smith, had only two more years of life left to him. On 13 April 1922 he and his mechanic on the Vimy flight, Lieutenant Bennett, took off from Brooklands, England, to try out a Vickers Viking amphibian in which they intended to fly around the world. Sir Keith Smith was to have joined them on this trial flight, but because his train was delayed by fog he arrived only in time to see the Viking crash, killing both its occupants. Sir Ross Smith was buried in Adelaide, where the Vimy is preserved today as a memorial to the London–Darwin flight. The first airmail service between Australia and Britain began on 10 December 1934, fifteen years to the day after the Vimy had landed at Darwin. The Brisbane–Singapore sector of this route was flown by the newly established Qantas Empire Airways, of which Sir Keith Smith was director until his death in 1955.

The anthropologist who was working among the Aranda in 1901, Sir Baldwin Spencer, reached the end of his life among a people scarcely less primitive than the Aborigines of Central Australia. At the age of 69, far from settling into comfortable retirement, Spencer set off in the steps of Charles Darwin to look for analogies to the Aborigines among the Yaghan Indians of Tierra del Fuego. He left England in February 1929 as a crew member on a frozen mutton steamer bound for Punta Arenas at the tip of Patagonia. From there, accompanied by his secretary, Miss

Jean Hamilton, Spencer crossed the Strait of Magellan to a snow-capped fragment of Tierra del Fuego, Hoste Island, where he hoped to find an old Yaghan woman who was believed to speak some English. On this island, at a place called Yaka-Shaka Cove, he suffered a heart attack and died on 14 July. He was buried at Punta Arenas.

Although King O'Malley retired from politics in 1919, he lived to become, at the age of 99, the last surviving member of the first Federal parliament – having outlived by more than a year his one-time colleague and later antagonist, W. M. Hughes. During his long retirement the King occupied himself with tasks as varied and idiosyncratic as making his own coffin and defending his dubious claim to have founded the Commonwealth Bank. Hughes once likened this claim to Bill Adams's tale, *How I Won The Battle Of Waterloo*. In reply the King said that Hughes knew less about economics and finance than any blackfellow knew about Euclid, and that the only bank he had ever had anything to do with was the Yarra bank.

Hughes remained in Federal parliament until his death, at the age of 88, on 28 October 1952. He had served as Prime Minister for more than seven years, a record broken only by the long reign of Sir Robert Menzies. Hughes resigned as Prime Minister in 1923 after the Country Party refused to continue supporting the National Party under his vestigially socialist leadership, and he was expelled from the National Party after engineering the downfall of the Bruce ministry. As there was no going back to the Labor Party for Hughes, he spent the rest of his parliamentary career in the United Australia Party (a right-wing grouping, but independent of the Country Party) and its successor, the Liberal Party. Obituary writers agreed that Hughes had been a prime example of the British-Australian duality. *The Sydney Morning Herald* called him 'a stalwart champion of Australia and what used to be called the Empire' and *The Times* said 'Australia loses one of the founders of Australian nationalism who was yet an ardent supporter of the Imperial connection.' His coffin was carried on a gun carriage through the streets of Sydney, covered with a union jack.

The longest lived of all the young Commonwealth's public figures was Archibishop Mannix, who died in his 100th year, 1963. In 1920 he set out from Melbourne to visit his aged mother in Ireland and the Pope in Rome. So turbulent were conditions in Ireland at that time, with the Irish Free State still more than a year away, and so uncompromising were the Archbishop's public statements on his way through the United States, that the British Government forbade him to visit the land of his birth. A Royal Navy destroyer took him off the steamer from New York and marooned him, like a pirate, at Penzance.

Even as late as the 1950s, when he was going on for 90, Archbishop Mannix probably played a part in Australian politics. Certainly his protégé, B. A. Santamaria, was largely responsible for the splitting of the Australian Labor Party in 1956, and during this period Santamaria frequently sought the old man's advice. It was said that Daniel Mannix managed to interfere in Australian politics even after death. He died on the day Sir Robert Menzies delivered his policy speech for the 1963 elections, and was buried on the day Arthur Calwell delivered his.

Anzac

No nation's military exploits have ever been recorded more meticulously than were Australia's in *The Official History Of Australia In The War Of 1914–1918*, on which C. E. W. Bean and his colleagues began work in 1919. The twelfth and final volume (Vol VI: *The AIF In France May 18 – The Armistice*) was not published for another twenty-three years, at the height of a second world war. The twelve volumes, bound in cloth of a colour which reminded one reviewer of dried blood, contained 9765 pages and 3,600,000 words. More than any other Australian, Bean was responsible for the apotheosis of Anzac. In the year after his death, 1969, I travelled to Gallipoli, crossing the Dardanelles by car ferry with a former Turkish soldier, Sureyya Dilmen, who had been on the peninsula when the Australians landed. Near Eceabat (formerly Maidos), where the ferry berthed, the huge exultant figure of a Turkish soldier had been exposed in white clay upon the khaki hillside. It was early April, the sun was out, and the sesame fields were in bloom. As we drove from one carefully tended war cemetery to the next, across hillsides strangely reminiscent of the kind of scrub one finds on the windswept headlands of eastern Australia, I surrendered meekly to the overwhelming emotional impact of that place. Here was the high ground reached by Lalor's company on the first day. Here was Lone Pine. Here The Nek. When Bean and Jack Howe visited The Nek in 1919, they found the remains of about 300 Australians in a strip of scrub no larger than three tennis courts.

Mr Dilmen said The Sphinx was now smaller than it had been in 1915, and that one day the wind and rain would fret it away completely. We drove down to Anzac Cove and past that shingly Aegean beach to the Australian cemetery at Ari Burnu, a slope of newly mown grass lined with row upon row of inscribed white plaques. It reminded me of the awful infinity of white crosses which I had seen only recently in the last few seconds of *Oh! What A Lovely War*. 'A clean straight life nobly ended – age 21,' read one plaque. They were all much the same: 'His friends bereft have only left his photo on the wall – Mother', 'Nearer my God to thee, gone but not forgotten', 'Far from home and all that love him, here lies a noble lad' . . .

Six years later, in June 1975, I went to Pozières. Taking a taxi from Albert, we drove past fields of green wheat which was still a few weeks away from the kind of stooks seen elsewhere in Picardy by Sister Alice Kitchen in the summer of 1916. The main road from Albert to Bapaume passes through a miraculously restored Pozières. So faithfully was the village rebuilt that one can recognise it today from a photograph taken before the war, and reproduced in Volume XII of Bean's *Official History*. Citroens and Renaults have replaced horses and carts, but the neatly tuck-pointed brick walls and shingle roofs look exactly the same. Roses bloom behind wrought iron fences, a baker delivers long loaves of bread, and an old man is scything grass outside the Eglise Mairie.

Our taxi drove beyond the village and left us beside a wooden gate carved with the insignia of the AIF. Inside was a grassy mound with an inscription reading: 'The ruin of Pozières windmill which lies here was the centre of the struggle in this part of the Somme battlefield in July and August 1916. It was captured on August 4th by Australian troops who fell more thickly on this ridge than on any other battlefield of the war.' How elusive is a dark past on a fine day! Looking out across the wheatfields, with larks rising and high tension wires disappearing into the morning haze, I could not imagine the summer's day which Jack Tarrant spent here in a crater with shrapnel flying overhead.

Before returning to Albert we called at a café opposite the village church. The old scytheman was there, taking a glass of wine, and a young labourer whom we had seen hoeing weeds in a beetroot field was throwing quoits in the backyard. Against one of the outside walls was a pile of what at first I took to be old agricultural pipes; in fact they were shell cases from the Great War. The farmers around Pozières still unearth these relics from time to time, and sell them as scrap metal. As I felt the weight of one, I remembered how hard Alec Raws had found it to sleep while six shells were bursting over his head every minute.

Back in Sydney I visited Jack Tarrant, who was then in his 82nd year and living at a war veterans' home in Narrabeen. After the war Mr Tarrant was a storeman and packer in a wool store, ending up as its manager. He and his wife lived at Allawah for more than thirty years, and after Mrs Tarrant's death he moved to Narrabeen. From the balcony of his flat Mr Tarrant looks out on primitive bush where flocks of rainbow lorikeets feed on angophora blossom and perch swaying on grass-tree spears. He has won the confidence of these birds to such an extent that they not only come to his balcony by the dozen, but often walk boldly into his lounge room.

The Governor-General

The three most controversial representatives of the British Sovereign in the Commonwealth of Australia have all been Australians: Sir Isaac Isaacs (1931–1936), Sir William McKell (1947–1953) and Sir John Kerr (1974–1991). Isaacs had controversy thrust upon him by the manner of his appointment, but lived it down by his conduct in office. McKell, as a newly resigned Labor Premier of NSW, could hardly avoid initial controversy (Menzies described the appointment as 'political jobbery . . . expressly designed to lower the Governor-Generalship in significance and esteem, and so weaken our vital connection with the Crown'), but he confounded his critics by behaving in office with the utmost decorum. Kerr brought controversy upon himself by the way he used vice-regal power, and, in the eyes of many of his fellow-countrymen, he never lived that down.

In 1930 the very idea of an Australian Governor-General seemed to many Australians a contradiction in terms, like an Australian grenadier guard or a British gum tree. It seemed natural enough, however, to the newly elected Scullin (Labor) government. The Balfour report had made it clear in 1926 that the Governor-General was the personal representative of the Sovereign, and not of the British Government. Nothing was said about the source of advice which might properly be taken by the King in appointing his Governor-General, so why should such advice not be taken from His Majesty's Australian ministers? When the Scullin cabinet in March 1930 came to nominate a replacement for Lord Stonehaven, it chose Isaacs (who was about to be appointed Chief Justice, a post which he held for only nine months) in preference to the only other short-listed candidate, Sir John Monash. The choice was fortunate, for Monash – who had become chairman of the State Electricity Commission of Victoria – had only another year to live.

J. H. Scullin suggested Isaacs to the British Government, and deliberately or otherwise allowed the suggestion to become public knowledge in Australia. The Federal Government did not officially admit that Isaacs's name had been sent forward, but neither did it deny rumours to that effect. Accepting the rumours as true, the Leader of the Opposition, J. G. Latham, condemned the choice of Isaacs as 'strident and narrow jingoism', and the Council of Combined Empire Societies sent a protest petition of 130,000 signatures to the Secretary of State for the Dominions. The principal objection was that an Australian could not help holding Australian political opinions of some kind, whereas a nominee from Britain would be more likely to remain politically impartial.

The King himself held this view. After a rather testy meeting with

Scullin at Buckingham Palace, however, His Majesty acceded to the appointment rather than run the risk of embroiling himself in Australian politics. He did so with 'great reluctance', and wrote of the appointment: 'I should think it would be very unpopular in Australia.' Australian misgivings were dispelled by the new Governor-General, who showed himself to be at least as capable of impartiality as any import. Nor was there yet any basis for the suspicion, which has been advanced as another argument against Isaacs's appointment, that future Australian governments would make the office of Governor-General a close preserve for native-born Australians. Between Isaacs and the next two Australian-born Governors-General – Sir William McKell (1947–1953) and Lord Casey (1965–1969) came a British baron, a Royal duke and two British viscounts. By 1965 – or at the latest by 1969, when an unsuccessful candidate for the parliamentary leadership of the Liberal Party, Sir Paul Hasluck, was appointed Governor-General – the idea of a British governor-general had come to seem as unnatural to most Australians as a local incumbent had seemed to many in 1930. George V and the Empire societies had apparently been mistaken: an Australian, even a newly retired Australian politician, could perform the musty rites of Yarralumla as circumspectly as any British nobleman.

Then came Sir John Kerr, breathing unexpected life into a reserve power which was thought almost to have withered away from lack of exercise. Kerr broke a legislative deadlock by the unprecedented act of dismissing a ministry with a majority in the House of Representatives;[1] yet in breaking the deadlock so abruptly he may well have strained, even broken, something vital in his own office. It is too early yet for any consensus about the wisdom or impropriety of the Governor-General's withdrawal of E. G. Whitlam's commission on 11 November 1975. My own opinion – and in case of bias, I ought to declare it – is that the Governor-General acted unwisely. Although he was within his constitutional rights – and in harmony with prevailing public opinion, as the subsequent election showed – his action was nonetheless a radical departure from accepted standards of vice-regal action. Judged within a context of past assumptions about the office of Governor-General, his sending of the Whitlam Government to an election that it had no hope of winning, although other options were available to him, must be considered improper; it may well, indeed, have changed the very nature of that office. But there is a paradox here. Reprehensible though one may consider the

[1] Unprecedented in federal politics. In 1932 the Governor of New South Wales, Sir Philip Game, dismissed the Lang Labor ministry which held a large majority in the NSW Legislative Assembly.

dismissal to have been, its effect on the governor-generalship may in the long run seem to have been beneficial. I shall return to this later.

Sir John Kerr came to Yarralumla, on the recommendation of the Whitlam Government, as a lawyer and former Chief Justice of New South Wales. He had a reputation for ambition and pragmatism (how else could a one-time republican have climaxed his career by swearing to well and truly serve Her Majesty?), and also for intellect and political insight; yet he was devoid of parliamentary experience, and history had shown that while the better governors-general of Australia had all been politicians in their time, most of the less successful ones had not. Kerr's response to constitutional crisis, when the time came, was open to criticism as being too narrowly legal. Whether he genuinely accepted the dubious proposition that the Constitution left him no other course; whether he regarded a judicial approach, handing down judgment as if from the bench, as the easiest way out of an undeniably difficult situation; whether he acted partly from personal motives (a place in history, etc); or whether he took part in some form of establishment conspiracy – all these are questions which may never be answered satisfactorily. The only question about which there will certainly be some eventual agreement is whether or not he acted in the best interest of his country.

The situation which confronted Kerr was one of considerable but not solely legal complexity. The Liberal and Country Parties rightly believed the political climate to be such that if a general election was held (that is, for both Houses) they would have an excellent chance of being returned to the government benches which they had occupied in coalition for twenty-three of the last twenty-six years. Labor had been in office only since December 1972, and during that short period had already been obliged to defend itself once at a general election brought about by the Opposition's obstruction in the Senate (May 1974). The Whitlam Government was prepared to countenance a normal Senate election (that is, for half the Senate seats) at its own timing, in the hope that it might gain control of that chamber; but it knew only too well how badly handicapped it would be at a general election there and then, for it faced not only unemployment and inflation, just as other western democracies did, but also certain electoral handicaps largely of its own making.

Controlling the Senate as it did, the Opposition decided to try to compel a general election by deferring Supply – that is, by deferring consideration of the annual Appropriation Bills sent to it from the House of Representatives. Although the Senate had never acted in this way before,[2] the Opposition majority argued that it could do so consistently

[2] Under Section 53 of the Constitution the Senate may send money bills back to the House

with the Constitution and with conventions governing relations between the two Houses. It also argued that if the Prime Minister tried to remain in office without the financial means to govern, the Governor-General would have a clear constitutional duty to dismiss him, dissolve both Houses of Parliament, and call another general election.

The situation was not in fact as straightforward as the Opposition asserted. The House of Representatives maintained that the Senate's deferral of supply to force the resignation or dismissal of a ministry violated the lower House's position relative to the Senate under the Constitution, violated its traditional supremacy on money matters, and was therefore a dangerous breach of convention. The Senate based its case upon Section 53 of the Constitution which provided that, although the Senate could neither originate nor amend money bills, it should with these exceptions 'have equal power with the House of Representatives in respect of all proposed laws.' Did this mean that it could defer supply? On 10 November the Chief Justice of Australia – Sir Garfield Barwick, a former Liberal cabinet minister himself – advised the Governor-General (after Sir John Kerr had asked him, alone among the High Court's seven justices, for an opinion) that the Senate was constitutionally able to defer supply. After Kerr's action, however, other opinions were expressed to the contrary – notably by Sir Richard Eggleston, a retired judge who was reportedly one of the candidates considered for the governor-generalship at the same time as Sir John Kerr.

Assuming that the Senate was right about its power to defer, and that the Prime Minister would remain firm in his proclaimed determination not to resign and not to advise a general election, what was the Governor-General to do? Should he, as many constitutional experts had stated in the past, act only on the advice of his ministers? Was it on the contrary his clear duty, as stated by a former Solicitor-General and now spokesman for the Opposition, to withdraw the Prime Minister's commission? Or should he play a less active role, as argued in an opinion given to the Governor-General on 6 November by the two principal law officers of the Crown, the Attorney-General and the Solicitor-General. In his own mind the Governor-General had settled on dismissal, and the Chief Justice's opinion reassured him in this by saying: 'The course upon which Your Excellency has determined is consistent with your constitutional authority and duty.'

No one had denied (or has denied with much conviction since) that

of Representatives with a request for amendment, and has often done so. Although the Senate had never previously deferred or refused Supply, it should be remembered that in 1970 and 1974 Labor leaders in both Houses acted and spoke as if the Senate could legitimately refuse Supply.

the Governor-General holds a reserve power of dismissal, though the law officers' opinion referred to the 'uncertain existence and unknowable constituents' of that power. The law officers' opinion argued strongly for vice-regal restraint, warning that intervention would – in the words of Asquith's memorandum to George V – drag the Crown into the arena of party politics. The law officers expressed 'the gravest doubt that the power to dismiss may properly be exercised solely to procure a forced dissolution', and said that its exercise would deny effect to the one provision of the Constitution (Section 57) expressly directed to the solution of deadlock by a joint sitting of both Houses of Parliament.

The advocates of vice-regal intervention pointed to sections of the Constitution which defined the Governor-General's basic role as maintaining the Constitution and Commonwealth laws on the advice of a ministry *holding office during His Excellency's pleasure.* As the law officers' opinion pointed out, however, these provisions did not, considered alone, 'afford any guide as to the circumstances when the extreme and abnormal reserve powers of dismissal of a ministry and consequent dissolution of the Representatives should or may be exercised or even that they still exist. This is the field of convention and discretion.'

To treat the exercise of these powers as obligatory, wrote the law officers, was to deny a vice-regal authority 'to offer suggestions where the circumstances have reached a stage sufficiently grave to warrant His Excellency's adoption of that course, bearing in mind that the cardinal rule is that the Crown should not *"withdraw these differences from their proper sphere".'* The words which I have italicised belong to a quotation, cited earlier by the law officers, from Alpheus Todd's authoritative *Parliamentary Government In The British Colonies.* Arguing that the real question for the Governor-General was not which of the disputants was correct, but rather that the two Houses were in real dispute about momentous matters, the law officers wrote: '. . . it can hardly be doubted that the Crown will not as a general rule take sides in such disputes for [as Todd states] "while it should be the Governor's earnest desire to contribute, as far as he can properly contribute to the removal of existing differences between the two Houses, it is clearly undesirable that he should intervene in such a manner as would withdraw these differences from their proper sphere, and so give to them a character which does not naturally belong to them, of a conflict between the majority of one or another of the two Houses and the representative of the Crown.'

One can imagine such earlier representatives as Lord Northcote or Sir Ronald Munro-Ferguson bringing their political skills to bear on such a deadlock. Certainly one doubts that they would have acted as arbitrarily as Kerr did, for he had at his disposal three options other than dismissal. Firstly, he could have done nothing, leaving the political contestants to fight it out as far as a joint sitting, or more likely until surrender by one side or the other before that stage was reached. The Whitlam Government was confident of winning such a contest, for public feeling was running against the Senate's deferral, and some Opposition senators were having second thoughts about their breach of convention. Secondly, the Governor-General could have recommended that the Senate take a vote on the Opposition bills. In view of the known reluctance of some Liberal senators to vote against Supply, this recommendation alone could well have broken the deadlock. Thirdly, the Governor-General could have accepted the Prime Minister's advice for a Senate election, which Whitlam had informed Kerr by telephone on the morning of 11 November he would be tendering when he visited Government House later that day. Instead of any of these courses which would have given the government at least a fighting chance of remaining in office, the Governor-General chose the course most likely to result in the government's defeat. When the Prime Minister arrived at Government House the Governor-General, knowing that Whitlam was without supply and was still resolute against a general election, was waiting for him with a letter of dismissal. He then invited the Leader of the Opposition to form a caretaker government on condition that Fraser should recommend a double dissolution. Parliament was dissolved, and at the general election of 13 December the Labor Party suffered catastrophic defeat.

To that extent the Governor-General may seem to have acted correctly, for the Whitlam Government was shown to have lost the confidence of the nation. Yet it is difficult to predict the long-term effect of Sir John Kerr's having appeared to take political sides by sending Labor to its third election in as many years (after twenty-three years in Opposition, be it remembered) with the disadvantage of having been dismissed from office by the Queen's representative. In explanation of his action, the Governor-General claimed it was 'the only solution consistent with the constitution and with my oath of office and my responsibilities, authority and duty.' But the considerable body of Australian voters who regarded themselves as having been disfranchised by the Governor-General knew very well that his claim was disputable.

'The Queen would never have done this,' said Mr Whitlam. Nor had any of her predecessors wielded such power since William IV dismissed Lord Melbourne in 1834, only to see him returned triumphantly to office at the ensuing election. In fact the Queen, in her capacity as Queen of the United Kingdom, could never be confronted with a parliamentary deadlock such as the one in Canberra, for the non-elected House of Lords cannot deny supply to a government with a majority in the House of Commons. Yet the real point about the Queen in her capacity as Queen of Australia is surely not whether she would have acted as her representative in the Commonwealth did, but rather that she had absolutely no say in the matter. She first heard about it after the event, and when Buckingham Palace later acknowledged a request by the former Speaker in the House of Representatives that the Queen should reinstate Mr Whitlam as Prime Minister it advanced an apparently new doctrine that the prerogative powers of the Crown rested with the Governor-General and not the Queen.

Whether one condemns or applauds Sir John Kerr, it may be argued that one effect of his action was to expose the Buckingham Palace-Yarralumla nexus for the fiction that it had become. Hopetoun, Northcote and Munro-Ferguson were the Crown's representatives in fact, responsible to it through the Colonial Office. But when an Australian governor-general faced a constitutional crisis for the first time, he did so without the slightest reference or accountability to Britain. Indeed he was acting like the president of a republic, not like the representative of some distant constitutional monarch.

Lion

One suspects that affection for things British, ever dwindling though it may be, would survive indefinitely even in an Australian republic. The British part of the British-Australian duality reminds me of the old mathematical paradox: if you travel half the distance from A to B, then half the remaining distance, and keep on halving it, when do you reach B? Answer: never. In finite time at least, some of the distance will always remain; and so too with the lion.

The lion drew back from its position of imperial supremacy in various stages at conferences in 1917, 1926, 1929 and 1930. For example, the imperial conference of 1926 adopted the Balfour report which defined Great Britain and the dominions as 'autonomous Communities within the British Empire, equal in status, in no way subordinate one to another in any respect of their domestic or external affairs, though united by a common allegiance to the Crown, and freely associated as members of the British Commonwealth of Nations.' In several respects, however, the existing status of the dominions fell short of this pious definition. Another conference in 1929 drafted a statute to correct some of the anomalies, and from its work came the Statute of Westminster, enacted by the British Parliament in 1931. The Statute of Westminster enabled the dominions to amend or repeal British legislation applying to them; it prevented the British parliament from legislating for a dominion unless requested to do so by that dominion's parliament; ended the doctrine of repugnancy, under which imperial laws had prevailed over dominion laws whenever the two conflicted (in the case of Australia, however, the removal of the *Colonial Laws Validity Act* applied only to Federal parliament, not to State parliaments); and declared that dominion parliaments had power to legislate extra-territorially. These provisions were not applicable to Australia until the Statute had been adopted by Federal parliament, and parliament was in no hurry to do that. It did not do so until 1942, under the wartime Curtin ministry.

Other changes between the wars included formal acknowledgment that the Sovereign was directly related to dominion governments, not indirectly through the British government; a declaration suspending in practice the Governor-General's power to reserve legislation and the Sovereign's power to disallow; and agreement by the British government to procedure whereby the dominions could appoint by Royal instrument diplomatic representatives answerable solely to their own governments. In this last matter Australia was also slow to act, preferring to operate externally through the British Foreign Office until World War II.

In 1939, just as in 1914, Australia was content to become involved in war automatically by Britain's declaration. 'Great Britain has declared war,' said the Prime Minister, R.G. Menzies, and 'as a result, Australia is also at war.' No one questioned this logic at the time, but when Britain declared war on Japan in 1941 the Curtin government made a separate declaration for Australia. Australia's shield against the onslaught of Japan – a recurrent nightmare suddenly come true – was not the Royal Navy but the navy whose battleships Deakin had once invited to Sydney and Melbourne over the head of the Colonial Office.

Contrary to the comforting fable in the *Commonwealth School Paper* forty years before, the lion was powerless to defend its kinsman, the young kangaroo, against the Asian dragon. The American rescue radically altered Australia's view of the world, but left intact many of its emotional ties with Britain. The Queen's visit in 1954, the first of its kind by a reigning British monarch, probably aroused more public interest than any previous royal tour, and as late as the 1960s the longest serving Prime Minister in Australian history, Sir Robert Menzies, was still proclaiming himself one of 'the Queen's men' and 'British to the boot-heels.' In 1963 Sir Robert's cabinet decided to call Australia's new decimal currency unit the royal, but was persuaded by public outcry to take another look at the short list, which consisted of austral, crown, dollar, pound, royal, regal and tasman. *God Save The Queen* was gradually going out of fashion during the 1960s, but in 1966 the prime minister, Harold Holt, claimed that it expressed Australian sentiment more faithfully than any 'synthetic national anthem'. According to a public opinion poll at that time, 57 per cent of Australians preferred *God Save The Queen* to other anthems. By 1974 this figure had fallen to 25 per cent, and in 1984 *Advance Australia Fair* was gazetted as the national anthem. Thereafter *God Save The Queen* was played only on vice-regal occasions.

Kangaroo

What Menzies and Holt did for the lion during the 1950s and 1960s, the Whitlam Labor government did for the kangaroo during the 1970s. There were initiatives in national policy, and innovations in symbolism and style. The Queen's portrait disappeared from definitive Australian postage stamps, though it could still be seen once a year on stamps commemorating her birthday. In 1973 Federal parliament altered the Queen's style and titles, with her concurrence, because, as the Prime Minister put it, they were 'not now sufficiently distinctively Australian.' Since 1953 the royal style and titles had been: 'Elizabeth the Second, by the Grace of God of the United Kingdom, Australia and Her other Realms and Territories Queen, Head of the Commonwealth, Defender of the Faith.' The new formulation was simply 'Elizabeth the Second, by the Grace of God, Queen of Australia and her other Realms and Territories, Head of the Commonwealth.'

The letters of credence which Australian heads of diplomatic missions present to foreign heads of state continued to carry the Queen's signature and titles, but without any confusing mention of the United Kingdom. The first Australian diplomat appointed to a foreign country was a minister to Japan in 1940. By the 1950s Australia's foreign service consisted of twenty-eight ambassadors and high commissioners, and by the 1970s seventy-four.

In the judicial sphere the Whitlam Government tried to block off the few remaining avenues of appeal from Australian courts to the Privy Council in Britain, but was only partly successful. 'The purpose of the Australian Government,' said Mr Whitlam in a ministerial statement, 'is to make the High Court of Australia the final court of appeal for Australia in all matters. That is an entirely proper objective. It is anomalous and archaic for Australian citizens to litigate their differences in another country before judges appointed by the government of that other country.' The Privy Council (Limitation of Appeals) Act of 1968 had already abolished appeals from the High Court to the Privy Council in all constitutional, Federal and territory matters, and in 1975 the Privy Council (Appeals From The High Court) Act precluded appeals in matters of a wholly State character.

A second bill introduced by the Whitlam Government, the Privy Council (Appeals Abolition) Bill, would have had the effect of abolishing appeals to the Privy Council from State courts, and excluding approaches being made from Australia for advisory opinions of the Privy Council under British legislation of the early 19th century. In 1973 the Tasmanian and Queensland governments had petitioned the Queen to refer the question of rights to the Australian sea bed (did they belong to the Commonwealth or the States?) for the Privy Council's advisory opinion. Not surprisingly, as the matter was soon to come before the High Court,[3] the Queen did not accede to this request. Queensland unsuccessfully sought another advisory opinion in 1974, this time in connection with a proposal that Her Majesty should be known as Queen of the United Kingdom, of Australia, of Queensland, and so on. Using powers available to the Australian parliament under the Statute of Westminster, the Privy Council (Appeals Abolition) Bill requested and consented to the enactment of British legislation abolishing appeals to the Privy Council in the remaining instances where such appeals still lay from Australian courts, and abolishing the means of bypassing the High Court through seeking advisory opinions from the Privy Council. This bill was blocked in the Senate, however, and thus in 1976 Australia still had a vestigial link with the Privy Council.

During its three years in office, the Whitlam government gave some of Australia's ceremonial trappings a more distinctively national character. Although knighthoods and other such distinctions continued to reach deserving Australians via the non-Labor State Governments, the Whitlam Government suspended the Imperial honours system and established in its place the Order of Australia, with a Chancellor (who else but the quasi-president of Australia, Sir John Kerr?), Companions, Officers and Members. The Governor-General adopted a new royal salute, the first six bars of *God Save The Queen* and the four last bars of *Advance Australia Fair*; and the Bureau of Statistics conducted an opinion poll which showed that of 60,000 respondents questioned about Australian anthems (not including *God Save The Queen*), 51.4 per cent preferred *Advance Australia Fair*, 19.6 per cent *Waltzing Matilda* and 13.6 per cent *Song of Australia*.

[3] After considering a challenge by all States to the validity of the Seas and Submerged Lands Act, the full bench of the High Court ruled that the Commonwealth had sovereign rights over the Australian territorial sea and continental shelf.

Advance Australia Fair moved uneasily into greater prominence, but its status in relation to *God Save The Queen* was never clearly defined. This uncertainty was removed by the Fraser Government, which announced that *God Save The Queen* would be reinstated as the sole salute on royal and vice-regal occasions. The Fraser Government also reintroduced a Commonwealth list for Imperial honours, coexistent with the Order of Australia, but the former was again suspended by the subsequent Labor government.

The Constitution and Federation

By reason of the electorate's innate conservatism and the provisos governing constitutional amendment, few changes have been made to the Constitution. Of forty-two proposals for amendment so far put to the Australian people by referendum, only eight have been carried, and none of these would have been likely to upset the founding fathers. The Constitution can be amended only by an amending bill passed by an absolute majority of either House, and then strong affirmation by referendums in all States. A referendum may be carried only by a majority of the electors as a whole and a majority in at least four of the six States.

Of ten proposals put to referendums between 1976 and 1991 only three were carried, dealing with senate casual vacancies, retirement of judges and referendum procedures. The other subjects – too daunting for the electorate – were rights and freedoms, fair elections, local government, parliamentary terms, interchange of powers between Canberra and the States, and terms of senators.

There have been several attempts to reassess the Commonwealth Constitution in the light of past experience and changing conditions, but so far these have been almost entirely fruitless. The first attempt, by a Royal Commission appointed in 1927, found little need for change, and produced hardly any effect; the second, by a constitutional convention meeting in 1973 and 1975, was no more than a charade. The Royal Commission, appointed largely as the result of criticisms of the Constitution by State premiers and secessionists, concluded that Australia's federal system provided a good balance between central authority and regional self-government. 'It seems to us,' reported the Commission, 'that the concentration of all legislative and executive functions in one authority would be likely to produce the paralysis at the centre and anaemia at the circumference which has been referred to by some writers on political science . . . We think that the loyalty of a citizen finds its fullest scope, in a country of the size of Australia, when certain important functions are assigned to local authorities, and those which are truly national to the central government.'

The Australian Constitutional Convention which met in Sydney during 1973 brought the three tiers of government together for what was described in advance as the first major review of the Constitution since Federation. It was inspired by the perennial financial embarrassment of the States, but also by dissatisfaction with the working of the Constitution at other levels of government. In his opening speech the Governor-General, Sir Paul Hasluck, said that the convention would be either 'a monumental flop or an honoured landmark.' It was a flop. The conflicting interests of centre and circumference could not be reconciled, and the principals soon retreated into political rhetoric. A session scheduled for 1974 did not take place because the Commonwealth could not agree on the political composition of its delegation, and a session held in Melbourne during 1975 was boycotted by the four State Liberal governments. After four more biennial sessions of the Australian Constitutional Convention failed to achieve any significant reforms, a six-member Constitutional Commission with secretariat and advisory committees was established in 1986 with a brief to report by 1988 on proposals for revising the Constitution. Four of the referendum proposals mentioned earlier were a consequence of this Commission's final report, and the electorate wanted none of them. Otherwise the report had no immediate results, although its wide-ranging research and recommendations were likely to prove of value to a Constitutional Centenary Foundation formed in 1991 for the purpose of encouraging review and development of Australia's constitutional system, to be completed by the year 2000. This Foundation, the product of a Constitutional Centenary Conference held in commemoration of the 1891 constitutional convention, was to be partly funded by the Commonwealth, and chaired by the former Governor-General Sir Ninian Stephen.

Although the 75th anniversary of Federation passed almost without notice, the jubilee in 1951 was celebrated with great assiduity throughout the Commonwealth. A commemorative plaque was erected on what remained of the pavilion in which the Commonwealth had been proclaimed in Centennial Park. This hexagonal wooden structure, minus its original white exterior, was moved in 1901 to Cabarita Park, beside the Parramatta River, where it stands to this day as a largely forgotten memento of proclamation day. The site of the pavilion in Centennial Park, southeast of the main Oxford Street gate, was still marked by a six-sided obelisk, originally part of the pavilion, inscribed with the names of the States.

The main jubilee function in 1951 was a state banquet in King's Hall at Parliament House, Canberra. In proposing the toast to the Commonwealth of Australia, the Governor-General, Sir William McKell, said he hoped he would live to see the day when 'a shrine will be erected upon the historic spot in Centennial Park, and in that shrine will be written in letters of gold the names of the great and courageous men who made the Commonwealth possible'. A domed and pillared pavilion was erected over the obelisk in 1988, but Sir William missed seeing it by three years.

Monarchy and Republic

Whether because of affection for this antipodean kingdom, or in calculated response to republicanism, the Royal Family has spent more time than usual in Australia since the disruptive events of 1975. In those fifteen years, there have been no fewer than ten Royal visits, including six by the Queen herself. None of these recaptured anything like the rapture of 1954, but it could not have been denied that the House of Windsor still commanded considerable respect and affection. Nevertheless, the symbolic role played in Australian life by a monarch who was not resident in this country, and who was required by the three-centuries-old Act of Settlement to be a member of the Church of England, had become increasingly anachronistic.

In 1986, at the formal request of all State legislatures, Federal Parliament passed the Australia Act, bringing 'constitutional arrangements affecting the Commonwealth and the States into conformity with the status of the Commonwealth of Australia as a sovereign, independent and federal nation.' The Attorney-General's Second Reading speech emphasised that nothing in this legislation would impair the position of the Queen as Queen of Australia. 'In fact,' he said, 'the Queen, instead of being formally advised on State matters by United Kingdom Ministers, will now be advised direct by State Premiers in her exercise of the power concerned.'

The Australia Act, and an identical act of the British Parliament, removed all outmoded constitutional links still existing between Australia and the United Kingdom, including those avenues of appeal from Australian courts to the Privy Council which the Whitlam Government had tried to abolish eleven years earlier.

Among other things, it also terminated any powers still remaining in the British Parliament to make laws that would have effect as part of Australian law; it removed certain British limitations upon the legislative powers of the State parliaments, in particular by repealing the *Colonial Laws Validity Act* in relation to the States; and it shortened procedure for the award of Imperial honours on State lists and the appointment of State governors.

Instead of being made by the Queen on advice from United Kingdom ministers, following recommendations by State premiers to the Foreign and Commonwealth Office in London, awards and appointments would be made by Her Majesty on direct advice from the premier of the State concerned. (By 1991, Imperial honours had been abandoned by all Australian Governments, even the Federation's sole non-Labor Government, that of New South Wales.)

Although the 1988 report of the Australian Constitutional Commission specifically recommended 'no change to Australia's status as a constitutional monarchy or to the position of the Queen of Australia as Head of State', some of its recommendations did refer to the Queen's powers under the Constitution. It recommended constitutional amendments to remove the Governor-General's rarely exercised power to reserve bills for the Queen's pleasure, and the Queen's power (never yet exercised) to disallow any Commonwealth law within one year from the Governor-General's assent. It also recommended amendments to confirm that most of the powers vested in the Governor-General are exercisable only on ministerial advice (in this context, it also expressed the opinion that vice-regal reserve powers, which a Governor-General may exercise without or contrary to ministerial advice, should be kept to a minimum); to confirm likewise that the Governor-General's role as Commander-in-Chief of the armed forces is essentially a titular one, in which he acts with the advice of the Federal Executive Council; and, finally, to provide that His Excellency's power to appoint deputies be exercised only on the Prime Minister's advice.

If the waning of support for the Monarchy had been gradual, the surging of republicanism was sporadic. The latter rose in the wake of 1975, with hopes of a 1988 republic to usher in the third century of European Australia, but subsided before the end of that decade. In 1982 a republican plank was inserted in the Australian Labor Party's platform, committing the Party 'to bring about the complete legal separation of Australia from the United Kingdom, Crown and Parliament.' It lay dormant, however, and the Bicentenary passed with scarcely any mention of the issue.

As the Bicentenary had not been spur enough for a republic, the next appropriate date – indeed the only comparably auspicious occasion for a long time to come – would be 1 January 2001, the day on which the world turns over a new millennial leaf and Australia celebrates the centenary of Federation. In June 1991 the ALP National Conference passed a resolution in accordance with the 1982 objective, calling upon the Hawke Government to 'embark upon a public education campaign, culminating in a referendum which would effect reform of the Australian Constitution and other political institutions to enable Australia to become an independent republic on 1 January 2001.' It also called on the ALP to begin community debate on this subject, and directed the National Executive to report to each National Conference held during the 1990s on the progress of such debate.

At about the same time, in July 1991, a diverse group of well-known Australians launched an Australian Republican Movement which, although not politically aligned, seemed likely to promote the kind of debate called for at the ALP National Conference. 'The exact terms of an Australian republic can only be decided by public debate and by the vote of a majority of the Australian people at a referendum,' said the inaugural chairman of the ARM committee, Tom Keneally. What the new movement advocated was not a denial of Australian national identity or Australian institutions, but rather a celebration of those things; nor was it advocating a republic such as the United States, where the head of state is also head of government, but rather a parliamentary republic with a formal (not executive) head of state, like those of India, Ireland, Italy and Israel.

Such republican status could be achieved by replacing the Queen and her appointive Governor-General with a head of state (still called 'Governor-General' if 'President' seemed too radical a change) either appointed by the Australian government, elected by popular vote or, more likely, chosen by some form of electoral college, probably consisting of Commonwealth and State parliamentarians. It would be necessary to amend those sections of the Constitution referring to the Queen, and to the Governor-General if his replacement were to be called something else. But otherwise the basic machinery of Commonwealth government – the Westminster parliamentary system, federalism, judicial review of legislation and so on – would stay as it is. State Constitutions would require some amendment for the introduction of State republican government, but that should not be beyond the wit of constitutional lawyers, nor the approval of voters.

An Australian Republic would presumably remain part of the Commonwealth of Nations. (Of the forty-seven member nations, no fewer than twenty-six are now republics, though they recognise the Queen as Head of the Commonwealth.) By the same token, individual Australians would presumably retain whatever respect and affection they already feel for the United Kingdom and its Monarch.

Certainly a change from monarchy to republic would not be as simple as is sometimes claimed, but neither would it be as difficult as some pro-monarchists warn. The main pro-monarchy argument is the traditional conservative question: why change something that works? Responding to the ALP's activation of the republican issue, the Liberal Party began a contrary campaign. By September 1991 two papers had been produced, one written by the shadow minister and former Leader of the Opposition, John Howard, and the other by a Victorian senator, Rod Kemp.

'The first and fundamental question to be asked,' wrote Howard, 'is why should this nation be plunged into a divisive, acrimonious debate about an institution whose continued existence is held very dear by a significant section of the population who will tenaciously oppose any attempt to change the status quo? At a time of great economic disarray and significant challenges to our competitive survival, it seems a grievous waste of effort and emotional resources to debate an issue so patently destined to divide our people.'

The republican reply to that, as expressed by Keneally, is: 'Some will say that there are more pressing issues – the economy, child poverty and a whole range of important social issues. We would reply that there is no denying the urgency of addressing these problems. But we can surely consider the important issue of constitutional reform at the same time. We can at last demonstrate that we are taking our destiny into our own hands. For the world is going its own way and Australians are the only ones who can provide a future for Australia. If we cannot discover loyalty, sanity, human decency and leadership amongst our own people, then we are finished as a nation.'

Briefly, the principal arguments for becoming a republic – as summarised by the constitutional lawyer George Winterton in his book *Monarchy to Republic* – are those concerned with national identity, opposition to the heredity principle, a preference for popular sovereignty (sovereignty derived from the consent of the Australian people rather than the British Parliament), and opportunity for wider constitutional reform (for example, by defining more clearly the President/Governor-General's discretionary powers).

'Because a head of state is a symbol of national identity,' writes Winterton, 'it is not surprising that many Australians should feel that their country's retention of the head of state of its former colonial overlord as its own head of state detracts from their sense of independent nationhood.'

Similarly, retention of the hereditary British monarch as Australian head of state may be seen as retarding recognition of Australia's role as an Asian-Pacific nation. It must also be puzzling or even repugnant to some Australians of non-Anglo-Celtic descent. This would undoubtedly apply to some of the many Australians of Irish descent.

The anti-republican reply is that Australia already has complete independence – as witness the Queen's denial in 1975 that she had any power to override the Governor-General. 'Australia has properly been described as a crowned republic,' writes Howard. 'This is a good description as in many ways we now have the best of both worlds. Those who do not care for the royal link do not find it is something which intrudes into their everyday lives. On the other hand, millions of Australians have a deep respect for the institution and admire the dedication and sense of duty displayed by the present occupant.' As for the non-British part of the population (23 per cent, but nearly 50 per cent if Irish-Australians are included), Howard argues that by no means all of them dislike the British Monarchy.

Anti-republicans also make much of the Crown's alleged unifying influence and political neutrality, to which republicans may well advance the contrary evidence of its divisive influence in 1975.

In return, anti-republicans may point out that an elective head of state would be no less capable of error than an appointive Governor-General representing a Monarch of Australia seated on a British throne.

Clearly there is much room for debate, and ample time to prepare the inauguration of an Australian Republic on 1 January 2001, given appropriate political intention and electoral endorsement. But it remains to be seen how seriously the ALP National Executive, Caucus and Federal Parliamentary leadership will take the resolution of the Party's National Conference. It must also be acknowledged that without a bipartisan political approach, the chance of a republican referendum being carried would be slim indeed. An Australian Republic is surely inevitable, but who can say with any confidence just when in the third millennium this will come about?

APPENDIX

Governors-General 1901-1919

John Adrian Louis, Earl of Hopetoun
  (afterwards Marquis of Linlithgow), P.C., K.T., G.C.M.G.
  1 January 1901–9 January 1903
Hallam, Baron Tennyson, P.C., G.C.M.G.
  17 July 1902–9 January 1903 (Acting)
  9 January 1903–21 January 1904
Henry Stafford, Baron Northcote, P.C.
  G.C.M.G., G.C.I.E., C.B.
  21 January 1904–9 September 1908
William Humble, Earl of Dudley, P.C.
  G.C.B., G.C.M.G., G.C.V.O.
  9 September 1908–31 July 1911
Thomas, Baron Denman, P.C., G.C.M.G., K.C.V.O.
  31 July 1911–18 May 1914
Sir Ronald Craufurd Munro-Ferguson
  (afterwards Viscount Novar of Raith), G.C.M.G.
  18 May 1914–6 October 1920

Commonwealth Ministries 1901-1919

Barton	1 January 1901–24 September 1903
Deakin	24 September 1903–27 April 1904
Watson	27 April 1904–18 August 1904
Reid-McLean	18 August 1904–5 July 1905
Deakin	5 July 1905–13 November 1908
Fisher	13 November 1908–2 June 1909
Deakin	2 June 1909–29 April 1910
Fisher	29 April 1910–24 June 1913
Cook	24 June 1913–17 September 1914
Fisher	17 September 1914–27 October 1915
Hughes	27 October 1915–14 November 1916
Hughes	14 November 1916–17 February 1917
Hughes	17 February 1917–10 January 1918
Hughes	10 January 1918–9 February 1923

BIBLIOGRAPHY

ALEXANDER, F. *Australia Since Federation*. Nelson, Melbourne, 1967.

AMERY, L.C.M.S. *Times History Of The War In South Africa*. London, 1900–1909.

ANSTEY, F. *Red Europe*. Fraser and Jenkinson, Melbourne, 1919.

ARTHUR, SIR G. *Life of Lord Kitchener*. Macmillan, London, 1920.

ATKINSON, L. Australian Defence Policy: a Study of Empire and Nation, 1897-1910. Thesis, Australian National University.

BARTON, SIR E. Correspondence. Edmund Barton papers MSS. National Library of Australia.

BASTIN, J. 'Federation and Western Australia'. *Historical Studies*, November 1951.

BEAN, C. E. W. *Anzac To Amiens*. Australian War Memorial, Canberra, 1946.
Flagships Three. Alston Rivers, London, 1913.
Letters From France. Cassell, London, 1917.
Official History of Australia in the War of 1914–1918. Vols I and II ('The Story of Anzac'), Vols III and V ('The Australian Imperial Force in France, 1916 and 1918). Angus and Robertson, Sydney.
Two Men I Knew: William Bridges and Brudenell White, Founders of the AIF. Angus and Robertson, Sydney, 1957.
With The Flagship in the South. William Brooks, Sydney, 1909.

BEAZLEY, K. 'The Labor Party and the Origin of the Commonwealth Bank'. *The Australian Journal of Politics and History*, May 1963.

BIRRELL, J. *Walter Burley Griffin*. University of Queensland Press, Brisbane, 1964.

BRENNAN, N. *Dr Mannix*. Rigby, Adelaide, 1964.

BUCHANAN, A. Typescript 'Prime Ministers Of Australia'. National Library of Australia.

BURGER, G. J. Spanning a Continent: the Transcontinental Railway from Kalgoorlie to Port Augusta. Honours BA thesis, University of Adelaide, 1962.

CARRINGTON, R. N. 'A True Story Of An Australian Journalist's Five Years Search For Fame in Fleet Street'. MSS. Mitchell Library.

CHAMBERLAIN, W. M. *To Shoot And To Ride: The Australian: The South African War 1899–1902*. Military Historical Society of Australia, Melbourne, 1967.

COLE, D. ' "The Crimson Thread of Kinship": Ethnic Ideas in Australia 1870–1914'. *Historical Studies*, April 1971.

COWEN, Z. *Isaac Isaacs*. Oxford University Press, Melbourne, 1967.

CRAWFORD, R.M. *A Bit Of A Rebel; The Life and Work of George Arnold Wood*. Sydney University Press, 1975.
'Tom Roberts and Alfred Deakin' in *In Honour of Daryl Lindsay*, ed. Philipp, F. Oxford University Press, Melbourne, 1964.

CRESWELL, SIR W. *Close To The Wind*. Heinemann, London, 1965.

CROWLEY, F.K. (ed.) *A New History of Australia*. Heinemann, Melbourne, 1974.
(ed.) *Modern Australia in Documents*. Vol I 1901–1939. Wren, Melbourne, 1973.

CUNNEEN, C. The Role of the Governor-General in Australia, 1901–1927. Ph. D. thesis, Australian National University.

CUTLER, T. 'Sunday, Bloody Sunday' in *Strikes: Studies In Twentieth Century Australian Social History*. Angus and Robertson, Sydney, 1973.

DAWSON, IDA. Diaries MSS 1901–1915. Mitchell Library.

DEAKIN, A. Notebooks MSS. Alfred Deakin papers. National Library of Australia.
Federated Australia: Selections from Letters to the Morning Post 1900–1910. Ed. J.A. La Nauze. Melbourne University Press, 1968.
The Federal Story, the Inner History of the Federal Cause 1880–1900. Robertson and Mullens, Melbourne, 1944.

DE MOUNCY, E. Recollections 1914–1918 MSS. La Trobe Library.

EVANS, G. 'God Save the Queen? Australia as a Republic'. Address to Counterpoint Forum, Murdoch University, 29 September 1982.

EVATT, H.V. *The King And His Dominion Governors*. Frank Cass, London, 1967.

FISHER, PEGGY. Recollections of her father, Andrew Fisher, MSS. Andrew Fisher papers. National Library of Australia.

FITCHETT, REV. W.H. *Deeds that Won The Empire: Historic Battle Scenes*. Bell's Indian and Colonial Library, London, 1897.

FITZHARDINGE, L.F. 'W.M. Hughes and the Treaty of Versailles, 1919'. *Journal of Commonwealth Political Studies*, July 1967.
'Hughes, Borden and Dominion Representation at the Paris Peace Conference'. *The Canadian Historical Review*, June 1868.
William Morris Hughes: a political biography. Vol I. Angus and Robertson, Sydney, 1964.

FITZPATRICK, B. *The British Empire In Australia 1834–1939*. Melbourne University Press, 1941.

FOXCROFT, A. Diary 1914–1918 MSS. La Trobe Library.

FRASER, J.F. *Australia: The Making Of A Nation*. Cassell, London, 1910.

FREEMAN, HILDA. *An Australian Girl In Germany*. Specialty Press, Melbourne, 1916.

GAMMAGE, W.L. *The Broken Years: Australian Soldiers In The Great War*. Australian National University Press, 1974.

GARRAN, R.R. *Prosper The Commonwealth*. Angus and Robertson, Sydney, 1958.

GILLEN, F.J. *Gillen's Diary: The Camp Jottings of F.J. Gillen on the Spencer and Gillen Expedition Across Australia 1901–1902*. Libraries Board of South Australia, Adelaide, 1968.

GOLLAN, R.A. *The Commonwealth Bank of Australia: origins and early history*. Australian National University Press, 1968.
Radical and Working Class Politics: a study of Eastern Australia 1850–1910. Melbourne University Press, 1960.

GOUGH, SIR H. *The Fifth Army*. London, 1931.

GRIFFITH S.W. *The Divina Commedia*, trans. by Sir Samuel Griffith. Henry Froude, London, 1911.
Correspondence of Sir Samuel Griffith MSS 1860–1914. Dixson Library.

GRIMSHAW, C. 'Australian Nationalism and the Imperial Connection 1900–1914'. *The Australian Journal of Politics and History*, May 1958.

HAIG, LORD. *The Private Papers of Douglas Haig 1914–1919*. Eyre and Spottiswoode, London, 1952.

HAMILTON, I. *Gallipoli Diary*. Arnold, London, 1920.

HANCOCK, I.R. 'The 1911 Imperial Conference'. *Historical Studies*, October, 1966.

HANCOCK, W.K. *Australia*, Ernest Benn, London, 1930.

HANKEY, LORD. *The Supreme Command: 1914–1918*. Allen and Unwin, London, 1961.

HART, R.A. *The Great White Fleet*. Little Brown, Boston, 1965.

HESELTINE, H. *Vance Palmer*. University of Queensland Press, 1970.

HIGGINS, H.B. Correspondence MSS. National Library of Australia.

HIRST, J. 'The Conservative Case for an Australian Republic'. *Quadrant*, September 1991.

HORNE, D. 'Power from the People. A New Australian Constitution'. Victorian Fabian Society Pamphlet No. 32, October 1977.

HOWARD, J. 'Some Arguments Against an Australian Republic'. NSW Liberal Party, September 1991.

HUGHES, W.M. *Policies and Potentates*. Angus and Robertson, Sydney, 1950.
Splendid Adventure: A Review of Empire Relations Within and Without the Commonwealth of Britannic Nations. Ernest Benn, London, 1929.
Correspondence MSS. W.M. Hughes papers. National Library of Australia.

HUNT, A. Correspondence MSS. Atlee Hunt papers. National Library of Australia.

HUTTON, SIR EDWARD. Military Forces of the Commonwealth: Minute Upon the Defence of Australia, 1901. Commonwealth Parliamentary Papers 1901–02.

JAMES, R.R. *Gallipoli*. Batsford, London, 1965.

JEBB, R. *Studies In Colonial Nationalism*. Arnold, London, 1905.

JOSE, A.W. *Official History of Australia in the War of 1914–1918*. Vol IX ('The Royal Australian Navy'). Angus and Robertson, Sydney.

KEITH, A.B. *Imperial Unity and the Dominions*. Clarendon, Oxford, 1916.

KEMP, R. 'Australia's Future: Constitutional Monarchy or Constitutional Chaos?' NSW Liberal Party, September 1991.

KENEALLY, T. 'God Save The Republic'. *Australian Author*, Spring 1991.

KENDLE, J. *The British Empire—Commonwealth, 1897–1931*. Cheshire, Melbourne, 1972.

KITCHEN, ALICE. Memoir 1914–1918 MSS. La Trobe Library.

KITCHENER, LORD. Memorandum on Defence of Australia, 1910. Commonwealth Parliamentary Papers, 1910 Vol II.

LA NAUZE, J.A. *Alfred Deakin: A Biography*. 2 Vols, Melbourne University Press, 1965.
The Making of the Australian Constitution. Melbourne University Press, 1972.
'The Name of the Commonwealth of Australia'. *Historical Studies*, October 1971.

LEE, J.E. *Duntroon, the Royal Military College of Australia*. Australian War Memorial, Canberra, 1952.

LLOYD GEORGE, D. *War Memoirs*. Vol I. Nicholson and Watson, London, 1933.

MACK, LOUISE. *An Australian Girl In London*. Fisher Unwin, London, 1902.

MACKENZIE, C. *Gallipoli Memories*. Cassells, London 1929.

MARRETT, R.R. and PENNIMAN, T.K. *Spencer's Last Journey*. Oxford, 1931.

MATTERS, L.W. *Australasians Who Count in London*. Truscott, London, 1913.

MATTHEWS, F. *Back to Hampton Roads*. Huebsch, New York, 1909.

M'CLURE, G. Diary 1901 MSS. Mitchell Library.

MEANEY, N.K. 'A Proposition Of The Highest International Importance'. *Journal of Contemporary Political Studies*. November 1967.

MEGAW, R. 'Australia and the Great White Fleet'. *Journal of the Royal Australian Historical Society*. June 1970.

MONASH, SIR JOHN. *The Australian Victories In France in 1918*. Hutchinson, London, 1920.

NEILSON, J.S. Autobiography MSS. National Library of Australia.

NICOLSON, H. *Peacemaking 1919*. Constable, London, 1933.

BIBLIOGRAPHY

NISH, L.H. 'Australia and the Anglo-Japanese Alliance, 1901–1911'. *Australian Journal of Political History*, November 1963.

NORRIS, R. *The Emergent Commonwealth*. Melbourne University Press, 1975.

O'COLLINS, G. *Patrick McMahon Glynn: A Founder of Australian Federation*. Melbourne University Press, 1965.

PALMER, J. (NETTIE). *Henry Bournes Higgins: A Memoir*. Harrap, London, 1931.

PALMER, VANCE AND NETTIE. Correspondence and papers MSS. National Library of Australia.

PANKHURST, A. *Put Up The Sword*. Women's Peace Army, Melbourne, 1915.

PARKER, R.S. 'Australian Federation – The Influence of Economic Interests and Political Pressures'. *Historical Studies*, November 1949.

PAUL, J.B. 'An Australian Republic? But Why?' *Quadrant*, September 1991.

PENNY, B.R. 'Australia's Reactions to the Boer War'. *The Journal of British Studies*, November 1967.
'The Australian Debate On The Boer War'. *Historical Studies*, April 1971.

PHILLIPS, R. *The White Feather*. Melville and Mullen, Melbourne, 1917.

PRICE, SIR A.G. *The Skies Remember*. Angus and Robertson, Sydney, 1969.

QUICK, SIR J. and GARRAN, R.R. *The Annotated Constitution of the Australian Commonwealth*. Angus and Robertson, Sydney, 1901.

RAWS, J.A. *Records of an Australian Lieutenant: a story of bravery, devotion and self-sacrifice, 1915–16.* 193?.

RAWSON, D.W. 'Political Violence in Australia'. *Dissent*. Autumn, 1968.

REID, G.S. 'God Save the Queen? Australia as a Republic.' Address to Counterpoint Forum, Murdoch University, 29 September 1982.

Report of the Advisory Committee on Executive Government to the Constitutional Commission, Canberra Publishing and Printing Company, 1987.

REYNOLDS, J. *Edmund Barton*. Angus and Robertson, Sydney, 1948.

ROBSON, L.L. 'Social Classes in Twentieth Century Australia'. *Hemisphere*, ed. Maguire, R.J. 1964.
The First AIF: A Study of its Recruitment 1914–1918. Melbourne University Press, 1970.

ROE, M. 'An Historical Survey of Australian Nationalism'. *The Victorian Historical Magazine*, November 1971.

ROYAL COMMISSION. Royal Commission on sites for the seat of Government of the Commonwealth, 1903. Commonwealth Parliamentary Papers 1903.
Royal Commission on Federal Capital Administration, 1916. Commonwealth Parliamentary Papers, 1917.

Royal Commission on Northern Territory Administration, 1919. Commonwealth Parliamentary Papers, 1920–21.

Royal Commission of Inquiry into the present conditions, including the method of government, of the Territory of Papua, and the best means of their improvement, 1906. Commonwealth Parliamentary Papers Senate 1970.

Royal Commission on the condition of the natives of Western Australia, 1905. Government Printer, Perth, 1905.

SAWER, G. *Australian Federal Politics and Law*. Vol I 1901–1929. Melbourne University Press, 1956.

The Australian Constitution. Australian Government Publishing Service, Canberra, 1975.

SCOTT, E. *Official History of Australia in the War of 1914–1918*. Vol XI ('Australia During The War'). Angus and Robertson, Sydney, 1936.

SERLE, G. *From Deserts The Prophets Come: The Creative Spirit In Australia 1788–1972*. Heinemann, Melbourne, 1973.

'Australia and Britain' in *Contemporary Australia: Studies in history, politics and economics*, ed. Preston, R.A. Duke University Press, 1969.

SHEPHERD, M.L. Typescript memoirs 1873–1936. Australian Archives.

SHOESMITH, D.R. Boom year: A Study of Popular Leisure in Melbourne, 1919. MA thesis, Australian National University, 1971.

SISSONS, D.C.S. Attitudes to Japan and Defence 1890–1923. Thesis, Australian National University.

SMITH, A.N. *Thirty Years: The Commonwealth of Australia, 1901–1931*. Brown, Prior and Co, Melbourne, 1933.

SMITH, SIR R. *14,000 Miles Through The Air*, Macmillan, London, 1922.

SPENCER, W.B. and GILLEN, F.J. *The Arunta: A Study of a Stone Age People*. Macmillan, London, 1927.

Northern Tribes of Central Australia. Macmillan, London, 1904.

SPENCER, W.B. Journal 1901–1902 MSS, diaries 1911–1913 MSS. Mitchell Library.

SPIELVOGEL, N. *A Gumsucker On Tramp*. S. Spielvogel, Ballarat, 1905.

SYMON, SIR J. Correspondence with Justices of the High Court, 1905. Commonwealth Parliamentary Papers Vol II 1905.

TENNYSON, LADY. Papers of Audrey Georgiana Florence, Lady Tennyson MSS. National Library of Australia.

THOMPSON, J. The Australian High Commission in London; its origins and early history 1901–1916. MA thesis, Australian National University, 1972.

THOMPSON, R.C. Australian Imperialism and the New Hebrides, 1862–1922. Thesis, Australian National University.

BIBLIOGRAPHY

TREVELYAN, G.M. *Grey of Falloden*. Longmans Green, London, 1937.

TURNER, I. *Industrial Labour and Politics: The Labour Movement in Eastern Australia 1900–1921*. Australian National University Press, 1965.
Sydney's Burning. Alpha Books, Sydney, 1969.

WARD, R. 'Two Kinds of Australian Patriotism'. *The Victorian Historical Magazine*. February 1970.

WELLER, P. (ed.) *Caucus Minutes 1901–1949: Minutes of the Meetings of the Federal Parliamentary Labor Party*. 2 Vols. Melbourne University Press, 1975.

WEST, F. *Hubert Murray, the Australian Pro-consul*. Oxford University Press, Melbourne, 1968.

WIGMORE, L.G. *The Long View: a history of Canberra, Australia's National Capital*. Cheshire, Melbourne 1963.

WINTERTON, G. *Monarchy to Republic*. Oxford University Press, Melbourne, 1986.

WOOD, G.A. 'Australia and Imperial Politics' in *Australia, Economic and Political Studies*, ed. Meredith Atkinson. Macmillan, London, 1920.

YARWOOD, A.T. *Asian Migration to Australia: the background to exclusion 1896–1923*. Melbourne University Press, 1964.

INDEX